The Human Condition

The Comparative Religious Ideas Project

Robert Cummings Neville, Director

The Human Condition

A Volume in the Comparative Religious Ideas Project

Edited by

ROBERT CUMMINGS NEVILLE

Foreword by

PETER L. BERGER

STATE UNIVERSITY OF NEW YORK PRESS

Published by
State University of New York Press, Albany

Printed in the United States of America

For information, address State University of New York Press,
90 State Street, Suite 700, Albany, NY 12207

Production by Marilyn P. Semerad
Marketing by Dana E. Yanulavich

Library of Congress Cataloging-in-Publication Data

The human condition / edited by Robert Cummings Neville; foreword by Peter L. Berger.
p. cm.—(The comparative religious ideas project)
Includes bibliographical references and index.
ISBN 0-7914-4779-0 (alk.paper)—ISBN 0-7914-4780-4 (pbk.: alk paper)
1. Religion—Philosophy. 2. Human beings. I. Neville, Robert C. II. Series.
BL51. H96 2000
291.2'2—dc21 00-020548

10 9 8 7 6 5 4 3 2 1

To

William Eastman, Publisher

Who, as Director of the State University of New York Press,
fostered the extraordinary variety and depth of studies of
world religions, and the careers of young scholars working
with novel approaches, that have made possible such
ambitious comparative inquiries as this one.

Contents

Foreword

Peter L. Berger

The present volume, which contains the results of the first year of a three-year project conceived and directed by Robert Neville of Boston University, constitutes an innovative contribution to the comparative study of religious traditions. As such, it will undoubtedly attract the attention of scholars in this field. Should it be of interest to a larger audience? The following remarks give a positive answer to this question.

The process of modernization, which by now has fundamentally affected virtually every society on earth, has as one of its most important consequences the situation commonly called pluralism. The term means quite simply that people with very different beliefs, values, and lifestyles come to live together in close proximity, are forced to interact with each other, and therefore are faced with the alternative of either clashing in conflict or somehow accommodating each other's differences. Pluralism in this sense is often applied to the cohabitation of different racial, ethnic, or linguistic groups, but the differences that give pluralism its name are very frequently religious in character. Religious pluralism is not a unique feature of modernity. It existed in the Hellenistic-Roman world along the great trades routes of Central Asia, in urban centers of the Islamic world, and elsewhere. What is distinctive about modern pluralism is its pervasiveness, both geographically and sociologically. Geographically, there are few places left today in which any one religious tradition holds an unchallenged monopoly. Where the attempt is made to maintain or restore such a monopoly under contemporary conditions, it requires heavy coercion and even then it is constantly threatened by the pluralizing forces or modernity (notably the modern media of mass communication). The fate of Franco Spain, which sought to restore the monopoly of traditional Catholicism, is instructive in this respect. More recent attempts, such as by the Islamic revolution in Iran, face very similar difficulties. And sociologically, modern pluralism leaves out very few groups within a society from its corrosive effects. Cosmopolitan groups, such as much-traveled scholars or merchants, have very often been affected by pluralism in earlier periods. Thus, for example, the religious mishmash characteristic of today's "New Age spirituality" has quite a few similarities with the syncretistic ideas that floated around the educated classes in the late Roman empire. Today, however, such ideas are as likely to be espoused by secretaries and truck drivers as by people with a college education.

The encounter with religious traditions other than one's own can be fascinating, intellectually stimulating, possibly leading to greater tolerance. It can also be very disturbing, because it is likely to undermine taken-for-granted certainties and thus threaten the guidelines by which people have organized meaningful lives for themselves. Put simply, pluralism *relativizes*. What in an earlier time was a belief held with absolute conviction now becomes an opinion or a matter of taste—in the wonderful phrase of American pluralism, it becomes a "religious preference." This relativization is often experienced at first as a great liberation; after a while it may come to be felt as a great burden. There appears then a nostalgia, a yearning for the comforting certainties of the past. Pluralism, the erstwhile liberator, now becomes an enemy, the "great satan" who must be fought in the name of timeless truths. This social-psychological process unleashes a curious dialectic between relativism and fanaticism. The end result of pluralistic relativization is an attitude of *total* tolerance, in which nothing is left of one's original beliefs, where anything goes, and where the only virtue still adhered to is, precisely, that of unlimited tolerance. As this attitude becomes burdensome to individuals (after all, nihilism is not a very practical worldview for most people), they become conversion-prone—to wit, prone to fall into whatever fanatical reassertion of uncompromising truth comes their way. The infinitely tolerant relativist now turns into the fanatic with non-negotiable cognitive and moral demands. The dialectic need not end there. Every fanaticism is vulnerable to relativization, just as every relativism may be cut short by this or that "Damascus experience."

While these two positions are psychological and sociological opposites, they share an important cognitive assumption: Both the relativist and the fanatic believe that there can be no reasonable communication between different worldviews, no worthwhile search for mutually acceptable criteria of truth by which the differences could be discussed. Given that assumption, there is no middle ground between challenging nothing that those others are saying and hitting them over the head until they surrender or disappear. Yet ordinary experience shows that this assumption of non-communication does not hold universally. There have been many cases in which there has been meaningful communication between people with widely differing beliefs and values, as a result of which a middle ground was indeed established so that the several groups could co-exist amicably without either open conflict or giving up everything in their cherished tradition. Indeed, the history of religious pluralism in American society, with some unfortunate exceptions, has been a considerable success story in these terms. The success has very rarely been the result of negotiations between theologians or other accredited theorists. The cognitive and moral compromises have rather been hammered out over lunchbreak conversations between fellow-workers, over backyard fences by neighboring housewives, or by parents coming in contact because of shared concerns for their children's schools or recreational activities. Nevertheless, all such communications *imply* a philosophical principle—something along the lines of the "natural reason" that, for example, the Jesuit missionary Matteo Ricci assumed as providing a common ground for Christians and Confucians. It is interesting that the aforementioned assumption held by both relativists and fanatics—namely, that there can be no reasonable communication between cognitive adversaries and therefore no common search for truth—has a curious correlate on the level of scholarship in particular. The recent history of Western and especially American academia has witnessed a massive assault on any notions of objective truth. Every proposition about the world is supposedly determined by one's location in history and society, and there is no method by which this determination could be overcome or even minimized. There have been various versions of this view—neo-Marxist, neo-Freudian, more recently feminist and "multiculturalist"; the somewhat dubious term "postmodernism" has been used to cover all of them. In the area of religious scholarship, this has had both practical and theoretical implications. Practically, it has changed the intentions of dialogue between religious traditions: While earlier there had often been the expectation that such dialogue might lead to new insights on the level of truth, this expectation must now seem futile; instead, all one can hope for is a degree of empathy with those others and perhaps, as a result, more friendly attitudes toward them. The theoretical implications are even more far-reaching: Any notion of truth in the area of religion is given up, and therefore any attempt to compare the way in which different traditions grapple with the truth; all that can happen is that one tells one's own "narrative" (the story of how one came to look at the world in a certain way) and listens to the others' "narrative" with as much empathy as one can muster. Religious traditions now appear as some kind of Leibnizian "monads," impenetrable to the outsider, sovereignly impermeable by generalizing concepts.

This point of view has great gains for the would-be spokespersons of this or that tradition ("nobody can speak for my people except me") and, slightly more mellowly, for the narrow specialist ("nobody understands my specialty except me—and I don't have to listen to anyone outside of my specialty"). It expresses, of course, an extreme relativism, legitimated now in terms of an epistemological theory. It is interesting, though, to observe that this relativism, far from inducing tolerance, leads to its own peculiar fanaticism, be it ideological (the more political form) or methodological (for those who are less interested in changing society than in denying tenure to those who disagree with them in the university department).

This cannot be the place to argue why this point of view is thoroughly mistaken. Suffice it to say that both its practical and its intellectual consequences are devastating. The Balkanization of theory leads logically to Balkan-like politics. And if there is no conceivable "natural reason" on the basis of which different ideas can be compared and assessed, there can be no such thing as "science": We can only talk at and past each other—until, frustrated by this exercise, we start bashing each other's heads in. The present project is a scholarly one. It has no immediate practical goals, such as more profound dialogue between religious traditions or more amicable relations between their adherents. Yet, indirectly, it is relevant to both of these aims. It presupposes the possibility of objective understanding and comparison, which also implies a middle ground between total relativism and fanaticism. Although Robert Neville, a scholar of impeccably irenic temperament, has had no polemical intention, there is here an implicit rejection of the "postmodernist" assumptions mentioned before. Both the method of the project and the title of this volume bear testimony to this. With one exception (which was a practical matter), each religious tradition was interpreted by a scholar who is not an adherent of it. This, of course, implies that this can be a valid enterprise and therefore shows a faith in the possibility of scientific reason that flies in the face of the "postmodernist" epistemology. And to speak of a "human condition" further implies that all human beings, and thus all religious traditions, share a common objective world that provides at least some categories by which different views of it can be compared and assessed.

These remarks do not necessarily imply a consensus on these matters within the project. Very probably they do not. They are only intended to show why the participant thinks that the project should be of interest beyond the area of religious scholarship proper.

Preface

Robert Cummings Neville

The Comparative Religious Ideas Project, based at Boston University, ran from the fall of 1995 through the spring of 1999, meeting as a seminar for twenty-five days in total. Its results are published in three volumes: *The Human Condition*, *Ultimate Realities*, and *Religious Truth*. The conclusion of the project was a conference in May, 1999, at which the participants in the project were joined by a number of distinguished scholars of world religions, including Anne Birdwhistell, Jose Cabezon, Julia Ching, Jordan Pearlson, Arvind Sharma, Jonathan Z. Smith, Max Stackhouse, Tu Weiming, and Lee Yearley, who had not been involved in the project save Stackhouse and Tu as mentioned below. The conference reflected on drafts of the volumes and produced helpful insights into what we had done and not done with the special virtue of external but experienced perspectives. Although the three volumes were drafted sequentially, they are published together and thus benefit from a retrospective overview in the form of this preface, which appears in each volume.

Two purposes motivate the project: to develop and test a theory concerning the comparison of religious ideas, and to make some important comparisons about religious ideas of the human condition, ultimate realities, and religious truth. These two aims are intimately connected: the theory cannot be tested without putting it to work making comparisons, and comparisons are not to be trusted without a justified second-order reflection on the nature of comparison.

In the study of religion in Western cultures today, the making of comparisons among religions on topics such as ours is not novel or surprising. Despite the fact that scholars are worried about the imperialism of interpretive categories, comparisons are standard fare in undergraduate religion courses—how else can people learn about religions new to them? Moreover, ignorance of the world's major religions is simply unacceptable today in any discipline within religious studies, even in confessional theologies, if only for the sake of keeping imperialist prejudices in check. The larger worlds of politics, economics, and cultural communications are deeply shaped by conceptions of how religions relate comparatively to one another, often conceptions that are unnecessarily ignorant and parochial. So what we propose here is to offer some better comparisons on very important religious topics, better for having been refined through the comparative methods of the theory.

The careful presentation of an elaborate theory of comparison for religious ideas, by contrast, is extremely surprising in religious studies today and a significant contribution if successful. Precisely because of raised consciousness about the imperialism of earlier comparisons and theories of comparison, theoretical approaches to religion and especially to comparison are highly suspect. Theory as such is unpopular. Our most unusual purpose, then, is to present a theory of comparison and make it work. This purpose itself has brought some serious qualifications and limitations to the project as will be indicated shortly.

The design of the project has been to assemble a working group of persons in the greater Boston area consisting of both tradition-specialists in different religious traditions and generalists of several types, along with graduate students, and then to set to work discussing the three large topics of religious ideas comparatively in structured ways, one each year, with a fourth year for editorial polishing of the three volumes mentioned.

The project's working group was selected to set in tension two contrary tendencies in thinking about the comparison of religious ideas. One is the tendency to see each religion, perhaps even each text within a religion's intellectual tradition, to be unique and special—and to be in danger of misconstrual when subjected to comparisons. For this purpose we recruited six specialists in different religions with a strong commitment to historical specificity: Francis X. Clooney, S.J., expert in Hinduism; Malcolm David Eckel, expert in Buddhism; Paula Fredriksen, expert in Christianity; S. Nomanul Haq, expert in Islam; Livia Kohn, expert in Chinese religion; and Anthony J. Saldarini, expert in Judaism. The contributors page in each volume gives the particulars of their affiliations. Of course, each of these scholars specializes in only some strands of his or her tradition and in only some periods, usually the ancient or medieval. Moreover, to emphasize the difference between scholarly comparative purpose and the worthy though different purpose of interfaith dialogue, these scholars were selected because their tradition of expertise is different from the tradition with which they primarily identify, with only one exception (Haq).

Each of these scholars was helped by a graduate assistant, sometimes to the extent of co-authorship of their papers; working with the scholars as listed above were Hugh Nicholson (with Clooney), John Thatamanil (with Eckel), Tina Shepardson the first year and Christopher Allen the next two (with Fredriksen), Celeste Sullivan (with Haq), James Miller (with Kohn), and Joseph Kanofsky (with Saldarini). The purpose of including the graduate students as full partners in the working group was not only to facilitate the research and writing but also to develop ways of teaching collaborative research in religious studies at the doctoral level. Whereas the natural sciences sponsor collaborative projects in which experts from very different fields come together on a common problem, the custom in religious studies, especially its humanistic side as involved in textual research, has been to gather like-minded and similarly trained scholars. Inspired by the sciences, our project explicitly seeks diversity.

The other tendency we sought for the working group was integration, synthesis, and generalization, a drive to raise new questions for each of the traditions that we bring into comparative perspective. Four of us represented this move, each in different ways: Peter Berger, a sociologist; John H. Berthrong, an historian of religions; Wesley J. Wildman, an historical and constructive theologian and philosopher; and myself, a philosopher, theologian, and theorist about comparison. In the first year of our study, we thought of this second group as the "comparativists" and the first group as "specialists." Quickly it became clear, however, that the specialists compared in their own ways and that the generalists had specialized religious perspectives behind their integrative work. We are pleased to find now that all of us engage in comparison, each in ways reflecting our beginning tendencies but even more what we have learned from one another in the collaboration. Moreover, as the group became conscious of itself as having an integrated identity, with habits of language and thought developed through time invested together, we came to think of our project in terms of the comparisons to which we all contribute rather than merely the comparisons each of us makes as influenced by the others. This process is by no means complete, but it is discernible and in fact described in each of the volumes in Wildman's appendices, "On the Process of the Project." In the original formulation of the project we were clear that the ways the group worked together would have to develop over time. What we had not anticipated in the original formulation of the project is the importance of the reporter, Wildman, who produced the seminar minutes and who called us continually to assess what we had accomplished, how stable our comparative hypotheses are on the one hand and how tentative on the other.

In addition to the working group the project had a board of senior advisors who reviewed the initial design and met with the working group at the end of the first year and in the concluding conference. These include Julia Ching, Jordan Pearlson, Max Stackhouse, and Tu Weiming. The outside advisors helped to bring our shared work into new and critical perspectives.

The thought was that, though both specialists and generalists are comparativists in one sense or other, the specialists would prevent too-easy generalized comparisons while the generalists would keep the specialists in comparative conversation with one another. There have been some discouraging times when we realized just how hard it is to learn to think together without dropping to a lowest common denominator, or giving in to pressures for consensus, or quickly agreeing to disagree without pushing the arguments as far as possible. The labor of joining these two kinds of approach is apparent in the progress through the three volumes. In *The Human Condition* the specialists discuss what their separate texts or traditions say about the topic, and the generalists' "conclusion" maps these and other points onto a comparative grid. In *Religious Truth*, the last volume, the comparisons take place within the specialists' chapters and the generalists' "conclusions" are indeed summaries and then reflections on important topics that emerged from the comparisons. The middle volume, *Ultimate Realities*, is truly transitional with the grid gone but the conclusions heavily formed up by the generalists. After much discussion, and with the encouragement of the outside experts at the concluding conference, it was decided to leave the form of the progressive collaboration as it was in fact, and indeed to gloss it more explicitly in appendices to each volume. These volumes thus reflect the learning process of the working group.

⟿

Why study the human condition, ultimate realities, and religious truth instead of other topics? Although each is explained and its importance outlined in the respective volumes, in a sense the selection is arbitrary. Our initial grant proposals put forward six topics of which these are only three. Salvation, food and diet, ritual, religious journeys, religious cosmologies, religious communities, illness and health, goodness and evil, the nature of religious practices such as meditation, the roles of women, social stratification, religious violence, religious beliefs as social constructions—these and many more major topics were suggested at various points and could just as well have been chosen. Most of these receive some discussion in one or more of the volumes, but each could have been treated as a major category.

In another sense the choice of topics is not arbitrary because these three lend themselves very well to investigation while laboring to develop effective collaborative strategies and to test our theory of comparison. The great religious traditions each have a literature about these topics, variously construed. These topics also have been under discussion in the Western academy for over two centuries, and there is a growing body of literature here, too. Therefore we could limit our work to examining texts, and doing so within academic traditions of interpreting these or like texts. We know, of course, that there are many non-textual expressions of ideas, but we simplified our work so as not to have to deal with them here.

To the question whether these topics and the categories that spell them out are *justified*, the answer is more complex. They certainly are justified in that they have a trajectory of scholarly analysis into which we have stepped with three volumes of further reflection that go a long way toward refining them. But have we shown that reality is such that the human condition, ultimate realities, and religious truth identify very important elements? In *Ultimate Realities*, chapter 7.1, and again in chapter 8.6, Wildman and I say that at least four tasks are required for justifying our kind of categories. First is to identify relevant plausible possibilities for comparison; second is to explore the logical or conceptual structures of the categories and to justify this conceptual or philosophical work; third is to provide a genetic analysis of the religious symbols compared and to relate this to the comparing categories, including within the genetic analysis accounts of historical, social, psychological, neurophysiological, and environmental evolution; and fourth is appropriate analysis of the circumstances that accompany the key shifts in symbolic representation during the history of the religious ideas. The Comparative Religious Ideas Project focused almost entirely on the first step in justification; nearly all of our debates were about the plausibility and relative importance of these categories. *Ultimate Realities* introduces a theory of contingency in chapter 8, and *Religious Truth* presents a theory of religious truth in chapter 8, both of which begin to address the approach to justification through logical and philosophical analysis; but these do not go far enough to justify our categories. The third and fourth steps are almost entirely absent except for an occasional genetic account of the history of ideas. The entire field of religious studies is decades away from a thorough justification of any categories in this rich sense. From time to time we have drawn close enough to see what real justification of our categories would mean, and have drawn back before the enormity of the project. Our contribution here is rather simple and fragmentary.

Why did we choose these six "traditions," and how do we study them? The religious traditions studied and compared in this project are, in alphabetical order, Buddhism, Chinese religion, Christianity, Hinduism, Islam, and Judaism. The obvious anomaly in this list is Chinese religion, because we might expect a distinction between Daoism and Confucianism, and maybe Chinese Buddhism. After all, contemporary scholars divide their expertise, intellectual styles, and professional loyalties into Daoist, Confucian, and Chinese Buddhist studies respectively. In our group, Livia Kohn is a specialist in Daoism and John Berthrong in Confucianism, so the temptation to distinguish Chinese religion into subtraditions is genuine. On the other hand, both Kohn and Berthrong take a stronger interest in Chinese Buddhism than David Eckel, our Buddhist specialist whose language expertise is in Indian and Tibetan tongues, suggesting that Chinese Buddhism is at least as Chinese as it is Buddhist. Moreover, Confucianism and Daoism share an ancient Chinese cosmology that is also vital to Chinese folk religions and an important influence on Chinese Buddhism. Thus, it seemed to us that the major literate traditions within Chinese religion should be considered together.

For the sake of comparison of the religions' ideas about our topics it is highly advantageous to be able to analyze some particular texts in detail. Yet these texts are meaningful as representative of the religions only when we also have in place some more general characterizations of the religions. And then of course the texts represent the religion of which they are a part in only one way, and other texts might develop the religion in quite different directions: Augustine, some of whose texts we discuss, interprets the Christian view of the human condition differently from Origen, for instance, or Mary Baker Eddy. So our strategy is as follows.

For the general characterizations of the religious traditions we go to their core texts and motifs. These are ancient scriptures and classics, events illustrated in them such as the Exodus and the Confucian revolt against disorder, or thought patterns such as yin-yang complementarity and the search for underlying unity. Religious traditions form around and take their initial identity from these core texts and motifs in such a way that all subsequent developments in each tradition have to come to terms with them. Religious traditions, as we know, are extremely diverse internally, often in contradictory, sometimes warring, ways. Yet all the kinds of Hinduism accept the importance, if not authority, of the Vedas, which are their core texts. Buddhism, a religion originating in the same South Asian environment, does not. Rather, its core texts and motifs have to do with the sermons and other teachings of the Buddha, early tales of his life, and the understanding of authority in terms of the Buddha, Dharma, and Saṅgha. Both Daoism and Confucianism base themselves on the ancient Chinese yin-yang cosmology and the classic texts of the Spring and Autumn and the Warring States periods; the *Yijing* is as Confucian as Daoist, and plays crucial roles in both throughout their histories. Sunni and Shi'ite Muslims war with one another but still define themselves as Islamic based on the core text of the Qur'ān. Orthodox, Roman Catholic, Protestant, and Radical Reformation Christians, as well as the Independent Christian Churches of Africa, identify themselves through the ways they interpret the Christian Bible, however different those ways are. Orthodox, Conservative, Reform, and Reconstructionist Jews take very different stances toward the Torah and the rest of the Hebrew Bible, but they are all forms of Judaism because that is their core text, especially in virtue of its motif of the Exodus and formation of the people of Israel.

Our strategy is to consider the six religious traditions on the one hand in terms of their core texts and motifs, and on the other hand in terms of some one or few texts that can be analyzed in detail for comparative purposes, especially in terms of how they relate to the core texts and motifs. Thus we avoid the pitfalls of attempting to describe the "essence" of a religious tradition and can still make general characterizations based on the core texts and motifs and the diverse ways they have been interpreted.[1] We also honor the nervousness of our specialists about making comparisons without specific texts to work on and their careful circumscription of the comparisons to the content of those texts.

There are two further advantages to this strategy of specific texts plus core classic texts and motifs. The first is that it invites other scholars to treat yet other texts as different representatives of religious ideas within a religion, and to make comparisons among different authors. The limitation of the texts we actually discuss here is an example of the fragmentariness of our enterprise, in the face of which our model invites supplementation. The second is that it makes our arguments vulnerable to correction by inviting criticism of our representations of the core texts and motifs, of our interpretations of how the specific texts relate to them, and of our comparisons.

It should be clearer now why we have chosen to examine six religions that have long intellectual traditions. Each has a rich mine of core texts and motifs and long, complicated histories of diverse interpretations of them. By contrast, we do not have core texts for Native American religions that have been supplemented by long traditions of diverse interpretation, although we do have core motifs for those religions that, with advancing scholarly interpretation, might soon make those religions candidates for our kind of comparison of religious ideas. Within the limits of the six traditions represented, therefore, the religious ideas we want to compare can be understood in terms of their histories and their polysemous qualities.

The experts in our group are all specialists in the ancient or medieval periods of their traditions, first millennium CE developments at the latest. We have depended on the specialists to emphasize historical and textual details. The generalists, by contrast, tend to have more philosophical interests and a higher tolerance for generalizations. Thus a healthy tension is induced in our work between the historian's concern for ancient identifications of the religions and the philosophically or sociologically minded generalist's concern for what about them is really important to compare in our late-modern historical situation.

⟡

The heart of our conception of the comparative enterprise is that it is an ongoing process, always proceeding from comparative assumptions, formulating comparisons as hypotheses, making the hypotheses vulnerable to correction and modification until they seem steady and properly qualified, and then presenting them for further correction while accepting them as the new comparative assumptions. This pragmatic approach to inquiry structured the design of the project, the actual course of our discussions, and the editorial composition of our books.

Closely related to this pragmatic emphasis on process and vulnerability is a particular conception of how a comparison is made, namely, by means of a vague category such as the human condition that is variously specified by different conceptions of the human condition. The different specifications are translated into the language of the vague category, with three resulting moments or elements: the vague category as such, the multitude of different specifications, and the restatement of the vague category as now enriched with specifications. Comparison and its problems are closely allied with translation and its problems. These issues of process and theory in comparison are discussed somewhat informally in *The Human Condition*, chapter 1, which is all the methodology a reader needs to get into the specific comparative chapters of that book or of *Ultimate Realities* or *Religious Truth*. But for those interested in a more explicit elaboration and defense of this approach, see *Ultimate Realities*, chapter 8, "On Comparing Religious Ideas," chapter 9, "How Our Approach to Comparison Relates to Others," and chapter 10, "The Idea of Categories in Historical Comparative Perspective." For how these methodological considerations relate to a theory of religion, see

Religious Truth, chapter 9, "On the Nature of Religion: Lessons We Have Learned."

The structure of the three volumes of The Comparative Religious Ideas Project is the following. Each is written to be read by itself, providing an extended multidisciplinary and comparative essay on its topic, the human condition, ultimate realities, or religious truth, and situated with a self-conscious methodology. Each has an introduction to the topic that also explains the specific structure of the book. Each book has six chapters by the specialists, with each of these chapters giving part of one tradition's perspective on the topic, followed by one or more chapters of conclusions and essays on topics related to comparison or the topics studied. Each volume has an appendix describing the process of the project and one or more annotated lists of suggestions for further reading.

Authorship is a complicated matter for a collaborative project. Nothing in any of the volumes is unaffected by the collaborative discussions of the working group and usually it is not possible to cite the origins of the ideas and influences. Nevertheless, each chapter is the primary if not sole responsibility of some one author. The six specialists had different working relationships with their graduate research assistants, and in several cases the assistants contributed texts to the chapters as secondary authors. These are indicated in the tables of contents with the formula "X with Y," where X is the primary specialist author and Y the contributing research assistant. The collaboration between Wildman and myself grew dramatically throughout the project. I was the first author of the methodological and summary chapters. He believes himself not to have made sufficient contribution to the second summary chapter in *The Human Condition* to be listed as a secondary author, although I myself know the influence of his ideas. He is a strong secondary author in all the others, and indeed those written later show his hand nearly as much as mine. The two chapters of which he is primary author and I secondary, *Ultimate Realities*, chapter 9, and *Religious Truth*, chapter 9, are strongly his own and are oriented to relating our project to larger ongoing comparative work. We have made no attempt to disguise the differences in temperament, approach, or conviction among our authors.

Important limitations of this project need to be discussed because they derive from the choices made about the project design itself. (These are in addition to limitations that come from our incompetence or plain foolishness, which we are not prepared to admit.)

Limiting our sources to literate traditions among the "world religions" means that we have cut ourselves off from the ideas of other traditions on our topics of the human condition, ultimate realities, and religious truth. We are limited to the Axial Age religions, for instance, and some scholars are now saying that the study of religion needs to move beyond the dominance of those religions and properly seek wisdom from Native People, traditional religions, or New Age religions. This is particularly important in light of ecological concerns, for instance. Although we are not attempting to compare contemporary religious ideas, particularly, our focus makes us vulnerable to the charge that the non-literate traditions may have been far more important for our topics than we indicate. We admit that this might turn out to be the case.

Limiting our sources to six literate world religions means also that we cut ourselves off from the methods and kinds of understanding that come from disciplines that deal with mainly non-literate religion, for instance, anthropology and other social sciences, ritual studies, art-and-religion, studies of popular religion, folk culture, and the rest. We focus on the old-fashioned approaches of textual studies, literary analysis, historical research, philosophy, and methodology itself. This was a deliberate choice on our part in order to work out effective collaboration. If collaboration has seemed difficult and occasionally baffling to us, think what it would have been if it had to include the vast array of other approaches to religious studies. That we do not include them does not mean that we reject them nor deprecate their importance. Rather, it means that our approach to the religious ideas of the traditions we cover is fragmentary. Moreover, it means that our analyses and conclusions are vulnerable to being greatly qualified or overthrown when those other approaches are finally brought into collaborative connection. The strength of our approach in this matter, however, is precisely here: we are clear about the limits of what our literary methods can do, and it will be a great advance when our comparisons are corrected by what arises from outside those limits.

Limiting our discussion of the relations among different religions' ideas on our topics to *comparison* does not do justice to the problem of *translation*. The extensive literature on translation, and the history of European translations of religious texts in the nineteenth century, come at many of our problems from another angle. By no means is translation identical with comparison, but there are many analogies and overlapping concerns. One difference is that, at least according to our theory of comparison, a vague comparative category has a moment of quasi-neutrality relative to the specific things compared, and can be assessed in that regard, whereas translation does not employ a third language to mediate between the two being related. Translation indeed exhibits what Jonathan Z. Smith calls "magic" when a speaker of two languages "just knows" how to say in one language what the other says and how that sometimes cannot be said. In our theory, as developed in *Ultimate Realities*, chapter 8, translation is a proper part of comparison but set within a larger process of checks.

The limitation of our project to comparing "basic ideas" such as the human condition, ultimate reality, and religious truth, makes it very difficult sensitively to register many of the points made by the "hermeneutics of suspicion." Most writers of our religious texts have been men and reflect the male point of view. Feminists have rightly argued that a text-based approach such as ours thus is cut off from what the women around the men were thinking, and the women's thinking might have been very important for shaping the religious realities. Feminists also have rightly pointed out that our approach reinforces the general patriarchal assumption that what is important in religion is the men's opinions, expressed in texts, and that this reinforcement is worse the more effective our approach is. Other liberation perspectives, speaking on behalf of marginalized voices and religious movements, rightly can criticize our choice to deal only with the "central" world religions. Our answer to these forms of the hermeneutics of suspicion is two-fold.

First, we plead for mercy in light of the difficulty of the task of comparison. We need to begin with the most elementary and direct expositions and comparisons that we can in order to get started. Unless we can bring some greater self-consciousness and a self-correcting procedure to comparison, comparative judgments will remain at the level of anecdote and prejudice.

The second answer follows from the first. The only way to make progress in comparison, from the standpoint of the hermeneutics of suspicion, is to have steady and well-formulated hypotheses to criticize. Does the hermeneutics of suspicion overturn these comparisons? Supplement them by comparisons on behalf of women and the marginalized? Reconstruct the intellectual causal boundaries? To respond Yes to any of these questions and to justify the affirmative answer would be to make solid and important progress. Our comparisons are aimed to be in a form vulnerable to precisely these corrections. (The forms of the hermeneutics of suspicion that consist in scientific reductionism and anti-colonial theory are spoken to throughout the texts of all volumes.)

One of the subtlest limitations of this project was pointed out at the concluding conference by Jose Cabezon. The very structure of the project, with a director, co-directors, senior scholars, and graduate students, with authorship shared as primary and secondary, reflects what he called a hierarchical Cartesian approach. He meant not only the obvious hierarchical organization but also the supposition of the importance of clarity, order, and classification. A Buddhist would not have done it this way. Others in the project earlier had pointed out what they called the Confucian orientation of the project itself as well as in the expressions of conclusions; I am a Boston Confucian and this complaint was made in good humor, but much to the point of Cabezon's remark. Cabezon focused on what he took to be our attempt to reduce comparison to filling in a comparative grid. He believes our procedure claims that a comparative hypothesis works by fitting things into their Cartesian places.

To this I admit first that the project is indeed organized hierarchically, that I do not know how else to get grants from funding agencies who want someone to be responsible, and that as a Confucian I believe it is the responsibility of those with age and power to foster those down the line, step by step. Moreover, it should be reported that a fairly constant refrain through the four years of the project was that I should be more directive and not let the seminar flow under the guidance of its format alone. Though perhaps embarrassed to admit it, most of the participants believed the academic process could benefit from a Confucian Daddy.

But Cabezon was right that all this nudges the process toward order and definiteness. In defense of this arrangement, we believe this is the way to make progress. If our hypotheses have a definiteness that is false to reality, that can be pointed out. An hypothesis without definiteness cannot be criticized. If the very process itself cooks its conclusions, then that can be pointed out by showing another possible process. This was a recurrent theme of our discussions from the first year, when it was proposed that we relate narratives rather than compare in our way, or that we suspend definiteness in favor of indirection. But we could never quite organize the alternatives. This means that our procedure is vulnerable, and possibly misguided, but that someone else needs to say just how this is so and to do better. For us, at least most of us, our procedure has advanced comparison and we offer these volumes for use and criticism.

Note

1. See M. David Eckel's argument in "The Ghost at the Table," *Journal of the American Academy of Religion* 63 (1995): 1085–1110, to the effect that it is possible to talk about what is essential in the sense of *necessary* to a religious tradition without presupposing an *essence*.

Acknowledgments

The Cross-Cultural Comparative Religious Ideas Project has been supported by generous grants from the National Endowment for the Humanities and the Henry Luce Foundation, Inc., as well as cost sharing on the part of Boston University. We are deeply grateful to these sponsors without which the Project would have been impossible.

We are also grateful to Dr. Susan Only who was the Project Administrator for the four years of its duration and who superintended finances and arrangements with great skill. We thank Ms. Shirley Budden, Financial Officer of the Boston University School of Theology, and the Boston University Office of Sponsored Programs, especially Ms. Phyllis Cohen, for their careful work on behalf of the Project. At various times, Christopher Allen, Raymond Bouchard, Mark Grear Mann, and James E. Miller performed valuable editorial services in the preparation of our publications, and they deserve great thanks.

Several people outside the Project read some or all of drafts of the three volumes that report its findings, and we thank them all for very helpful advice that has guided revisions. They include Anne Birdwhistell, Jose Cabezon, Julia Ching, Jordan Pearlson, Arvind Sharma, Jonathan Z. Smith, Max Stackhouse, Tu Weiming, and Lee Yearley. Ching, Pearlson, Stackhouse, and Tu were senior advisors to the Project from the beginning.

Our colleagues at the State University of New York Press have been extraordinary in bringing our publications to light, beginning with our acquisitions editor, Ms. Nancy Ellegate. We also thank our production editor, Ms. Marilyn Semerad, and the marketing manager, Dana E. Yanulavich. We dedicate these volumes to William Eastman, whose daring in the publication of religious studies made projects such as this possible.

Introduction

Robert Cummings Neville
and Wesley J. Wildman

To understand the human condition in its deepest and most mysterious respects we rightly look to religion. Religion helps to form elementary imaginative structures about how we do or should orient ourselves in the cosmos. Religion shapes and rehearses in ritual our most important affiliations with one another and with nature, and it provides the rationales both for why those affiliations are important and for what it means to be obligated to them. To be human is to lie under obligation in some sense and religion allows us to imagine and enact this in detail. Religion addresses the most basic questions of the meaning of life or its lack of meaning, of individual grounding and destiny, of personal fulfillment or ultimate frustration, pain, and suffering. Religion articulates what is most real, harmonious, and ideal about human life as well as why human beings usually suffer so from illusion and sick craving, from imbalance and disharmony, and from social injustice and personal sin. When we want to do something about this sad contrast between the normative side of the human condition and its ordinary actual failure, religion gives us maps (myths), models (saints and rituals), and methods (of spiritual growth), even if they amount only to a counsel of resignation.

Of course much about the human condition is not related directly to religion. We need a planet with a favorable ecological niche, gravitic and atmospheric conditions within a small range of tolerance, and resources for food and shelter. We must cope with parents, endure adolescence, and get along with others so as not to be thrown to the wolves. Communities are vulnerable to dislocation and destruction. Most people get sick and everyone dies eventually. The human condition is an adventure in search of beauty and excellence; it requires institutions of governance, education, and justice; it involves the pursuit of knowledge for its own sake and for utilitarian ends; and it is entangled with issues of personal and social maturation, the cultivation of prosperity, and defense of one's place. All of these aspects of the human condition involve non-religious dimensions of life such as biological maintenance, interpersonal relations, plain pain and suffering, human expansiveness, the arts, politics, law, education and learning, psychology, economics, and the successful use of force. How foolish it would be to attempt to treat all of these dimensions of the human condition as functions of religion! And yet, when any of these other dimensions of the human condition gets threatened or questioned in a radical way, or when coping with them pushes the institutions that address them to their margins and beyond, these dimensions re-raise issues of the human place in the cosmos, of the nature and justification of elementary affiliations, and of the meaning and identity of human life—and these are the religious aspects of the human condition.

Alas, alas, the previous two paragraphs are sadly naive and misleading. This is all the sadder because what they say is largely true and would be accepted as common wisdom by nearly everyone who understands them and is not a scholar trained to pick up their naiveté.

The chief reason for their naiveté is that there are many religions, not just "religion in general," and adherents of those religions do not necessarily say the same thing. Whether they agree on the generalizations asserted above in the name of "religion" cannot be known until we discover what each says in its texts and debates about the aspects of the human condition under discussion and compare those assertions. Until we compare them, we do not know and cannot assert responsibly whether they agree or not, and in what respects. And so it is dangerous, or at least naive, to talk much about aspects of the religious dimension of the human condition in general. Instead of saying "religion is such and so," we should be open to saying "some religions are such and so" and "other religions are something else again." The very distinction between religious and non-religious dimensions of the human condition is complicated.

The other reason for the naiveté is that the language of those two paragraphs arises out of a particular intellectual and social context, namely the existential situation of late modernity in Western cultures characterized by the collapse of Christendom. The seeds of that collapse were sown in the late Renaissance critique of religion that initiated the privatization of religion and its steady withdrawal from public life. World War I demonstrated that "Christian Civilization" in Europe was a contradiction, and a dangerous one. Samuel Huntington has recently detailed the criticisms levied by East Asian, South Asian, and Islamic critics against fallen Christendom as being morally and spiritually bankrupt, existentialism to the contrary notwithstanding.[1] European civilization's intellectual and cultural responses to the collapse of Christendom have been diverse and somewhat frantic. Paul Tillich is perhaps the pivotal European figure to interpret the collapse of Christendom in terms of the human condition.

In the tradition of mediating theology since Schleiermacher, Tillich asked what broader dimensions of human religiosity Christianity is supposed to address. Tillich's was an explicitly philosophical move, asking questions that he thought were more general (or vague) than the particular concerns of Christianity, Judaism, and secular European culture, and that in fact were asked in particular passionate ways in all religions. Instead of using categories such as "sinners rendered up to judgment," Tillich talked about the human condition and about God as the ground of being that makes the human condition possible. Christianity was interpreted as an expression of a broader phenomenon, or as a specific (and for Tillich, uniquely correct) religious response to a broader religious need. His explication of this took advantage of the deep spiritual vocabulary of European existentialism. But its power was not limited to that. Japanese scholars of the Kyoto school as well as Orthodox Christian scholars influenced by Dostoyevsky plumbed the depths of late modern existential Angst, and were in dialogue with Tillich's categories such as the *human condition.*

Perhaps Tillich's categories characterize much that is important about late modern society in general, including those non-European cultures reacting to modernization or about to do so. At any rate, the notion of "the human condition" and the associated references to existentialist literature, art, ethics, and the critique of traditional religion through generalization, is a twentieth-century idea. It has a European origin and global dissemination through the effects of modernity. How can such an historically and culturally limited concept serve to reveal something basic about religion in general or importantly common to all or most religions? Eighth-century Christianity would no more have recognized talk of "the human condition" than would have eighth-century Buddhism, Islam, or Vedānta. Is it not naive, then, for the opening paragraphs of this section to talk about "the human condition" at all if they are intended to be explications of "religion" or even "all religions?"

Critiques of naiveté, however, are cheap. As Ricoeur and others have pointed out, realism requires the acquisition of a "second naiveté."[2] By paying attention to criticisms, insisting that doubts be based on as much concrete evidence as positive assertions, and disciplined engagement with the real subject matter under discussion rather than merely generalized rumors about it, a legitimate route is open to substantive "critical commonsensist" embrace of the subject matter.[3] From that embrace comes new knowledge that is, at the very least, an improvement over both what is claimed in the "first naiveté" and what is left after its skeptical rejection. All this is to say that, self-mortifying suspicions aside, we know a lot about the human condition and about religion and religions. We do not need to ask whether we know enough that is trustworthy to get started because we already are started. We do need to ask how to make what we think we know vulnerable to correction. One important way to do this is to compare what religious people and their sacred texts say about the human condition.

Starting with the vague theme of the human condition, the specialist scholars of our project seminar used their selective approaches in an effort to determine how the human condition is conceived in each of the six religious traditions being studied.[4] Then we asked what subcategories articulate important comparative relations among the traditions or subtraditions that our experts had analyzed. The discussion was wide-ranging with many dozens of candidate hypotheses considered, usually arising from the rhetoric of the specific text under discussion. It was obvious from the start that an idea or term common to several traditions, such as the self, often means quite different things. This caused us to become clearer about how a category is vague insofar as it is differently specified in the several traditions and how it is specified differently when made concrete in terms of them. The discussion involved a constant tacking back and forth between vague and specific formulations.

In the end—really at the end, in the last revisions of this manuscript—we settled on a scheme of categories as expressing what we most want to say about how the religious traditions compare concerning the human condition. The comparisons fell out under three main heads: *cosmological dimensions* of the human condition, *personal dimensions*, and *social dimensions*.

Issues concerning the *cosmos* that bear upon the human condition grouped themselves around interpreting the cosmos in four principal respects: the *unity* of the cosmos (including God plus the world in traditions that distinguish them), *ontology* or the problems of existence, the *value* of the cosmos and things within it, and *causation* or patterns of origination and change in senses that bear upon the human condition.

The personal and social dimensions sometimes seemed quite distinct from one another, as when we discussed the Buddhist no-self doctrine for which social matters seem not so important, or the Jewish notion of the people of Israel for which the niceties of self or no-self seem beside the point. But in the end we came to see the distinction as intolerably artificial and so here treat the personal and social dimensions together. We interpret these in four comparative respects as they bear on the human condition: How they define *personal identity,* including issues of community, substantiality, continuity, and body-mind-soul relations; how human beings lie under *obligation,* with a stress on the very different ways religious cultures articulate what is normative, ideal, or binding; how the human condition involves a *predicament* that religions address as a problem; and how all the above are a function in part of human *affiliation* with other people, with social groups as such, with institutions of various sorts, and with nature variously encountered.

Obviously, some of these categories are more natural for some religious texts and traditions than for others. For instance, it requires a significant leap of interpretation to apply the category of "obligation" to Buddhism, even though the category does register important Buddhist themes. Again, questions of ontology typically are secondary in Jewish thought and texts, though the category is still needed to account for important Jewish ideas. Overall, we agreed that the categories themselves, the ordering that places the cosmic categories first, and even the propensity to present the categories schematically was rather Confucian in character. As we hope to show in the rest of the book, however, useful results can come of this scheme and its tendency to distort can be checked by subjecting every result to the dialectic of correction. After all, no scheme will be free of implicit commitments and this particular scheme is at least as richly encompassing and capable of registering diverse ideas about the human condition as others that we considered.

Only at the end, we should stress, did this scheme become settled enough to count as a provisional result of an ongoing process. It was not a guide to the discussion or papers throughout, although predecessor candidates were operative from early on. Chapters 2–7 should not be read as illustrating the scheme of categories but as providing the discussions from which the scheme emerged. Chapters 8 and 9 express comparative hypotheses in terms of the scheme that emerged from the earlier chapters and seminar discussions and from their author's own analyses. The tentativeness of both the scheme and the organization of the comparative hypotheses should be recognized; but the comparative process as we understand it makes the scheme vulnerable to nuancing and correction.

The tentativeness of the scheme, and the comparisons that fall within it, are illustrated in the following way. We noticed early on that an alternative approach to the human condition could be generated from a narrative reading of this distinction in which a human life begins somewhere, goes somewhere, and encounters various situations along the way. This kind of narrative formulation of the elements of the human condition is particularly congenial to Buddhist emphases. We also recognized that the rubric of cosmos-society-individual is especially congenial to Chinese emphases; indeed this rubric emerged from our early discussions of Kohn's paper for this volume. The cosmic-social-individual pattern of categories was adopted for what seems to us now to be a number of reasons: partly because most of our specialists favored this rubric, partly because we felt it more directly addressed cosmic and social topics, and partly because of a previously undiagnosed Confucian disposition among most of the project's generalists. Becoming aware of the contrast between this rubric and the more narrative proposal just described helped us to understand that our decision had a specific history and context. This in turn helped us to find ways to overcome the limitations of perspective associated with the rubric adopted for this volume. Rubrics inevitably invite limitation of perspective; the trick is to avoid being trapped by those limitations by finding ways to enrich the perspective.

But all this turns on comparison. Comparison of religious ideas is as much the topic of this book as the human condition. We begin with an introduction to the problem of comparison and to the theory that guides our approach.

Notes

1. See Samuel P. Huntington's *The Clash of Civilizations and the Remaking of World Order* (New York: Simon & Schuster, 1996).
2. See Paul Ricoeur's *The Symbolism of Evil* (Boston: Beacon Press, 1969), especially the conclusion, "The Symbol Gives Rise to the Thought." See also the essays in Part IV of his *The Conflict of Interpretations: Essays in Hermeneutics,* ed. Don Ihde (Evanston, Ill.: Northwestern University Press).
3. "Critical commonsensism" is the title Charles Sanders Peirce gave to his philosophy. By "critical" he meant that any claim to knowledge had to be treated as an hypothesis and made vulnerable to correction when there is reason to do so; he attributed this philosophic theme to Kant, who used the term "critical" in a different sense, however. By "commonsensist" he referred to the philosophy of the Scottish commonsensists Thomas Reid and Dugald Steward and adopted from that the thesis that thinking is always in the middle of life, never at its beginning or foundation. Therefore we are assuming many things as commonsense dictates, and legitimately do so, until

there is concrete reason to doubt them. The crucial points for Peirce are to determine what a good reason for doubt consists in, what its occasions are, and how to make the process of reflective living vulnerable to correction. See the various papers with “critical commonsensism” in the title in volume 5 of the *Collected Papers of Charles Sanders Peirce*, ed. Charles Hartshorne and Paul Weiss (Cambridge, Mass.: Harvard University Press, 1934).

4. For the technical meanings of “vagueness” and “specificity,” see 1.2; cross references in this volume are to chapter and section.

1

On Comparing Religious Ideas

Robert Cummings Neville
and Wesley J. Wildman

1.1 On Comparison: Why It Is Important

To understand another person, to negotiate a business deal, to settle a trade dispute, to avert a war, to generate cross-culturally feasible solutions to global ecological problems, to cultivate habits of tolerance in a local community—these are all activities in which people must grasp what is important to each other in terms that all participants can understand. Consider the complex task of forging international resistance to torture, for instance. Torture may be repudiated by one person on the basis of an inalienable right to personal safety, by another because of divinely guaranteed dignity of human life, by another because of long-term pragmatic concerns for social stability, and by yet another because it destroys the honor of everyone involved. Nevertheless, all may reach an understanding that can be expressed in terms general enough to encompass everyone's particular interpretation. That agreement might be expressed by saying that "torture is wrong and must be stopped." Each of the key terms in this sentence ("torture," "wrong," "must," "stop") is vague, because each is understood differently by the various people who affirm it. Nevertheless, the sentence as a whole and each term within it are meaningful.

This illustrates the value of common terminology for mutual understanding and solving problems cross-culturally. The terminology does not need to apply univocally to all of the instances it must cover; nor can it be equivocal, because no mutual understanding would then occur. Rather, such common terminology must be vague in just the right way: vague enough to be specifiable differently in each case it describes, but not so vague as to be meaningless. Very often terms with the right sort of vagueness do not already exist before a practical problem draws attention to the need for them. In that case, diligent work can yield new concepts or perhaps modify the nuances of old language to create the needed terminology.

The central component of such diligent work is comparison, for comparison is required both to detect the need for better terminology, and to generate and test proposed terminology. Yet comparison itself requires common terminology, so a complex dialectical process is implied here: as the terminology improves, comparison gets more nuanced; and as comparison is more adequate, the terminology gets more accurate. This dialectical process is prevented from becoming viciously circular by the specific character of the things or approaches that are engaged in comparison, and to which the terms apply.

That the process of comparison is dialectical in this sense means that comparisons are never complete or fixed, but rather provisional through being dependent upon the subsequent stability of the comparative terminology. Moreover, a particular statement of a comparison is an abstracted part of the larger dialectical process of developing and criticizing the limits of the terminology. The terminology thus needs to be understood not only in its stipulated meaning but also through the history of its development. Comparison is a *process* of making, evaluating, and correcting comparative assertions, not merely the assertions themselves lifted from the process. The critical process renders the terminology vulnerable just as it does the assertions made within it. Perhaps the most important methodological theme of this book is that comparison is a process that is all the better the more vulnerable it is to correction. The research project of which this book is a partial expression centers around the critical process of probing the vulnerabilities of the comparisons it considers.

In this book, the objects of study are religious ideas about the human condition. Comparison is used to develop, probate, and improve appropriately vague terminology, most of which (like the phrase "human condition" itself) is inherited from past discussions, and then semantically tweaked. The terminology about the human condition produced in this way is presented here ready to serve three main purposes: deepening mutual understanding of the religious traditions discussed through accurate description, elaborating a comparative understanding of religious traditions that allows us to say how they are similar and different in relation to the human condition, and enhancing well-established traditions of interpretation about the human condition in cross-cultural perspective. Other goals for this flexible, multipurpose terminology can be imagined easily enough, but do not figure explicitly in this book. For example, detecting what is religiously important about the human condition connotes a kind of systematic, normative inquiry into the human condition that lies outside the goals of this volume. Presumably, the terminology produced by diligent comparison here will be of use to others who might wish to pursue such a task.[1]

A further word should be said here about what is to be compared in this volume, namely, religious ideas about the human condition. Religions involve much more than ideas, and in fact it is difficult to find a situation in which religious ideas are deemed more important than their intended practical purposes. Typical representatives of even intensely philosophical traditions such as Madhyamaka Buddhism and Medieval European Christianity would say that religious ideas are for the sake of guiding practice, sometimes paradoxically so. Accordingly, *comparative religions* is a far broader project than *comparative religious ideas*, our topic here. For those traditions comfortable with the word "theology," the topic discipline is "comparative theology," and for those traditions uncomfortable with that word, the comparison is with the ideas and ways of thinking that either take the place of theology or exclude theology and its analogues. A more exact statement of what falls within the category of "religious ideas," considering diverse traditions of world religions, is itself part of the project's inquiry (although it falls within the research projected for the third year). We have chosen to compare religious ideas rather than the many other religious phenomena and practices that might be compared in order to narrow the project somewhat and to be able to employ traditional disciplines of analysis that themselves have a critical history, namely the analysis of texts in various traditions. As noted in the preface, this approach to comparative religious ideas limits the religious traditions that we can study to those with extended textual intellectual traditions—although surely religious people from primal or traditional religions and popular and marginalized religious groups have interesting religious ideas to compare. Whatever conclusions we reach should be qualified by the recognition of the fragmentariness of the project: ideas are only a fragment of religious reality, and religious traditions with extensive literatures are only a fragment of religious life.

1.1.1 Comparative Method

"Comparative method" means at least three things. One is the conception of comparison, what comparison consists in, what counts as a comparison. Another is the ongoing process of comparison whereby comparisons are proposed as hypotheses, refined, tested from as many angles as possible, and related to one another. Yet a third is the procedure our specific project has followed, the character of our seminar discussions and the writing and rewriting of papers.

Jonathan Z. Smith has suggested to many people that there is no method in comparison, only a "magical" leap of imagination, and therefore that talk of comparative method such as we venture in this project is necessarily self-deceptive.[2] That Smith's argument does not serve the ends of those who would exorcise comparison from the study of religion is evident from the fact that he himself makes intriguing comparisons, even in the same volume. Nevertheless, a challenge is issued to those such as ourselves who would defend the possibility of methodical comparison. Actually, Smith's objection is most forcefully pronounced against comparison as a science in the sense of Geisteswissenschaft, something we do not mean here at all. There is a lot of territory between comparison as strict science and comparison as magical leap, however, and our project has been cultivating a patch of ground in that middle territory.

To be clear, we agree with Smith that comparison of religious phenomena is ill-served by a method offering an algorithm for moving from demonstrably true premises to a thereby demonstrably true conclusion. Descartes grandly defended that conception of method in relation to all forms of inquiry in *Discourse on Method* and *Meditations*. Aristotle and Boethius earlier had also conceived of method in that narrow, logical way. It was understandable that discussion of methods for inquiry at first did not clearly distinguish method from logic, being content to focus on the complex debates over which forms of argument really succeed in extending truth from premises to conclusion solely by virtue of the argument's formal structure. But logic in that narrow sense is merely the aspect of method that deals with the validity of argumentation. Ongoing debates in logic bear out its importance; logicians want the validity of argumentation to be rightly described by logic regardless of the field in which argumentation is used. Method for inquiry, by contrast, must be attuned to the specifics of each field of inquiry, including the relevant data, modes of interpretation, and strategies for correction of proposals. Logic is merely the beginning of method. Therefore, to agree with Smith that narrowly logical conceptions of method are not useful for guiding the comparison of religious phenomena is merely the beginning and not the end of discussions of comparative method. For us, comparative method must attend faithfully to the complexities and frustrations inherent in comparing religious ideas.

1.1.2 *Vulnerability and Stability*

Comparing religious ideas begins in confusion with possibly misleading verbal comparative similarities and interpretive biases of which there are good reasons to be suspicious. Beginning *in medias res*, comparative method by various devices imagines new and potentially improved hypotheses about comparisons, and then proceeds to reflect on them and test them from many points of view. The final status of the hypotheses is not that they are guaranteed by the structure of some method but that they are formulated in such a way as to be vulnerable to correction. Whatever stability and justification they possess derives from how they have been tested so far. Their worth depends on their vulnerability, which is the degree to which they can be sustained or corrected by new tests and perspectives as these are put into play. In our pragmatic approach, a comparative hypothesis that seems to have been guaranteed by the method through which it was produced is likely to have been made somewhat invulnerable to correction. An invulnerable hypothesis suffers from the fact that its limitations and possible falsity are obscured, perhaps as a result of delight or relief at having something seemingly firm to hold onto while at sea in the genuinely baffling world of religious ideas. If Jonathan Z. Smith is sometimes misread as being opposed to all comparison of religious phenomena, it may be most often by those who have developed a visceral allergy to the obscuring of the vulnerability of comparative hypotheses by surreptitious ideological biases. We share the allergy but advocate a method for comparison that helps maintain vulnerability and diagnose bias.

Our comparative method aims to produce *stable* comparative hypotheses without endangering the virtue of vulnerability, a matter of delicate balance. On the one hand we need to present hypotheses supported by good reasons in order to take them seriously for further study. Vulnerability to future correction thus cannot mean hypotheses so silly that any fool can see through them. On the other hand the comparative hypotheses might very well be corrected radically in the future, shown to have great limitations that were not immediately apparent, or revealed to be more projections of the comparativists' conceptions than genuine features of the phenomena. Stability does not imply no exceptions: quite the contrary, an hypothesis is stable if many exceptions to it are noted and yet on balance the comparative point holds. We have discovered that almost anything in a religious tradition has some analogue in the other traditions and that, even though configuration and weighting of shared elements varies among traditions, generally stable comparative distinctions between traditions and texts can be made, at least for the purpose of further exploration. Thus, part of the meaning of *stability* is that the comparison can become *destabilized* by attention to details without always causing the wholesale collapse of an hypothesis. Resorting and reconfiguring might be the way to register the complexity of the phenomena while preserving the insight of the extant hypothesis. When that fails, abandoning or replacing the hypothesis is demanded. Comparative method is a process of framing stable hypotheses, destabilizing them in properly empirical fashion, amending them and recovering stability where possible, and scrapping the hypothesis in favor of a new idea when the time comes.

1.2 Vague Categories

When two or more things are compared, they are compared in the same respect. We call the respect of comparison a "vague category," which is to say a category used vaguely enough to allow room for the coexistence of different kinds of things within it. A category is vague if it allows things that contradict one another to fall within it; a category is merely general if it requires the things that fall within it to be mutually consistent.[3] So, to compare our six religious traditions in respect to what their representatives think about the human condition is to treat "the human condition" as a vague category. Just what the various traditions say about the human condition are the ways they specify the vague category. What they say might be in contradiction with one another but still fall under the vague category of the human condition. A comparative category, therefore, has at least two modes, moments, or levels: the vague and the specified. (There is a third, to be discussed shortly.)

To be clear about this distinction is extremely important, and unfortunately this clarity is not common in the comparative traditions of the nineteenth and twentieth centuries. What has been common is to take one tradition, usually Christianity, to be the source for vague categories and then to construe all the traditions as specifications of those categories as determined by their source-tradition, in which process Christianity gets preferential treatment and all traditions (including Christianity) are distorted. This is a literal description of Hegel's comparisons, though not of the order of his exposition.[4] The vague category properly must be no more biased toward one specification than toward another. Therefore, part of the process of comparison is the continual reformulation of the category as vague so as to be neutral to the ideas compared within it. Nearly every vague category has some particular historical roots—"the human condition" is heavily influenced by twentieth-century existentialism—but the category needs to be abstracted and purified so as to be as neutral as possible in registering what is compared by means of it.

Another common mistake has been to rest content with applying a vague category to traditions being compared without bothering to make clear how each tradition specifies the vague category in its own way. This blinds us to the details, which is disastrous because nuances are often the most important features of a tradition. To say that the West Asian traditions and many of the South Asian ones are "theisms" is vaguely true; but this does not say how or in what sense any of those traditions are theisms, and no tradition is a theism in general, not even Western Enlightenment deism. Comparisons require attention to the concrete details. None of this presumes that the details of religious ideas are always more important or more real than the vague categories they specify. Indeed, in certain interpretive contexts the relatively vague fact that all those religions are theisms, in contrast to Confucianism, say, might be far more important than the differences between them and the commonality might point to the metaphysically more fundamental reality. In general, making progress in comparison requires moving back and forth between the details and the vaguer commonalities. Although things need to be compared in a common respect in order for differences to be noted, if what the things compared have in common is vague, the most fundamental question is whether and if so how they are different or similar in respect to it. Clarity regarding the logical place of the relatively vague and specific is crucial.

Comparison requires a third logical step, mode, or moment beyond articulating vague categories and how each of the traditions compared variously specify them. The specifications need to be translated into the language of the vague comparative category. That is, whatever the comparativists decide are specifications of the human condition needs to be translated into the language of the human condition. Thus, the language expressing the vague category gets enriched and filled in so as to register the distinctions in the various specifications. As this step advances, the category itself becomes rich and concrete, expressing how all the traditions compared articulate it. From this vantage point both the category vaguely articulated and the separate specifications are abstractions from what the comparativists now know about the human condition, expressed in at least momentarily stable hypotheses.

Only when the specifications are translated into the language of the vague category, enriching that language, is it possible to make comparisons. Only then is it possible to see whether the traditions say the same, radically different, partially overlapping, contradictory, or virtually incommensurate things. To say that the various religions fall under the same vague category is not comparison. To say that the specifications sit side by side is not comparison. Comparison is to say how the specifications are similar and different in terms of the category in respect to which they are compared.

To be clear in this way about what would be a successful comparison is not automatically to establish that successful comparisons are possible. Our judgment about the prospects for successful comparison of religious ideas can be summarized in a triply conditional statement, as follows. If the category vaguely considered is indeed a common respect for comparison, if the specifications are made with pains to avoid imposing biases, and if the point of comparison is legitimate, then the translations of the specifications into the language of the category can allow for genuine comparisons. It must be stressed that even this conditional judgment is a provisional, empirical result and not somehow guaranteed in the abstract by some theory of how much human beings can know about religious matters. The real challenges to successful comparison are the three conditions, however, and the test of any comparative method is whether that method helps to detect commonalities without bias for a legitimate purpose. While some thinkers have philosophical commitments for or against the possibilities of meeting these conditions, we do not. Our comparative method does not guarantee that the three conditions can be met; it only optimizes the process of comparison. It is our experience, not our philosophical commitments, that suggests that the three conditions can be met, sometimes, and so that genuine comparisons can sometimes be made.

1.3 Criteria for Success

Success in comparing religious ideas is a more elusive goal than success in comparing other features of the world, such as cars, economic policies, or even human personalities. The problem can be expressed in terms of the three conditions that we think must be met before successful comparisons can be achieved.

First, it is hard to tell in relation to religious ideas whether or not we have genuine commonality in the vague categories presupposed in a comparison. The main reason for this is two-sided. On the one hand, religious ideas can be interpreted descriptively, as affirming something about reality. On the other hand, they can be interpreted in terms of the qualities with which they carry what is important in their referents over into the interpreters. "Getting a true description" is one kind of carryover. But conforming one's soul to God, giving up attachments, shaping liturgies for their proper effects, affecting the moral life of a community—all these are potentially "true" carryovers that are not ordinarily descriptive.[5] Again and again we have noted the importance of the soteriological purposes of religious ideas, in contrast to their descriptive purposes. Symbols used non-descriptively say something about their referents, but often it is hard to determine what this is, for the sake of comparison, even when a descriptive interpretation of the symbol is silly ("God is the *rock* of my salvation"). Accordingly, special care needs to be taken when translating highly symbolic ideas into the language of the comparative category.

Second, personal investment in religious matters makes the avoidance of bias more difficult than in many other areas of comparison. Even with the best will in the world, religious convictions run deep and are multiply, invisibly, connected to the criteria we bring to bear on judgments of many kinds. And sometimes the will is not at its best, even among comparativists. Special care is needed here, too, and our comparative method is an asset in detecting and correcting bias.

Third, legitimacy of the purposes of comparison is often difficult to judge. The usual reasons people compare religious ideas are to satisfy curiosity, to increase understanding, and to serve other theoretical purposes such as the construction of theories of religion or theories of religious realities. While there are other reasons, some perhaps more noble and some less, there are problems even with the usual reasons, and here are two. First, comparison asks questions of tradition's religious ideas that those traditions themselves may not ask. Even when the tradition itself is involved in comparison the questions we ask may be differently voiced. Leaving aside how adherents feel about it, this can be of concern to some thinkers because the very act of comparison alters at least the expression if not the substance of the specific texts and traditions. Second, comparing religious ideas can have implications for the comparers' own existence and distortion occurs when the quest for impartiality robs the ideas of their natural relevance for transforming people's lives, even when the people in question are those comparing the ideas in a scholarly way. This is the intriguing opposite of the problem of bias: distortion can also be the result of the struggle to be unaffected by the ideas we compare. How serious are these two problems? Our provisional viewpoint is that, if done carefully and vulnerably, allowing comparative questions to draw out implications and reveal new aspects of the subject can be helpful for everyone and everything concerned—adherents, scholarship, personal lives. Comparison is an act that changes things and we hold that our comparative method helps us take responsibility for those changes.

Whether the value of our purposes in comparing religious ideas finally justifies such distortion or changes as might occur in the resulting processes of translation and evaluation is a matter of moral judgment informed by experience. We think our purposes valuable enough in our context to justify comparison. We can imagine contexts in which our moral compass would point in the opposite direction.

The goal of success in comparing religious ideas is a truly adventurous one. It is problematic, at least in these three ways, but these are problems appropriate to such an adventure. Our empirically grounded conclusion continues to be that all three problems can be managed with the aid of a good comparative method and that successful comparison is possible.

1.4 Process and Strategy

From what has been said it is apparent that the work of coming to understand religious ideas comparatively is a process within which a presentation such as this book is a report on progress. This should not be construed to mean that the same authors will keep revising and revising, never finally meaning what they say. On the contrary, the process should be reported out when the comparativists think they have done the best they can with their material. Further corrections will be done when new perspectives, new questions, new data have been found, and often this will have to be done by others. That it is a report on progress means that our project is part of a larger cultural comparative enterprise.

A particular comparative project, dealing with a finite set of subjects as in our study here, needs to be considered as part of a larger intellectual and social milieu, as we began to do above in reflecting on the morality of comparing religious ideas. There are many assumptions about other comparative topics that are in play as we study the human condition and we assume things about parts of religions other than those under focused discussion here. At any given moment there are assumptions shaping the background of comparisons, often assumptions unique to each of the fields represented—Chinese studies, Indian studies, Jewish studies, sociology of knowledge, metaphysics, history of Christian theology, and so forth. Although these masses of background assumptions are easily engaged with one another, they are never clearly exposed except when attention turns from the focused topic to them directly. Yet being provoked by our shared struggle with the material under comparison also serves to call into question and alter our background assumptions, especially as we learn from one another. In the long run, perhaps the most critical tests for vulnerable ideas come not when they themselves are the focus of attention but rather when they are critical elements in the background of a project engaging something else. The solid, nuanced pragmatic tests of hypotheses come when the hypotheses are put into play in a larger arena.

Having said this much about the place of our kind of study in the ongoing process by which a society comes to understand and relate to its various cultures, more can be said about the process of comparison internal to our project. The process begins with the methodological affirmation that several different disciplines are needed to make progress and that a multidisciplinary approach is better pursued together than by any of us working alone. The process then picks up some obvious comparative topics, for instance, the human condition, ultimate realities, and religious truth, that nearly everyone would agree cut across most religions and in respect of which they can be compared. But then the process encounters different understandings of those topics, even at the vague level, which need to be talked through. The differences among the specialists come from the tendency to see the vague category in terms of the *prima facie* exemplifications or specification in their respective traditions and texts. For the generalists, the differences come from the cultures of their different disciplines. Yet all of us operate in the same general late-modern academic world so that these discussions move quickly and productively.

The process of comparison then turns to explicit discussion of the specifications of the comparative category proposed by the specialists in each tradition. Suggestions are entertained and criticized. Criticism is usually double-edged, pursuing two questions, often both at once. One is whether some religious idea is really an instance of specifying the human condition. The other, in light of ambiguities or puzzles regarding the first question, is whether we have correctly parsed the human condition at the vague level. At this point, it is helpful to break the main comparative category down into subcategories and thus come to a multidimensional understanding of the vague categories, such as the cosmological, social, and personal aspects of the human condition. Such a division then calls for new attempts to locate and relate specifications, and thus a constant back-and-forth critical dialectic is established, only slowly coming to steady articulations of the vague categories and settled specifications.

Yet another dimension of the process is the translation of what is learned through specifying the vague categories into the language of the categories themselves, for instance, the human condition. At no point is the comparative process wholly devoid of this translation procedure in which the actual comparison is expressed. But the translation process becomes more systematic and fulsome as the comparative hypotheses are formulated and tested.

Vulnerability within this process characterizes each of the moments. We might discover that we have misstated the vague category, or misidentified and misdescribed a specification, or mistranslated the significance of that specification for the vague category and the other specifications. In our own conversations, as well as in the larger process of comparison that has been flourishing for at least two centuries, it is sometimes difficult to identify just what is wrong: the category for comparison, the identification and analysis of a specification, or the development of a language to treat the specifications in comparative fashion relative to the category. It is easier without being easy in the context of self-consciousness about the nature of comparison made possible by a comparative method.

In this process, we have attempted to build in not only the dialectic of criticism between specialists and generalists but also that of continually reassessing the vague categories as grounds for comparison, the selection and interpretation of specifications from the various traditions, and the interpretive translation of the specifications into the language of the human condition and the drawing of comparative conclusions. We believe this is the logic of how good comparison gets done in the larger comparative-religions conversation. We have tried to operationalize and epitomize it in our project procedures.

This is sufficient anticipation to key in readers to the selectivity in the six chapters ahead. The selectivity will be emphasized once again at the beginning of chapter 8.

Notes

1. Extended discussions of the nature and purposes of comparison, the special terminology it can produce, and its historical and philosophical background, are to be found in *Ultimate Realities*, chap. 8.
2. See "In Comparison a Magic Dwells," *Imagining Religion: From Babylon to Jonestown* (Chicago: University of Chicago Press, 1989).
3. The language of "vagueness" comes from the philosophy of Charles S. Peirce, and it is discussed, with the references to Peirce, in *Ultimate Realities*, chap. 8.
4. See, for example, his *Lectures on the Philosophy of Religion*, 3 vols., ed. Peter C. Hodgson (Berkley: University of California Press, 1984, 1985, 1987).
5. In *Religious Truth* we distinguish three kinds of truth, or rather three problematics for understanding truth: epistemological truth, scriptural and revelational truth, and truth in practice. The last has to do with realizing truth, becoming true, manifesting truth, living in the truth. See especially chaps. 7 and 8.

2

Chinese Religion

Livia Kohn

2.1 General Considerations

Chinese religion has been divided into several traditions, different to the point that many scholars speak of Chinese religions in the plural rather than of a singular religious system of China.[1] The major traditions commonly acknowledged are the so-called high religions of Confucianism and Daoism, joined further by the foreign creed of Buddhism in its heavily sinicized form, and complemented by popular religion, the day-to-day beliefs and practices of the Chinese people. These four, although both by the Chinese and by scholars distinguished as discrete entities and studied in their particular forms, have continuously interacted with each other and formed an integrated religious system that shares certain fundamental principles of classical Chinese cosmology and stands united in a uniquely Chinese view of the universe.

The human condition in this system is normatively seen in an overwhelmingly affirmative mode: it is good to be alive, it is most precious to be born human, it is not only desirable but possible to realize oneself humanly in and through this world. A second major characteristic of the human condition in Chinese religion is that it is closely tied in with other beings, such as plants, animals, people, and even ghosts and spirits, and with other levels of existence. The individual in China never stands alone—some scholars even go so far as to deny the existence of true individuality in traditional China[2]—but moves always along in interrelations with others in a social context and with the forces of nature and the divine in a supernatural dimension. This facet of the human condition in China is directly related to the fact that the Chinese worldview in general is more oriented toward process than substance, that it focuses more on correlations and synchronicity than underlying entities and ultimate causes.

These basic characteristics have certain consequences for the way the human predicament is viewed in Chinese religion. First, the Chinese are eminently self-conscious about the division into cosmos, human affiliations (society), and individual (heaven, earth, and humanity), distinguishing at every step the forms and processes of interrelatedness both within and among these levels. Second, they pay close attention to the human mind, since the active awareness of interrelation, the conscious adaptation to or deviation from the interactive patterns of body, society, and cosmos, holds the key to the attainment or loss of harmony—normatively defined as the ideal and original state of human beings in the world.

Chinese religion thus offers a world-friendly vision of the human condition, a vision of interaction and process rather than individuality and substance, and a vision of a body-mind unity wherein one's conscious perception of self and world determines the degree of the human enterprise. The human task in this world then is to maintain a balance, to stay in continuous and harmonious interaction with self, others, nature, and cosmos without disturbing the various interlocking circles and maybe even remedying whatever disturbances may already have occurred. Harmony is always a goal, achieved only partially and forever to be worked for—but a real goal nonetheless, something that is felt and experienced at times in everyone's life to a greater or lesser degree.

This-worldly and fundamentally positive in its evaluation of the human condition, Chinese religion has yet also a transcendental level, a dimension of other-worldliness. This aspect of the big world picture, stimulated by Buddhism and actively taken up by religious Daoism in the middle ages (220–960 CE), has become a firm part of mainstream Chinese culture, manifesting itself both in Neo-Confucianism and popular religion since the Song (960–1260). It proposes an ideal level of pre-being, an ultimate state before creation, which represents the ideal state of being. The human predicament in this vision, then, means the loss of this pure state of pre-existence. The main task of people is accordingly to recover it by reaching out to the higher spheres. The goal is to leave the interrelatedness of the realm of harmony behind and find a place at the source of cosmic creation and the center of life, to become part of something higher, other, and latent, something that is present in the world but not identical with it.

All three higher religions of China share this vision of transcendence, finding it realized in Buddhist nirvana, Daoist immortality, and Confucian sagehood. They also all agree on the continued importance of the realm of harmony, so that anyone who has attained the higher spheres can come back to the world to help other beings—whether as Buddhist master, Daoist immortal, or Confucian sage. The superimposed layer of transcendence, originally imported with an alien religion and as a completely different dimension from the classical model, therefore did not diminish or fundamentally alter the basic Chinese vision of the human condition but enriched it by raising it to a more divine level and by opening new paths and worldviews in traditional China.

2.2 The Chinese World and the Human Predicament

The Chinese world in its normative dimension is fundamentally good and inherently harmonious. Created in a series of transformations and without an active break from the pure, formless Dao, it manifests itself in a wondrous and mysterious combination of manifold forces and beings that—as and when each realizes its nature as originally part of the Dao—work together to constitute a perfect cosmos.[3] The essential basis for this inherently harmonious world is an energy known as *Qi* (*ch'i, ki*), the life force, vital breath, inner pneuma of all existence. Qi, as part of the Dao before creation called "primordial Qi" (*yuanqi*), carries the inherent qualities of each and every living thing, determines its nature and activities. It is the matrix of life, the DNA of the universe's genetic structure.

The Chinese view regarding the root of all life is monistic and unity-oriented: all is ultimately one, and the One is manifest in all. In this respect it is a clear example of what Maria Colavito has called the "mythic model of the One"[4] as opposed to that of the Zero. In a world rooted in the One, "everything manifest would of necessity be a copy of that which exists within the One . . . with the One the only original."[5] Any object or being consequently partakes of the One yet can never be the One itself, which remains formless at the root of creation. Everything thus has always only partial access to the unity of the original, is never fully whole. One-centered cultures typically rest their entire thinking on the One and strive for the return to wholeness and completion. Accordingly, the Chinese count everything from one (they are one year old at birth), see creation as a division of the One in manner of the amoebae (*Daode jing* 42: "The Dao produces the One; the One produces the two; the two produce the three . . ."), and strive for the return to the unity of the origin.[6]

Human beings in this world are yet another manifestation of partial oneness—specific phenomenal outcroppings of the true all-encompassing One (Dao) at the center. Since they have this nature in common with everything else (stars, mountains, governments), it follows that their inherent structure exactly mirrors, or is isomorphic with, the organization of everything else. In other words, as correlative thinking is fundamental to all Chinese thought, the movements and manifestations of Qi within the human being are structurally identical with those in society, the natural world, and the stars. The human body as a result is used as the predominant metaphor for institutional, geographical, and astronomical realities—and vice versa. The human body is described as an administrative organization including ruler, civil ministers, and the military, as a natural landscape complete with mountains, rivers, and plowing farmers, and as a replica of the stars on the firmament.[7] The gods and spirits and even demons, moreover, that inhabit the wider world are equally present within the human body, from where they easily communicate with their counterparts in the stars, the mountains and rivers, and the families and communities of humanity.

There are, therefore, four areas of life: the body, society, nature, and the sky. All equally grounded in the same original Oneness through Qi as their common constituent, they follow the same organizational principles. They moreover reverberate in close mutual interaction, causing reactions and developments as part of an overall pattern of "impulse and response."[8] The comparison of such a universe has, moreover, been made in contemporary physics with a gigantic jelly bean, in which various condensed elements, all made up from the same primordial stuff but placed in different positions, vibrate at different yet ultimately harmonizing frequencies that each make a clear contribution to the whole and, if ever distorted, jolt the entirety of the system.[9] The notion of vibrating frequencies is useful here and has, in a musical metaphor, been made by the Chinese themselves.[10] It expresses how underlying unity and manifest diversity can be joined in one system. All vibrating frequencies are ultimately made from the same stuff (vibrations) yet can hum at quite different speeds (high or low). In the same way, all things in the Chinese universe hum along but some do so more intensely than others. Qi, in other words, has various levels of density and speed of flow, which are each suitable for specific entities and change with time and space. This, in turn, means that the Qi can be either too thick or too thin, flow too fast or too slow. The Chinese, having codified the movements of Qi on all levels and in all niches of life, have provided its most sophisticated analysis within the human body in the context of their traditional medicine. Here the variations in Qi density are expressed as "full and empty" (*xushi*), more technically called "excess and deficiency," while the differences in speed of flow are described in terms of temperature as "hot and cold" (*rehan*).[11]

Any given entity, and that includes people as well as houses and landscape features, communities and institutions, weather patterns and starry constellations, can thus deviate from its Oneness-given course or inherent frequency pattern and exhibit an irregularity. This, therefore, is the key to defining the human predicament in the Chinese world. Typically a deviation begins with a perfectly harmonious tendency that is taken too far. Caution, for example, the proper attitude to cultivate in the iciness of winter, may go to extremes and turn into the excessive emotion of fear. Future-planning and the reasonable storage of goods, the thing to do in the fall, may get out of hand and turn into greed. Similarly, to take an example from a different area, the movement of tectonic plates, a gradual and natural performance within the earth, can intensify to a sudden grinding and result in an earthquake. Greed, fear, and earthquakes as well as all other types of negativity and misfortune (hatred, envy, sickness, wars, political upheaval, etc.) are therefore equally viewed as derailments of Qi. Causation in the Chinese system is thus understood as an impulse of Qi—whether good or bad, harmonious or deviant.

This view leads to two further observations: First, the derailment of Qi on one level—remember the vibrating jelly bean—emits an impulse that stimulates irregularities on the others, so that an earthquake or eclipse becomes the expression of, or the omen for, a major sociopolitical upheaval. A recent example of this is the 1976 earthquake, the biggest in China in the century, that was linked immediately with the death of Mao Tsetung a few weeks later. Second, while all natural entities, such as planets, tectonic plates, and even rivers that flood, undergo a temporary irregularity and then bounce back to their regular course without much trouble, human beings, having consciousness and memory, tend to perpetuate the irregular patterns above and beyond the crisis situation. A first spurt of greed or fear, brought forth in a particular situation, is duly relieved through acquisition of goods and the calming of nerves, but then is remembered and becomes part of the individual's repertory of reactions. Thus the human predicament arises with emotions and desires, which in turn influence conscious thinking and give rise to evaluations of things as profitable or harmful, good or bad. Self-perpetuating, these emotions, desires, and conscious evaluations are much harder to get rid of than to acquire. Far from being only a temporary burst of deviance, they become encrusted and solid, and take over the thinking and behavior of the person—a continuous thorn in the flesh of the universe, an unending dissonance in the vibrations of the cosmic bean.

A universal response to the human predicament so defined is the admonition, found in Chinese sources of all traditions, "to know when to stop" (*zhizu*), to learn how to do things at the right time and in the right measure. The great divination classic of the *Yijing* accordingly specifies when "perseverance furthers" and when it is auspicious "to cross the great water."[12] Confucians express the same idea as the ability of the ideal minister to come forward and serve at the right time yet retire again when his task is done without clinging to his position. Daoists, appealing to the inborn intuition in people, find it in the natural sense of how much effort to expand on what project and at what point. The popular tradition, finally, has it in detailed calendar regulations, which tell people exactly when to plant and sow (and for how long) and when to harvest and to store (and how much).

Once, however, the decline into emotions and desires has been made, "knowing when to stop" is no longer enough and a battle has to be fought to restrain, control, and suppress the deviating forces. To this end, different traditions have suggested various means. The Confucians take recourse in propriety (*li*), the correct behavior within the existing hierarchies and fulfillment of obligations to the social community; the Daoists advocate a lessening of sensory inputs and outward actions in a state of tranquillity and "nonaction" (*wuwei*); the Legalists find the solution in sets of detailed laws that punish excesses and force people to stay in line; the cosmologists, finally, establish a system of "seasonal commandments" that order every detail of life in accordance with the ongoing interaction of yin and yang (aspects of Qi activity) described in a pattern of five phases (wood or lesser yang, fire or greater yang, earth or yin/yang in balance, metal or lesser yin, water or greater yin).[13]

In addition, popular culture has developed a veritable plethora of control mechanisms, including both ways to find accordance with the inherent cosmic rhythms and means to remedy an existing deviation. Fortunetelling with the help of dreams, facial features, and natural omens, and geomancy, the science of placing tombs and houses for maximum harmony of Qi, are preventive in this respect, representing the attempt to guard against baleful influences and stay on the right side of the universal pattern. Medicine and rituals, on the other hand, serve to reestablish regularity, stimulating or blocking off the flow of Qi with the help of acupuncture, moxibustion, exorcism, and prayer.

Taking off from this ancient and all-pervasive understanding of the human condition, the religious Daoists made it their task to see to the return of the splintered human Qi to its original home in the Oneness of creation. To do so, they proposed a worldview that expanded the pure, formless Dao at the root of all into a primordial manifestation at the nub of creation—a manifestation that was still pure but no longer quite so formless. Heavens of vague, glittering materials, gods that change shape continuously, and scriptures that blend in and out of existence in celestial caverns make up this divine realm. Here the Oneness is still intact, and all heavens, gods, and scriptures participate in it fully and not just in part. They therefore have the ability to merge back into ultimate formlessness, just as they can go forward and become solidified in worldly appearances (e.g., scriptures appearing in human script on the walls of grottos).

The human task from this perspective is a much more onerous one: not just to abandon all desires and conscious evaluations to return to one's inherent Qi-balance, not just to maintain and serve this balance to the best of one's ability, but to go far beyond it and recover the original purity of the Dao and establish oneself firmly in the heavens, reaching a state "as immortal as heaven and earth, living as long as the sun and moon." This process of transcendence and recovery necessitates the complete transformation of the human being in all physical, sensory, and conscious aspects. The socially determined and desires-defined "I" must give way to a cosmic, indeterminate, and ultimately formless oneness with the One, a state in which immortal identity is only a metaphor for a level of pure so-being that can neither manifest nor be imagined by ordinary means. To this end, Daoists prescribe diets that eliminate common food, gymnastic and breathing exercises that make the body supple and soft, meditations and trances that raise the level of interior awareness, and visualizations of the gods and the heavens that allow the adept to see the details of his new home.[14] They thereby transform the person from a physical and sensory human being to an eternal and formless divinity, providing for the return of the partial to the ultimate One.

2.3 Resolution of the Human Predicament

2.3.1 *A Textual Example*

Many texts, in different ways and focusing on different aspects of this complex, two-layered system, describe the human predicament in China and offer various ways to resolve it. Some concentrate entirely on the ways and means by which to curb desires and emotions in either social or individual contexts, others emphasize the best methods to maintain inherent harmony, others again—especially those of religious Daoism—give precedence to transcendence and detail the routes from ordinary to immortal life. Still, there are some that describe the system as a whole, and among these is a set of two Daoist texts that, dating from the Song dynasty (960–1260), provides a comprehensive example of how the workings of harmony and transcendence are described in indigenous terms. The texts have parallel titles, "The Venerable Lord's Wondrous Scripture of Exterior Daily Practice" and "Of Interior Daily Practice" (*Taishang Laojun wai/nei riyong miaojing*) and occur in sequence in the Daoist Canon (DZ 645 and 646). Part of the famous "harmonizing of the three teachings" (Confucianism, Daoism, Buddhism) that dominated Song-dynasty thinking, they contain both Confucian and Buddhist tenets, while at the same time following inner alchemy, the dominant Daoist practice of the time. The scripture on "exterior practice" accordingly specifies a total of forty-seven rules of conduct that allow the dissolution of desires and establishment of harmony, while its counterpart on "interior practice" describes meditative exercises that, through the revolution of yin/yang or water/fire energies in the body, result in the creation of an immortality elixir or "great medicine" that will transform the adept into an immortal. But first the texts:

Taishang laojun wai riyong miaojing

(*The Venerable Lord's Wondrous Scripture of Exterior Daily Practice*, DZ 646)

Respect heaven and earth
Honor the sun and the moon
Fear the law of the land
Follow on the way of the kings

Obey your father and mother
To your superiors be honest and withdrawing
To your inferiors be harmonious and kind
All good things do

All bad things eschew
From perfect people learn
Debauched people avoid
High knowledge is dangerous

Deep knowledge is enriching
Be calm and always at peace
Be restrained and always content
Be cautious without worrying

Be patient without shame
Give up all luxury

Devote yourself to perfection
Conceal others' flaws

Praise others' virtues
Practice skillful means
And teach your neighborhood
Befriend the wise and the good

Keep away from sounds and sights
In poverty, stick to your lot
In wealth, give charity
In action, be even and deliberate

In repose, rely on others
Always battle your ego
Never give in to jealousy and hate
Reduce stinginess and greed

Give up cunning and craftiness
Those oppressed help to liberate
Those who hoard try to change
Never break your promises

Always speak the truth
Think of the poor and orphaned
Give aid to the homeless and indigent
Save those in danger and trouble

Accumulate hidden merit
Always practice compassion
Never kill any beings

Listen to words of loyalty
And be free from a scheming heart
Follow these rules
And ascend to the beyond

Taishang laojun nei riyong miaojing

(*The Venerable Lord's Wondrous Scripture of Interior Daily Practice*, DZ 645)

Now, as regards daily practice,
Keep your food and drink firmly regulated

And sit silently in meditation,
Never allowing even a single thought to arise.
As the ten thousand affairs are all forgotten,
You can visualize the gods and firm up your intention.

Keep the lips close to each other
And the teeth lightly touching.
Your eyes don't see a single thing,
Your ears don't hear a single sound.

Thus your mind is unified and focused within.
Now harmonize your breathing into a regular rhythm,
Let it become subtler and subtler, issuing lightly,
Almost as if it wasn't there at all,
And without the slightest interruption.

Then naturally the fire of your heart
Will sink down to the water of your kidneys
And ascend to the cavern of your mouth,
Where sweet saliva will arise of itself.
Then the numinous perfected will support your body,
And spontaneously you know the path to eternal life.

During all the twelve double-hours of the day,
Always maintain purity and tranquillity.
Keep the numinous terrace of your heart free from all affairs: This is purity.
Stop even a single thought from arising in your mind: This is tranquillity.

The body is the residence of the qi-energy,
The mind is the harbor of the spirit.
When intention stirs, the spirit is agitated;
When the spirit is agitated, the energy disperses.

In the same way
When intention is stable, the spirit remains firm;
When the spirit is firm, the qi-energy gathers together.
The perfected energy of the five phases
Thus gathers together and forms a pinch [of pure stuff].

Then naturally in the body
Sound can be heard stirring.
Then, sitting and lying down one is aware
Of a movement in the body like wind blowing,
Of a rumbling in the stomach like thunder booming.

Harmonious energy becomes superb,
And its sweet cream trickles to the top.
Then with ease you can drink from the pure pinch
And your ears will begin to hear the tunes of the immortals.

They are melodies never plucked on strings,
Sounding spontaneously without clapping,
Reverberating of themselves without drumming.

Spirit and energy then combine
Like forming a boy child in the womb.
If you can spot them in your interior realm,
Spirit will start speaking to you
From the true residence of emptiness and nonbeing,
Where you can reside at ease with all the sages.

Next, refine the combination in nine transmutations
And you will produce the great cinnabar elixir.
Spirit will leave and enter freely
And your years will match those of heaven and of earth.

The sun and moon will join to shine on you,
And you are liberated from all life and death.
Every day you do not practice this
You lose something of your power.

So, during all twelve double-hours of the day,
Always maintain purity and tranquillity.
Energy is the mother of spirit, Spirit is the son of energy.
Like a chicken hatching an egg,
So you visualize spirit/gods and nourish energy—
Then, how can you ever be far from the Wondrous?

Mysterious and again mysterious—
In the human body, there are seven treasures.
Use them to support the state and cherish the people,
Grow them from the fullness of your essence, energy, and blood.

Essence is quicksilver [silver];
Blood is gold [gold];
Energy is jade [lapis lazuli];
Marrow is crystal [crystal];
The brain is numinous sand [agate];
The kidneys are jade rings [rubies];
And the heart is a glittering gem [carnelian].

Keep these seven treasures firmly in your body
Never letting them disperse.
Refine them into the great medicine of life—
And among the ten thousand gods
Ascend to the immortals.

2.3.2 *Obligation to Nature and Society*

The first of these two short texts responds to the human predicament by establishing a way to live harmoniously within the world of nature and society, to interact successfully by fulfilling one's obligation toward all surrounding entities. In narrowing concentric circles, it moves from "respect for heaven and earth" and the sun and the moon to "fear of the law of the land" and the way of the kings, on to obedience to "father and mother" and the correct behavior toward one's superiors and inferiors. More specifically, the adept is admonished to honor social relations and obey the social mandate, to do good and eschew evil, to stay away from the debauched and learn from the perfected. In this, as in most of the remainder, the text reflects a traditional Confucian vision, in which, while the planets and universal forces are honored, human behavior is determined largely in the context of obligation to family and the social hierarchy. Here society as a whole is the religious community, the locus for the attainment of harmony and the perfection of social relations is the way to resolve the human predicament.

Confucians thus center their teaching on the five relationships of ruler and minister, father and son, husband and wife, older and younger brother, and friend and friend. They encourage the pursuit of five major virtues, the so-called constancies of humanity, righteousness, propriety, wisdom, and faithfulness.[15] Together the relationships and the virtues, together with seasonal rules and detailed prescriptions of dress and formal conduct, constitute the key norms of the Confucian system, established in the classics on the authority of the sages of antiquity but not derived from a divine source. Nor are they given in the form of unalterable laws but are rather vague guidelines, the meaning of which depends on changing circumstances (as one may be at some time a father, at other times a younger brother) and on the degree of personal rectitude achieved (as some people may find it easier to give up material benefits for the sake of righteousness than others). Thus establishing an overarching standard for the formal relationships and behavior within nature and society, the Chinese define obligation as an exercise in mutuality between a superior and an inferior, between the individual and the group, between human beings and the natural and spiritual forces of the world. Norms in this system are thus guidelines to an ideal of interactive harmony, something to hold dear in one's heart and practice to the best of one's ability in a continued effort that lasts a lifetime.[16]

For this reason, all central precepts of Confucianism regulate human relationships and behavior,[17] and the major salvific activity of the tradition consists in conscious and historical learning. Learning about the world and the great men of the past causes people to become more virtuous, raises their awareness of social and natural harmony, and thus provides the necessary knowledge of how to do the right thing at the right time and in the right measure.

This kind of knowledge also appears in our text on "exterior practice," where it is described as deep and "enriching" as opposed to a knowledge that is "high" and "dangerous" because it creates the illusion of power and ego-independence. This deep knowledge further manifests, as the text describes it, in an overall freedom from emotions, apparent in pervasive calmness and restraint, by being "cautious without worrying" and "patient without shame." To make sure the balance is not only reached but kept, the text warns against "all luxury" and encourages devotion to "perfection," another word for harmony in this context. This harmony within society is moreover maintained by being considerate of others, never pointing out their mistakes but always lauding their virtues, and by behaving appropriately in different life situations, resigned in poverty, generous in wealth, deliberate in action, and grateful for others' help.

Harmony, once won, is yet always on the brink of dissolution, the Qi-flow, however steady, easily falls into deviation. For this reason, the text, closely echoing other Confucian documents, emphasizes that one must "always battle the ego" and clearly warns against the desires, emotions, and unpleasant character traits that develop so easily yet will ultimately prey on one's inner peace: jealousy and hate, stinginess and greed, cunning and craftiness. While fighting against these negativities on the inside, one should also exhibit a socially responsible behavior without, a behavior that is not only the key of Confucianism but in this text also bears distinctly Buddhist overtones. To be always honest in one's dealings and true to one's words, to help the poor and oppressed—those are maxims on which both religions readily agree. But "those who hoard try to change" reflects the understanding that the rich and oppressing are also in need of help, are suffering from inner tensions, and thus constitute a danger to overall harmony because of their strong desires and emotions. Similarly, the notion that by helping the poor and troubled one will "accumulate hidden merit" as well as the encouragement to "always practice compassion" and "never kill any beings" clearly reflect Buddhist influence.[18] Still, the text returns to a more Confucian note by again emphasizing the virtues of loyalty and honesty before indicating, in the final note, that all of this is not to be practiced for the sake of harmony on earth but to "ascend to the beyond."

The "exterior practice" in this Daoist scripture thus conforms closely to the understanding of human beings as parts of an intricate system of obligation and norms as defined through relations and interactions, reaching from different tendencies within the individual through the family, community, and state to the cosmic forces in the sky. The more the parts work together in harmony, the more the vibration frequencies get along, the more auspicious the world is and the more good fortune there is for everyone. This harmony, however, is continuously in danger of derailment, and one must not only guard against the emotions and desires within but also against improper behavior and oppression without. Following the social rules, developing high moral standards and good virtues, is as much part of the establishment of harmony as the control of the desires within—although the former is quite impossible without the latter. Ultimately the social rules are nothing but an expression of the same universal Qi-patterns that also work in nature and in the individual, so that any deviation within (where it is most likely to occur) will render them defunct. Harmony on all levels ultimately depends on the human being, placing him into a condition not only of ultimate connectedness but also of highest responsibility.[19]

2.3.3 *Realization of Oneness with the Cosmos*

On a more celestial and cosmic level, the human predicament is further resolved by transforming the human being back into a pure cosmic being. This is undertaken through "interior practice," which begins where "exterior practice" ends. The second of the two texts, therefore, first admonishes the practitioner to carefully "keep his food and drink regulated" so as to avoid disturbing Qi influences from nourishment. In a technical Daoist context, this means periods of fasting and the replacement of more common foods, especially grains, with the pure herbs and minerals of the Dao, among which pine needles, mica, and "numinous fungus" are the favorites. Next, it specifies a concentrative meditation exercise, during which the adept sits silently and "never allows even a single thought to arise." This level of control of the mind within, just as the changing of the bodily diet, is beyond the harmonization effort of "exterior practice," reaching above mere balance and integration into the realm of formlessness. Only in such a purified condition, free from the "ten thousand affairs" of the world, will the pure gods of the Dao appear in visualization.

To achieve communication with them, the body has to be firm and quiet, and the senses have to be withdrawn completely. As the mind, too, is at rest and unified, the breath becomes so subtle it is hardly noticed anymore. Then attention can be paid to the manifestations of cosmic Qi within, and the fire-Qi of the heart, a warm energy of yang nature, is felt to rise and fall in circulation with the water-Qi of the kidneys. Through these energies, the body participates in the cosmic movements of Qi and becomes part of a purer, more celestial level of existence. Supported by the forces of the Dao, the "numinous perfected," the adept can then maintain the state of inner calm and increase the formless meditation on the circulation of the energies.

Continuing this state, with intention stable and the spirit firm, the circulating energies, revolving in the pattern of the five phases, will coagulate and bring forth a pure substance, the first "pinch" of the immortal elixir. Often described in terms of sexual union, this "pinch" is also called the "mysterious pearl" and forms the core of the immortal embryo that will grow in the adept's divine womb.[20] Its successful coagulation is apparent to the practitioner as a deep rumbling in the body, the first independent movement of primordial Qi as it is reintegrated from its yin and yang aspects. This, although part of the classical tradition, is still happening today, as the 1914 report of Jiang Weiqiao, also known as Master Yinshi, demonstrates. Himself a weakly child and battered by various illnesses, he sought last recourse in inner-alchemical methods and practiced a meditation called "quiet-sitting," during which he would focus his attention on the lower abdomen, where after a while he could feel a "cloud of hot power." At one point, however, the Qi began to move—quite unexpectedly. As he describes it,

> Then, on the twenty-ninth of the fifth month, during the evening sitting, it happened first: All of a sudden there was this intense rumbling movement in the cinnabar field in my lower abdomen. I had been sitting in quiet meditation as usual, but this was something I really couldn't control. I was shaken back and forth helplessly. Then an incredibly hot energy began to rise at the bottom of my spine, climbed up further and further until it reached the very top of my head. I was startled and alarmed.[21]

What Master Yinshi witnesses here and, being himself a modern man with an interest in biochemistry, cannot quite believe is the establishment of the so-called microcosmic orbit, during which the Qi rises up through the spine, passes through the head, and again descends to the abdomen.[22] It does so in a primordial cycle that increases the purity of the entire body and gives rise to more and better drops of the divine elixir. Sipping from it, the adept begins to develop immortal qualities, his senses now attuned to the pure spheres of the Dao, or as the text has it: "Your ears will begin to hear the tunes of the immortals, they are melodies never plucked on strings, sounding spontaneously."

The higher purity reached with this cycle in turn forms the basis for the evolution of the immortal embryo who, as the representative of the adept's pure spirit, will become his divine persona and serve as his vehicle to the realm of the immortals. This is attained through continued revolution of energies, the "transmutation of the cinnabar elixir," and results in the utter merging of the adept with the Oneness at the beginning of the universe. This, in turn, makes him a true immortal: living as long as heaven and earth, happily joining the sun and the moon, and "fully liberated from all life and death."

Having outlined the high point of the adept's career, his merging back into Oneness and utter transcendence of the cycles of the world, the text concludes with a variety of admonitions. First, it warns against laxity and laziness, exhorting students to keep to the practice "during all twelve double-hours of the day," or what we would call "round the clock." Next, it restates the relationship between energy and spirit, the personal manifestation of Qi and the divine aspect of the individual, describing the former as the mother of the latter. In other words, there is no immortality without the physical basis of the body, and only through the purification and transformation of Qi-energy can the spirit be set free and return to the primordiality of the Dao.

A third concluding note once more emphasizes the high value placed on the human body by describing its different parts as the "seven treasures." An originally Buddhist notion (*sapta ratna*), these are seven precious substances, fine metals and gems that are indestructible and of high purity. The Daoists adapt this notion, insert their own metals and minerals in place of the Buddhist ones (listed in brackets), and link the list with different parts of the human body. Retaining the basic substances of the body, such as essence, blood, and marrow, and holding on the heart and the kidneys as the source of pure yang and yin energies, the adept is guided to refine the elixir and attain celestial immortality at the root of all.

2.3.4 *Harmony and Transcendence*

Taken together, the two texts on "exterior" and "interior practice" present a comprehensive description of the human path in Chinese religion. Beginning with a state of deviation from the cosmic patterns, they train adepts through a set of moral encouragements to control their emotions and desires and live as socially responsible individuals, full of compassion for all living beings. Once this positive state of alignment with the universal flow has been achieved, adepts are taught to move beyond all outer manifestations and develop a sense of formlessness within. The body is weaned from normal food as the mind is freed from thoughts, then the pure energies of the Dao, in a more primordial form than they appear in the outer world, are envisioned. Circulating these energies through increasing levels of purity, a divine elixir and an immortal embryo form within, core essences of the energy of Oneness. Joining them fully, the adept attains immortality, first hearing and seeing what is ultimately without sound or sight, then ascending to the heavens and joining them in a life as eternal as the universe itself.

While the first part of the practice can be described as the recovery of, or the return to, a harmonious state of life in close interaction with all living beings, the second part is both a return and a progression, a recovery of primordial oneness and the creation of a new, transcendent entity. What was unconscious immersion of spirit in energy before, now emerges as the conscious immortal realization of this spirit. The heavens and gods of the Dao, primordial and formless at the beginning of all, are also the endpoint of a cosmic unfolding of spirit that transforms while it returns. The spirit of the ascended immortal, having passed through the impurities of worldly life and the hardships of Daoist training, forms now a richer part of the universe. He hums, as it were, at a higher and more powerful frequency, and is thus able to enrich the universe, to support a significantly larger portion of the cosmic bean in harmony. It is because of this enhanced harmonizing power that Daoist sages—immortals who have attained the higher stages but have not yet ascended—bear such a large share of social responsibility and are looked upon by the tradition as the harbingers of prosperity and harmony in a state of universal great peace. The ultimate goal of the Daoist universe is thus not only the transformation of individuals into immortals, but also the creation of a harmonious cosmos of celestial dimensions, the establishment of the heavenly halls on earth through the complete transcendence of all. The ideal of harmony, dominant in mainstream and popular Chinese thinking, is thus never lost even in the Daoist world, only realized from a different angle.

2.4 Categories for Comparison

The human condition in Chinese religion is basically viewed in an affirmative mode. It is good to be human, it is natural to be human, it is real to be human. Within this framework, human life is described primarily as an ongoing process of joining and interaction. Human beings are part of the universe and function in exactly the same way as all other existing things: they are not separated from natural existence, they are not created special, and they are not different in structure or organizing principle. If they functioned as they were ideally intended, intelligent yet non-evaluative, responsive to nature's changes yet without getting upset, the world would flow along in perfect harmony and to the benefit of all.

This normatively described ideal, however, is not actual, ordinary life. The human predicament, what sets people apart from the rest of creation, is that they have consciousness. Consciousness, moreover, arises from memory through which temporary deviations of Qi are stored as useful reactions to life. These are then activated on many occasions, even when they are not called for, thus increasing the deviation of Qi-flow and the disturbance of harmony. To unlearn these reactions, commonly called emotions and desires, but also including conscious evaluations, such as likes and dislikes and considerations of profit and loss, is the central task in much of Chinese thought, while popular practice has tended to focus on damage containment after the fact (through healings, exorcisms, and confessions).

Key categories in this vision of the human condition can be divided into the three levels of cosmos, society, and individual. Let us look at each of them in turn.

2.4.1 *Cosmological Categories*

Among cosmological categories, there is the nature of the Chinese cosmos as one, as basically dynamic, and as inherently harmonious. Oneness, to begin, can be contrasted both with the Zero, the kind of thinking that does not allow for an underlying force or spirit at the root of creation, and with the Many, the diversity of manifest existence. While the One and the Zero are clear-cut opposites, the One and the Many are complementary, the One reappearing in all single aspects of the Many, and the Many in their combined total making up the One. In addition, the One can also be contrasted with the Two, which can be expressed as the division between unity and duality or monism and dualism. In this case, the Chinese come down firmly on the side of the One, not acknowledging any separation between creator and creation. Their view is thus fundamentally different from those found in Western theistic or Hindu traditions, where a major distinction is made between the godhead and the created world.

Another key category in regard to the cosmos is dynamic versus static. This can also be expressed as the contrast between the natural flow of things and their substantiality, or between becoming and being. There are no "elements" in the Greek sense in the Chinese universe, no firm indissoluble entities that exist from the beginning and remain forever. All life consists of a continuous flow of dynamic energy interaction (according to the five phases) that never stops and always moves in one direction or the other, manifests with one set of characteristics or another. This category has significant consequences for the Chinese universe, since recovery of purity is not the return to some original substance but the reestablishment of a smooth and harmonious flow. It also means that much of Chinese worldview is synchronistic rather than causal, a fact especially emphasized in studies of Chinese medicine, where diagnosis does not look for an underlying root cause but observes the mutual relationship between all symptoms manifest at any given moment.[23] Causation, in other words, is not so much the linear stimulation of a series of firm and enclosed entities, as it tends to be seen in Western traditions, but a simultaneous spread of Qi-impulses throughout the entire world, which in itself consists of energy vibrations and flow, is an intricate and interlinked network, not a conglomeration of substances.

A third important overall category is that of harmony versus disharmony, the acknowledgment of a true and pure state of natural flow that can be disrupted—typically either through excess or deficiency, torrents or obstructions. The key to this category, not unlike the second, is the close cooperation and smooth interaction of a large number of individual entities (all participating in the flow). Through it, not only is the ideal human condition not static but it is also never alone. The human being, to be true to himself, must interact with others—other people, natural forces, the divine Dao. It is the interaction that is central, not the being itself. Disharmony can be caused naturally by an occasional excess or deficiency in Qi, it can also be the result of intentional or willful human action. The power to think and act in a disharmonious way is what sets human beings apart from the rest of creation. Potentially a great source of disharmony in the cosmos, humanity is not only in a position of central importance but also in one of highest responsibility. Earthquakes, floods, and tornadoes are thus entirely our own fault, indications that all is not well in the lives of people and the government of the land. The category of harmony thus includes the notions of interactivity and of responsibility for the state of the world. This again contrasts sharply with Western notions of separate and unique individuals and Hindu ideas of soul-entities. Personal realization in China is therefore never really personal but always interactive, be it in obligation to society or in reaching oneness with the cosmos, depending on the level of harmony attained.

2.4.2 *Social Categories*

On the level of human affiliations, the Chinese vision of the human condition is clearly hierarchical as opposed to egalitarian, focuses on groups and people's obligations to them rather than on the rights and autonomy of individuals, and sees human activity as bound by cosmic commandments instead of personal decisions. Here the Confucian vision predominates, especially as it is linked with Chinese cosmology in the Han dynasty and becomes the leading form of social thought in traditional China.

The five key relationships of Confucianism thus stand for a complex system that ranks people by seniority and closeness of family relationship. Standing and activities in the world are determined by this hierarchical structure, in which there is no notion of equality. The same hierarchical thinking also applies to humans vis-à-vis animals, so that humans are considered the most "numinous" of all creatures without, however, being thought of as their masters. The continuity of all life and its manifestation in different patterns of Qi ensures a clear structure of ranks while at the same time reaffirms the basic commonality among all living things. In addition, the hierarchies ensure that all obligation is circumscribed firmly by the individual's rank, while the interactivity of the system causes virtues to be predominantly social (loyalty, filial piety) rather than of personal character (honesty, perseverance).[24]

Groups predominate in all respects over individuals in Chinese society. That means that anyone is first a member of a family, clan, village, or state before he is an individual with needs and wishes. Justice, as a result, is a group affair; often entire families are executed for the treason of one, and typically groups of five families stand responsible for neighborhood order. Even the individual's intention in committing a breach is ignored in favor of the effect of his deed on the harmony of the whole. Thus, in formal legal codes the killing of a father is not measured according to its being accidental, manslaughter, or murder, but taken as a major disruption of social coherence and punished accordingly.[25] Tragedy in the Western sense is thus unknown—conflicts between two contradictory inner inclinations commonly being resolved by the social rightness of one over the other.

Above and beyond the social rightness are the "seasonal commandments," a set of rules and regulations that detail which actions should be undertaken at what times of the year. Divided according to the twelve months, they spell out exactly which color should be worn, what kind of food eaten, which administrative measures taken (executions only in the fall, when nature itself is killing vegetation), which physical weaknesses expected, which taboos observed, and so on. Much of the practical living of people is thus tied in closely not just with their social group but also with the larger rhythms of the year, reducing personal decisions to a minimum. The system, developed in ancient China and observed at least partially for much of her history, is still quite active in Japan, where one must not heat one's house or wear boots before mid-November, the traditional beginning of winter (Chinese seasons peaking rather than beginning at the solstices and equinoxes), however cold it may be in actual fact. Similarly there are whole ranges of food available only during certain months, and ideally a formal meal during any season should be arranged to reflect the predominant color and taste of that season (sour and green in the spring, for example). The effect of these practical measures is a certain rigidity in daily living, but they also create an active seasonal awareness and a sense of rightness in living along with the patterns of nature.

On the level of human affiliations, therefore, the Chinese understanding of the human condition shows a certain similarity with other socially focused religions, as, for example, Judaism, Islam, or Hinduism. Religious realization is attained through a wholesome and lawful life within society, the religious community is the same as the social, many aspects of daily life (attire, food, rites) are defined by rules, and the key religious authority is held by wise men or priests who ideally also function in the government of the state, be it as rulers, ministers, or advisors. In contrast to the other religions, on the other hand, norms in China are not derived from a divine source but depend on the cycle of nature and the patterns of human interaction; their main commandments are not unchangeable laws but vague rules that are adjusted according to changing circumstances. The main purpose, moreover, of social obligation is the attainment of harmony both in nature and society and not obedience to a deity or the improvement of karma, making the Chinese idea of obligation similar to and yet different from that found elsewhere.

2.4.3 *Personal Categories*

On the personal level, finally, that is, within the self of the person, a self that society and cosmos are trying hard to keep to a minimum, there is the understanding that the body is structured in exactly the same way as the rest of the world, that there is a basic dichotomy between energy and spirit, which can also be, and has been in China, expressed as the split between body and mind, or yin and yang souls, and that there are two major kinds of knowledge: evaluative knowledge about the world and intuitive wisdom in regard to its inner workings.

First, the human body, as already mentioned earlier, is described as an administrative organization including ruler, civil ministers, and the military, as a natural landscape complete with mountains, rivers, and plowing farmers, and as a replica of the stars on the firmament. It is inhabited by a variety of souls (yin and yang), by body gods and spirits, as well as by parasitic demons that wish it to die. All the various aspects and dimensions of the larger world are present in the body, which in turn is the dominant metaphor for descriptions of the universe and society—the ruler being the head, the various inner organs the ministers, and so on. The human body, wondrous and fascinating as it may be, is thus not anything special but repeats in a microcosmic form what is present elsewhere. Human beings are not substantially or essentially different from the rest of creation, even if they occupy a key position in it. This is significantly different from Western notions, which assign humanity the place of ruler of all creation and find in the human body a design inspired by divinity.

The same holds true for the body-mind dichotomy commonly established in Western and Indian religions. Although the Chinese distinguish between body and mind, the basic division they make is not so much between a material, physical entity and a spirit or soul but between body versus physical Qi, mind versus spirit. That is, in light of the overall monistic vision of the Chinese, spirit is just another form of Qi-energy (and thus mind of body), albeit a more subtle one that moves at a much higher velocity. For this reason, there is no essential or substantial difference between mind and body, which are merely different aspects of the same basic underlying force. On the other hand, human beings as participants in the pure Qi of creation consist of a grosser (physical) force called "physis" (*xing*) and a more subtle (spiritual) force called spirit (*shen*).

These two, ultimately of the same source and closely interrelated, disintegrate under the impact of desires and evaluative consciousness into body (*shen*) and mind (*xin*), negatively charged terms that indicate personalized, ego-centered versions of the pure energy coagulation that the human being originally is.[26] The main contrast in the culture is thus not between body and mind, but between them as one unit and physis and spirit as another. The effort of religious practice, on whatever level, is accordingly to reduce, minimize, or even eradicate body and mind as personalized deviations and restore physis and spirit in their full power—Confucians and popular practitioners concentrating on reduction, Daoists preferring total elimination in favor of transcendence.[27]

Closely related to this division of the human being into physis and spirit is the dichotomy of knowledge versus wisdom. The material aspect of the person, needing food and sustenance from the outside world, feels desires and anxieties and makes judgments as to the potential benefit and harm of various people and objects. It gives rise to a knowledge that is analytical, divisive, and judgmental, works in binary opposites, and has only one goal: the satisfaction and aggrandizement of the ego-centered self. This knowledge is evaluated negatively and should be controlled, either by placing the interests of the community and others on an even level (through Confucian learning), by subjecting it to the advice of fortune-telling (through popular shamans), or by abolishing it altogether (through Daoist quietism).

Wisdom, on the contrary, means "knowing when to stop," being aware of the self in the larger context of society and the cosmos, and having an inherent, either learned or intuitive, sense of what is right at any given moment. This requires a great sensitivity to the social context (Confucian propriety), to the movements of Qi in the seasonal cycle (medicine, popular lore), and to the way nature has meant oneself to be (Daoist spontaneity). In all cases, intentional action prompted by selfish aims is to be avoided and benevolence (other-centered action) or nonaction (nonintentional action) are to be preferred. The memory of self-aggrandizing activities is to be reduced, while the mindfulness of present interrelative circumstances should be enhanced. Wisdom, whether socially conscious and learned or inner-centered and intuitive, makes people let go of the ego and helps them perform the balancing act of being human in a process-centered, closely interrelative universe.

This distinction between conscious knowledge and intuitive wisdom is also familiar from other religions, in which knowledge is associated with the practical and wisdom with the spiritual aspects of life. What is special about the Chinese understanding of it, though, is the notion that knowledge tends to serve the self whereas wisdom leads to selflessness, and that selflessness is much preferable to any form of self. In other traditions, both knowledge and wisdom are placed at the service of the self, the latter granting higher and more spiritual levels of "self-realization" than the former but not denying or destroying it. The Chinese, favoring harmony and thinking in interrelated energy processes rather than substances and individuals, find nothing about the self to recommend and ultimately see personal categories in a rather negative mode. Affirmation, in other words, of human life in the wider context of the universe means the negation of personal forms of individual existence and realization.

The human condition in Chinese religion, to summarize, is characterized by a continuous effort to match the ever-changing evolution of circumstances and factors in individual, society, and nature. It is an ongoing act of balancing, away from static and egotistic accumulation and toward a smooth interaction with others, nature, and the Dao. Cosmos, society, and individual, acknowledged as the three central dimensions of life, can and will live in perfect harmony, provided everyone fulfills his or her part—by being individual yet interactive, conscious yet wise, human yet selfless. As a result, it demands comparative categories that take the different levels of life into consideration and are highly conscious of interaction and the role of the human mind. It cannot easily be related to Western notions of a fully transcendent deity, a substantial self, and a rigid distinction between body and mind, and any attempt to apply such Western concepts must give rise to confusion and lead to devaluating Chinese culture. The same holds true also for the rather negatively focused approach of Buddhism to the human condition, which cannot be fruitfully applied to the Chinese case: whatever is not is by definition not and therefore of no interest to a culture that sees the processes of life and interaction in an affirmative mode and as central to the human condition.

Notes

1. The debate is old and goes back to the nineteenth century, when J. J. M. DeGroot first published his book *The Religious System of China* (Leiden: E. Brill, 1892). The present *Journal of Chinese Religions* uses the multiple approach to the problem, but more recent scholarship is favoring again a singular vision, as exemplified in the book by Jordan Paper, *The Spirits Are Drunk: Comparative Approaches to Chinese Religion* (Albany: State University of New York Press, 1995).
2. This view is especially common among German scholars, who have written variously on the subject. For example, Wolfgang Bauer, "Icherleben und Autobiographie im älteren China," *Heidelberger Jahrbücher* 8 (1964): 12–40; and Rolf Trauzettel, "Individuum und Heteronomie: Historische Aspekte des Verhältnisses von Individuum und Gesellschaft in China," *Saeculum* 28.3 (1977): 340–64. For a discussion, see my "Selfhood and Spontaneity in Ancient Chinese Thought," *Selves, People, and Persons*, ed. Leroy Rouner, Boston University Series in Philosophy and Religion, Vol. 13 (South Bend, Ind.: University of Notre Dame Press, 1992), 123–40.
3. One thinker who expresses this vision most clearly and consciously is Guo Xiang, the third-century commentator on the *Zhuangzi*. This has prompted Isabelle Robinet to describe his view as " Kouo Siang ou le monde comme absolu," *T'oung-pao* 69 (1983): 87–112.
4. Maria M. Colavito, *The New Theogony: Mythology for the Real World* (Albany: State University of New York Press, 1992), 13.
5. Ibid., 15.
6. Zero cultures, in contrast, hold on to two basic principles: "that each thing is independent unto itself; and that that which is, is that which manifests" (ibid., 18). In a world based on these principles, the role and importance of all things would only be determined by themselves; they would work only for their own interest; there would be no need to justify any action; and "if things *could* be done, or created, they *would* be" (ibid., 18). As death would not be

a return to one's true home in the One but the end of all existence, there would be an endless struggle for stability and solidity, found only in the things of this world.

7. For texts, especially from the Daoist tradition, documenting all these views, see my *The Taoist Experience: An Anthology* (Albany: State University of New York Press, 1993), 161–88. A more general discussion of Chinese body visions is found in my "Taoist Visions of the Body," *Journal of Chinese Philosophy* 18 (1991): 227–52; and in Kristofer Schipper's "The Taoist Body," *History of Religions* 17 (1978): 355–87.

8. The Chinese term for this is *ganying*. A comprehensive discussion is found in Charles Le Blanc, "Resonance: Une interpretation chinoise de la realité," *Mythe et philosophie à l'aube de la Chine impérial: Études sur le Huainan zi*, ed. Charles Le Blanc and Rémi Mathieu (Montréal: Les Presses de l'Université de Montréal, 1992), 91–111.

9. A corresponding physics theory is proposed by Itchak Bentov in his *Stalking the Wild Pendulum: On the Mechanics of Consciousness* (New York: Dutton, 1977). For the jelly bean, see especially page 20.

10. Based on the observation that if two lutes are placed next to each other and the string of one is plucked, the same string on the other will begin to vibrate, the model has been applied to the variety of beings on earth. *Zhuangzi*, chap. 2, has: "[Heaven] blows on the ten thousand things in a different way, so that each can be itself" (Burton Watson, *The Complete Works of Chuang-tzu* [New York: Columbia University Press, 1968], 37). For a general discussion, see DeWoskin, *A Song for One or Two: Music and the Concept of Art in Early China* (Ann Arbor: University of Michigan Center for Chinese Studies, 1982). A note on the Daoist use of the metaphor is found in my *Taoist Mystical Philosophy: The Scripture of Western Ascension* (Albany: State University of New York Press, 1991), 104.

11. For a comprehensive discussion of the various forms of Qi and its modes of movement, see Ted Kaptchuk's *The Net That Has No Weaver: Understanding Chinese Medicine* (New York: Congdon & Weed, 1983), especially page 178. Another area in which the Chinese have codified universal patterns is divination. Especially the *Yijing* (*Book of Changes*) gives advice on when to act how in the most harmonious way. For a translation and study, see Richard Wilhelm, *The I Ching or Book of Changes,* Bollingen Series XIX (Princeton: Princeton University Press, 1950).

12. Wilhelm, *I Ching*, op. cit.

13. For discussions of these various viewpoints, see Fung Yu-lan and Derk Bodde, *A History of Chinese Philosophy*, 2 vols. (Princeton: Princeton University Press, 1952). A detailed description of the seasonal commandments of the cosmologists is also found in John Major's *Heaven and Earth in Early Han Thought: Chapters Three, Four, and Five of the Huainanzi* (Albany: State University of New York Press, 1993).

14. See Livia Kohn, "Transcending Personality: From Ordinary to Immortal Life," *Taoist Resources* 2.2 (1990): 1–22.

15. For a discussion of these in Neo-Confucianism, see Wing-tsit Chan, *Neo Confucian Terms Explained* (New York: Columbia University Press, 1986), 17.

16. See Tu Wei-ming, "The Confucian Perception of Adulthood," *Adulthood*, ed. Erik Erikson (New York: W. W. Norton, 1978).

17. See Michael Kalton, *To Become a Sage: The Ten Diagrams on Sage Learning by Yi T'oegye* (New York: Columbia University Press, 1988), 103.

18. While the idea of "hidden merit" is clearly Buddhist and indicates the notion that good deeds, although without obvious reward now, will bear auspicious karmic fruit in the future, the concept of merit and demerit or divine reward and punishment is very ancient in China. It reflects the supernatural transposition of the workings of the administrative bureaucracy and is known as far back as the fourth century BCE (Donald Harper, "Resurrection in Warring States Popular Religion," *Taoist Resources* 5.2 [1994]: 13–28). Usually calculated in points, merits resulted in a longer life expectancy on earth, while demerits accumulated cause early death.

19. This is clearly reflected in the vision of the ideal human being in Confucianism, as described, for instance, in Zhu Xi's characterization of Master Mingdao, described in Wing-tsit Chan's translation, *Reflections on Things at Hand: The Neo-Confucian Anthology Compiled by Chu Hsi and Lü Tsu-ch'ien* (New York: Columbia University Press, 1967), 299–302. It comes out again, in a different perspective, in the Confucian insistence that the best state is to be fully at one with the cosmos, "regarding heaven, earth, and the myriad things as one body, the world as one family, and the country as one person." See Wing-tsit Chan, *Instructions for Practical Living and Other Neo-Confucian Writings by Wang Yang-ming* (New York: Columbia University Press, 1963), 272.

20. For a description of the inner alchemical process and the development of the embryo, see Farzeen Baldrian-Hussein, *Procédés secrets du joyau magique* (Paris: Les Deux Océans, 1984) and Lu Kuan-yu, *Taoist Yoga—Alchemy and Immortality* (London: Rider, 1970).

21. The translation is taken from my "Quiet Sitting with Master Yinshi: Medicine and Religion in Modern China," *Zen Buddhism Today* 10 (1993): 86.

22. This practice, in modern nomenclature and with the express purpose to "turn stress into vitality," is taught in the United States by Mantak Chia, a Chinese immigrant from Thailand. See, for example, his *Awaken Healing Energy Through the Tao* (Huntington, N.Y.: Healing Dao Books, 1983); or his *Taoist Ways to Transform Stress into Vitality* (Huntington, N.Y.: Healing Tao Books, 1985).

23. For a highly theoretical discussion of this, see Manfred Porkert, *The Theoretical Foundations of Chinese Medicine* (Cambridge, Mass.: MIT Press, 1974).

24. Honesty in this context is still a virtue but interactive rather than of charac-

ter. Instead of referring to a person's allegiance to a generally acknowledged objective and irreversible reality, it indicates the best possible behavior in the light of social harmony. For example, "if a Japanese host is caught by his guest with his pants down, there is no apologizing or confusion; instead there is a social agreement that the event simply never happened." See Robert A. Paul, "The Place of Truth in Sherpa Law and Religion," *Journal of Anthropological Research* 33 (1977): 172. Similarly, the Tibetan Sherpa rewrite history in favor of social harmony rather than ferreting out an objective truth that can, as absolute, "only exist in the realm of Buddhahood" (ibid., 173).

25. For an extensive discussion of this aspect of Chinese culture, see Derk Bodde and Clarence Morris, *Law in Imperial China* (Philadelphia: University of Pennsylvania Press, 1973).

26. Kohn, *Taoist Mystical Philosophy*, 99.

27. The same pattern holds true for the two types of souls—yin and yang, material and spirit. While the seven yin or material souls (*po*) are energies of earth that represent physical needs and instinctive behavior, the three yang or spirit souls (*hun*) belong to heaven and represent good moral and high spiritual aspirations of people. They come together at birth to form an individual and disperse again at death, *po* returning to earth through the burial of the body, *hun* going back to heaven through the installation of the deceased as an ancestor.

3

Beginningless Ignorance

A Buddhist View of the Human Condition

Malcolm David Eckel
with John J. Thatamanil

3.1 Introduction

The Buddhist tradition offers many possibilities for a comparative study of religious approaches to the human condition. If you think that the biggest problem in human life is simply ignorance, Buddhists have a lot to say about the misapprehensions that lead people into a perpetual cycle of craving, frustration, and death. If you would rather focus on the possibility of a moral order, with its attendant rules and obligations, Buddhist views of karma and moral responsibility make attractive points of contrast and comparison. If you think that the problem of human life lies in its fragility or contingency, Buddhists have a great deal to say about impermanence and the conditioned quality of human existence. If you would rather approach the human predicament as one of impurity, illness, or imbalance, Buddhists can tell you many things about ways to heal your ills, remove impurities from the mind, or seek a balance between extremes. If you would rather approach the human condition through its possibilities rather than its difficulties, Buddhists can tell you a great deal about the possible goals of human life, ranging from the classic understanding of nirvana as the cessation of desire to the Mahāyāna visions of Emptiness and the Pure Land. The problem, in the face of such rich possibilities, is to know where to begin.

In deference to the Buddhist tradition, I will start at a point that Buddhists themselves consider to be the beginning. This beginning is not the moment of creation or the beginning of time. Buddhist authors are relatively unconcerned about the origins of the cosmos or even of human life itself. The beginning I have in mind is the beginning of Buddhist *tradition*, the moment when Siddhārtha Gautama met five of his friends in the Deer Park at Sarnath and gave verbal expression to the realization that had made him a Buddha. Traditional accounts of this event in the Buddha's life give one of the most basic and authoritative doctrinal statements of the Buddhist attitude toward the human condition. I will begin with an account of this doctrinal formula, then I will step back and consider the implications of Buddhist attitudes toward life for our comparative project on the human condition, not merely to supplement or modify the growing list of "vague categories" but to reflect from a Buddhist perspective on what constitutes a useful category in the comparative study of religion.

3.2 Primary Doctrinal Evidence—The Four Noble Truths

Buddhist canonical tradition provides the following account of the Buddha's first sermon:[1]

> Thus have I heard. The Blessed One was once living in the Deer Park at Isipatana (The Resort of Seers) near Bārānasi (Benares). There he addressed the group of five bhikkhus:
>
> Bhikkhus, these two extremes ought not to be practised by one who has gone forth from the household life. What are these two? There is devotion to the indulgence of sense-pleasures, which is low, common, the way of ordinary people, unworthy and unprofitable; and there is devotion to self-mortification, which is painful, unworthy and unprofitable.
>
> Avoiding both these extremes, the Tathāgata has realized the Middle Path: it gives vision, it gives knowledge, and it leads to calm, to insight, to enlightenment, to Nibbāna. . . .
>
> The Noble Truth of suffering (Dukkha) is this: Birth is suffering; aging is suffering; sickness is suffering; death is suffering; sorrow and lamentation, pain, grief, and despair are suffering; association with the unpleasant is suffering; dissociation from the pleasant is suffering; not to get what one wants is suffering—in brief, the five aggregates of attachment are suffering.

> The Noble Truth of the origin of suffering is this: It is this thirst (craving) which produces re-existence and re-becoming, bound up with passionate greed. It finds fresh delight now here and now there, namely, thirst for sense-pleasures; thirst for existence and becoming; and thirst for non-existence (self-annihilation). . . .
>
> The Noble Truth of the Path leading to the Cessation of suffering is this: It is simply the Noble Eightfold Path, namely right view; right thought; right speech; right action; right livelihood; right effort; right mindfulness; right concentration. . . .
>
> As long as my vision of true knowledge was not fully clear in these three aspects, in these twelve ways,[2] regarding the Four Noble Truths, I did not claim to have realized the perfect Enlightenment that is supreme in the world with its gods, with its Māras and Brahmas, in the world with its recluses and brahmanas, with its princes and men. . . . And a vision of true knowledge arose in me thus: My heart's deliverance is unassailable. This is my last birth. Now there is no more re-becoming (rebirth).
>
> This the Blessed One said. The group of five bhikkhus was glad, and they rejoiced at his words.

This basic summary of the Buddha's enlightenment is almost tailor-made for a comparative investigation of the human condition. It begins with a claim about the nature of suffering, it states that suffering has an origin and a cessation, and it indicates that there is a path to follow to bring suffering to an end. The text also shows the close connection between traditional Buddhist accounts of the human condition and the Indian doctrine of transmigration or rebirth. Thirst or craving produces re-existence and re-becoming. The Buddha himself, by understanding and enacting his understanding of the Four Noble Truths, escapes the process of re-becoming. His craving is gone, he is no longer reborn, he has achieved nirvana.

To probe these doctrinal concepts more deeply, it is tempting to ask how the process of death and rebirth began: How does a person come to be in a condition of suffering? An answer to this question can be found by elaborating the second of the Four Noble Truths. According to the standard Pali summary of the twelvefold chain of Dependent Origination (*paṭicca-samuppāda*), ignorance (*avijjā*) gives rise to volitional states (*saṃkhāra*), volitional states give rise to consciousness (*viññāna*), consciousness gives rise to mental and physical phenomena (*nāmarūpa*), mental and physical phenomena give rise to the five senses plus the mind (*saḷ-āyatana*), the five senses plus the mind give rise to sensory contact (*phassa*), sensory contact gives rise to feeling (*vedanā*), feeling gives rise to craving (*taṇhā*), craving gives rise to attachment (*upādāna*), attachment gives rise to becoming (*bhava*), becoming gives rise to birth (*jāti*), and birth gives rise to decay and death (*jarāmaraṇa*). It would not be wrong to interpret this sequence of causes as meaning that the root cause of suffering is ignorance. Ignorance is the place to begin if one wants to unravel the chain and escape its effects. But Buddhists insist that the chain of Dependent Origination is less of a linear process than a circle. Ignorance gives rise to the other elements of the chain, and they in turn give rise to ignorance. When Indian Buddhists were asked to explain the primordial origin of suffering, they simply said that it is "ignorance without beginning."

The notion of beginningless ignorance has led the Buddhist tradition to avoid unnecessary speculation about the origin of things and focus instead on how to make them better. There is a well-known story in the Pali Canon about a disciple named Māluṅkyaputta who approached the Buddha and asked him ten questions: Is the universe eternal? Is the universe not eternal? Is the universe finite? Is the universe infinite? Is the soul identical to the body? Is the soul different from the body? Does the Buddha exist after death? Does the Buddha not exist after death? Does he both exist and not exist after death? Does he neither exist nor not exist after death?[3] Rather than answer the questions directly, the Buddha responded with a story. Suppose someone is shot with a poisoned arrow and brought to a physician. Would he say: "I will not let this arrow be pulled out until you tell me the caste of the person who shot me, how tall he was, the color of his complexion, what kind of bow he used to shoot it, what kind of bowstring it had, what the arrow was made of," and so forth. If he insisted on getting answers to all these questions, he would die before the questions could be answered. The same is true of Māluṅkyaputta's questions about such things as the finitude of the universe. They are not helpful for the task at hand, which is to pull out the arrow of suffering by applying the insights of the Four Noble Truths and the Noble Eightfold Path.[4]

A more useful way to explore the doctrinal categories of the Four Noble Truths is to scrutinize the concept of suffering itself. A common analysis of the concept of suffering (found in the Sanskrit Abhidharma and Pali Abhidhamma) divides suffering into three separate categories: the suffering that is clearly suffering (*dukkha-dukkha*), the suffering that is due to change (*vipariṇāma-dukkha*), and the suffering that consists of conditioned states (*saṃkhāra-dukkha*). The first two types of suffering are easy to interpret. The first category refers to a sensation or feeling (*vedanā*) whose identity is clear: it involves physical or mental pain. The second kind of suffering is the sensation of losing something pleasurable. The Abhidharma tradition tells us that the third kind of suffering is more subtle and can be perceived clearly only by saints:

> People do not feel an eyelash when it is sitting in the palm of the hand, but when it falls into their eye it causes discomfort and pain. Foolish people are like the palm of the hand: they are as insensitive to the suffering of conditioned states as they are to an eyelash. Wise people are like the eye: they are deeply disturbed by this [suffering].[5]

For those who do not yet count themselves among the saints, the texts only hint at what they mean about the suffering of conditioned states. In the commentary on *The Treasury of the Abhidharma* (*Abhidharmakośa*), Vasubandhu says only that, when sensations are neither painful nor pleasurable, they still are "suffering" because they always pass away: "If something is impermanent by virtue of the fact that it is causally conditioned, it is suffering."[6]

To understand what it means to say that "conditioned states" are suffering, it helps to set the three types of suffering next to the list of the three "characteristics" (*lakkhaṇa*) of existence: everything is suffering (*sabbaṃ dukkham*), everything is impermanent (*sabbam aniccam*), and nothing has a self (*sabbam anattā*).[7] The first two characteristics correspond to the first two types of suffering: one has to do with sensations that are downright painful, the other with pleasurable sensations that become painful when they pass away. The third characteristic takes us into another realm of Buddhist thought. Not only do things cause suffering now or in the future, they are not what they seem to be: they have no identity or "self" (*ātman*). Here the analysis of the First Noble Truth converges with the analysis of the Second. The twelvefold chain of Dependent Origination begins with ignorance. What is one ignorant of? Certainly it is important to avoid the mistake of thinking that anything is permanent, but the most important and most fundamental form of ignorance is the mistake of attributing a "self" to things including, of course, oneself.

What does it mean to say that things have no self? We find a useful account of this concept in a semi-canonical Pali text known as *The Questions of King Milinda*.[8] In one of the chapters, a king by the name of Milinda (Gk. Menander) located somewhere in what is now Afghanistan asks a Buddhist monk named Nāgasena what he means by no-self. Nāgasena answers with another question: "Did the king come on foot or in a chariot?" The king says that he came in a chariot. Nāgasena asks: "What does the word 'chariot' refer to? Does it refer to the wheels, the floor, the reins, or some other part of the chariot?" The king says that the word "chariot" is a conventional designation (*vohāra*) or term (*paññatti*) that depends on (*upādāya*) all of these parts together. Nāgasena then echoes the king's language and says that the word "Nāgasena" also is a conventional designation that refers to the different, changeable components of his personality. There is no single, enduring "self" to be called "Nāgasena."

Here in rudimentary form are the components of a classic Buddhist theory of no-self. The investigation begins with a question about the referent of a word: is there an enduring, unified reality to which a word like "chariot" or "Nāgasena" can refer? The answer is no, for two reasons. First, both the chariot and Nāgasena are complex entities: they consist of parts. The "combination" (*saṃghāta*) made up by these parts is not in itself a real entity. The words do not refer to any single part individually and the "combination" of the parts is an imaginary construct that "depends on" (*upādāya*) the individual parts. Second, the parts themselves are constantly changing. While it may seem that there is some continuity in the personality of Nāgasena, the parts of the personality, like the parts of the chariot, are constantly in flux. The word "Nāgasena" refers not only to an imaginary construct in space but to an imaginary construct in time: the "stream" (*santāna*) of the personality of "Nāgasena." It would be correct to say, then, that the theory of no-self involves a theory of language encased in a theory of reality. To be literally true, words have to refer to enduring, unified things, but because things are constantly in flux, there are no enduring, unified things. This point is expressed by saying that words are merely a form of conventional usage (*vohāra*), agreement (*sammuti*), or designation (*paññatti*), but do not refer to the ultimate (*paramattha*) reality of things. In other words, there are two truths, conventional truth and ultimate truth, and words belong to the realm of conventional truth.

Someone who is feeling argumentative on this point might ask whether the words in the preceding paragraph are conventional or ultimate, and also ask, if these words are merely conventional, how they can express an ultimate truth. *The Questions of King Milinda* does not address these questions directly, but it suggests an answer that later texts develop more extensively. Words that express the distinction between the two truths belong, like all words, to the realm of conventional truth, but they can have a useful function in removing misconceptions about the nature of reality. As Mahāyāna writers are accustomed to say, words function as illusions to remove other illusions, and the best illusions are the ones that also remove illusions about themselves. The driving force behind this process of disillusionment is not mere curiosity about the nature of things. The process grew from the traditional analysis of the origin of suffering mapped by the chain of Dependent Origination. If the root cause of suffering is ignorance, the removal of ignorance is the most basic step a person can take toward the cessation of suffering. Wisdom (*paññā*), the understanding of no-self, removes the cause of suffering and leads eventually to the cessation of suffering that is known in the Buddhist tradition as nirvana.

Not all Buddhists would agree with this analysis of no-self. It comes from a combination of late Pali canonical sources with a hint of the two-truth theory of the Madhyamaka to illuminate some of its more important implications. The vocabulary represents the state of the tradition in Pali and Sanskrit sources about the year 200 CE, when Buddhism had become well established throughout Southeast Asia and the first important Buddhist connections had been made between India and China. The transmission of Buddhism to Japan and Tibet had to wait another six hundred years, as did many of the important Buddhist philosophical developments in India and China. But it is not an overstatement to say that most Buddhists who trace their traditions back to this period would recognize the importance of this complex of themes: suffering, impermanence, ignorance, craving, no-self, wisdom, nirvana. I suspect that they also would acknowledge that the most important thing a person should know about the human condition—to recognize the depth of difficulty in the human life and to prepare oneself to change it—is the idea of no-self.

The significance of the no-self doctrine does not make the process of comparison an easy matter. Buddhists offer many useful concepts to think about aspects of the human condition, but at the core of the tradition lies a concept that others find puzzling and problematic. In fact, Buddhists intend the concept to be puzzling and problematic. They apply the no-self doctrine like a critical principle to many of the categories that other religious traditions hold dear. When the Hindu philosopher Udayana shook his fist at a temple door and said to God, "Drunk with the wine of your own Godhood, you ignore me, but when the Buddhists are here, your very existence depends on me,"[9] he was not making a gratuitous insult. He was involved in a bitter dispute with Buddhists about the existence of God and was one of the chief defenders of Hindu theology against the Buddhist critique. Buddhists in India used the no-self doctrine to deny the epistemic value of scripture and the significance of the Upaniṣadic doctrine of the self. The doctrine sits uneasily in the setting of comparative theology.

One way to deal with the difficulty of the no-self doctrine would be to follow the example Nomanul Haq has set for us in his response to the position of the *Vivekacūḍāmaṇi*. Dr. Haq said that the Vedānta critique of the divine-human disjunction "would be considered *shirk*, pure and simple," and he added a cautionary note about the fate of al-Hallāj, lest we overlook the significance of such accusations. It is possible that the no-self doctrine poses what Christians were once proud to call a theological "scandal" over which other religious traditions have no choice but to stumble. I am more inclined, however, to follow a different comparative strategy: to ask whether the Buddhist doctrine allows us to look in new ways at the traditions we have studied, to see things in them that are genuinely significant but would not strike us as having the same importance if we were not seeing them through Buddhist eyes. Buddhists seem to be telling us that the most important thing for human beings to understand about themselves is not what they are but what they are not. Could this be a useful question to advance the discussion of the human condition?

In some comparative settings the Buddhist doctrine of no-self can call forth important echoes from the religious traditions of the West. In the summer of 1981, I was asked to introduce the Dalai Lama for a series of lectures on Buddhist philosophy in Emerson Hall at Harvard.[10] To set the scene I told a story about the inscription over the north door of the building. When the building was originally built, I was told, the philosophy department asked the architect to inscribe the doorway with the words: "Man is the measure of all things." During the summer, when no one but tourists and administrators is abroad in Harvard Yard, the president changed the inscription to read: "What is man that thou art mindful of him?" (Psalm 8:4). To convey the force of these words to the Dalai Lama, I translated them into Tibetan in words that might be retranslated as: "What are you referring to when you use the word 'man'?" The word I used for "man" (*gang zag*, Sanskrit *pudgala*) was meant to recall a long Buddhist controversy about an aspect of the personality known as the *pudgala* (commonly translated as the "person" but literally "man") that some Buddhists thought capable of continuing to the next life. The doctrine of the *pudgala* has long since faded from view as a legitimate option in Buddhist philosophy, but its memory lingers on as a symbol of the classic mistake to be avoided when thinking about the nature of the self. It is, as it were, the fundamental heresy of the Buddhist tradition. The question "What is man that thou art mindful of him?" especially when it is used to challenge a philosopher's assertion of the importance of "man," sets up an uncanny resonance with the basic Buddhist question about the use of the word "man": "What could you possibly be referring to when you use the word 'man'?"

What is the connection between these two questions? Are they asking the same thing? It is hard to imagine, from the Buddhist side, what could count as an affirmative answer to this question. There ultimately is no "thing" for these two questions to ask. But the juxtaposition of the two questions does set in motion some useful lines of comparative investigation. Are there comparable negations in other traditions? If so, what do they mean? Nomanul Haq has given us two fascinating examples of negation in Islamic accounts of the human condition. The *shahāda* begins with a negative particle: "There is *no* god but God." Whatever else human beings may be, they must know that they are not God. Dr. Haq has helped us understand how the negation of the *shahāda* echoes another negative particle in the Primordial Covenant between God and human beings: "And when the Lord extracted from the children of Adam—from their spinal cord—their entire progeny and made them witness upon themselves, saying, *Am I not* your Lord? and they replied, No doubt, You are, we bear witness." (Qur'ān 7:172–73). The *Vivekacūḍāmaṇi* (cited by Francis Clooney) is quite remote from the theological world of the Qur'ān, but it too starts with fundamental negation: "[God is] the object of the doctrine of all Vedānta, and *he is not* an object" (*sarva-vedānta-siddhānta-gocaraṃ tam agocaram*).[11] The distinction between *gocaram* ("object") and *agocaram* ("no object") establishes the dialectic that will yield eventually to the *non*-dualistic (*advaita*) awareness of Brahman. Livia Kohn could have drawn our attention to the opening line of the *Daode jing* in her exposition of Chinese philosophy. It too starts with a well-known negation: "The Way that can be told of *is not* the eternal Way."

Are these negations mere accidents, or do they share a significant and comparable function? A phenomenologist of religion would say that the negative force of these statements is far from accidental. The sacred manifests itself as *different* from the profane, and the most fundamental form of religious awareness is the differentiating negation, the sense that the sacred or holy is set apart as other, as *not* being the profane. Even nondualistic traditions are *not* dual, in opposition to the dualities of ordinary understanding. But it is not necessary to put on the garb of a phenomenologist to recognize that there is something significant in these negations. The traditions that flow from these statements cultivate an awareness that the human condition is unsatisfactory and, at the same time, open to some kind of transcendent possibility. To say "there is no god but God" suggests radical judgment on any human inclination to elevate anything (including oneself) to the status of God, but it also suggests that "God's in his heaven—All's right with the world." To say that the "object" of the Vedānta is "no object," negates the ordinary uses of language and thought that objectify the divine and attempt to bring it into the sphere of ordinary human awareness, but the words also suggest that God is not object but subject, that is, that God is identical to the individual's own awareness. In the Buddhist case, the doctrine of no-self criticized any human tendency to reify and cling to the things of this world, including the self that does the clinging, but it also initiates the possibility of freedom, the cessation of suffering, and nirvana. To know that there is no self is to be free to change and discard the habits of mind and heart that generate the cycle of rebirth.

In the sessions of the seminar, we often have asked ourselves whether the human condition is defined best as the predicament in which the religious life begins or as the goal at which it ends. Our initial response to this question was to say that the first year of the seminar should be concerned with beginnings and should focus on the human predicament rather than on human possibility. But it has proved impossible to set aside considerations of human striving—impossible, in other words, to speak of what human beings are without speaking of what they hope to become. I wonder whether this is not in itself a fundamental feature of what we call the "human condition." Could it be that the human condition is defined precisely at this point of balance, where one is aware that one is not what one was but has not yet become what one hopes to be? If so, it comes close to what Buddhists mean by an awareness of no-self, the awareness that one is not bound by what one was and is free to evolve into something new.

3.3 The Form of a Buddhist Narrative—The Middle Way

In my presentation to this seminar in the fall semester, I argued that the doctrinal investigation of Buddhist attitudes toward the human condition should only be a starting point. Doctrine has its value, but the Buddhist tradition reveals its nuances more fully in the stories Buddhists tell about their saints and, finally, in the stories they tell about themselves. For an indication of what this shift of attention might mean, one needs to look no further than the text of the Buddha's first sermon. The sermon is not simply a doctrinal discourse: it tells a story. Or rather, it tells a series of stories, strung together in sequence and nested within one another. The narrative frame is provided by the oral transmission embodied in the formula: "Thus have I heard." To hear the words of the text (rather than reading them on a page) is to participate in the act of "tradition," the act of hearing and passing on the words of the master. Inside this frame lies the story of the Buddha's encounter with five monks, the preaching of a sermon, and the monks' response to his words. Within the sermon itself lies a condensed story of a journey, a "Middle Path" that leads to the experience of nirvana.

What do Buddhists mean by the Middle Path? The text explains that it is the avoidance of two extremes: the extreme of self-indulgence and the extreme of self-denial. Behind the formula lies a story about the discipline that led Siddhārtha Gautama to become a Buddha.[12] When the future

Buddha left the palace to become a renunciant, he practiced a discipline of extreme fasting and self-mortification. As the sermon says, he found this practice to be "painful, unworthy, and unprofitable": it did not lead him to the goal he was seeking. So he accepted nourishing food from a young woman and sought a balance between indulgence and denial. According to Buddhist tradition, his meditation flourished, and he achieved the meditative breakthrough that constituted his "awakening" (*bodhi*), the awakening that was expressed in the Four Noble Truths. From this narrative foundation, the concept of the Middle Path has been carried into many other areas of Buddhist life and thought. One of the important philosophical schools of the Mahāyāna is called the Madhyamaka or "Middle" School, not only because it seeks a balance in discipline but because it seeks a cognitive balance between excessive denial and excessive affirmation. According to the Madhyamaka, complete denial of the reality of things leads to a sterile nihilism and complete affirmation leads to a paralyzing fatalism. If truth lies anywhere, it lies in the avoidance of these two extremes.

The idea of the "path" runs even more deeply in Indian civilization than this. Buddhists share a general Indian conception of *saṃsāra* as a "wandering" through the forest or ocean of rebirth. The challenge of the religious life is to "cross" (*tṛ*) the ocean of rebirth to reach safety on the other side. A savior, like the goddess Tārā, is one who helps a person across, and a bodhisattva is often defined as someone who has "already crossed" and turns back to "bring others across."[13] When *saṃsāra* is visualized as a forest rather than an ocean, the challenge is to find the proper route, a process that is intimately related to finding a guide (*nāyaka*) and developing the vision to find the proper path. One of the earliest Mahāyāna scriptural texts, the *Ratnaguṇasaṃcayagāthā*, gives a vivid picture of the relationship between the path and clarity of vision:

> How can a large group of people, who have been blind from birth, have no guide, and do not know the way, ever find their way into the city? Without wisdom the five perfections are blind, have no guide, and cannot reach enlightenment.
>
> When they achieve wisdom, they receive their sight and can be called by the name ["perfection"]. They are like a painting that is completely finished except for the eyes: [the painter] receives no payment until he paints the eyes.[14]

Here wisdom functions as a guide: it helps find the way and keeps the other Buddhist virtues from straying off the path. Wisdom is also like the final act in the painting of a deity: adding the eyes brings the painting to life and earns the painter his fee.

Howard Nemerov has described a metaphor as "the compact, allusive form of a story or fable."[15] Buddhist metaphors are no exception. They tell a story about the path to Buddhahood and about the discipline used to chart the way. To say that wisdom is a "guide" for the path, for example, suggests that practice is gradual and moves through a series of stages. It also suggests that the understanding appropriate for one stage may not be appropriate for another. To speak of wisdom as a form of vision (*darśana*) suggests a hierarchical relationship between seeing and hearing. In Buddhist philosophy (which also goes by the name of "vision") there is a preference for direct, analytical vision over the experience of hearing the teaching from someone else. In the account of the Buddha's first sermon, the movement from hearing ("thus have I heard") to seeing ("vision, knowledge, calm, insight") reflects a common Buddhist progression from the reception of a teacher's words to the cultivation of direct insight.[16]

It is useful to ask whether these simple narrative sequences of following a path or developing a clear view of things represent what the cognitive linguist Mark Johnson calls "the bodily basis of meaning, imagination, and reason."[17] Certainly a basic fact of the human condition is that human beings all have bodies. Like other thinkers in other traditions, Buddhist philosophers picture cognitive processes in images drawn from the body. To know is to go and see. Truth is up, error is down, and so forth. But such basic bodily images are difficult to separate from more complex cultural practices. Buddhist texts often refer to practitioners as yogis, and stipulations about the practice of philosophy are often tied to yogic disciplines of posture and breath. Buddhist processes of mental cultivation also can be based on a symbolic connection between the human body and the cosmos. Indian Buddhists share the general Indian image of the yogi as an island of stability and immovability in a sea of change. Indian temples, both Buddhist and Hindu, represent the mountain of reality, the palace of the deity, and the form of a human body. The practice of yoga can be understood as a way to realize the stability of the mountain and palace of the cosmos in one's own mind and body. Even the yogic image of stability, however, is too simple to capture the complexity of the Middle Path. Among other things, it would contradict the no-self doctrine, which tells us, if it tells us anything at all, that an attempt to cling to the realities of this life as stable and immovable is doomed to failure. In actual application, the Middle Path involves a much more dynamic and complex series of opposites, with stability found in the midst of instability, reality in the midst of unreality, and affirmation in the midst of negation.

To illustrate this point, let me turn to the work of the sixth-century Indian philosopher Bhāvaviveka. Bhāvaviveka represents the Madhyamaka

("Middle") School of Mahāyāna Buddhism. He is a follower of Nāgārjuna and the principal source for the discussion of Buddhahood in my book *To See the Buddha*. Bhāvaviveka begins his most detailed account of his own philosophy with a long statement about the goal of his philosophical quest. Images of vision are interspersed not only with images of moving and climbing but with a host of other metaphorical expressions of Buddhist cognitive discipline.

> To have the eye of wisdom and none other is to see [truly]. An intelligent person is intent on seeking the knowledge of reality.
>
> An intelligent person, even if he is blind, sees the whole universe without obstruction. He sees anything that he wants to see, even if it is far away, subtle, or concealed.
>
> Without intelligence, even [Indra], who has a thousand eyes, is blind. He does not see the right and wrong paths to heaven and liberation.
>
> To open the eye of wisdom is to avoid falling into the six perfections as if they were thorns poisoned with a desire for different kinds of results.
>
> To be disciplined in the perfections is to be pure in three ways, with compassion as the motive and omniscience as the goal, yet one's mind is not fixed (*sthita*) on that [goal].
>
> Wisdom is the ambrosia that brings satisfaction, the lamp whose light cannot be obscured, the steps on the palace of liberation, and the fire for the fuel of the defilements.
>
> There are two kinds of intelligence, according to the two truths. Correct relative [wisdom] has to do with the discrimination of real things.
>
> Conventional wisdom fulfills the prerequisites of merit and knowledge, beginning with generosity, it discriminates causation and the characteristics [of things].
>
> It also brings sentient beings to maturity through the practice of great friendliness and compassion.
>
> Ultimate wisdom requires a negation of the network of all concepts, and it moves without moving in the clear sky of reality.
>
> It is peaceful, directly experienced, non-conceptual, imperishable, and neither one nor many.
>
> It is impossible to climb the tower of the palace of reality without the steps of correct relative [wisdom].
>
> One focuses one's intelligence with relative truth, then analyzes the individual and universal characteristics of things.
>
> An intelligent person should be disciplined in concentrating the mind and also in the knowledge that comes from listening [to the scriptures] because [the knowledge that comes from listening] is the cause of other knowledge.
>
> It is impossible to see one's face in muddy or turbulent water, and it is impossible [to see] reality in a mind that lacks concentration and is covered with obstructions.

When the mind strays from the right path like an elephant, it should be bound to the post of the object [of meditation] with the rope of mindfulness and brought slowly under control with the hook of wisdom.

When [the mind] is excited, one should quiet it with thoughts of impermanence. When its attention span is too short, one should extend it by practicing on a large object.

When it is distracted, one should focus it by considering the causes of the distraction. When it is depressed, one should arouse it by displaying the benefits of courage.

When it has been soiled by the mud of passion, hatred, and delusion and is out of control, one should cleanse it with the water of meditation on impure objects, friendliness, and dependent origination.

When one knows isolation, stability, peace, intentness on the object, skill and suppleness, one should be indifferent.

When the mind has been concentrated, one should investigate with wisdom. One should analyze whether the identity of the things that are grasped conventionally is [also grasped] ultimately. If so, it is reality. If not, [reality] should be pursued [elsewhere].[18]

Bhāvaviveka clearly saw his own work as following a path to a goal. Even Indra, the god who has a thousand eyes, cannot see the difference between the right path and the wrong one, but the bodhisattva who practices the Mahāyāna and has the eye of wisdom not only sees the right path but enters it without being caught by the thorns of desire. To stay on the correct path, the bodhisattva needs not only vision but the concentration (*samādhi*) to keep the mind from wandering. Lest one imagine that this process is easy, Bhāvaviveka reminds us that the mind is like a wild elephant and has to be bound to its post with the rope of mindfulness and the hook of wisdom. The motion in all these images takes place, it seems, on the horizontal plane. It responds to the image of the human predicament as a process of aimless wandering and tries to give this wandering a direction and purpose. Superimposed on this image of horizontal movement is an image of ascent. To become wise is to use the categories of conventional wisdom to climb the tower of the palace of reality and reach the clear sky above.

The metaphor of vision also has two dimensions: the eye of wisdom shows a person how to find the correct path, but it also looks upward into the clear sky of reality at the top of the temple tower. Here the purpose of the philosopher's discipline is not simply to get to another place but to remove the obstacles or coverings that obstruct the eyes, making it impossible to see things clearly. The obstacles are not identified in this sequence of verses, but the reference to muddy or turbulent water gives a hint of what they might be. Here the mind is like water and needs to be purified by removing things that "cover" or obscure it. The same image of a "covering" recurs in Madhyamaka accounts of enlightenment as the cure of an eye disease in which "layers" are removed from the eye so that a person can see clearly. The commentarial literature explains that these "coverings" (*āvaraṇa*) come in two forms: there are the "defilements" (*kleśa*) that are discussed in traditional Buddhist literature (consisting chiefly of passion, hatred, and ignorance) and the "coverings" that obscure objects of cognition (*jñāeya*). These seem to be the cognitive barriers and limitations that keep a person from experiencing the omniscience of a Buddha.

As Bhāvaviveka develops his argument, the images of the solid palace and the discriminating eye take on a different appearance. The palace tower that here requires a gradual and diligent ascent becomes the palace seen in a dream, where the challenge is not to climb the tower but to wake up from the dream.

> Someone who feels drowsy and falls asleep sees such things as young men, women, and a palace, but does not see them when he wakes up.
>
> Likewise, someone who has opened the wisdom-eye, stopped the sleep of ignorance, and woken up does not see things as they are seen conventionally.[19]

At this second stage in the argument, the correct vision of the palace is no vision: one sees it best by not seeing it at all. Bhāvaviveka gets to this place by an elaborate analysis of the Mahāyāna version of no-self: the doctrine of Emptiness. He shows that all the categories of traditional Buddhist doctrine, from the gross elements to the constituents of the personality and nirvana, are empty of any identity (*svabhāva*). After he has shown the Emptiness of all existing things (*bhāva*), he does the same for their absence (*abhāva*), and finishes with a demonstration of the Emptiness of Emptiness. To understand all of this (and realize that it is nothing to understand) is to wake up from the sleep of ignorance and not see anything at all.

This is not the end of the story, however. Bhāvaviveka continues his exploration of image of vision with what can best be described as the bodhisattva's returning glance. After realizing that the palace of reality is nothing but a dream, the bodhisattva looks back on the world and weeps tears of compassion.

> [The bodhisattva] has climbed the mountain peak of wisdom and is free from grief but looks with compassion on ordinary people who suffer and are burned by grief.

> Then, with eyes wet with compassion, [the bodhisattva] sees that ordinary people are covered by an imaginary net created by the art of conceptual thought.
>
> The ambrosia of reality, the happy cessation of conceptual diversity, is as clear as the autumn sky. But [ordinary people's] minds move in darkness and they do not see.[20]

The bodhisattva's vision does not stop here. The bodhisattva also looks forward toward the Buddha and weeps tears of devotion.

> To bring benefit to the world, [the bodhisattva] worships the perfectly enlightened and awakened Buddhas with [eyes] moist with devotion and praises them continually with hymns.[21]

At this point the bodhisattva's palace also takes on a new kind of reality. It is not the solid palace that started the text, nor is it the dream palace from which the bodhisattva awoke. It is a devotional object that is created by the power of the bodhisattva's imagination, arrayed with beautiful decorations, and offered as an act of devotion to the Buddha.

The combination of images in the last stage of the text is the one that finally makes the force of the Middle Path clear. The first stage, with its palace-tower and real vision, functioned as the extreme of affirmation. The second stage, with its image of the dream palace, functioned as the extreme of negation. Here the eyes that weep over the unreality of other's illusions and the imagination that creates devotional offerings to the Buddha hover on the boundary between reality and unreality, between affirmation and denial. To follow the logic of Emptiness, it is precisely because bodhisattvas realize the unreality of these things that they are able to respond to them with their unique sense of power and compassion. They have achieved a state that is called *apratiṣṭhita-nirvana*, a nirvana that is unstable or is not located in one place as opposed to another.[22] They do not leave *saṃsāra*, but they are free from the harm of *saṃsāra*, and they do not attain nirvana, but it is as if they were located in nirvana. The significance of the Middle Path is found in precisely the instability of this awareness. It is impossible to put one's feet down in either an unqualified affirmation or an unqualified negation. Both have to be held together and let go together in an experience that is both serious and playful. To hold them and also let them go is to experience the dynamic sense of opposites that gives the Mahāyāna tradition such energy and breadth. It is a way to be wise and compassionate, to be detached and engaged, and above all to be free.

In the first section of this chapter, I argued that the concept of no-self can provide a useful comparative category to draw out the implications of negation in other religious traditions. Could the same be said of the concept of the Middle Path? Fortunately, Bhāvaviveka has saved us from the danger of what Paula Fredriksen has called "speculative and fictive" comparison by embedding his own model of comparative discourse inside his own text. For reasons too complicated to explain, having to do with an obscure *lectio difficilior* in the Tibetan translation of Bhāvaviveka's text and my own misguided attempt at emendation, my interpretive relationship with this text did not end when I published my translation. In tracking down the origin of a particularly problematic word, I became aware of a more general poetic relationship between Bhāvaviveka and the Hindu tradition, particularly the *Bhagavad Gītā*. Bhāvaviveka sets the relationship in motion in the second chapter (called "Taking the Vow of an Ascetic"), in which he describes the bodhisattva in the guise of a brahmanical ascetic. The bodhisattva bathes in the water of morality, wears patience like a white ring of hemp, ties his matted hair with fortitude. He carries compassion like a dark deerskin, faith like a water jug, and endurance like a reed mat, and he worships the sun in the form of the perfectly enlightened Buddha.[23] In later chapters, Bhāvaviveka speaks of the bodhisattva as a practitioner of yoga. Like Arjuna in the *Gītā*, the bodhisattva grapples with issues of compassion (*kṛpā*) and grief (*śoka*). The bodhisattva's goal is called *brahmacaryā*.[24] At the highest levels of the path, the bodhisattva weeps tears of *bhakti*. The climax of Bhāvaviveka's text comes with a great vision of the Buddha, like the vision of Kṛṣṇa in the eleventh chapter of the *Gīta*, but flanked in this case by Śrī and Lakṣmī (in the form of the primary and secondary characteristics of the Buddha's body).[25]

Why would Bhāvaviveka play so aggressively with Hindu categories in his account of the bodhisattva path? I found some useful guidance in an article by Emiko Ohnuki-Tierney on the image of the monkey as an image of the self in Japanese society.[26] She argues that there is an oscillation in meaning between a metaphoric and a metonymic identification of monkeys and human beings. In one (the metaphoric) the monkey is treated as a different category of being (animal as opposed to human) that shares certain similarities with the human. In the other (the metonymic) both the monkey and the human are treated as members of the same category, and one is used to stand in for or represent the other. Ohnuki-Tierney says that the tension between the metaphoric and metonymic relationship gives Japanese self-definitions a distinctive sense of fluidity. You can point to differences in anatomy between a monkey and a human and say, "I am a human because that is not me." But you can also look at the monkey as a kindred creature and visualize human beings as a part of a single sacred cosmos with animals and gods. Could Bhāvaviveka be engaging in a comparable play of similarity and difference?

From one perspective, Bhāvaviveka's philosophical project, with his elaborate descriptions of rival philosophical schools, can be viewed as an attempt to place himself on the map of Indian philosophy, to say that the Madhyamaka tradition deserves a place among the other recognized schools of Indian thought. But his aggressive analysis of the positions of rival schools also lays claim to a position of intellectual dominance. More, perhaps, than any other philosopher who had gone before him, he gave systematic definition to the differences between the Indian schools, and he laid out the field on which they would have to contest one another. One dimension of his work (the metonymic) was to say that all, including himself, were representatives of the same category, and whatever symbols or practices seemed important to other sects or movements were ones that he shared. It was as if he were saying, "If you carry a deerskin and a water jug, so do we, and if you worship Brahman or the sun, so do we. The difference between us, however, is that I get to define the difference, and define it in such a way that our relationship is merely metaphoric: We may seem to carry a deerskin or water jug, but they actually are the virtues of compassion and faith."

The relationship between metonymy and metaphor or similarity and difference is particularly clear in Bhāvaviveka's treatment of the relationship between the Buddha and Brahman. At one point in his discussion of the Buddha, he asks whether Emptiness (referred to here as the Dharma Body of the Buddha) is the same as the supreme Brahman (*paraṃ brahman*) of the Upaniṣads. His answer is yes.[27] But he adds that the gods Śiva, Viṣṇu, Brahmā do not understand it. Only the highest bodhisattvas, Avalokiteśvara, Maitreya, Samantabhadra, and Mañājuśrī, worship it correctly, and they worship it without worshipping it. Here the apparent assertion of similarity shifts to an assertion of difference. Bhāvaviveka says that the two traditions may seem to be members of the same class, but they differ in a crucial respect. Bhāvaviveka belongs to the class of thinkers who realize the truth, and the others do not grasp it. Even here, however, the ground is not stable. To say that Śiva, Viṣṇu, and Brahmā do not grasp the supreme Brahman is to say that they grasp it correctly—by not grasping. All they would need to do is understand the significance of their "not grasping." The truth is in the play of difference and similarity rather than in one side to the exclusion of the other.

To move beyond the confines of Bhāvaviveka's text but remain within the historical boundaries of the Buddhist tradition itself, we could use the same model to explore the resonance between the Middle Way in Mahāyāna Buddhism and the concepts of balance and harmony in the religious traditions of China. The Chinese were certainly able to hear the music in the concept of the Middle Way. Much of the dynamism in

Ch'an Buddhism and later in Zen came from what Arthur F. Wright calls "a complex amalgam of Buddhist and Taoist ideas."[28] How much of this is "Buddhist" and how much is "Taoist"? Superficially it seems possible to identify various borrowings and transformations. But at deeper levels, in which both traditions apply their critiques of real, stable categories, the labels "Buddhist" and "Taoist" cease to have clear meaning. To be called "Buddhist" might be the last thing one would want to have happen if one were following the dynamic movement of the Middle Way. The key to these comparisons is to recognize that Buddhists view the human condition as one of being "on the way," and the "way" is defined as much by an attitude or approach to life as it is by the concrete conditions of life itself.

3.4 What Makes a Useful Category in Comparative Theology?

What conclusions can we draw from this brief and selective investigation of Buddhist attitudes toward the human condition?

First, I have attempted to show that it is not sufficient merely to collect categories, as if the sum of all relevant terms would add up to a serious comparative statement about the human condition (in the singular or the plural). We have to make interpretive choices and identify key elements in the traditions in question. We have to ask, in Nomanul Haq's words, about the "proper part": not just what we find under the hood that looks like a wheel, but what the wheel is that drives the car. In the case of the concept of "suffering," there are many possible lines of comparative investigation: suffering comes from ignorance; it has to do with craving and desire; it is connected to a doctrine of rebirth; and so on. I have argued, however, that there is a key idea behind all of these ideas: the doctrine of no-self. Ignorance is ignorance about the self: one falls prey to craving and desire out of a mistaken sense of self-importance; and the process of rebirth is driven by the sense of self. Buddhists could give fascinating responses to any number of interesting comparative questions about the human predicament, but the place at which Buddhists themselves would attempt to focus the questioning is the sense of self.

Second, I have attempted to illustrate that the concept of a "category" should include not merely what might be called single descriptive terms, such as "obligation" or "loyalty," but interpretive principles or orientations. The doctrine of no-self seems at first to name a concrete claim about the nature of the human personality: "sentient beings have no permanent identities." But in the Buddhist tradition it stands for a larger approach toward negation in general that has much in common, in a structural or phenomenological sense, with negations in other traditions, even with negations that have radically different doctrinal content. The point is even more true of the concept of the Middle Path. Its significance cannot be limited to a particular judgment about the value of self-denial and self-indulgence. It names an interpretive principle that, for Buddhists, applies to every aspect of human life and thought, including their relations with their neighbors and with themselves.[29]

Third, I hope to have suggested, implicitly if not directly, that the comparative enterprise itself needs to be informed by the insights and interpretive techniques of the traditions under study. These traditions are not objects under a microscope to be analyzed and dissected in service of a comparative classification, but subjects who can talk back. When the Buddhist tradition is allowed to speak for itself, it levels a pointed critique at any attempt to create substantial and stable categories that purport, in some definitive sense, either to exclude or to include. The best categories are the ones that put both similarities and differences into play without attempting to settle the issue one way or the other.

In this respect the part of the Buddhist tradition that I have attempted to elucidate here has much in common with the argument that, through Jonathan Z. Smith, has come to dominate much of the theoretical thinking among "comparativists" in the American Academy of Religion. In the essay "In Comparison a Magic Dwells," Jonathan Z. Smith argued that the old comparative project of arriving at a scientific determination of the similarities that bound together different religious traditions was based on a cognitive fallacy. It was not science but magic, in the sense outlined by J. G. Frazer when he said that "homeopathic magic is founded on the association of ideas by similarity."[30] This is to say that the old project of determining comparative "similarities" is only a small step removed from the project of sticking pins in an effigy of an enemy to give him a headache. But like a good Buddhist, Smith sees the other side of the word "magic" in the word "imagination." In the final essay of *Imagining Religion*, "The Devil in Mr. Jones," he explores resonances between the mass suicide in Jonestown, Dionysiac cults in Euripides' *Bacchae*, and cargo cults in the New Hebrides, all in the service of removing from Jonestown what he calls "the aspect of the unique."[31] Are these phenomena the same? Are they different? The radical distances between them, in spatial, historical, and conceptual terms, make the questions particularly strange. But these phenomena do illuminate one another in their similarity as well as their difference, and this process of mutual illumination is worth pursuing by anyone who intends to interpret a phenomenon to circles of observers who share more than the identity of a single discipline. The term "condition" in the phrase "human condition" has its origin in the Latin *condicio*, meaning "to stipulate, agree, talk things over together." This is an etymology that Buddhists would find congenial. It is the human "condition" to talk things over, to discover how large a gap there is between words and the "things" to which they are presumed to refer, and to discover, in the process, a sense of wisdom and compassion that is, if not a common human inheritance, at least a common human possibility.

Notes

1. *Saṃyutta Nikāya* 56.11. Translation quoted from Walpola Rahula, *What the Buddha Taught,* 2nd ed. (New York: Grove Weidenfeld, 1974), 92–94.
2. The text explains that, for each of the Four Noble Truths, the Buddha has understood the truth itself, has understood that one should perform a certain action with regard to that truth, and has understood that he himself has performed that action.
3. *Cūla-Māluṅkya Sutta*, in *Majjhima Nikāya* 63. The story is summarized in Rahula: 12–15.
4. Note that the example of the arrow focuses on the situation in the past that caused suffering in the present, while Māluṅkyaputta's questions focus on the future. The suggestion is that either form of speculation, whether it is about the past or the future, can distract a person from the practical challenge of removing suffering in the present.
5. The verse is quoted in *Abhidharmakośabhāṣyam of Vasubandhu*, ed. P. Pradhan, Tibetan Sanskrit Works Series 8 (Patna: K. P. Jayaswal Research Institute, 1975), on verse 6.3. It also is quoted by Candrakīrti in *Prasannapadā*, ed. L. de La Vallée Poussin, Bibliotheca Buddhica 4 (St. Petersburg, 1903–13), 476. The same comparison appears in the commentary on *Yogasūtra* 2.15. See *The Yoga System of Patañjali,* trans. James Haughton Woods, Harvard Oriental Series 17 (Cambridge: Harvard University Press, 1927), 132.
6. *Pratyayābhisaṃskaraṇād yad anityaṃ tad duḥkham*: commentary on vs. 6.3.
7. *Anguttara Nikāya* I, 286.
8. *The Questions of King Milinda*, trans. T. W. Rhys Davids (1890–94; reprint ed. New York: Dover Publications, 1963).
9. *Aiśvaryamadamatto 'si mām avajñāya vartase / upasthiteṣu bauddheṣu madadhīnā tava sthitiḥ*, quoted in George Chemparathy, *An Indian Rational Theology: Introduction to Udayana's Nyāyakusumāñjali* (Vienna: De Nobili Research Library, 1972), 28.
10. The lectures have been published in *His Holiness the Dalai Lama of Tibet*, Tenzin Gyatso, *The Dalai Lama at Harvard*, trans. and ed. Jeffrey Hopkins (Ithaca: Snow Lion, 1988).
11. *Vivekacūḍāmaṇi of Śrī Śaṅkarācārya*, trans. Swami Madhavananda (Calcutta: Advaita Ashrama, 1992).

12. Edward J. Thomas, *The Life of the Buddha as Legend and History*, 3rd ed. (London: Routledge and Kegan Paul, 1949), 62.

13. For example, Bhāvaviveka's *Madhyamakahṛdayakārikā* 1.8: "[The bodhisattva] sees that the wisdom-eye of the whole world has been concealed, and when he himself has crossed over the unholy hell of rebirth, he causes [the world] to cross over as well" (*lokam ālokya sakalaṃ prajñalokatiraskṛtam / saṃsārāmedhyapātālāt tīrtvā tārayituṃ svayam*). The Sanskrit is quoted from V. V. Gokhale, "Madhyamakahṛdaya Tarkajvālā," *Miscellanea Buddhica*, ed. Chr. Lindtner (Copenhagen, 1985), 88.

14. The Sanskrit verses are found in *Prajñā-pāramitā-ratna-guṇa-saṃcāyā-gatha*, ed. Akira Yuyama (Cambridge: Cambridge University Press, 1976), 35. Note that the verse just quoted from Bhāvaviveka also begins with an image of blindness.

15. Howard Nemerov, "On Metaphor" *A Howard Nemerov Reader* (Columbia: University of Missouri Press, 1991), 232.

16. I have explored these issues more extensively in *To See the Buddha: A Philosopher's Quest for the Meaning of Emptiness* (San Francisco: HarperCollins, 1992; reprint ed. Princeton: Princeton University Press, 1994).

17. Mark Johnson, *The Body in the Mind: The Bodily Basis of Meaning, Imagination, and Reason* (Chicago: University of Chicago Press, 1987).

18. *Madhyamakahṛdayakārikā* 3.1–21. The Sanskrit has been edited by Yasunori Ejima in *Development of Madhyamaka Philosophy in India: Studies on Bhāvaviveka* (Tokyo, 1981). The translation is mine.

19. Ibid., 3.253–54.

20. Ibid., 3.296–97, 300.

21. Ibid., 3.340.

22. The concept of *apratiṣṭhita-nirvāṇa* is discussed in *To See the Buddha*, 172–75.

23. V. V. Gokhale, "The Second Chapter of Bhavya's *Madhyamakahṛdaya* (Taking the Vow of an Ascetic)," *Indo-Iranian Journal* 14 (1972): 40–45.

24. *To See the Buddha*, 172–88.

25. Ibid., 192.

26. Emiko Ohnuki-Tierney, "Embedding and Transforming Polytrope: The Monkey as Self in Japanese Culture," *Beyond Metaphor: The Theory of Tropes in Anthropology*, ed. James W. Fernandez (Stanford: Stanford University Press, 1991), 159–89.

27. *To See the Buddha*, 169–71.

28. Arthur F. Wright, *Buddhism in Chinese History* (Stanford: Stanford University Press, 1959), 78.

29. Responding to Wesley Wildman's attempt to name the kinds of categories we have turned up to date (minutes 2/26/96, section 5.2), it might be useful to attempt to specify the kind of category indicated by the term "Middle Path."

Madhyamakakārikā 24.18 says: "Dependent Origination is what we call Emptiness. It is a dependent designation (*upādāya prajñapti*), and it is the Middle Path (*pratipad madhyamā*)." This verse tells us that the three primary terms in the verse (Dependent Origination, Emptiness, and Middle Path) are "dependent designations." The word "chariot" in *The Questions of King Milinda* also was a "dependent designation": it referred only to a series of parts. The difference in the Madhyamaka is not the notion of dependence or secondary reference but the idea that any analysis of reference can ever be grounded in real "parts." The terms in this verse (and all other terms) are "mere names" (*nāmamātra*) and depend for their meaning only on other terms like themselves. The word "path" (*pratipad*) in "Middle Path" gets its meaning from a root that means to "go." To "go" in Sanskrit can mean both to "move" and to "know." A more accurate translation of Bhāvaviveka's understanding of the term "Middle Way," incorporating both of these two meanings, would be "Middle Approach," suggesting that the path is not a road to be traveled through the forest of *saṃsāra* but the "manner," "approach," or "cognitive procedure" by which the road is traveled. This is one reason why it is common in Mahāyāna literature to elide the distinction between "way" and "goal": to have found the correct approach to life is already very close to having found the goal. From a comparative perspective, there are interesting similarities between this concept of the correct "approach" and Aristotle's concept of *orthos logos* as the "rational principle" or "right reason" by which one finds the mean (*Nicomachean Ethics* 1103b31). In my book on the Buddha, I argue that the Madhyamaka understanding of states of awareness and rational principles comes down to earth, as it were, in the consciousness of actual sentient beings. It would not be inconceivable to follow the verbal echo of Aristotle's *orthos logos* all the way to John 14.6.

30. Jonathan Z. Smith, *Imagining Religion From Babylon to Jonestown* (Chicago: University of Chicago Press, 1982), 21.

31. Ibid., 111.

4

To Be Heard and Done, But Never Quite Seen

The Human Condition According to the Vivekacūḍāmaṇi

Francis X. Clooney, S.J.
with Hugh Nicholson

4.1 Introduction: The Text and Its Challenge

The *Vivekacūḍāmaṇi* is a Sanskrit text in the Advaita Vedānta tradition of Hindu India, composed after the year 800 CE. As Sanskritic, it is a refined and disciplined document meant for the small minority of Indians, mostly male, who could read Sanskrit; as a Vedāntic text it combines attention to the ancient Upaniṣads (c. 900–300 BCE) with later systematizations of the upaniṣadic teachings on ritual, self, and reality, a system most importantly formalized in the *Uttara Mīmāṁsā Sūtras* of Bādarāyaṇa; as advaitic, it insists on the ultimate unity of interior reality (the *ātman*, self) and the ultimate cosmic reality (*brahman*); as a text that points the way to the ultimate truth about us and our world and lasting bliss, it is in principle relevant for all human beings who seek knowledge and happiness. It is, indeed, a product of the human condition, a masterful reflection on it, and a bold effort to change it.

Throughout this chapter, I shall use the *Vivekacūḍāmaṇi* as the instrument of an inquiry into the Hindu view of the human condition—as "Hindu," and therefore as inherently diverse and liable to multiple constructions that need not be reduced to a single viewpoint. The *Vivekacūḍāmaṇi* is representative of widely shared Hindu views regarding what the world is like, and how one is to understand and respond to it. It is a paradigmatic blend of the dour pessimism and articulate hopefulness that one often finds in Hindu texts. Yet, as an Advaita Vedānta text that is explicitly elitist, it presents itself as quite unlike other Hindu texts, marking out a quite different view of what the world is like and what one is to do about it. But even in this self-presentation as having little to do with the common run of Hindu identity and religious practice, it is very much like other Hindu texts that also delight in placing restrictions on their potential audience.

The *Vivekacūḍāmaṇi* is divided into two major parts. The first describes and analyzes the non-self, as the teacher shows his disciple what all that he seems to be, but really is not. The second offers a comparable description and analysis of the nature of the true self, along with instruction on the need to overcome the deeply rooted and habitual wrong understanding we have of ourselves. As such, the *Vivekacūḍāmaṇi* is a well-wrought but by no means unique *advaita* text. Within the *advaita* tradition, the *Vivekacūḍāmaṇi* is most aptly compared with the *Upadeśasahasrī* ("Thousand Teachings") of Śaṃkara. The first two of the three prose sections that conclude that earlier text take the form of instructions of a disciple by his teacher, and the second has the feel and tone of the *Vivekacūḍāmaṇi*; both texts have the same double goal of giving a correct view of a wide range of religious and philosophical issues and also illustrating the proper, clear, and effective instruction of the disciple. Yet the *Vivekacūḍāmaṇi* is far more developed and rhetorically ample and effective; it is perhaps most memorable for its narrative frame, which shows us both the style of teaching and the effect this has on the ideal student. The *Vivekacūḍāmaṇi* invites concerted efforts to think its meaning through; it offers a practical agenda, and asks its readers not merely whether they understand, but whether or not they intend to change. As a specific, specialized text, however, it also suggests that one must be educated properly even to understand the human condition and what it signifies. As we proceed, let us keep in mind the universality *and* narrowness of the choice we have made in focusing on this text.

At the beginning of the *Vivekacūḍāmaṇi,* the disciple seeks out the teacher in desperation, and the teaching that follows in response is presented as a great act of compassion that rescues the student from the conflagration of the world. His speech effectively presents his torment in his afflicted situation, the world as a place of pain, *saṃsāra*: the ocean in which one drowns, or from which one is saved, and the fire by which one is withered and burnt:

> O Master, O friend of those that bow to you, you are an ocean of mercy, I bow to you; lift me, fallen as I am into this sea of becoming, with a straightforward glance of thine eye, which sheds nectar-like supreme compassion.
>
> Save me from death, afflicted as I am by the unquenchable fire of the blaze of *saṃsāra*, and shaken violently by the winds of an untoward lot, terrified and so seeking refuge in you, for I do not know any other man with whom to seek shelter. (35–36)
>
> O lord, with your nectar-like speech, sweetened by the enjoyment of the elixir-like bliss of *brahman*, pure, cooling to a degree, issuing in steams from your lips as from a pitcher, and delightful to the ear—sprinkle me who am tormented by worldly afflictions as by the tongues of a forest-fire. Blessed are those on whom even a passing glance of your eye lights, accepting them as your own.
>
> How to cross this ocean of becoming? what is to be my fate? which means should I adopt? regarding these, I know nothing. Have mercy on me, lord, and bring to an end the misery of *saṃsāra*.
>
> He speaks thus, and takes refuge, scorched by the heat of the burning fire of *saṃsāra*. . . . (39–41a)[1]

The text closes with the enlightenment of the student, his achievement of bliss, and the departure of both student and teacher, to wander freely throughout the world on their own.

Throughout the first major part of the text, the intellectual project of communicating an awareness of non-self is accompanied by that of inculcating a felt repugnance for the corruptible body and its many flaws; the non-self must be felt to be repulsive:

> This body of ours is the product of food and comprises our material layer. It lives on food and dies without it; it is a mass of skin, flesh, blood, bones, and filth, and can never be the eternally pure, self-existent Self.
>
> How can this body, being a pack of bones, smeared with flesh, full of filth, and highly impure, be the self-existent Self, the knower, which is ever distinct from it?
>
> It is the foolish man who identifies himself with a mass of skin, flesh, fat, bones, and filth, while the man skilled in reflection knows his own self, the only reality there is, as distinct from the body. (154, 158–59)

And nearer to the end,

> Realizing the Self, the eternal, pure knowledge and bliss, throw far away this limitation which is the body, inert and filthy by nature. Then remember it no more, for something that has been vomited excites but disgust when called to memory. (414)

The *Vivekacūḍāmaṇi* is a pedagogical masterpiece, intended to enable competent readers to recognize and appropriate the great claims that it presents—either directly, or more probably by undertaking the disciplined student life commended by in its verses. It is filled with repetitions and refrains that mark the persuasive dimension of its agenda; points are repeated in order to inculcate the right way of thinking in the student. Even if the learned brahmin reader is capable of learning the true meaning of Vedānta, he still needs to be persuaded to follow through on its practical agenda in a way that ensures lasting personal appropriation. By extension, prepared, privileged readers are invited to identify intellectually and emotionally with the disciple who comes to the teacher, to work through the highly delicate intellectual inquiry presented there, and also to live in a way that leads to the idealized state that occurs at the end of the conversation.

Here is a brief outline of the *Vivekacūḍāmaṇi*, which will be a useful referent throughout our consideration:

A. Narrative introduction: the disciple seeks a teacher (#1–70)

B. The preparatory teaching on the non-self (#71–211)

1. The teaching on the non-self

2. The practice of discrimination: charting the path to the real Self according to an analysis of the layers of the non-Self, based on *Taittirīya Upaniṣad* 2, concluding with a stark awareness of the emptiness of non-self

C. The major teaching on the comprehension of the true self, in theory and practice (#212–478)

1. The new question regarding the true Self

2. Response: non-dualism in theory

3. The meaning and application of the great correlation, 'that you are,' in *Chāndogya Upaniṣad* 6

4. Non-dualism in practice

5. Summation of the major teaching

6. At the end of the major teaching on the self, the disciple reaches enlightenment.

D. Narrative conclusion: the liberation of the disciple and the concluding exchange (#479–577)

4.2 The Human Condition, Perceived and Real

Our first task will be to trace an understanding of the *Vivekacūḍāmaṇi*, with an eye toward how each of its key dimensions is both distinctive and yet also common, shared with other systems; I will do this by tracing several dimensions of the text. First, its statement of the perceived and real nature of the human condition, by attention to *māyā*, the human problem and *advaita*, the non-dualism that marks the true human condition. In subsequent sections I will examine the role of *viveka*, as that discriminating knowledge that uncovers the falsities of *māyā*; and the practical process of *bhāvanā*, the inculcation of right understanding.

4.2.1 *Māyā: The Human Problem*

It is easiest to begin as the *Vivekacūḍāmaṇi* itself does, with a statement of the human problem although, as we shall see, in reality there is no such problem. We have already seen the torment that prompts the student to seek out a teacher, and in a way the *Vivekacūḍāmaṇi* is dedicated to the assuagement of that torment. To present this persuasively, however, it must first generalize the problem so that it can be understood and responded to: personal confusion is symptomatic of *māyā*, and *māyā* subsists in that dismal non-self that constitutes the ordinary process of human nature.

The *Vivekacūḍāmaṇi* suggests that the problem of anguished existence can be formalized as the problem of an ignorance that is both epistemological and ontological. In stating the problem of human existence, one could dwell simply on the epistemological fact of ignorance, *avidyā*, but the *Vivekacūḍāmaṇi* rephrases this as the problem of *māyā*, the epistemological but also ontological, and experienced, confusion to which human nature is subject.[2]

In the course of explaining the gross and subtle bodies—which comprise the non-self—the teacher refers a number of times to ignorance, particularly the seemingly substantial power of *māyā*. *Māyā* is presented as including the three constituent strands (*guṇa*) that in turn comprise the three material-psychological realities out of which all complex realities are made, lucidity (*sattva*), passion (*rajas*), and dark inertia (*tamas*):

> Ignorance, also called the undifferentiated, is the power of the Lord. She is without beginning, is made up of the three constituent strands (*guṇa*) and is the highest. She is to be inferred by one of clear intellect only from the effects she produces. She is *māyā*, by whom this entire universe is brought forth. (108)
>
> The world is the production of *māyā*:

> The body, organs, breath, mind, ego, etc., all modifications, the sense-objects, pleasure and the rest, the gross elements such as the ether, in fact, the whole universe, even undifferentiated matter, all of this is the non-self.
>
> From the prime matter down to the body, everything is *māyā* and the effect of *māyā*. Know these and *māyā* itself to be the non-self, and therefore unreal, like a mirage in the desert. (122–23)

Through darkness (*tamas*) and passion (*rajas*), *māyā* distorts reality, by respectively *concealing* its non-dual truth and *projecting* instead a wrong, deceptive version of the way things are:

> *Tamas* has the concealing power, which makes things appear other than what they are. It is this that causes the repeated human transmigrations and starts the action of the power of projection.
>
> *Rajas* has the power of projection, which is of the nature of an activity, and from which this primeval flow of activity has emanated. Mental modifications such as attachment and grief are continually produced from this. (113, 111)
>
> One who is overpowered by ignorance mistakes a thing for what it is not; it is the absence of discrimination (*viveka*) that causes one to mistake a snake for a rope. Great dangers overtake him when he seizes it through that wrong notion. Hence it is the mistaking of transitory things as real that constitutes bondage—listen my friend!
>
> This veiling power, comprised of *tamas*, covers the Self. . . .
>
> When his own self, endowed with the purest splendor, is hidden from view, a man through ignorance falsely identifies himself with this body, which is the non-self. And then the great power of *rajas* called the projecting power sorely afflicts him through the binding fetters of lust, anger, etc. (138–40)

Even lucidity, a preponderance of which leads one toward what is clearer and better, is part of *māyā*:

> Pure *sattva* is like water, yet in conjunction with those two [*rajas* and *tamas*] it makes for transmigration. The reality of the self becomes reflected in *sattva* and like the sun illumines the entire world of matter. (117)

Difference—as objective, as projected by the mind—is due to *māyā* (238); it is the power of the Lord experienced as the material world on the one hand, and embodiedness on the other (243). The world as we know it is knowable only in and through *māyā:*

> All of this duality consists of *māyā*, and is in reality non-duality; thus says scripture, and thus we experience it in deep sleep. (405)[3]

Certainly here too a great deal of nuance is possible, in comparison with the meanings rendered to *māyā* by a broader range of Hindus. In the *Gītā* and related texts, for instance, *māyā* is the Lord's marvelous power. In the *Gītā* the experience of amazement comes to the fore, instead of "confusion" or "illusion":

> Though I myself am unborn and undying, though I am the lord of creatures, I fashion nature as my own, and I come into being through the *māyā* of my own self. (*Bhagavad Gītā* 4.6)
>
> Divine, composed of nature's qualities, my *māyā* is hard to escape; but those who seek refuge in me cross over this *māyā*. (*Bhagavad Gītā* 7.14)

In theistic contexts as well as in Advaita, *māyā* represents both a subjective condition and problem, and a cosmological or ontological dimension of the world as such: *our* ignorance is never just mental, and it is never just a private property. Because of its wider scope, it is considered more terrible, yet also more amenable to solutions that can be worked out for people (however narrowly identified) in general.

The torment of the disciple lies in the fact that he is living according to this distortion that affects not only his way of thinking, but also his complete way of being: his ignorance is *māyā*. Until he finds his teacher, his efforts at solutions are too narrow and private, and only further contort and worsen his situation. Vedānta of course offers a solution to this situation, one that proceeds by two stages: through a changed way of thinking, and consequently through a changed way of living.

Māyā and other forms of "Hindoo illusionism" have been written about abundantly in the West. The idea that Orientals think of the world as a dream has been popular for a long time. To a large extent this view is very wrong indeed, because even the full-blown theory of *māyā* that we find here does not translate directly into a practical, everyday view that the world is merely illusory; we are talking theory, not a dull devaluation of ordinary reality. Yet a core portion of this misconception may be retained, since *māyā* has ontological roots; it is always about who and what we and our world are as much as what we think and say. *Māyā* is ignorance with body and with power; it is comprehensive, functioning on multiple levels, as a powerful, world-disfiguring force that requires a comparable response. But the solution is possible, precisely because ignorance is not essential to human nature; it is a mistake that can be remedied, dispelled. How this is so is the truth of *advaita*.

4.2.2 *Advaita as Simple Non-dualism: The True Human Condition*

I began with the *problem* of human existence in order to facilitate our approach to the questions at issue. In fact, the most direct way to present the human condition in the Non-dualist—Advaita—Vedānta is to state that there is an all-inclusive unity underlying reality. There is no problem; we just think there is.

As an Advaita Vedānta text, the *Vivekacūḍāmaṇi* argues for an original and eventual complete identification of the knower and the known, a realization that inevitably and without delay overturns ordinary consciousness:

> It is this supreme oneness (*parama advaita*) which alone is real, since there is nothing else but the self. Truly, there remains no other independent entity in the state of realization of the highest truth.
>
> Through ignorance all this universe appears in diverse forms; but it is nothing but *brahman*, which is absolutely free from all the flaws of imagining (*bhāvanā-adoṣa*).
>
> "This universe is truly *brahman*," such is the august pronouncement of the *Atharva Veda*. Therefore this universe is nothing but *brahman*; for that which is superimposed on something has no separate existence from its substratum.
>
> "It is not this, not this"—for such things are imagined and not real. They are like the snake seen in the rope, and like dreams. Perfectly eliminating the objective world in this way by means of reasoning, one should next realize the single being that underlies both lord and self. (226, 227, 231, 246)

And, near the end of the text, the absence of diversity is proclaimed over and over:

> It is full, without beginning or end, immeasurable, unchanging, it is only one, not two, *brahman*; here there is no diversity whatsoever.
>
> It is not to be avoided nor taken up nor accepted nor relied upon; it is only one, non-dual, *brahman*; here there is no diversity whatsoever.
>
> It is without qualities or parts, subtle, unvarying, without color; it is only one, non-dual, *brahman*; here there is no diversity whatsoever. (464, 467, 468)

Advaita is recognized by the *Vivekacūḍāmaṇi* as the original truth underlying the human condition.

By reason of various historical convergences, Advaita Vedānta, though difficult and rare, is the system of Hindu thought that has attracted the earliest and most sustained interest in the West, which itself has been fascinated with theories of pantheism and monism that seem akin to Vedānta.[4] Certainly, the claim that non-dualism is the deepest truth of the human condition—and that it is not be personalized as a divine being—provides a clear referent for comparison and contrast with various Jewish, Christian, and Muslim views of the world. If this is truly a starting point and not a conclusion, we have here a first foothold for understanding the Vedānta view of the human condition—and therefore an honored and legitimate entrance into Indian views of the human condition. But there is more to be said, even in the context of the *Vivekacūḍāmaṇi*, before "non-dualism" could become a useful tool in a comparative project.

4.3 The Function of Right Knowledge (*viveka*) in the Apprehension of the Truth of the Human Condition

The preceding analysis of *māyā* and *advaita* is abstract, even as a presentation of the human condition as a problem that can be solved. No one profits, really, from the mere postulation of oneness and its obscuration. Rather, *advaita* must be accomplished, realized, through a disciplined process of coming to understand the world differently, all that we are not and all that we are. The *Vivekacūḍāmaṇi* is therefore a typically pragmatic Hindu text: the human condition is never improved merely by postulations about what is, should be, the case, for the human condition is constructed in such a way as to elicit a certain kind of understanding that is in turn a certain kind of action.

The practical remedy offered by the *Vivekacūḍāmaṇi* is first of all the project indicated in its title: the practice of skilled discrimination, a sorting-out (*viveka*) that proceeds by distinguishing things one from the other, most important the Self from all else, the non-self:

> A firm conviction to the effect that *brahman* is true and the universe mistaken: that is designated as discrimination (*viveka*) between the permanent and the impermanent. (20)

The *Vivekacūḍāmaṇi* is committed to the possibility and value of right knowledge, and it specifies this knowledge as *viveka*: accurate, discriminating knowledge as the key transformative and liberative power in human life. Subtle and discerning knowledge is the primary tool by which one can unveil *māyā*'s distortions of reality and accordingly make evident the fundamental truth of *advaita*. The teacher explains to the student:

> It is truly through your connection with ignorance that you, who are the supreme Self, find yourself bound to non-self, whence alone proceeds the flow of this world (*saṃsṛti*). The fire of knowledge, kindled by discrimination (*viveka*) between these two [self and non-self], should burn up the effects of ignorance together with its roots.

Now I am going to tell you fully about what you ought to know, the discrimination between Self and non-self. Listen to it and confirm it in your own self. (47, 71)

Discrimination is the means to the destruction of *māyā*:

Māyā can be destroyed by the realization of pure *brahman*, one without a second, just as the mistaken idea of a snake is removed by the discrimination of the rope. . . . (110)

Bondage can be destroyed neither by weapons nor by wind nor by fire nor by millions of actions—by nothing except the great sword of knowledge that is discrimination, sharpened by the grace of the lord. (147)

The cessation of superimposition takes place through perfect knowledge, and by no other means. Perfect knowledge (*saṃyak jñāna*), according to scripture, consists in the realization of the identity of self and *brahman*.

This realization is achieved by perfect discrimination between the self and the non-self; therefore one must discriminate between the individual self and the true self. (202–3)

When something conjured up in error is subjected to discrimination, then it is nothing but that [*brahman*], and not at all different from that. (253)

Perfect discrimination brought on by direct realization distinguishes the reality of the seer from the seen object, and it cuts through the bond of delusion created by *māyā*; and there is no more experiencing this world for one who has been freed from this. (345)

That in which something is imagined to exist through error is, through discrimination, that thing itself, and not distinct from it; when the error is gone, the reality of the falsely perceived snake becomes the rope; similarly, all of this has as its proper nature the self. (387)

Viveka is most prominently displayed in the first part of the *Vivekacūḍāmaṇi,* where it is a process of careful, inquisitive inquiry that can be undertaken only by the educated and self-controlled person who gradually learns how to see things—sense-objects, mental impressions and developed ideas, dreams and fancies, the words and injunctions and practices of religious life—exactly for what they are, nothing less or more. It is a kind of observation that, by shedding light on reality as it is, banishes wrong understandings of every object of knowledge. *Viveka* is primarily useful in the deconstruction of the non-self described in the first major section of the *Vivekacūḍāmaṇi*.

Let us examine the key example of *viveka* at work in the *Vivekacūḍāmaṇi*, where it is used to uncover, one by one, the layers of the non-self. This endeavor is based on a reading of *Taittirīya Upaniṣad*, which speaks of the five "layers" of the (non)self. In the second part of that very old upaniṣad, we are led through a series of five material and psychological layers that are also layers of self: food, vital self, mind, intellect, bliss. In the upaniṣad, the meditation simply posits these five increasingly interior layers of self, inviting the meditator to travel inward, from one to the other. With the fifth layer, the process simply stops; the inquirer is left with the knowledge that the deepest core of the self—*brahman*, on *brahman*—is blissful. The puzzling fact that each of these selves is in the shape of a bird is explained by an additional note: the upaniṣad is psychologizing the fivefold fire of the old sacrificial system, in which bricks were laid out geometrically in a five-layer altar, each layer bearing the shape of a bird, for the altar itself is the bird that takes the sacrificer to heaven. In the upaniṣad, while the movement of getting there is a kind of meditative ritual, the route is speculative and leads right into the inner self.[5]

In the *Vivekacūḍāmaṇi,* the whole of the teaching on the non-self is built around this *Taittirīya* text, though differences are evident. The architectural structuring of the five-layered bird altar and its mythic cosmology have been put aside, for the sake of a spare, rationale analysis. So too, the transformation of the five-layered bird and the corresponding deeper levels of self into a series of five layers of *non*-self indicates a turning away from the upaniṣadic confidence that there can be positive continuity in the quest for interiority. Rather than a series of claims that there is "still more," in the *Vivekacūḍāmaṇi* the challenge is rather a series of "nots." The process has been rationalized and reduced; it is less imaginatively accessible, yet more yielding to the work of the rational mind. Instead of altars, we find a series of analyses and arguments as to why the body, vital self, mind, understanding, and experience of bliss cannot be the true self. Each of the five arguments concludes with a summary verse as to why this version of self-identity is not adequate:

1. *Food:* This body of ours is the product of food and comprises our material layer. It lives on food and dies without it; it is a mass of skin, flesh, blood, bones, and filth, and can never be the eternally pure, self-existent Self. It does not exist prior to birth or posterior to death, it is born in a moment, it dies in a moment, it is changeful by nature; it is not one, it is inert, a sense-object, like a jar; how can it be one's own self, the knower of changes in being? (154–55)
2. *Vital self:* The vital layer is not the Self, because it is a modification of air, and like the air it is inside and outside, and because it never knows in the least either its own weal and woe or those of others, being eternally dependent on another. (166)
3. *Mind:* The mental layer also cannot be the supreme Self, because it has a beginning and an end, is subject to modifications, is characterized by pain and suffering, and is an object; whereas the seer can never be seen as the object of seeing. (183)
4. *Intellect:* This knowledge layer which we have been discussing cannot be the supreme Self for the following reasons: it is subject to change, is insentient, is a limited thing, is the object of seeing, and is not constantly present. The impermanent cannot be taken as the permanent. (206)

5. *Bliss:* Nor is the blissful layer the supreme Self, because it is endowed with changeful attributes, is a modification of material nature, is the effect of past good deeds, and is located within the other layers which are modifications. (209)

Careful analysis is both necessary and possible if one is to understand and discard the non-self, entirely. This realization is the achievement of *viveka*; the layers of the onion have been gently peeled away, and there is nothing inside them. It is a stark, more immediate, and personal realization of *māyā* and the futility of the postulations humans make regarding their identities. *Viveka* achieves its primary Vedāntic purpose, to uncover the non-self in its deceptive multiplicity; as an intellectual practice, it thus includes a series of judgments about what the self is and is not.

Has Vedānta thus become more accessible to the interested reader? Yes and no. Although this is not a reductive rationalism, the *Vivekacūḍāmaṇi* does trust the ability of humans to sort out reality intellectually and see the human condition for what it is. We have seen that *viveka* marks the insistently rational dimension of Vedānta. There is a way of thinking that the educated person can undertake that will resist and eventually conquer the power of *māyā*. Reason can expose the apparent self, the non-self, and also make intelligent use of scripture in order to achieve a comprehension of the true self. I suppose we can say that most religious traditions, particularly those with long and literate traditions, are committed to a moderate reliance on reason. There is no claim or evidence in the *Vivekacūḍāmaṇi* that *viveka* is an entirely peculiar or idiosyncratic version of reasoning, even if the style of reasoning seen in the *Vivekacūḍāmaṇi* depends on contextual suppositions drawn from the Upaniṣads and generations of readings of the Upaniṣads; it is careful thinking, a careful sorting out of what is and what is not.

But *viveka* is not enough. By reasoning, the student sorts out what is before his eyes and strips away every illusion. At the end of the first major part of the text, the student is left with a stark realization: *viveka* has led him to see that none of this is self, none of it matters. All that is left for him is to hope for a new response from the teacher, which can take him beyond the quandary he has fallen into. This discernment of non-self ends in perplexity, the posing of a further question, as the disciple cries out,

> After these five layers have been eliminated as false, teacher, I find nothing here but the absence of anything! What entity is there left with which the wise knower of the self should realize his identity? (212)

Although Vedānta is a committed intellectual tradition, the desired clear apprehension of non-self cannot in itself constitute the liberative experience the disciple seeks: because *māyā* is not just ignorance but also a distorted way of being, its remedy must also be a transformation of one's way of being human. Thus the need for the second major section of the *Vivekacūḍāmaṇi,* which seeks to describe how one is to integrate oneself in self-knowledge. To achieve a positive sense of what *is*, steps must be taken beyond the accomplishments of *viveka*, for the reintegration of mind and life in the Self.

Viveka is very demanding indeed; its prerequisites are impressive—anguish at the world as it is, and a certain austerity and detachment. It is an intellectual procedure that requires careful practice; if carried through rightly, as in the first part of the *Vivekacūḍāmaṇi*, it leaves the student with a stark sense of non-self. As texts more ample and less irenic than the *Vivekacūḍāmaṇi* indicate, it is no easy task to understand clearly the nature of body and mind and differences of opinion are stubborn. Because the problem is comprehensive, the solution cannot be simply epistemological; one must cultivate this way of right knowing and extend it, gradually transforming even one's own identity.

Now it should be obvious that this kind of knowing is very rational indeed; there is nothing esoteric about it, such that it would stand alone, apart from the ways in which other human beings in other times and places have thought, discerned, distinguished apparent and deeper realities. One might suggest that as a way of knowing, *viveka* can be learned and practiced by anyone among us. Yet here too there are limits to the significance of this achievement: in the *Vivekacūḍāmaṇi*, *viveka* does not provide mere information about reality, and a regimen of *viveka* does not conclude in results that can be summarized and passed around. Rather, it is a way of reopening the question of one's own self, beginning—as in the case of the anguished student—with one's particular discontents and anxieties and their presuppositions. Since *viveka* here is presented as fruitful in the context of a disciple-teacher relationship, there must also be some assessment of the sociology of this kind of knowledge: among whom can it happen, as modeled here? We shall return to this question in section 4.5, but first we must attend more closely to the agenda that is imposed upon the person who practices *viveka* and understands where it leads.

4.4 The Transformation of Human Living and the Project of Transformation (*bhāvanā*)

The narrative frame of the *Vivekacūḍāmaṇi* marks its concern to change the reader. Its analysis of the human condition—ontological and epistemological alienation from our true, ever-present identity—requires that it also instruct the student on the actual transformation of self, toward a real-life appropriation of what the text teaches; here I refer to this project of transformation by just one of the distinctive terms for it, *bhāvanā* ("making-be," "effecting a way of being").

Transformation is primary to the agenda of almost half of the text, the lengthy section from verse 264 to verse 463. Imperatives are used quite liberally in this section. For example, each verse from 277 to 285 ends with the command, "Be done with this superimposition," that is, stop confusing your self with extrinsic, distracting factors:

> The mind of the yogi perishes, being constantly established in his own self; thence follows the cessation of impressions. Therefore, be done with this superimposition on your self!
>
> By means of scripture, reasoning, and your own realization, realize your self as the Self of all, even if a trace remains; be done with this current superimposition on your self! (277, 281)

286 is a command to think, and 287–90 enjoin the reader to become a certain kind of person. The Vedānta view that there is an obligation at the heart of scripture is hardly novel; its great intellectual predecessor, Mīmāṃsā ritual theory, had built its entire exegesis around the idea that there are central, core commands in the scriptures, in reference to which everything else is to be understood. Of course, the Vedāntins have to find their way carefully here—encouraging a course of action while discouraging the notion that knowledge can be guaranteed by any predictable set of actions.

The section of the *Vivekacūḍāmaṇi* on the true self is channeled through a presentation of the famous *tat tvam asi*—"that you are"—from the *Chāndogya Upaniṣad* 6. In the context of the upaniṣad as it has been understood traditionally, "that you are" is explained by a series of evocative images and comparisons that a father put before his son in order to get him to understand the simpler, higher truth. The upaniṣad repeats *tat tvam asi* eight times, each according to a different illustration. Section 6.8 offers the teaching as the conclusion to a discourse on sleep and death. In 6.8.6, everything is rooted in *brahman*, to which one returns through death, reversing the process of creation; it is then that the correlation is made: *tat tvam asi*, "Śvetaketu, you are that Self, that Reality." In 6.9–16, each example adds to Śvetaketu's understanding:

> the essences of different flowers become a single honey . . . rivers do not keep their identity in reaching the ocean . . . the sap is everywhere in the tree . . . the finest seed from which the tree grows is invisible . . . salt dis-

> solved in water, though unseen, can be tasted everywhere in the water . . . a man abandoned and blindfolded in the forest can find his way home . . . the dying man retreats into himself, losing worldly consciousness . . . an honest man is not burnt by the red-hot axe. . . .

The pattern for all eight is given in the first:

> ". . . that which is the finest essence—this whole world has that as its soul. That is reality. That is the self. That you are, Śvetaketu." "Sir, cause me to understand even more." (6.8.9 part)

The use of the *Chāndogya* text in the *Vivekacūḍāmaṇi* is marked by three stages.

First, there is a process of rationalization similar to what we have already seen regarding the *Taittirīya* text; here too, an old upaniṣadic teaching is removed from its mythological context, and its pedagogical context, and presented as a strictly rationally accessible teaching. The eight examples are removed, and no mention is made of them as the topic is generalized, abstracted. Instead, the *Vivekacūḍāmaṇi* sets forth a formal and simple linguistic tension between the *tat* ("that," *brahman*) and the *tvam* ("you," individual self), and emphasizes the creative possibilities provoked by the tension between them:

> The wise realize the highest reality which is devoid of knower, knowledge, and known, which is infinite, undifferentiated, pure and undivided consciousness.
>
> It is that which can be neither thrown away nor taken up, which is beyond the reach of mind and speech, immeasurable, without beginning and end, *brahman*, the fullness, the "I," the great one; if so, then the text, "That you are" repeatedly establishes the absolute identity of *brahman* and the self, denoted by the terms 'that' and 'you' respectively, divesting these terms of their relative associations; it is the identity of their implied and not literal meanings which is meant to be inculcated; for they are in attributes contrary to one another, like the sun and a glow-worm, the king and a servant, the ocean and a well, Mt. Meru and an atom. (239–42)
>
> Hence those two terms must be carefully considered according to their implied meanings, so that their absolute identity may be established. Neither the method of total rejection nor that of complete retention will do. One must reason it out through the process which combines the two. (247)

In showing how reason helps to overcome the evident differences between the *tat* and the *tvam*, the *Vivekacūḍāmaṇi* models a developed Vedāntic way of reasoning, which can be examined also in other important Vedānta texts, such as the *Upadeśasahāsrī* and the *Vedāntaparibhāṣā*.

Second, there is the appeal to the disciple to remake his way of being. The simple truth of the identity of *brahman* and the self must be gradually inculcated and thereby realized. Once the truth of non-dualism is announced, it is made the subject matter of a series of appeals for interiorization. At a key point in the major teaching we find a refrain in ten verses that encourage *bhāvanā*, the "making-be" or inculcation within oneself of this new attitude toward self and world and *brahman—brahma tat tvam asi bhāvaya ātmani*, you are that *brahman*; establish this attitude in your self:

> That which is beyond caste and creed, family and lineage; devoid of name and form, quality and flaw; transcending space, time, and sense-objects—*you are that brahman; establish this attitude in your self*;
>
> that supreme *brahman* which is beyond the range of all speech, but accessible to the eye of pure realization; which is pure, the embodiment of knowledge, the beginningless entity—*you are that brahman; establish this attitude in your self*;
>
> that which is free from birth, growth, development, waste, disease, and death; which is indestructible; which is the cause of the projection, maintenance, and dissolution of the universe—*you are that brahman; establish this attitude in your self*;
>
> that beyond which there is nothing, higher than the highest, the inmost self, of unitary essence, the real, conscious, joyful, infinite and immutable—*you are that brahman; establish this attitude in your self.* (254, 255, 258, 263)

What one reasons to by appeals to the implied, secondary meanings of *tat* and *tvam* must nevertheless be inculcated gradually, practiced until it becomes habitual.

Third, the remainder of this positive exposition of the self (as far as 463) is a Vedāntic yoga; the immediate appeal to impress upon one's mind the truth of the *Chāndogya* claim is elaborated as a meditative process and way of life that aims at changing the mind even to its deepest habitual levels: this change is urged upon the disciple as the way to interiorize and appropriate the truth that in theory is already available due to the nature of the self and the clarity of scripture. The achievement of the new attitude indicates a rich notion of *viveka* as rational in a full and embodied form, since *māyā* is more than an epistemological problem. The goals of this Vedāntic yoga is the project of concentration and ultimate integral unity (*samādhi*); a series of verses, 352–66, describe Vedāntic discipline around the principle of *samādhi*:, as these concluding verses suggest:

> Reflection should be considered a hundred times superior to hearing, and meditation a hundred thousand times superior even to reflection, but [integration] without differentiation (*nirvikalpa*) is infinite.

By integration without differentiation, the reality of *brahman* is clearly and firmly realized, but not otherwise; for then the mind, being unstable by nature, would be mixed up with other perceptions.

Therefore, with senses controlled, integrate (*samādhatsva*) [yourself] continually, with mind quieted and turned within; destroy the darkness made by beginningless ignorance by seeing your oneness with being. (364–66)

This integral attainment of self must be cultivated in a way of life, by way of meditation:

This imaginary world has its root in mind, and never persists after the mind is annihilated. Therefore integrate (*samādhehi*) the mind in the supreme Self, which is your inmost essence.

The wise one realizes in his heart, through total integration (*samādhi*), the infinite *brahman*, which is of the nature of eternal knowledge and absolute bliss, which has no exemplar, which transcends all limitations, is ever free and without activity, and which is like the limitless sky, indivisible, absolute. (407–8)

With mind integrated (*samāhitāntaḥkaraṇaḥ*), behold in your self the Self, of infinite glory, and cut off your bondage scented with the scents of previous births; strive for the fruition of your birth as a man.

The Self is devoid of all limiting adjuncts, existence, consciousness, bliss, one without a second: firmly establish your self in the Self, and you shall no more come this way.

Realizing the Self, the eternal, pure knowledge and bliss, throw far away this limitation which is the body, inert and filthy by nature. Then remember it no more, for something that has been vomited excites but disgusts when called to memory. (411–12, 414)

At the end of the *Vivekacūḍāmaṇi*'s appeal and summation of the theoretical and practical teaching on the self, the disciple reaches enlightenment, as the truth of self illumines him completely; he rises and begins a hymn of praise and delight:

Realizing the supreme truth through these instructions of the guru, the authority of the scriptures, and his own reasoning, with his senses quieted and his mind integrated, he became immovable in form and perfectly established in the self.

Having integrated his mind for some time in the supreme *brahman*, he rose and out of supreme bliss spoke as follows:

My mind has annihilated, and all its activity has melted, because I have realized the identity of self and *brahman*; I known neither this nor that, nor what or how much is this infinite bliss. (479–81)

His way of being and his way of thinking are transformed, for the powerful team of *viveka* and *bhāvanā* have broken the epistemological and ontological power of *māyā*. The remainder of the *Vivekacūḍāmaṇi* is devoted to praising this new, totally free state. Just as the experience of *māyā* was revealed as entirely loathsome, a life of realized self-knowledge is now made as attractive as possible. The teacher responds with a long description of the ideal way of life of the realized sage who continues to live in this world that is now bliss, no longer misery. These two verses indicate the teacher's tone and intent:

> The sage lives alone, enjoying the sense-objects while yet being the very embodiment of desirelessness; he is always satisfied with his own self, and himself is established as the self of all; sometimes a fool, sometimes a sage, sometimes possessed of regal splendor, sometimes behaving like a motionless python, sometimes wearing a benign expression, sometimes honored, sometimes insulted, sometimes unknown—thus lives the wise one, ever happy in the highest bliss. (541–42)

If *māyā* was both ignorance and a deformation of the world, realization of self is both mental clarity and a transformation of world. Because the disciple has not realized the self, his experience of human condition has been utterly transformed, in wisdom and behavior, personally and in social interaction; he has become what he had always been, unknowingly.

The rhetorical and narrative dimensions distinguish the *Vivekacūḍāmaṇi* among Vedānta texts. The underlying human reality (*advaita*) is terribly obscured (by *māyā*), yet the application of discerning reason (*viveka*) by a person persistent in self-transformation and vulnerable to the implications of knowledge can retrieve that underlying and liberative unitive experience—after which, if we attend to the end of the *Vivekacūḍāmaṇi* narrative, ordinary life as we know it is forever finished and done with. If the text is understood properly, it will be put into practice; if it is practiced properly, one's life will be changed. The meaning of life is not merely there to be observed and assented to; rather, it is a project to be undertaken for the sake of a still deeper recognition.

Of course, the quest to keep together the arduous use of reason and the transformation of the heart are not unique to either Vedānta or the Hindu tradition, although the matrix of relevant terms would be different in other examples one might adduce. At first glance it would seem that the *Vivekacūḍāmaṇi* invites comparison—conversation, engagement, mutual illumination, real change—more comfortably with religious traditions in which integral wisdom is at stake—for example, the medieval Christian tradition, the rabbinic tradition, the Daoist tradition, many of the Buddhist meditation traditions—and less the analytic, speculative, and comparative traditions of the modern academy. After one comes to some preliminary understanding of the text, perhaps, the next agenda item is to discern where one stands in relation to one's own potential communities of learning, religious, philosophical, academic, and where the various wisdoms praised by those communities seem likely to end up.

4.5 Exclusions, and the Force of the Text

However inviting we find the *Vivekacūḍāmaṇi*, in the end we must face the obstacles it places in our way; from its beginning, it severely limits its audience. Most human beings are judged fundamentally unprepared to carry forward the great project of liberative self-knowledge, and unable to remedy their lack of preparedness in this life.

The most striking exclusion that marks *Vivekacūḍāmaṇi* is the exclusion of all but male brahmins. The *Vivekacūḍāmaṇi* does not invite us—that is, those of us who have not been born male brahmins—to read it at all. Even when we do read it, we are told that its message does not really pertain to us, for we cannot do what it talks about unless we happen to be interested male brahmins:

> Human birth is rare among those born, being male is more rare, being a brahmin, more rare. Beyond that is focus on the path of vedic *dharma*, while knowing is beyond that. Distinguishing between the self and the non-self, experience of one's self, firmness in being *brahman*, liberation: this cannot be attained without good deeds done in billions of births. (2)

Knowledge may seem to be universally available, but the human condition is such that most people are simply incapable, in this birth, and the power of knowledge is not enhanced by imagining it to be actually available to everyone. The qualified person is a rare and solitary being; while the entire range of life forms is held in view at the start, the actual possibilities are inevitably narrowed down to the one or two people who might actually take advantage of what the *Vivekacūḍāmaṇi* makes available. Life is marked intrinsically material and social from the start, and the knower is always an embodied knower, defined in terms of certain realistic possibilities and impossibilities proposed and determined by society. According to the *Vivekacūḍāmaṇi*, being a brahmin and being male are realistically necessary concomitants of being a potentially successfully knower.

The point is made even more forcefully in the next verses, which urge these male brahmins to take seriously the unique opportunity they have before them:

> Hard to get are these three things which have as their cause divine favor: being a human, desiring liberation, and taking refuge with a great man. (3)
>
> Even if one gets that hard to get human birth, and is a male and the intent of the scriptures, the foolish person who does not strive for the liberation of his own self is a suicide, destroying himself due to grasping what is not real. (4)

The description/prescription of the student—and thus the reader—continues all the way through the introductory portion of the *Vivekacūḍāmaṇi*, interwoven with the description of the burning, tormenting nature of this world mentioned at the beginning of this chapter.

In his modern commentary on the *Vivekacūḍāmaṇi*, Chandrasekhara Bharati[6] says that verse two—"human birth is rare among those born, being male is more rare, being a brahmin, more rare . . ."—aptly summarizes the entire *Vivekacūḍāmaṇi*. He attends faithfully to each restriction indicated in the verse, defending without hesitation the privileged role of male brahmins, who alone will have the undistracted time and devotion to explore the self. He quotes the sage Vasistha: "This body of a brahmin is not intended for enjoying sense-pleasures. It has to be subjected to strict disciplines here which will lead after death to unlimited bliss." (6–7) Others, he suggests, can ultimately be reborn as brahmins. (13) Since those who are not prepared were not, traditionally, likely to be readers of the *Vivekacūḍāmaṇi* at all, verse two is inviting its already elite readers to reflect on their special status and take advantage of its advantages.

By doing so the *Vivekacūḍāmaṇi* draws on older themes of preparedness and exclusion, aligning itself with other Indian systems that similarly restrict their audience by praising the rarity of truly worthy listeners—with the right lineage, with sufficient knowledge, with intense enough devotion. Both the similarities and differences among the various systems' restrictions are instructive. The issue is traditionally expressed by the Sanskrit term *adhikāra*, which signifies eligibility, preparedness: who is competent for this act or knowledge, and what are the qualifications that must be in place first? In the realm of orthodox practice (the *vaidika*, which represented in differing ways by the ritual practitioners, the Mīmāṁsā ritual theorists, and the *Laws of Manu*, there is a concern to limit orthodox ritual practice to the twice-born, and in effect to brahmins.

The extension of the restrictions from ritual to knowledge was fairly immediate. The primary Vedānta text, the *Uttara Mīmāṁsā Sūtras* of Bādarāyaṇa, prepared the way for the *Vivekacūḍāmaṇi* by insisting upon the exclusion of *śūdra*s from the study of the Upaniṣads even though it might seem that knowledge should be subject to fewer restrictions. The argument there seeks a balance between a mere replication of the ritualist exclusion that would align the liberative knowledge and ritual too closely, and a universalist view of knowledge, which would make that knowledge available to all and thus preclude consideration of the qualifications for knowing. The *Vivekacūḍāmaṇi* is reaffirming the earlier Vedānta position, though highlighting it all the more forcefully by placing the restriction on the knower at the beginning of its exposition: knowledge is the human way to liberation; humans have the capacity to know; few are actually ready for this knowledge, or to follow through on what it entails.

The *Vivekacūḍāmaṇi* is interestingly compared on the matter of exclusivity with the *Bhagavad Gītā*, a text highly admired for its inclusiveness. In chapter 9, Kṛṣṇa states that even women, the low-caste, and evil-doers can reach him; indeed, it is actually impossible to avoid reaching Kṛṣṇa who is the final referent of every human path. While the *Vivekacūḍāmaṇi* opens into what seems to be a universally accessible knowledge of self, the *Gītā* presents a God who reaches out to all and allows himself to be reached by all. These are two paths of devotion, *bhakti*: in the *Gītā*, the premium is on love of God, and the solution is in divine grace; in the *Vivekacūḍāmaṇi*, the premium is on the desire for the true self, and it is skillful practiced knowledge that leads to the solution. In both, however, there is a realistic recognition of difficulties, while the *Vivekacūḍāmaṇi* makes access impossible for most people, in any given lifetime. The human condition is such that optimism has a very solid basis, while immediate prospects are always less favorable. In the *Gītā*, the warrior Arjuna, the disciple, is gradually transformed through his encounter with the divine charioteer, Kṛṣṇa. But even the *Gītā*, revered for its universality, has a restrained view as to who is really capable of the knowledge it offers to all:

> Few among thousands strives for success, and of those who are successful few know me truly. (7.3)
>
> Even at the end of the *Gītā*, there is a warning about welcoming casual observers:
>
> You must not speak of this to one who is without penance and devotion, or who does to wish to hear, or who finds fault with me. (18.67)

Even when they seek to improve the human condition, Indian texts are usually sober and skeptical, setting a high price of admission.[7] The *Gītā* and the *Vivekacūḍāmaṇi* have this in common.

Throughout the rest of the introductory portion of the *Vivekacūḍāmaṇi* there are additional verses that reinforce the second verse's exclusory intent, while yet making it clear that even being a male brahmin is not in itself the whole solution.

First, *bhakti*—which ordinarily would be understood as devotion to a deity like Kṛṣṇa, and which would therefore be widely popular—is redefined as a commitment to self-knowledge, pursued with one's teacher:

> Among the things conducive to liberation, devotion alone is most honored. Seeking after the real form of one's nature is designated "devotion."
>
> Others maintain that the inquiry into the truth of one's own self is devotion. The inquirer about the truth of the *ātman* who is possessed of the above-mentioned means of attainment should approach a wise teacher, who confers emancipation from bondage. (31–32)

Yet even so, the cult of a guru—even the teacher in the *Vivekacūḍāmaṇi* itself—is also unacceptable:

> The true nature of things is to be known personally, through the eye of clear illumination, and not through the learned ones; the real nature of the moon is to be known with one's own eyes. Can others make one know it?
>
> Who but one's own self can get rid of the bondage caused by the fetters of ignorance, desire, action and the like, yes, even in a billion cycles? (54–55)

Any articulated and established pathway to the divine is necessarily relegated to second place, as are these standard systematic approaches:

> Neither by yoga, nor by calculation (*sāṃkhya*) nor by rites nor by knowledge, but only by realization of one's identity with *brahman* is liberation possible, and by no other means. (54–56)

Although the *Vivekacūḍāmaṇi* is very much an exegetical text, even scripture is not a sure guide, by itself:

> The study of the scriptures is fruitless so long as the highest truth is not realized, and it is equally fruitless when the highest truth has already been realized. (59)
>
> Even a commitment to careful reading is not a sure pathway into the text.

The *Vivekacūḍāmaṇi* is perplexing in its exclusions. On the one hand, it stresses *advaita*, simple and straightforward knowledge about the way things really are. On the other, it wants to define real ability and real limitation, in particular real-life situations: truth is universal, knowledge possible for all, but only male brahmins prepared for an arduous, disciplined way of life will manage to know things as they really are; the life of the brahmin is the sure way to knowledge, but nothing in that life can be entirely depended on. Despite the fragility of every restriction, failing to announce them would serve no good purpose. The matter of exclusion is therefore central to the *Vivekacūḍāmaṇi*, for it problematizes the human condition as ordinarily experienced, and narrowly limits its own audience, the set of those capable of responding to the situation. Most human experience, and indeed most Hindus' experience, has to be excluded; what is left is not dependable. Such is the exigency of the human condition and how we are compelled to think about it; and such is the *Vivekacūḍāmaṇi*, which is thus strikingly characterized by what it excludes and denies.

4.6 Integral Acts of Learning across Cultural and Religious Boundaries: Hearing, Knowing, Doing, But Not Speculating

Now let us see where this study of this single text has left us. The *Vivekacūḍāmaṇi* is not a mysterious text. Its individual words and concepts, such as *māyā, advaita, viveka,* and *bhāvanā,* have clear enough meanings, and we can begin to compare and contrast them with other things we know. The *Vivekacūḍāmaṇi* puts forward intelligible claims: there is a wonderful underlying truth to human existence, non-duality; we are alienated from our true reality and no longer know who we are; this ignorance twists both our knowing and way of being; the solution is clear thinking, the cultivation of concentration, and perseverance on the path to knowledge; but there are also prudent restrictions on this knowledge that must be cultivated and learned gradually, since not everyone is capable either of beginning to apprehend it or of following through on it.

Much of the *Vivekacūḍāmaṇi* can be understood even by people from outside the Advaita, Vedānta, Hindu traditions, provided they know Sanskrit or are willing to trust translations. All kinds of smaller and larger comparisons can be undertaken. It is obvious, for instance, that *advaita* can be compared with various kinds of mysticism and monism, since the idea of non-duality seems intelligible across cultural boundaries. But the idea of *advaita* is deceptively simple, and a vigorous corrective is required if we are to understand it properly against its Sanskritic and brahmanical background, and in relation to one or another version of monism, etc. The *Vivekacūḍāmaṇi* offers its own particular brand of non-dualism as a truth to be apprehended and a reality to be constructed in an orderly fashion: *advaita* is rationally accessible, radically transformative, usefully based on the Upaniṣads but only in terms of the learning process; it is best learned in the context of a guru-disciple relationship; it is accessible only to male brahmins who rise to the occasion and take seriously the opportunity occasioned by their discontent. Because this non-dualism occurs only in the context of a necessarily concomitant understanding of *māyā*—and the corresponding remedies to which we shall now turn—there is no value in the common selective comparisons. For example, it does little good to compare non-dualism with monotheism—"humans as finite and created," with "humans as *brahman*"—and then decide that these are very different, even irreconcilable ideas.

The preceding point may be generalized as follows. Whether or not the individual elements are intelligible, Advaita Vedānta—or any such developed discourse—must be approached as a system, and not merely as a collection of interesting concepts. *Advaita, māyā, viveka, bhāvanā* are individually intelligible, but it only is *together* that they truly distinguish the *Vivekacūḍāmaṇi*, even among Advaita texts that are comparable in character. Were any of the terms in the matrix to be altered, the others too would have to undergo significant transformation, even while retaining much of their original identity. The terms form an integral context; they require one another, and do not make sense nor appear useful when taken separately. Change one term, and the whole set of categories will have to be adjusted. If reality were to be defined in a theistic fashion and *advaita* effectively discarded, the problem marked by *māyā* would have to be rephrased, and then the cooperative action of *viveka* and *bhāvanā* would be rephrased in some other terms, for example, an approach to true knowledge of God or a scientific ideal of knowledge.

Moreover, the matrix represents an agenda. By defining the human problem and human possibility in terms of this matrix of concepts, the *Vivekacūḍāmaṇi* proposes a set of tasks to be undertaken, drawing readers into particular ways of re-thinking the human condition; in turn, this re-thinking opens into particular ways of responding, acting, living; in turn, these eventuate in a totally transformed and free life, in which all previous habits and habitual ways of viewing the world become impossible. The intended, ideal reader—the interested male brahmin—is put on the spot, challenged to change his life: first, in order that he can come to understand; and second, because he has in fact begun to understand. If one does not get involved, it is because one just does not understand, sufficiently.

For the *Vivekacūḍāmaṇi*, a reflective apprehension of the human condition is therefore in part marked by the achieved inability to remain standing at a distance, to observe reality and explain human existence speculatively, without acting. Life, in its various cultural manifestations and constructions, is never a spectacle merely to be observed and discussed from a privileged position, outside or above it. Experience is rather an integral whole, to be heard, listened to, participated in, obeyed—and speculated on only in the context of those activities. *Advaita* as theory does little to alleviate the human condition, for *māyā* reaches too deep to be dispelled by good ideas; *viveka* is a kind of engaged knowing that changes reality, leading to a radical transformation of one's sense of self; yet *viveka* too would be merely destructive—the realization of an extreme sense of "what is not"—if it is not complemented by a further task, the project of *bhāvanā*. Since persuading the disciple to see reality differently and interact with it differently is key to the *Vivekacūḍāmaṇi*, its exposition of the human condition is rhetorically "heated," and is intended to bring about transformed way of living.

While it is obviously a mistake to confuse Advaita Vedānta's worldview with some general "Hindu worldview," the *Vivekacūḍāmaṇi*'s combination of very broad and accessible claims (we all can be confused, we all can know) plus by some impossibly narrow exclusions (only brahmins, only males) represents a typically Hindu way of organizing reflection on the human condition as an agenda rather than a conclusion. As a bold, idiosyncratic document that does not represent a mainstream view of the human condition, the *Vivekacūḍāmaṇi* nevertheless successfully represents the kind of specific vantage point from which Hindus look at life: that is, in just one of many ways, always to the exclusion of other ways, and always within the frame of a specific program of action. A generalized overview of how Hindus regard the human condition would be inherently inadequate and misleading, unless the perspectival and partial force of that worldview and its expectations remain clear.

Unfortunately, the comparativist may confuse a legitimately preliminary and necessarily incomplete understanding with an adequate apprehension that provides a sufficient basis for discourses on Vedānta, Hinduism, the human condition, etc. But then, the effort to understand the *Vivekacūḍāmaṇi* would become nothing more than an elegant act of intellectual cannibalism, as various bits and pieces of it are excerpted and consumed, made part of another intellectual system, either a traditional one, or a new comparative system that consumes all that it studies. Or, perhaps, the *Vivekacūḍāmaṇi* may become a tourist site, the occasion for a few memorable snapshots and then a travel memoir. But in the process this very interesting "other" will die, as the consumers of religious ideas merely become more, more of themselves. This would be unfortunate, since the distinctive value of the *Vivekacūḍāmaṇi* lies in the matrix and the radical transformation of ordinary consciousness—the surrender of the non-self—that this demands of its intended readers.

In the end, the *Vivekacūḍāmaṇi* will provide no handy "Hindu view of the human condition" that can be merged into an enriched, post-comparative understanding of the human condition. There is no paradise for comparativists at the end of this road, no best, panoramic viewpoint; the joys and insights of comparison will have to be attained here, there, and yonder, too, in the course of many individual acts of taking "the other" to heart, with discrimination, *because we want to know*. If one reads carefully, one is exposed to a particular, somewhat rarified, but still emblematic Hindu view of the human condition; and one is also led into an argument with the author of the *Vivekacūḍāmaṇi* about the nature of the human condition and how one is to react to it. Fundamental decisions need to be made, about how we know, and how we live our lives, and these need to be stated in an open fashion, from somewhere, for some particular audience. One may in the end reject the *Vivekacūḍāmaṇi*'s worldview, or give in to it, or settle for a compromise, or even decide that having a set, coherent worldview is not so good an idea after all, because it would ask too much of us. But such gains—or losses—are achievable only through a series of specific involvements, and not by the adherence to an overall scheme that would explain everything that matters, in advance or from above:

> A disease is not cured if one simply utters the name of the medicine without drinking it; one cannot be liberated by words about *brahman*, without direct realization.
>
> Without making the apparent world vanish and without knowing the reality of the self, how can men gain liberation as a result of merely talking about *brahman*? (62–63).

Notes

1. Throughout, I use Swami Madhavananda's 1921 translation, with slight modifications: *Vivekacūḍāmaṇi of Śrī Saṇkarācārya* (Calcutta: Advaita Ashrama, 1992).
2. The prominent and developed understanding of *māyā* evident in the *Vivekacūḍāmaṇi* is one of the main reasons for distinguishing it from the earlier, normative works of Śaṇkara, to whom it was traditionally attributed. *Māyā*, more than *avidyā*, is a distinctive feature of a particular systematization of *advaita*. So too, this distinctiveness has primarily to do with describing the human problem as a complex distortion of reality that is ontological as well as epistemological—and that therefore will require a certain kind of *viveka* and, most important, the praxis that is *bhāvanā*. On *māyā* in Advaita Vedānta, see Paul Hacker, "Distinctive Features of the Doctrine and Terminology of Śaṃkara," *Philology and Confrontation: Paul Hacker on Traditional and Modern Vedānta,* ed. Wilhelm Halbfass (Albany: State University of New York Press, 1995), 78–85.
3. See also verses 67, 324, 345, 391, 496, 514, 569, 573.

4. At the end of the nineteenth century Swami Vivekananda brought *advaita* to a popular audience in the West. As long ago as Rudolph Otto's classic *Mysticism East and West* and as recently as Michael Stoeber's *Theo-monistic Mysticism: A Hindu-Christian Comparison* (New York: St. Martin's Press, 1994), numerous scholarly comparisons have been made between *advaita* and various versions of monism and unitive mysticism in the West.

5. See Francis X. Clooney, *Theology after Vedānta: An Experiment in Comparative Theology* (Albany: State University of New York Press, 1993), chapter 2, and also "From Anxiety to Bliss: Argument, Care and Responsibility in the Vedānta Reading of *Taittirīya* 2.1–6a," *Authority, Anxiety and Canon: Essays in Vedic Interpretation*, ed. Laurie Patton (Albany: State University of New York Press, 1994), 139–69.

6. In his commentary on verse two, in his *Vivekacūḍāmaṇi of Sri Sankara Bhagavadpada* (Bombay: Bharatiya Vidya Bhavan, 1988), as trans, P. Sankaranarayanan.

7. Perhaps because of the severe restrictions enunciated at the beginning of the text, however, the *Vivekacūḍāmaṇi* can afford to be less restrictive in the end: "Thus by way of a dialogue between the teacher and the disciple, has the nature of the *ātman* been ascertained for the *easy* comprehension of seekers after liberation. . . . For those who are afflicted . . . here is the triumphant message of Śaṇkara which points out, within *easy* reach, the soothing ocean of nectar, Brahman, the one without a second, to lead them on to liberation (578, 580; my emphasis).

5

Religious Dimensions of the Human Condition in Judaism

Wrestling with God in an Imperfect World

Anthony J. Saldarini
with Joseph Kanofsky

5.1 Introduction

The "Religious Dimensions of the Human Condition" in Judaism must be sought within the complex, multilayered web of traditional Jewish literature that begins with the biblical collection of narratives, laws, prophecies and wisdom writings, most of which were edited in the sixth–fifth centuries BCE and extends through the narratives, laws, commentaries, mystical visions, instructions, and prayers that have been composed from then to the present. The category "human condition" is neither indigenous to traditional Jewish thought, nor a foundational, generative question that is independently treated in Jewish religious literature. Thus assumptions and analyses about the human condition must be extricated from discussion of a variety of topics that are important to the tradition including God as creator and ruler of the world; God's revelation of the Bible and the commandments (collectively called Torah) that guide human living; human response to God through fidelity, obedience to, and study of Torah; human responsibility and weakness in the face of temptation; human disobedience to God through sin; and God's justice and mercy in punishing sin.[1]

A selection of salient themes and passages related to the human condition will provide the material for a comparison of religious views of the human condition. Illustrative texts will be drawn from the Second Temple, early Rabbinic, and modern periods. The Second Temple period (fifth century BCE–first century CE) saw the development of narratives, laws, commentaries, apocalyptic visions, prayers, and instructions based on the biblical tradition. The Wisdom of Ben Sira, also called Sirach and Ecclesiasticus, incorporates many themes of Second Temple Judaism and will be treated first. After the destruction of the Jerusalem Temple by the Romans in 70 CE, earlier traditions reached an important synthesis in the legal and exegetical works of early Rabbinic literature (second–sixth centuries CE). A few key passages will represent this literature. Limitations of space dictate that the rich variety of commentaries, codes, mystical reflections, philosophical essays, moral exhortations, and instructional treatises composed during the medieval and early modern periods be omitted. However, a brief synopsis of contemporary Jewish responses to the Holocaust, the destruction of six million Jews under Hitler, and the decimation of European Jewry will give some sense of the vitality of the tradition today. These select texts represent the central concerns of the Jewish tradition and provide an entree into this self-referential, tightly interwoven symbolic system in which narratives, laws, oracles, and images build on and conflict with one another while functioning as one dynamic imaginative and intellectual whole.[2]

5.1.1 *The Human Condition as Obligation under Torah*

A Jewish analysis of the "human condition" depends directly on the Jewish apprehension of God. *Human life and the human condition in all its complexity may be defined as life under, in relation to, and responsive to God or as a deviation from that divinely ordered relationship.* Fidelity, obedience, and love keep the relationship of Israel (Judaism's name for itself) with God healthy and orderly; sin, disobedience, and human weakness cause disorder, suffering, and evil. For the most part the first five books of the Bible (the Pentateuch or Torah), supported by the Former Prophets (Historical Books) and Latter Prophets, interpret the positive and negative aspects of human life in terms of divine commands and instructions. Humans either obey and enjoy God's favor with its attendant success or sin by disobeying God and suffer failure and disaster that is interpreted as divine punishment. By contrast, modern Western analyses of the human condition emphasize negative aspects of human existence such as alienation and death. Christian theology understands humans as fatally sinful and in need of divine salvation through Jesus Christ. But neither human weakness nor modern existential anthropology are the traditional starting point for a consideration of the "Religious Dimensions of the Human Condition" in Judaism. For example, Rabbi Joseph Soloveitchik, who was the spiritual and intellectual leader of modern orthodox Jews, responded to the Kantian, romantic, and existential philosophies of this century with the concreteness of Torah as constitutive of the Jew and as the cure for human failure.[3] The term "Torah" (literally "instruction") is here a comprehensive symbol that includes the Pentateuch (the first five books of the Bible) and the whole subsequent exegetical, legal, and instructional tradition that gives shape to Jewish life and thought. Torah is ultimately divine revelation and thus has priority over human reason and experience. Soloveitchik treats anxiety and repentance only at the end of his treatise, *Halakic Man*, in the light of Torah, such that repentance is the reconstituting of the self and the rectification of the human-divine relationship.

The roots of Soloveitchik's modern synthesis of the Jewish tradition can be seen in the literature of early Judaism. To anticipate the course of this study for the sake of the comparative task, the Jewish tradition orients all discussions of humans toward the point of ultimate reference, God, who represents the infinite reality that transcends the observable experience of human life. The uncertainties of life are usually resolved in favor of cosmic order, articulated through narratives and metaphors of creation out of chaos and divine governance and care for humanity. Although questions about divine justice arise, for example, in the Book of Job, they do not develop into the insistent modern passion to fully and rationally comprehend both God and evil ("How could God allow . . . ?"). Human identity and society derive from divine-human communication and relationship symbolized by Torah and the divine image and commandments define what is usually called human "nature." Social disruption and human deficiency in this system arise from infidelity to the human-divine relationship resulting in sin and evil.

5.1.2 The Human Condition as Relationship with God

The Jewish tradition, analyzed according to the comparative categories in chapter 1, affirms a cosmological order presided over by a just and provident God. Humans participate in that world as a social, communal whole and among humans Israel has a special place constituted by God's choice of the people of Israel and Israel's obedient response to God. Israel's sense of itself as God's people and its very knowledge of God and how to live as humans are deeply rooted in communal memory of God's activities on behalf of Israel, especially the Exodus from Egypt and God's self-revelation to Israel at Mount Sinai. Israel and all humanity experience a common human conflicted nature that suffers various limitations in the world, some natural and some caused by human evil. Though the justice of God has been challenged, sometimes severely, in the Jewish tradition, in the end God's rule over the world and good will toward humans is affirmed in various ways. Finally, and most important, the central symbol of Rabbinic Judaism is Torah, that is, revelation from God in the Bible and subsequent Jewish teaching. Torah is understood as law that obligates Israel (and to a lesser extent all humanity) to a pattern of behavior and a communal relationship with God (the covenant). Disorder in human society and life derive from failure to respond positively to God's commandments and inability to remain faithful to the covenant with God. With the guidance of Torah, however, Israel can live in harmony with God and the universe and deal effectively with the tensions and contradictions of human life.

5.2 Sirach (Ecclesiasticus)

The Wisdom of Jesus Ben (son of) Sira, also called the book of Sirach or of Ecclesiasticus neatly summarizes many themes of the Biblical tradition. It is recognized as a canonical book of the Bible by the Orthodox and Roman Catholics, but not by Jews and Protestants. Part of the Hebrew original, dating from the early second century BCE, has survived in several manuscripts along with a complete second century BCE Greek translation. The author, Ben Sira, synthesized but also strongly interpreted the teachings of the Bible and its wisdom tradition for Jerusalem Jews during the Hellenistic period. He is typical of many Judean interpreters and provides a good starting point for exploring the human condition.

5.2.1 Harmonies of Opposites in Human Life

All human beings come from the ground,
  and humankind was created out of the dust.
In the fullness of his knowledge the Lord distinguished them
  and appointed their different ways.
Some he blessed and exalted,
  and some he made holy and brought near to himself;
but some he cursed and brought low,
  and turned them out of their place.
Like clay in the hand of the potter,

to be molded as he pleases,
so all are in the hand of their Maker,
to be given whatever he decides.
Good is the opposite of evil,
and life the opposite of death;
so the sinner is the opposite of the godly.
Look at all the works of the Most High;
they come in pairs, one the opposite of the other.
(Sirach [Ecclesiasticus] 33:10–15)

Living in Jerusalem in peace (c. 180 BCE), he could confidently attribute the inequities and unintelligibilities of life to a good, provident divine creator and sustainer of the world. God's design and decisions determine the elements and the course of the universe. By simple observation, pairs of opposites, even of good and evil, seem natural and inevitable. Evil and death accompany the good life. The facts of life are attributed to divine wisdom, not to chance, independent natural laws, or human efforts. Knowledge of good and evil is merely a part of wisdom and a gift from God. For Ben Sira the ongoing pattern of divine creation and providence dominates Jewish history. He stresses the continuity and consistency of the ultimate power in the universe as guarantor of natural and social harmony.

5.2.1.1 Adam Rehabilitated

Ben Sira's serene world faces historical and exegetical challenges. His almost breezy review of life's tensions and contradictions under God's sovereignty contrasts ironically with the corpses of the Jews killed in battle and tortured by the Seleucid ruler in Syria, Antiochus IV Epiphanes, twenty years later. For reasons that are obscure Antiochus sought to introduce the worship of traditional Syro-Palestinian Gods into the Temple in Jerusalem and suppress the Judean way of life found in the biblical laws and customs. This historical assault threatened the world of Ben Sira and the confidence of his elegant, balanced, trusting poem. It caused significant adjustments in the outlook of many Jewish groups. Ben Sira's seemingly innocuous affirmation of God and the goodness of human existence is a radical reinterpretation of the story of human origins and the human situation in Genesis 1–3, as the following poem shows. Although his benign and confident acceptance and interpretation of the biblical tradition is not blind to the burdens and inconsistencies of human life (40:1–41:13), he incorporates negative human experiences into the flow of life and seeks to justify them as prepared for humans by God. In doing this he slides away from the biblical account of human disobedience and sin in order to affirm divine oversight and responsibility.

Hard work was created for everyone,
  and a heavy yoke is laid on the children of Adam,
from the day they come forth from their mother's womb
  until the day they return to the mother of all the living.
Perplexities and fear of heart are theirs,
  and anxious thought of the day of their death.
From the one who sits on a splendid throne
  to the one who grovels in dust and ashes,
from the one who wears purple and a crown
  to the one who is clothed in burlap,
there is anger and envy and trouble and unrest,
  and fear of death, and fury and strife.
And when one rests upon his bed,
  his sleep at night confuses his mind.
He gets little or no rest;
  he struggles in his sleep as he did by day.
He is troubled by the visions of his mind
  like one who has escaped from the battlefield.
At the moment he reaches safety he wakes up,
  astonished that his fears were groundless.
To all creatures, human and animal,
  but to sinners seven times more,
come death and bloodshed and strife and sword,
  calamities and famine and ruin and plague.
All these were created for the wicked,
  and on their account the flood came.
All that is of earth returns to earth,
  and what is from above returns above.

(Sirach 40:1–11)

In this poem the difficulties of human life, from birth to death (vv. 1 and 11), especially the anxieties and fears caused by fellow humans, pile up one on another. The first human symbolizes the common human condition (Genesis 3:17–19), but is not blamed for causing what Ben Sira takes for granted: all humans are born and die, work and suffer amid conflict and fear.[4] Contrary to the explicit teaching of Genesis (3:19) death and hard labor are not treated as punishment for Adam's sin. This poem subtly undermines the biblical view of the first humans in the Garden of Eden (Genesis 2–3). Ben Sira suppresses the deep symbolic resonances of Adam and Eve's desire for knowledge and immortality, their consequent disobedience to God's command not to eat of the tree of the knowledge of good and evil, their exile from paradise, and loss of the tree of life, that is, immortality (Genesis 3). A more positive view of human life and potentialities replaces the story of loss and punishment in Genesis.

Even death is domesticated as a natural release from the burdens of life for the good, though it can also function in its traditional role as a punishment for the wicked (40:8–10).

5.2.1.2 *Knowledge Affirmed*

Consistent with this poem, Ben Sira's climactic review of Israel's past heroes (chaps. 44–50) presents Adam not as the one who disobeyed God, was expelled from the Garden of Eden, and brought death to the world, but as an exalted creature: "Above every other created living being was Adam (Genesis 1:26; Sirach 49:14–16 [Greek]). The Hebrew is even more graphic: "Above every living thing was the splendor of Adam." Ben Sira gives unqualified approval of the ancestor of all humans and thus to humanity in general, despite the stories of human disobedience and punishment in Genesis 3. His positive interpretation of Adam and humanity and his acceptance of evil as a constituent part of life are explicitly articulated in another poem (17:1–24) in which God "filled them [humans] with knowledge and understanding, and showed them good and evil" (17:7). This pious picture of the divine gift of knowledge contrasts strikingly with Genesis 2–3 where God forbids the first humans to eat from the tree of good and evil and banishes them from the garden when they do so because they are too close to becoming like God and his heavenly court (Genesis 3:22–23; cf. 3:4–5). Ben Sira's reversal of Genesis and acceptance of knowledge of good and evil as part of life is based on a comprehensive appreciation of divine wisdom from the opening poem to wisdom (1:1–10) through the final autobiographical poem about the author's search for wisdom (50:13–30). Ben Sira counsels respect for God ("fear of the Lord") and good behavior as the road to a good life, as does Genesis, but cannot conceive of any kind of wisdom ("the knowledge of good and evil") as a liability.

5.2.2 *Cosmic Wisdom and Order*

Ben Sira has posited a transcendent, cosmic setting with an intelligible purpose and structure for human life. Order in the universe leads to intellectual and moral order in human life. Ben Sira, writing in the Hellenistic world, has probably been influenced (indirectly?) by the Greek virtues based on human nature. Early classical Greek thought stressed divine governance of the world and human subordination to fate. Combined with the biblical tradition of a beneficent God, the sufferings and uncertainties of life are subordinated to an overarching order. Ben Sira merges wisdom with the Book of the Law (24:23) and thus integrates the obligations deriving from the commandments into the obligations incumbent on humans as part of the created, natural universe. The human predicament, whether understood as foolishness, wickedness, or sinful disobedience to the commandments, can be securely overcome by knowledge of and acquiescence to a predictable cosmic order (cf. also the poems in Sirach 39–43).

5.2.2.1 *Human Evil Tendencies*

The emphasis on suprahuman wisdom and a reliable cosmic order creates a tension between the ultimate power in the universe and responsible human activity and conflicts with the human experience of evil and suffering. In the monotheistic setting of the Jewish tradition unexplained evil and sin caused by human deficiency inevitably raise the problems of theodicy, that is, God's justice and power. Both Ben Sira and the Rabbinic tradition acknowledge the human tendency to evil, but do not ascribe to Adam's sin in the garden the catastrophic effects attributed to it in Christian tradition in the doctrine of "original sin." Rather, Ben Sira responds to these problems with a sequence of diatribes and poems that mediate the mutual obligations between God and humans and the relationships between order and disorder, good and evil (15:11–18:14). For example, the charge that God leads humans to sin (15:11–12) provokes a double peremptory assertion concerning God's rectitude and human responsibility, "The Lord hates all abominations; such things are not loved by those who fear him" (15:13), followed by an explanation of the human situation in relationship to God.

> 14. It was he who made man in the beginning,
> and he left him in the hand of his own deliberation.
> 15. If you choose, you can keep the commandments,
> and faithfulness is to do [God's] good will. . . .
> 17. Before each person are life and death,
> and whichever one chooses will be given.
> (Sirach 15:14–17)

This passage has compressed a number of debates concerning human nature and divine rule of the universe. God's creativity in making humans in verse 14 (cf. Genesis 1–2) is completed in verse 15 by human creativity in doing God's will (both verbs are *poieo* in Greek). "Man" in verse 14 is the generic *adam* in Hebrew and *anthropos* in Greek, so it is individual humans including but not limited to the first Adam (the first human being) who cause sin, rather than the first Adam alone. God has left the human "in the hands of his own deliberation (*diaboulios*)," that is, free. However, this awkward Greek expression, which translates the Hebrew idiom, "in the hand of his own impulse (*yetzer*)," contains the very tensions Ben Sira seeks to resolve. The word *yetzer* comes from the verb to create or design and thus refers to the thoughts and intentions of the designer. Ben Sira understands the term in its most neutral meaning as human free choice. Like God the creator, man the designer makes his own life. However, the tradition before and after Ben Sira stresses the conflict and tendency to evil in human free choice. In Genesis *yetzer* is treated as an evil intention of the mind (6:5; 8:21) that leads inevitably to sin and in Rabbinic literature it is the powerful, non-rational tendency or impulse toward evil (see below). Ben Sira acknowledges that human choice is crucial, that is, a choice of life or death (15:17, an allusion to Deuteronomy 30:15–20), and he places responsibility for evil on humans, not God: "He has not commanded anyone to be wicked, and he has not given anyone permission to sin" (15:20). Although this conclusion may seem piously inevitable in a system with one good God, the Books of Job and Qohelet (Ecclesiastes) in the Hebrew Bible challenge it and Rabbinic literature, with great anguish and debate, apportions to God greater responsibility for evil and sin than Ben Sira by making God the author of the "evil inclination" in humans. Ben Sira chooses the opposite tactic here by neutralizing "natural" human tendencies and putting extra weight on human will and responsibility, that is, on humans understood as lying under obligation to the creator and ruler of the world.

5.2.2.2 *Wisdom and Torah*

Although Ben Sira attributes serious consequences to human life and decision, he still keeps ultimate reality, God and the cosmos, at the center of his world through the symbol of authoritatively revealed law (Torah) that remains present in Israel's communally affirmed memories and recitations. Concretely, Ben Sira anchors his understanding of a wise and good human life on the Torah (law) revealed by God to Moses and Israel at Mount Sinai. In this way he combines the rational affirmation of cosmic order with the dominant revelatory tradition of the Bible and he links Israel to God through obligatory commandments that cement their relationship established when God freed Israel from slavery in Egypt (Exodus 1–15). According to Ben Sira's interpretation of God's appearance to Israel on Mt. Sinai (Exodus 19–24),

> He [God] bestowed knowledge upon them,
> and allotted to them the law of life.
> He established with them an eternal covenant,
> and revealed to them his decrees.

Their eyes saw his glorious majesty,
and their ears heard the glory of his voice.
He said to them, "Beware of all evil."
And he gave commandment to each of them
concerning the neighbor.
(Sirach 17:11–14)

The expression "law of life" refers to the Deuteronomic interpretation of the revelation at Sinai (Deuteronomy 30:11–20) according to which God's law will bring life if it is obeyed and death if it is broken. The same point is made in the wisdom poem in the Book of Baruch (probably second century BCE), which may be dependent on Sirach: "[Wisdom] is the book of the commandments of God, the law that endures forever. All who hold fast to her will live, and those who forsake her will die" (Baruch 4:1). The identification of wisdom with the revelation of God and God's law at Sinai in the passage from Baruch is also the climax of a wisdom poem in Sirach: "All this [wisdom] is the book of the covenant of the Most High God, the law that Moses commanded us as an inheritance for the congregations of Jacob" (Sirach 24:23). Ben Sira stresses the positive effects of Torah on Israel and passes over the problems of sin and death lightly. Only the final verse of the first section of Ben Sira's poem (17:14) hints at evil and sin. The next few verses of Sirach 17, which in the view of some commentators are another poem, affirm God's knowledge of human actions and God's justice in responding to them. However, Ben Sira softens the threat of divine justice by claiming explicitly what he implied by using Sinai imagery above: Israel has a special status before God. God knows Israel's evil deeds, but good deeds such as almsgiving (17:22) and repentance (17:24) will win God's favor. The references to sin, punishment, and divine justice and human evil in Sirach are so lightly touched that a later editor of the Greek text has interpolated three verses that recognize human evil more frankly and stress God's mercy more clearly than the original author and translator did (Sirach 17:16, 18, 21).

5.2.3 Sirach in Context

Ben Sira introduces many concerns and themes that echo through later Second Temple and Rabbinic literature. His identification of wisdom with Torah leads eventually to the Rabbinic embrace of Torah as the central symbol for human knowledge of God, the divine-human relationship and human life and behavior. Ben Sira reworks both Israel's wisdom tradition and the account of human evil and sin in Genesis to support his optimistic and orderly view of human life and divine providence according to which humans have the responsibility and opportunity to choose

God, God's law, and life because God has given them the gift of wisdom. Sin and evil are facts of life that are neutralized by human fidelity to the commandments and wisdom and by divine justice and providence. Human impulses to sin and punishments for sin, such as death, are reinterpreted and subsumed into a larger scheme of balanced pairs prepared by a benevolent creator.

Ben Sira's synthesis of the biblical tradition is classically conservative in that it confirms the dominance of God as the point of ultimate reference and as the cause of all that is. Human nature, social relations, goals, knowledge, behavior, and life take shape in relation to God concretized as the wisdom that is specified as the Bible. The biblical covenant and law, as divinely authorized communication, guide the thinking and behavior of Israel. Thus the mature human ideally responds to God's transcendent self-communication that encompasses the natural and social orders. Human deficiencies, social disruption, and natural (from a human point of view) disorder are subsumed into the scheme of cosmic order or reduced to epiphenomena subordinate to the ultimate reality, God. The law of God guides human living away from the tensions of evil and death to vital relationships within human society and with God.

In Ben Sira's synthesis the ancient Near Eastern wisdom tradition is sharply focused through the Jewish tradition. Humanity as a whole melds gradually into Israel as wisdom becomes coextensive with the law or Torah revealed on Sinai. For example, in the poem from Sirach 17 partially cited above, Ben Sira begins by speaking of all humans being created from the earth (Sirach 17:1), but halfway through, without explicit notice, the subjects of the poem ("they") have become Israelites who have received the biblical covenant and law from God. To be fully human, that is, fully related to God, requires the reception and acceptance of divine revealed law. Other nations who lack that revelation and the covenant with God are known by God, but lack the close relationship of Israel and God. Consequently Gentiles (non-Jews) tend to be seen as evil at worst or marginal at best to Israel's special relationship with God. In the Jewish tradition non-Jews are a peripheral topic that arises occasionally as laws are worked out or apologetic stances crafted. This tight focus enhances the coherence and impact of Ben Sira's interpretation of his audience's world but limits his audience explicitly to adherents to his tradition. His view continues in Rabbinic literature, which for the most part treats Gentiles as part of the social background, as a political and social threat or as a boundary category with implications for how Jewish law is to be applied. Non-Jews are not a major topic of independent interest in most Jewish Rabbinic literature because most of the Biblical laws apply only to Israel, that is, to Jews.[5] Later Rabbinic literature developed a legal location for Gentiles through the seven Noahide commandments, that is, commandments applicable to all humans, who are descended from Noah (Genesis 6–9). The contents of the Noahide commandments vary slightly in the sources (murder, robbery, incest, blasphemy, etc.) but provide a conceptual framework for thinking about Gentiles.[6] However, the focus of the Jewish tradition and of this chapter is on Israel in the world, not on all humanity.

5.3 Rabbinic Literature

Rabbinic Judaism began to arise in the late first century CE, and its influence endures to the present. Its vast literature incorporated many biblical and Second Temple themes, such as those just reviewed in Sirach, but subjected them to further scrutiny and development. Rabbinic treatises and collections contain diverse materials, including aphoristic sayings, often in the name of a sage, stories about the sages, parables, rewritten biblical narratives, isolated exegeses, and citations of proof texts from the Bible, etc. Rabbinic literature is not systematically organized according to Greek or modern criteria but it is highly self-referential. A limited set of concepts, metaphors, symbols, traditional teachings, laws, hermeneutical rules, scriptural interpretations, narratives, laws, practices, and teachers are used and reused, cited and cited again in a variety of contexts for different purposes in seemingly limitless combinations. They form a self-contained, coherent thought world with ample room for questions, disagreements, and conflicting theses.

5.3.1 Torah as Central Symbol

According to the Rabbinic view, human life under God is constituted by Torah. The Rabbis affirmed the continuing relevance of God's power, love, and choice of Israel. After the destruction of the Jerusalem Temple by the Romans in 70 CE, they reconstituted the community of Israel through a renewed commitment to Torah. Torah served the Rabbis as an all-encompassing central symbol that included God, creation, revelation, history, and human life and behavior. They actualized Torah through dedicated and detailed study and enthusiastic observance of its requirements.

Although the word *torah* is often translated as law, it has a much broader meaning than the English word. "Law" derives from the narrower Latin word, *lex*, and is most often associated with the legal system or empirical scientific hypotheses. The noun *torah* comes from the Hebrew verbal root *yrh*, which means to teach or instruct. In the Bible it is used for instructions given by a priest, prophet, or wise teacher. It also denotes a group of laws, for example, the torah or instruction for celebrating Passover (Exodus 12:49). In Rabbinic literature *the* Torah is the Pentateuch, the first five books of the Bible. But Torah is most frequently used for the teaching of the Rabbis contained in Rabbinic literature, especially the Mishnah and Tosefta, which are systematic collections of laws and disputes, midrashim that are interpretations of biblical books and passages and the two Talmuds that gradually took shape in Palestine and Babylon in the third through sixth centuries. The Talmuds ostensibly comment on the Mishnah, but actually contain many stories, sayings, exegeses of Scripture, apologetics, polemics, disputes, etc. In the medieval and modern periods Torah encompasses all the commentaries on the Talmuds, the law codes that systematize their contents, and any other congruent literature. A person devoted to "Talmud Torah," the study of Torah, is devoted, at least in principle, to the contents of the whole tradition.

In Rabbinic thought Israel derives its very identity through Torah, and the individual Israelite male, ideally a learned sage, also achieves authentic personal identity through identification with Torah. In a sense, without Torah Israel does not exist and without obedience to Torah Israel is out of contact with God and thus sinful. Human proclivity toward sin, which is disobedience to God's law and implicitly rejection of God, is the central problem of the human condition to be resolved by acknowledgment of one's obligation to God's Torah and obedience to its commandments.

5.3.2 *Tractate Abot*

Mishnah Tractate Abot (also called Pirke Abot) with its commentary, the Fathers According to Rabbi Nathan (extant in two versions), gives a rationale for the Rabbinic way of life, which consists of study and observance of the Torah, and links many aspects of the Bible, Rabbinic teaching, and life to these themes. It contains a particularly dense concentration of teachings, exegeses, and exhortations that may be associated with the human condition. Tractate Abot consists of five chapters[7] and in its final form probably dates from the mid-third century when Rabbinic literature in general began self-consciously to defend its interpretation of Jewish law and life, that is, Torah and identify it with an oral Torah received by Moses on Sinai and passed on faithfully through the generations from Moses through the Prophets to the Rabbinic sages of the Greco-Roman period (Abot 1:1).[8] The sages preserve and develop the tradition through the study and practice of Torah.

5.3.2.1 *The Threefold Foundation of the Age*

The sages' world is anchored in a few biblical core symbols that are found in the second saying in Tractate Abot. Significantly the saying is attributed to Simeon (II) the Righteous, the high priest at the beginning of the second century BCE who was idealized by Ben Sira (Sirach 50). Under Simeon, in Ben Sira's view, worship was being conducted as it should, on the basis of the Torah, and Jewish society, which had not yet been rent by civil war and imperial persecution, was guided by the commandments and behaviors mandated by the Bible.[9] The Rabbis synthesized Ben Sira's classic view in a pithy saying attributed to Simeon: "On three things the age stands: on the Torah, on the Temple service and on acts of piety" (Abot 1:2). In this translation *ʿolam* retains the biblical meaning "age" rather than the later Rabbinic meaning "world" and *gemilut hasidim* is interpreted as "acts of piety" prescribed by the Torah in relation to fellow human beings rather than the more general "deeds of loving kindness."[10] Simeon's saying typifies the stability of prewar Judea. Israel is established on a triple traditional foundation, the Torah (the Pentateuch), the prescribed sacrificial worship at the Temple in Jerusalem, and traditional expressions of piety toward God and fellow humans. This triad of core symbols (Torah, Temple, and obedience to the commandments) spans the centuries from Ben Sira in Jerusalem to the Mishnah (c. 200 CE) after the Temple and Jerusalem have been destroyed. A substantial portion of the Mishnah is devoted to laws concerned with Temple festivals, sacrifices, and purity, even though the Temple had been gone over a century when it was written. Ideally Jewish society and religion form one seamless world in which priests, sages, and people all fulfill their duties to God and one another under the guidance of God's revealed law.

5.3.2.2 *The Threefold Foundation of the World*

Thus Simeon's saying may be read with a different nuance and retranslated as "On three things the *world* stands: on the Torah, on the Temple service and on acts of *loving kindness*." Since the politically independent Judean state no longer stands, the community's core symbols are related to the world at large with its many nations and Roman empire. As the commentary on Tractate Abot puts it, "From the very first the world was created only with loving kindness," as it is said, "For I have said, 'The world is built with loving kindness; in the very heavens you establish your faithfulness' (Psalm 89:2 [Eng.])."[11] Like Torah and the Temple, loving kindness is assigned a cosmic and foundational role that reaches back to creation and continues through the biblical and the Second Temple periods and on into the early Rabbinic period. The mundane obligation to do deeds of loving kindness takes on an enlarged role with the cessation of the biblically mandated sacrifices after the Jerusalem Temple was destroyed in 70 CE. According to a famous anecdote, Johanan ben Zakkai, a teacher in the late first century, was leaving Jerusalem when one of his students lamented the destruction of the Temple where sins were atoned. Johanan answered, "We have another atonement as effective as this. And what is it? It is acts of loving kindness, as Scripture says, 'I desire loving kindness and not sacrifice' (Hosea 6:6)."[12] In the absence of the Temple, the Torah, and obedience to the Torah, study and practice of loving kindness will atone for sin. Just as the Qumran community could understand themselves as atoning for the sins of Israel by their communal life,[13] Johanan understands faithful observance of the biblical social norms, instead of the lost rituals of the Day of Atonement, as atoning for the sins of Israel.[14] The obligation to foster proper social relations substitutes for the mandated Temple rituals.

Torah is also a remedy for the loss of the Temple. Among Temple sacrifices the burnt offering [holocaust] is the sacrifice most beloved by God, but according to Hosea 6:6 God desires "knowledge of God rather than burnt offerings." Knowledge of God comes from studying Torah, which is God's self-revelation so "the study of Torah is more beloved by God than burnt offerings. For if a man studies Torah he comes to know the knowledge of God, as it is said, 'Then you shall understand the fear of the Lord, and find the knowledge of God' (Proverbs 2:5). Hence, when a sage sits and expounds to the congregation, Scripture accounts it to him as though he had offered up fat and blood on the altar."[15] Although the world and the age in which the Rabbinic authors live is supposed to be founded upon Torah, acts of loving kindness, and the Temple service, Torah is so important to God and so essential to the order of the world and its history that the mere study of it can compensate for the loss of the Temple ritual. Study of Torah leads to knowledge of God that is a prerequisite for worship and to observance of the commandments that constitutes good behavior and promotes "acts of loving kindness" that establish and strengthen the link between humans and God.

5.3.2.3 *Temple and Torah as Generative Symbols*

Behind the comments in Tractate Abot and its commentaries lies a generative symbolic complex with God at its center and the Temple and Torah playing all-encompassing roles. The Torah is the wisdom, plan, and divine instrument of creation (Abot 3:14; Genesis Rabbah 1:1; Sifre Deuteronomy 48). Torah and its acknowledgment by Israel at Sinai preserve the world from chaos (b. Shabbat 88a). The Temple in Jerusalem was central for many of the biblical understandings of Israel, crucially important in much of second Temple literature, and, even after it had been destroyed by the Romans, central to the early Rabbis' vision of Israel's life according to the law. Even the loss of the Temple, one member of the foundational triad, could not destroy Judaism because study of all the laws given by God, even those that could not be applied, and acceptance of them as the proper order of the world led to the continued existence of the world and of Israel. The laws of Torah are thus not just practical obligations incumbent on adherents of Judaism but expressions of the underlying order of the universe. The human person, society, and knowledge of ultimate realities are all constituted by Torah in all its complexity and depth and actuated by conscious conformity to the authority of Torah and the obligations it implies.

5.3.3 The Torah Community

The working out of this integral vision of human life under God takes place in a community of male scholars, the subjects par excellence of most of the commandments, within a Torah-centered society that supports them. But the path to a Torah-centered society and its maintenance are beset with difficulties and dangers. To guide scholars and people along the right path Tractate Abot and its commentaries promote the study of Torah, the master-disciple relationship, putting Torah before all else, communal study, methods for clarifying uncertainties in Scripture and the law, a rational mode of carrying on discourse, good deeds based on Torah, the ordinary virtues of hospitality, generosity, compassion, sexual restraint, and patience and they warn against the vices that alienate a person from Torah, God, and his fellow humans. For example, the first of the five pairs of leaders in the chain of tradition are assigned a set of sayings balanced between the ideals of study and practice.

Jose ben Joezer of Zeredah and Jose ben Johanan of Jerusalem took over from them.[16]

> Jose ben Joezer says:
> Let your house be a meeting place for the sages, and
> sit in the very dust at their feet, and
> thirstily drink in their words.
> Jose ben Johanan of Jerusalem says:
> Let your house be open wide, and
> let the poor be members of your household, and
> talk not overmuch with women.

In both sayings the house, which is the center of activity and life, is to be open to the community. Scholars should be welcomed and listened to so that Torah is learned.[17] The needy should be welcomed and cared for so that Torah may be practiced. Together they constituted the religious society envisioned by Torah.

5.3.3.1 A Hedge against Sin

The final clause of Jose ben Johanan's saying reveals the traditional Near Eastern male-centered world of these sayings in which women are confined to the household, viewed as a distraction from important public matters, especially study of Torah, and regarded with suspicion as a source of "evil" (sexual sins?). More fundamentally, it and many sayings in Abot contrast sin, temptation, punishment, and the dangers of human weakness with the ideal of a humane, devout community devoted to Torah. Even with the best of intentions human weakness, desires, and even inadvertence may easily lead to infractions against the law. As a remedy for this human condition of weakness and sinfulness, "the men of the Great Assembly," a legendary transitional group that links the biblical period with the early sages, counsel teachers to "make a hedge about the Torah" (m. Abot 1:2), that is, create laws and customs ("a hedge" or "fence") that promote the observance of the mandated practices in Scripture. One vivid didactic story from the Palestinian Talmud (Shabbat 1:6 [3b]), which quotes Tractate Abot, will illustrate the hedge, again using male sexual passions as symbolic of the unending human susceptibility to temptation.

> There (in the Mishnah) we have been taught:[18] "Do not trust yourself until the day of your death" (m. Abot 2:4).[19]
>
> *There is a story*[20] about a pious man who used to sit and recite: "Do not trust yourself until the time of your old age." (He thought:) Like me.
>
> A spirit (female) came and tempted him (and he gave in).[21] Then he began to regret it. She [the spirit] said to him: Do not be troubled. I am a spirit.[22] Go and be attentive to your fellows.[23]

This story links resistance to temptation with the guidance given by Rabbinic teachings and devalues any wisdom that disagrees with or mitigates authoritative instruction. Thus the pious man who had prudently distrusted himself until his old age in the end failed to resist temptation because he had modified the teachings ("hedge") of the sages. The little vignette of the sage's temptation in old age encapsulates much of Rabbinic teaching about evil. First, no matter what one's age or motivation human weakness will lead to an inadvertent or willful infraction of the Torah. One must always take into account the human inclination to sin symbolized by the "evil inclination or impulse" (see below). Second, the antidote for this innate tendency toward evil is Torah (meaning revelation, God's commandments, study of Torah, and obedience to Torah).[24] The sage must study and accept God's commandments and develop the discipline to observe them rigorously.[25] Only then will the tendency toward evil be controlled.[26]

5.3.3.2 *Divine and Human Responsibility for Evil*

The image of the ideal human, responsive to the obligations deriving from the nature of creation, the explicit commands revealed by God, and actively remembered in traditions of the Jewish community, is fundamentally qualified by the pervasive human proclivity toward rejection of a wide array of obligations and of Torah and God. This paradoxical and conflictual human predicament prompts serious and sustained reflection on the origin, nature, and power of evil in human life, especially moral evil. Although the Rabbis have a robust sense of human frailty and of the prevalence of sin, their assignment of responsibility for sin, temptation, and human weakness varies according to the ambiguities of life. God as creator of humans is both blamed and exonerated for the evils in human life. The Rabbis complain about God's arrangements for humans, especially his creation of the evil impulse in humans that leads them to sin and destructive behavior, even as they grudgingly concede that God is justice. They fully embrace human freedom and responsibility for sin even as they bitterly lament the inexorable conflicts between good and evil in human life.

5.3.3.2.1 DIVINE-HUMAN COOPERATION

The story of Adam's sin in the Garden of Eden serves as a paradigm for the human condition, but, contrary to Christian theology, not as a cause of human evil, sin, and suffering.[27] Rather, the inevitability and pervasiveness of evil raise the problem of theodicy for the Rabbis. A neat summary of the ambiguities of human existence may be found in Tractate Berakot ("Blessings"), which teaches about the occasions and forms of blessings, that is, prayers. Praying or blessing implies an active relationship between God and the worshiper. Blessings sanctify numerous occasions and acknowledge God's interest and agency in human life. But the bad things that happen to people raise the theodicy question that is dealt with at the end of Tractate Berakot.

> A person is bound to bless [God] for the evil even as he blesses for the good, as Scripture says, "You shall love the Lord your God with all your heart and with all your soul and with all your strength" (Deuteronomy 6:5). "With all your heart" means with both your impulses, with the good impulse and with the evil impulse; "with all your soul" means even if [God]

> takes away your soul; "with all your strength" means with all your wealth. Another explanation: "with all your strength" means with whatever measure [God] measures out to you, give thanks to him greatly (m. Berakot 9:5).[28]

This biblical exegesis compresses the human situation into three stages. First, humans experience good and evil in life and cannot fully control the results because the human heart, which is the seat of thought, higher emotion, and will, is divided between tendencies to good and evil symbolized as the good and evil impulses. Second, evil constantly threatens the soul, which is the principle of life, with death. Third, to preserve life and resist evil and temptation requires divinely given strength that is beyond human resources. Thus, according to Berakot, the pious, prayerful person trusts God and thanks God for what God sends, both good and evil. The solution to the tensions in human nature and the path to mature integrity ("achieved personal identity") requires an active relationship with God.

But this very vague, general response does not adequately explain the problem of human evil because human weakness and sin are not simple matters. Adam's disobedience to God in the Garden of Eden (Genesis 3) does not explain the origin of evil and sin but only provides an example of human frailty. Despite his failure, Adam the first human is most often presented in a positive light in Second Temple and Rabbinic literature, either as a cosmic figure or as the archetypal human created by God.[29] Adam's tendency to evil and sin raises as many questions about God as about Adam.

5.3.3.2.2 Divine Responsibility for Good and Evil

The Rabbis held God, not Adam, responsible for the general state of human life with its ambiguities and evil and thus the complexity of life was to be explain through complexity in God. In the very act of creation God was faced with a paradox:

> In the hour when the Holy One, blessed be He, came to create Adam, he saw righteous and wicked people arising from him. God said: If I create him, wicked people will arise from him; if I do not create him, how are the righteous to arise from him?
>
> What did the Holy One, blessed be He, do? He removed the way of the wicked from before his face and he associated with himself the quality of mercy and he created him [Adam].[30]

Because humans inevitably bring about evil along with good, God governs the world (and even creation) according to two complementary norms, justice and mercy. If God governed only with justice, the evil world would be condemned and destroyed. If with mercy alone, sin and evil would dominate. Thus God juggles the realities of the world to enable humans to exist. God has accepted and must continue to accept human evil and temper justice with mercy because "from the very beginning of the world's creation the Holy One, Blessed be He, foresaw the deeds of the righteous and the deeds of the wicked" (Genesis Rab. 3.8). Good and evil are constitutive of humans and the human world from the beginning, inevitably and according to divine decision.

5.3.4 *The Evil Inclination*

The dynamic conflict in humans between good and evil tendencies and behaviors is symbolized by the metaphor of a good inclination or impulse (*yetzer ha-tov*) and an evil inclination (*yetzer ha-ra'*). But even here, the evil inclination is not all evil. Understood as desire, it motivates people to farm, build houses, and have families.[31] Some texts dramatize its destructive effects on humans and even personify it as an evil spirit while others place significant responsibility for the evil impulse on God. The evil impulse is not a tidy, coherent theory of evil, but an imaginative, evocative response to it. Various solutions are proposed for controlling the evil inclination, especially study and observance of Torah. As the tradition develops, repentance is proposed as the solution to the inevitability of sin along with making restitution to fellow humans. Both the situation of Israel in exile and of human life in an evil world also receive detailed development. A few sayings from Rabbinic literature will sketch out the main lines of this metaphoric complex[32] that addresses the nature of humans and their quest to achieve mature personal integrity and identity.

5.3.4.1 *The Effects of the Evil Inclination*

The idea of a tendency, impulse, or inclination (*yetzer* in Hebrew) to evil comes mainly from two statements about human corruption in Genesis. Before the flood that destroyed almost all humanity "the Lord saw how great man's wickedness on the earth had become, and that *every inclination of the thoughts of his heart was only evil all the time*" (Genesis 6:5). After the flood the survivors, Noah and his family, offered God a sacrifice. In response "the Lord smelled the pleasing aroma and said in his heart: 'Never again will I curse the ground because of man, even though *every inclination of his heart is evil from childhood*. And never again will I destroy all living creatures, as I have done'" (Genesis 8:21). The evil impulse or inclination, from *ytzr*, the root meaning create, make, fashion, refers to bodily, emotional, and personal urges toward human goals. Although the term may be used neutrally, it is biased toward the human passions, such as sexual urges and anger, which can easily become selfish or destructive. In Tractate Abot Rabbi Joshua warns about three dangers to social relations: "The evil eye and the evil impulse and hatred of humanity put a person out of the world" (Abot 2:11). Later Ben Zoma defines the mighty person as one who "subdues his impulse" (Abot 4:1). Ben Zoma's saying cites Proverbs 16:32 concerning anger as a way of characterizing the evil impulse. Rabbi Joshua's saying implies that a tendency toward envy or cupidity destroys human society. Other texts relate the evil inclination to lust (see the story from Palestinian Talmud above and b. Berakot 61a) and idolatry (b. Yoma 69b).[33]

5.3.4.2 *Combating the Evil Inclination*

In general, the evil impulse or inclination is envisioned as enduringly and increasingly powerful if not combated with determined resistance. It is treated as a negative force that must be countered by human effort and divine help embodied in the obligations of the commandments. Some texts trace the origins of the evil impulse to the moment of birth. It increases in strength year by year and overpowers the good inclination.[34] Only discipline, vigilance, and devotion to Torah can counteract its influence. But even if the evil impulse inevitably causes human sin and disorder, humans are responsible for their behavior. In a famous saying in Abot, Akiba teaches "Everything is foreseen, yet freedom of choice is granted. With [divine] goodness the world is judged and everything is according to the preponderance of deeds" (Abot 3:15). For the Rabbinic sages the moral order communicated through Torah was fundamental to the nature of God and the world. To deny that God judges between good and evil was equivalent to denying the reality of God. In this world humans, caught between the evil impulse and Torah, choose freely. They choose rightly if they are faithful to the obligations incumbent on them as humans and they are faithful if they learn and obey God's commandments.

5.3.4.3 *The Necessity for the Evil Inclination*

Although the evil impulse is often treated as an enemy to human goodness and life, the Rabbis recognized it as necessary for life and so not totally evil. The sages explain that "without the evil impulse a man would not build a house, take a wife and beget children." And Solomon verifies this: "And I saw all labor and all skill in work, that it is a person's envy of his neighbor" (Genesis Rab. 9:7). The most "natural" state of humans, raising a family, proceeds from sexual desires that are necessary for human survival. The "natural" coexistence of good and evil in the world, found earlier in Ben Sira, is affirmed through a forced interpretation of

Genesis 1:31, "And behold it was very good," a phrase said originally of the created world. This summary statement concerning the goodness of God's creation would seem to exclude the evil impulse, but the Hebrew contains the connective particle "we-," meaning "and." In Rabbinic hermeneutics this particle can be understood as including something not obviously implied. In this case the sages interpret this particle as inclusive of the evil impulse that was also created by God (Genesis Rab. 9:7). A Talmudic story catches the ambiguity of human desires more sharply than Genesis Rabbah. Israel was allowed to imprison the impulse toward idolatry in a lead pot because idolatry had led to the destruction of the Temple and Jerusalem and the exile of Israel. (Note that the impulse is personified as an evil spirit.) But with the impulse imprisoned, no eggs are laid because the evil impulse also motivates reproductive activity among animals (and humans). The production of human food and human life require the evil impulse. Consequently Israel frees the impulse so life can go on, but only after blinding it to reduce its power (b. Yoma 69b).

5.3.4.4 *Integrating the Evil Inclination into the Created Order*

Even with the evil impulse, in a monotheistic system God is ultimately responsible for both good and evil. In Genesis 8:21 God admitted that "every inclination of [humanity's] heart is evil from childhood." In response a Rabbinic commentator quipped "How wretched must be the dough when the baker himself testifies it to be poor!" (Genesis Rab. 34:10). In another saying God regrets creating the evil impulse because of all the trouble it causes (b. Suk. 52b). Genesis Rabbah explores the interweaving of God's good creation with tendencies to evil and sin at great length through biblical history. The very act of creation encapsulates the sins of humanity.

> "And the earth was formlessness and emptiness (*tohu va-vohu*) and darkness was on the face of the deep" (Genesis 1:2). Rabbi Judah son of Rabbi Simeon interpreted the text as referring to the generations.[35]
>
> "And the earth was formlessness (*tohu*)" refers to Adam (Genesis 3) who was reduced to complete nothingness (through his disobedience to God).[36] "And emptiness" refers to Cain (Genesis 4) who desired to turn the world back to formlessness and emptiness (through his murder of his brother).[37] "And darkness" refers to the generation of Enosh[38] (Genesis 5:6–11): "And their works are in the dark" (Isaiah 29:15).[39] "On the face of the deep" refers to the generation of the flood (that is, the majority of humanity destroyed by a flood because of sin and corruption—Genesis 6–9): "On the same day all the fountains of the deep were broken open" (Genesis 7:11). (Genesis Rabbah 2.3)

Subsequent phrases from Genesis are associated with the founding patriarchs of Israel and the next section of the commentary (2.4) continues Israel's history through the four evil world empires (Babylonia, Media [Persia], Greece, and Rome) to the coming of the Messiah (a leader anointed by God) as national savior at the end of the world. From the beginning of creation God foresaw the Temple built, destroyed, and rebuilt in the Messianic era (2.5). Good and evil, order and sin are firmly linked to one another from creation throughout history to the end of the world, in a manner reminiscent of Sirach above. The account of creation and creation itself contains the underlying pattern of history that is a relationship with God ruptured by sin and restored by repentance. Evil is always present, but subsumed into a good creation by a good creator.

5.4 The Modern Period

Jewish perceptions of the human condition, especially of evil and suffering, developed noticeably in the modern[40] West due to the enlightenment emphasis on human reason and the medieval and modern anti-Semitic persecutions that culminated in the destruction of most European Jewish communities by Hitler during the Second World War. Traditional writings on suffering and persecution often urged acceptance of these events as mysterious divine decrees or as punishment for sins. They questioned God's purposes and their sufferings in the way the Talmud wrestled with the Roman destruction of the Temple and domination of Jewish life. Some authors, such as Joseph Soloveitchik (cited at the beginning of this study) hardly raised the problem of suffering or the Holocaust, but continued to seek what Torah requires the Jew to do in all circumstances, even the most tragic.

5.4.1 Post-Holocaust Theodicy

But after the enlightenment many Jews began to question suffering in a way that presumes a reality outside of God, such that the suffering and evil and even God might be evaluated according to external, objective criteria. Reflection on the Holocaust perhaps reached its most extreme when Richard Rubenstein declared that in the light of the Holocaust God was dead (in the Nietzschean sense), that is, the traditional idea or myth of God was no longer viable.[41] Emil Fackenheim, by contrast, advised Jews not to hand Hitler a posthumous victory by ceasing to live as Jews.[42] Observant Jews have expressed their sorrow and hope in elegies and laments that have been incorporated into daily prayer and annual festivals, especially the Day of Atonement and the Ninth of Av, which commemorates the destruction of the Temple and by extension many other disasters in Jewish history. Thus a central response of the tradition has been to remember and incorporate both the good and evil in Jewish history (see the analysis of m. Berakot 9:5 above).

5.4.2 *Rationalist and Traditionalist Responses*

Two broad approaches to the problem of evil and suffering have evolved since the Holocaust. One frankly and insistently poses the problem of suffering and evil in the light of the horrors of the Holocaust, demanding a satisfactory answer of God, reason, or history. This approach reflects the enlightenment's confidence that human reason can answer any question, comprehend any problem, and, implicitly, fully understand God and the universe. The other, more similar to the Talmudic tradition, poses the question of suffering and evil in all its ambiguity and paradox without demanding an answer. The first insistently protests to or against God or at least against the traditional (and inadequate) divine figure who cannot answer the question. The second treats the question of evil like any other Talmudic question that provokes a plurality of responses and eludes a decisive solution. The truth is approached through the sophisticated study of the question and the wrestling with conflicting answers. In the words of an old saying, "The question remains a question, but we go on." This second approach may be summed up succinctly and poetically in Elie Wiesel's *Gates of the Forest*. The protagonist, who is a Holocaust survivor, meets a Hasidic Rebbe (a charismatic spiritual leader) and asks him: "After all that has happened to us, how can you believe in God?" The Rebbe looks deeply into his eyes and replies, "And how can you *not* believe in God after what has happened?"[43]

5.4.2.1 *Wiesel's Traditionalist Challenge to the Tradition*

But as comforting as the traditional approach may be, with its mobilization of prayer and study, the central resources and activities of the orthodox tradition, the question of evil and suffering, of the worth and meaning of human life, still confront modern Jews, whether traditional or liberal. Elie Wiesel, a European Jew and boyhood survivor of the Nazi concentration camps, has turned to narrative, the most powerful biblical genre, in order to summon God to earth to give an account of himself and his stewardship of his chosen people, Israel. In *Night,* his intensely reflective and symbolic memoir of his time in the labor and concentration camps of Europe, Wiesel tells the story of an execution of three people suspected of resistance.[44]

> The three victims mounted together onto the chairs.
> The three necks were placed at the same moment within the nooses.
> "Long live liberty!" cried the two adults.
> But the child was silent.
> "Where is God? Where is He?" someone behind me asked.
> At a sign from the head of the camp, the three chairs tipped over.
> Total silence throughout the camp. On the horizon the sun was setting.
> Then the march past began. The two adults were no longer alive. Their tongues hung swollen, blue tinged. But the third rope was still moving; being so light, the child was still alive. . . .
> For more than half an hour he stayed there, struggling between life and death, dying in slow agony under our eyes. And we had to look him full in the face. He was still alive when I passed in front of him. His tongue was still red, his eyes were not yet glazed.
> Behind me, I heard the same man asking:
> "Where is God now?"
> And I heard a voice behind me answer him:
> "Where is He? Here He is—He is hanging here on this gallows. . . ."
> That night the soup tasted of corpses.

In his own life Wiesel first responded to the inhumanity of Nazi genocide and to God with a ten-year silence during which he did not publish. Then he published *Night,* which contains this horrifying, challenging, elusive story. For Wiesel, the mature Jewish author after the Holocaust, the stakes are higher than for Ben Sira, with whom we began this study, but the answers are more elusive. Wiesel's God is more ambiguous and dangerous than Ben Sira's. A God who serenely presides over good and evil in a rational world (Sirach 33 above) will not do in Buna, the slave labor camp that kills its innocent prisoners. Nor will Qohelet's subtle criticism of God and diffident acceptance of a comfortable life without real knowledge of God satisfy or comfort the dehumanized world of Birkenau (alive in Wiesel's memory) where babies were burned in a ditch.[45] "Never shall I forget those flames which consumed my faith forever. . . . Never shall I forget those moments which murdered my God and my soul and turned my dreams to dust."[46] In this crisis the God of the Jewish tradition must reestablish his relationships with his people Israel and get his hands dirty with the pain and suffering of humanity if he is to maintain his covenants with his people. Wiesel stands in a long line of Jewish storytellers, stretching back to the Book of Job, the midrashic interpretations of Scripture, and the Babylonian Talmud, who confront God by forcing him into human life. But even here Wiesel bends the boundaries. The death camps were filled with Jews whom the Nazis sought to eradicate. But in a deep and ironic way, the climactic execution of the boy, which provokes the question about God, addresses all humans, not just the Jews who were the special object of the Nazis' hate. The boy, the servant of a Dutch camp officer discovered resisting the Germans, is not specifically identified as a Jew or Gentile (just as Job's identity is left vague). He, the Jews in the camp, and the Gentile prisoners too, all belong to God the creator—or do they, Wiesel asks?

A voice inside Wiesel answers the anonymous prisoner's question: "Here He is—He is hanging here on this gallows. . . ." Christians may be initially comforted by the superficial parallel to Jesus on the cross, but they have not listened to the voice. Is the voice God's or Wiesel's? Does the voice speak the truth? If God does speak the truth to Wiesel, has God too been overcome by evil as his people were? Is the strangling child hanging from the gallows a testimony and a sign of God's dethronement as the powerful and provident king of the universe? Is God dead with the child? Or is God's presence a sign of his mercy and is Wiesel's ambiguous, troubled memory, his story of the death camps, his *Night* a prelude to a new or deeper apprehension of God, growing from the Jewish tradition to encompass yet again the tragedy and vitality of human life?[47] God's presence in the Israelites' camp in Exodus protected escaping Hebrew slaves from Pharoah's armies (Exodus 13–15), but not in Germany in 1944. God's "presence" in the labor camp and on the gallows raises questions, but solves nothing definitively. The ellipsis at the end of the sentence ("He is hanging here on this gallows . . .") is an unspoken part of Wiesel's statement, leaving it open, unfinished, and uncertain. And even if the voice did speak the truth, it answers the spoken question silently within Wiesel. The prisoner behind Wiesel who asked a question out loud and those who heard his question could not hear the voice within Wiesel. And so, despite the voice, "that night the soup tasted of corpses" and at the end of *Night,* after his liberation Wiesel looks in a mirror and sees a corpse staring back at him.[48]

5.4.3 *Wiesel within the Jewish Tradition*

More than thirty years later Wiesel explicitly reaffirmed his anger at God, so much so that in his books "the presence of God is accompanied by a protest, and I hope that as long as I live I shall somehow be able to formulate, to articulate, that protest. But from within me, not from without."[49] Wiesel, like Ben Sira and many authors in the Rabbinic tradition two thousand years before him, encapsulates, challenges, and extends the Jewish tradition. Ben Sira rationalized the Jewish tradition in the face of the Greek culture and philosophy of the Hellenistic period in the eastern Mediterranean. The Rabbis wove the biblical traditions into a rich, nurturing world that sustained Jews for centuries. Wiesel combats the destructive irrationality of the descendants of the Hellenistic tradition and questions the certainties of the Talmudic world. All wrestle with God, an imperfect world dependent on God and the human proclivity to evil and all are inexorably associated with God for better or worse.

In the modern period the supposedly ordered cosmos and its ruling deity have come under more searching and sustained criticism than in Rabbinic literature. The world that should sustain human society has become chaotic and the God who should protect the obedient, responsive Jew (or human) has become less reliable and more dangerous. With the fading of the cosmic background and the disintegration of human society the human individual has been left standing alone, the center of attention, but weakened by ambiguities and threats from within and without. The communal memories that sustained personal and social identity and carried along the authoritative revealed commandments have faded so that the prisoner who asked the question out loud hears no public answer, no authoritative voice from Sinai giving direction to the prisoners in the camp. Rather, an individual hears an ambiguous, uninterpreted voice of doubtful authority within (did the others hear something too?) and still tastes death that evening and thirty years later. The urgency and depravity of the human condition thrust themselves upon the reader, but still the questions, the outrage, and the painful search for an answer take place within the complex, multiform traditions of the Jewish community.

5.5 Conclusion

In the Talmudic tradition that became normative for the Jewish community until the enlightenment a Jew is identified and constituted by Torah, God's self-revelation that articulates the shape of human life through law. Behind the boring particularities of a Torah-observant life lies the God, the creator and ruler of the universe who guarantees the unity and order of the cosmos in which the Jew lives. The Jewish community, in turn, is linked to God and the universe by Torah, specifically by the concrete obligations that guide all aspects of its members' lives. The order of the universe replicated in the orderly lives of Jews ensures the ascendancy of goodness. The covenant that binds Israel and God to one another defines the community's place in the universe and minimizes the inevitable disruptions in the relationship between earth and heaven. The limitations, frustrations, sufferings, and evils of human life are more than balanced by the integral and authentic life of Torah that is the wisdom of God and the rational structure of the universe.

The ideal peace of an Israel living according to Torah has been frequently disrupted by the evils characteristic of the human condition on earth. Sin, the refusal to follow faithfully the stipulations of the covenant between God and Israel, disrupts the harmony of human society and God's world as well. The rejection of obligation, that is, disobedience to God's commandments, directly harms Israel and disrupts its protective relationship with God. Suffering, death, destruction, and alienation ensue. From the beginning in the story of the Garden of Eden (Genesis 3) through the Rabbinic symbol of the evil inclination and on to the stunning inhumanity of the Holocaust the Jewish community and intellectual tradition have struggled to understand, respond to, and reconcile the cosmic power, presence, and concern of a God dedicated to order with the persistent, painful, and intractable propensity toward disorder and destruction in human desire and behavior.

Notes

1. Human nature and the human condition have been treated in a variety of syntheses of traditional Jewish thought, but the problem and solution is usually influenced heavily by modern concerns. See Samuel Belkin, *In His Image: The Jewish Philosophy of Man as Expressed in Rabbinic Tradition* (Westport, Conn.: Greenwood Press, 1960); George Foote Moore, *Judaism in the First Centuries of the Christian Era* (3 vols.; Cambridge: Harvard University Press, 1927–30), Vol. 1, 445–552, treats Man, Sin, Atonement under a variety of topics taken from Christian systematic theology as does Kaufman Kohler, *Jewish Theology Systematically and Historically Considered* (New York: Ktav, 1968; original 1918). Though E. E. Urbach, *The Sages: Their Concepts and Beliefs* (2 vols.; Jerusalem: Magnes, 1975) and Solomon Schechter, *Some Aspects of Rabbinic Theology* (New York: Macmillan, 1909) use indigenous Rabbinic categories, the arrangement of these topics is heavily influenced by the modern West.
2. For an analysis of how symbols work and mean, see Robert C. Neville, *The Truth of Broken Symbols* (Albany: State University of New York Press, 1996), 87–90; 132–33.
3. Joseph Soloveitchik, *Halakic Man* (Philadelphia: Jewish Publication Society, 1983; original Hebrew *'Ish Ha-Halaka*, 1944).
4. Contrary to Christian tradition, Jewish literature usually does not blame Adam for the sins of later generations, but rather attributes to him the biblical punishment for sin, death (Genesis 3:19).
5. Gary Porton, *Goyim: Gentiles and Israelites in Mishnah-Tosefta* (Atlanta: Scholars, 1988); Sacha Stern, *Jewish Identity in Early Rabbinic Writings* (Leiden: Brill, 1994).

6. For a thorough study, see David Novak, *The Image of the Non-Jew in Judaism: An Historical and Constructive Study of the Noahide Laws* (Toronto Studies in Theology 14; New York and Toronto: Edwin Mellen Press, 1983). For early stages in this line of thinking see Markus Bockmuehl, "The Noachide Commandments and New Testament Ethics with Special Reference to Acts 15 and Pauline Halakhah," *Revue Biblique* 102 (1995): 72–101.

7. A sixth chapter, Qinyan Torah, was added to later versions because Pirke Abot was read a chapter a week during the six Sabbaths between the feasts of Passover and Weeks (Pentecost).

8. Some sayings and sections probably date from the first and second centuries. The same may be said of the two versions of the Fathers According to Rabbi Nathan, which is a commentary on Abot. Though they contain some clearly late materials, certain blocks of sayings and comments seem to be early. The version of Abot on which the Fathers According to Rabbi Nathan comments is different from and probably earlier than authoritative version found in the Mishnah. Thus the commentary's roots go back to the late first and the second centuries.

9. Soon after the time of Simeon and Ben Sira (200–180 BCE) Simeon's family, the Oniads, was overthrown by Hellenizing priests who were in turn defeated by a subordinate priestly family, the Hasmoneans. Judas Maccabee and his brothers led a series of successful military and diplomatic struggles with the Seleucid rulers in Syria from 167 to 140 BCE which led to relative autonomy for Judea.

10. See Judah Goldin, "The Three Pillars of Simeon the Righteous," *PAAJR* 17 (1958): 43–58, for the meaning of the saying when applied to Simeon's time. Goldin considers the saying to come from the historical Simeon, a proposition which is doubtful.

11. Abot de Rabbi Nathan (*The Fathers According to Rabbi Nathan*), Version A, chap. 4.

12. Ibid. A similar interpretation of Hosea 6:6 appears in the late first-century Gospel of Matthew 9:13 and 12:7.

13. The Community Rule (1QS), 8–9.

14. Originally the sacrifices and "scapegoat" of the Day of Atonement (Yom Kippur) in Leviticus 16 were to remove impurities caused by inadvertent infractions of Temple rituals, but increasingly the festival was associated with repentance for sins related to social behavior.

15. Abot de Rabbi Nathan, Version A, op. cit., chap. 4.

16. They received Torah from their predecessors and passed it on to the succeeding generation and their successors, thus keeping the chain of tradition intact.

17. In antiquity much schooling took place in the home. Advanced studies took the shape of a few students reading, reciting, and discussing with a teacher who was usually supported by wealthy families.

18. The Aramaic expression, *taman teninan*, has a technical meaning in which "there" is understood to be the Mishnah, the authoritative collection upon which the Talmud is commenting.

19. This saying is one of several attributed to Hillel in the Tractate Abot.

20. "There is a story" (*ma'ase b-*) is a technical introduction to a narrative, historical or fictional, that authorizes by precedent or illustrates a Mishnaic rule.

21. The unstated implication is that he in some way gave in to sexual temptation.

22. Since the spirit is not a real human, the pious man's presumed sexual act was not a violation of the commandment which deals with acts among humans.

23. That is, recite the saying the way the rest of the sages recite it.

24. b. Bab. Bat. 16a; b Kidd. 30b; Sifre Deuteronomy 45.

25. b. Suk. 51b–52a.

26. Steven D. Fraade, "Ascetical Aspects of Ancient Judaism," *Jewish Spirituality from the Bible to the Middle Ages,* ed. Arthur Green (New York: Crossroad, 1986), 252–78.

27. Adam appears as a positive figure in Second Temple Jewish literature. See John R. Levison, *Portraits of Adam in Early Judaism From Sirach to 2 Baruch* (JSPSS 1; Sheffield: JSOT Press, 1988).

28. The Hebrew words for "strength," "measure," "thanks," and "greatly" are all either spelled or pronounced similarly, so this interpretation is based on wordplay.

29. See Levison above for Adam in Second Temple narratives and exegeses. For Adam as a cosmic figure in Rabbinic literature, see Susan Niditch, "The Cosmic Adam: Man as Mediator in Rabbinic Literature," *JJS* 35 (1982–74): 137–46.

30. Genesis Rabbah 8:4. Genesis Rabbah is a Rabbinic commentary on the Book of Genesis from the fifth century or so. It contains numerous comments on biblical words and verses, brief homilies, stories, sayings, and other materials. The original dates of the materials gathered in Genesis Rabbah are very difficult to establish.

31. Genesis Rabbah 9.7.

32. The many and varied stories, interpretations and sayings concerned with the evil inclination are assembled and interpreted in Frank C. Porter, "The Yeçer Hara: A Study in the Jewish Doctrine of Sin," *Biblical and Semitic Studies: Critical and Historical Essays by the Members of the Semitic and Biblical Faculty of Yale University* (New York and London: Scribner's/Arnold, 1901),

91–156; E. E. Urbach, *The Sages: Their Concepts and Beliefs* (Jerusalem: Magnes, 1975), 471–83; Solomon Schechter, *Some Aspects of Rabbinic Theology* (New York: Macmillan, 1909), 242–92. See Roland E. Murphy, "Yeser in the Qumran Literature," *Biblica* 39 (1958): 334–44; A. P. Hayman, "Rabbinic Judaism and the Problem of Evil," *Scottish Journal of Theology* 29 (1976): 461–76.

33. Michael L. Satlow, "Shame and Sex in Late Antique Judaism," *Asceticism*, ed. Vincent L. Wimbush and Richard Valantasis (New York: Oxford University Press, 1995), 535–43.

34. b. Suk. 52a-b; Abot de Rabbi Nathan, Version A, chap. 16 and Version B, chap. 30.

35. The last line of this first story of creation says in conclusion: "These are the generations of the heavens and the earth in their being created" (Genesis 2:4a). R. Judah takes generations to mean human generation and reads Genesis 1 as a code for humanity up to Jacob/Israel.

36. *Lemah we-lo' kelum*. *Tohu* in other places in the Bible means something that is in vain or nothing. Presumably the nothingness is because of sin.

37. Cain's fratricide brings about chaos.

38. Enosh is the son of Seth and grandson of Adam (Genesis 5:6–11). Nothing is said about his generation in Genesis 5. Since Adam sinned in the first generation and Cain in the second, the author assumes that there was sin in the third generation, which he connects with darkness in Genesis 1:2.

39. Is. 29:15 says "Woe to those who seek to hide deeply their plan from the Lord and their works are in the dark and they say, 'Who sees us, who knows us'." Such people are mocked for thinking they can deceive God who created them.

40. This survey of some trends in modern Judaism is based on the research and critical comments of Joseph Kanofsky.

41. See his essays in *After Auschwitz: Radical Theology and Contemporary Judaism* (New York: Bobbs-Merrill, 1966). His significantly different second edition, entitled *After Auschwitz: History, Theology, and Contemporary Judaism* (Baltimore: Johns Hopkins, 1992), is more conciliatory toward the tradition, but still stresses an immanent rather than transcendent God (e.g., pp. 171–74).

42. Emil Fackenheim, *To Mend the World: Foundations of Future Jewish Thought* (New York: Schocken, 1982), 299.

43. Elie Wiesel, *Gates of the Forest* (New York: Holt, Rinehart, Winston, 1966), 194.

44. Elie Wiesel, *Night* (New York: Bantam, 1982), 61–62.

45. Ibid., 30.

46. Ibid., 32.

47. Richard Rubenstein has answered that the God of the tradition is dead. See his essays in *After Auschwitz: Radical Theology and Contemporary Judaism* (New York: Bobbs-Merrill, 1966).

48. Wiesel, *Night*, op. cit., 109.

49. "Questions and Answers: At Brandeis-Bardin, 1978," [an institute in Simi Valley, California] in *Against Silence: The Voice and Vision of Elie Wiesel*, ed. Irving Abrahamson (New York: Holocaust Library, 1985), vol. 3, p. 246.

6

Embodiment and Redemption

The Human Condition in Ancient Christianity

Paula Fredriksen
with Tina Shepardson

6.1 Introduction

To explore the history of ancient Christianity is already to engage in the comparative study of religion. An energetic subspecies of late Second Temple Judaism, the new movement early on crossed over the borders of its rural, Aramaic-based, overwhelmingly Jewish context-of-origin into the urban, Greek-speaking, ethnically mixed synagogue communities of the eastern Mediterranean. The earliest documentation we have from this period—the letters of Paul, written roughly mid-century—attests to the dynamism of a new social and religious world in the making, to a rich variety of competing interpretations of shared symbols and traditions, and to an extreme internal contentiousness. These traits characterize the new religion from the beginning, continuing without diminution throughout its classical period (first–fifth century) and beyond.

In this chapter, I intend first to survey a range of Christian ideas about the human condition, particularly as these find expression in theological reflection on the nature and status of the body. We shall proceed through various thinkers, texts, and movements in rough chronological order:

first, the apostle Paul in the mid-first century; next, various dualist Christianities and the Catholic responses to them (late first to second century); then Origen through his systematic theology, the *Peri Archōn* ("On First Principles"; early third century); and finally to Augustine and *de civitate Dei* (*City of God,* 413–27).[1] My description will encompass as well an ongoing comparison of these different types of Christianity in terms of theological categories native to it: sin, redemption/resurrection, Christology, canon, and so on. My second, shorter section will survey our terrain through terms that have emerged from group discussion of other traditions: memory; obligation; loyalty; transformation; utopian vision. Any further conclusions I leave to the theorists editing this volume.

6.2 Paul

Paul fervently proclaims to his Gentile communities the Crucified, Risen, and about-to-return Son of God. This message of salvation, so urgently broadcast, brings with it a necessarily gloomy assessment of the circumstances that Paul's listeners would otherwise find themselves in. "Condition" designates too neutrally the target of the dramatic redemption envisaged here: humanity finds itself, in Paul's view, in a terrible, all-but-overwhelming *plight* so severe that nothing less than direct divine intervention—God sending his Son—could turn things around.[2] It is in the obverse of Paul's descriptions of what God has worked in Christ that we find, scattered, his views on the human condition.

People live in a sinister environment, trapped in the sway of "the god of this world" (2 Corinthians 4:4); of pagan gods, who are demons (1 Corinthians 10:20; Galatians 4:8–9); of enemy astral forces (1 Corinthians 15:24; Galatians 4:3), the elements of the universe (Romans 8:38–39); of cosmic rulers so powerful that they have even crucified "the Lord of glory" (i.e., Christ, 1 Corinthians 2:8); of sin, decay, and death. But while Paul speaks specifically to Gentiles who, as former idolaters, had conspired in their own enslavement to "beings that by nature are no gods" (Galatians 4:8), his sweeping characterization of humanity as universally mired in futility must encompass as well that community that God had sanctified, through the giving of the Law, to himself: Israel. Was the Law itself sin (Romans 7:7)? Had God's promise of redemption to Israel, recorded in Scripture and embodied in Torah, been reversed or annulled (cf. Romans 11:29; 15:8)? Impossible, answers Paul. But Law itself, though good because from God, has fallen under the dire influence of Sin, working through the Flesh (Romans 7 passim; 8:2–3). Flesh, Sin, and Death have compromised even God's Law: to defeat these evils, God finally had to send his own Son (Romans 8:3).

As a Jew—indeed, a Pharisee (Philippians 3:6)—Paul held that God was the unique Creator who, upon making the world and everything in it, had pronounced all things "good" (Romans 1:20; Genesis 1:3–31). How, then, had Creation come to such a pass? Paul implies that the cosmos in general and humanity in particular had been negatively transformed by the sin of Adam: "Thus as sin came into the world through one man and death through sin. . . . As one man's trespass led to condemnation for all men. . . . By one man's disobedience many were made sinners" (Romans 5:12,18,19). He nowhere develops this view, or accounts for why God allowed things to go on in this way for so long. He focuses, rather, on the ways that Christ has and will put things right.

In some passages of Paul's letters, Christ undoes the harm done by Adam by behaving in the opposite way: Adam was disobedient, Christ obedient; Adam brought death, Christ brought life, and so on. Elsewhere, Paul appropriates the language of Temple worship whereby through the offering of his death—the ultimate measure of obedience—Christ served as a form of blood sacrifice, expiating sin through his blood (Romans 3:25), thereby making humans "righteous" or "justified" (*dikaiothentes*) (5:9). Through his coming in the flesh (or seeming to),[3] and his dying in the flesh, Christ has begun a transformation of the cosmos and of humanity. The cosmos, subjected to futility and decay, "groans in travail" as it awaits the consummation of the redemption begun in and by Christ's resurrection (Romans 8). Once he returns to complete this work—descending from heaven "with a cry of command, with the archangel's call and the sound of the trumpet of God" (1 Thessalonians 4:16)—Christ will defeat the cosmic powers[4] that have enslaved all things,[5] including and especially the last enemy, Death itself (1 Corinthians 15:26).

Meanwhile, those "in Christ" experience a proleptic liberation through an infusion of God's, or Christ's, Spirit, whether through baptism (thus joining with Christ's cosmic body, the Church[6]) or by eating his body and drinking his blood in the eucharistic meal (1 Corinthians 11:23–27—done with the wrong attitude, a punitive death can result, v. 30). Joining this body means that the believer has "died" with Christ to the evil forces abroad in the world—to sin (Romans 7:20–22), to the Law (8:1–3), to the flesh (Galatians 5:24)—and can thus with confidence look forward, ultimately, to the transformation of his or her own body at Christ's Second Coming (1 Thessalonians 4:13–18; 1 Corinthians 15; Romans 6:5). The infusion of God's Spirit achieved by these means *should* lead to a moral and social transformation in the brief meantime, in which the *ekklesia* acts as one body (Galatians 3:28; 1 Corinthians 12:13), and individuals sin no more—especially and most important with respect to sexual misconduct (*porneia*) and idolatry, in Jewish perspective the "sins of the flesh" par excellence. But baptism does not in itself effect this transformation, as Paul well knows: his letters swell with exhortations, threats, scoldings, and condemnation as various members of the *ekklesia* fail to live morally as Paul thinks they should.[7] Their righteous conduct, together with their baptism in Christ, guarantees that they will be spared the impending wrath of God.[8]

The human condition, then, according to Paul, is fraught with danger and corruption, destined for wrathful destruction by the Almighty. Those saved in Christ, in the brief period before his return defeats evil and destroys the works of the flesh, can only "groan" as they await their "adoption as sons"—and, most specifically, the redemption of their bodies (Romans 8:23). What does this mean? *The transformation of the human condition will be marked, indeed effected, by the transformation of the believer's body.* The "resurrection like [Christ's]" that the believer will have merited through his mimetic and moral death to this sinful age in and through baptism (Romans 6:5) means that the flesh of his or her "lowly" body will change into a "glorious" or "spiritual" body (Philippians 3:21; 1 Corinthians 15:44). To the degree that Paul holds the resurrection of the dead to be somatic, he is typically Pharisaic; to the degree that he holds the raised body to be spiritual rather than fleshly, he imprints his conviction with his own experience of the Risen Christ (1 Corinthians 15:7). Flesh and blood belong to humanity as constituted in the old aeon; in the new, it has no place. "Flesh and blood cannot inherit the Kingdom of God" (15:50).

Paul's ideas—episodically communicated in letters, passionately held, and inconsistently expressed—serve as a peculiar apocalyptic commentary on the book of Genesis: the earlier scriptural figures of Adam and Abraham, of Isaac and Ishmael are all reread in light of his new convictions about Christ. Later generations, both gnostic and catholic, each justly claiming the Pauline legacy, would perforce reread Genesis too. Their views on God, physical creation, Jesus, redemption, *and on Paul himself*, would mark out two different, though coordinate, ways of understanding the human condition.

6.3 Christian Dualism and the High God

In an effort to make Paul consistent and, within an increasing Gentile Greek context, coherent, some later Christians took his condemnation of judaizing (the controversy in Galatians), his repudiation of "the flesh" (and thus circumcision as a way of glorying in the flesh, Galatians 3:3), and his descriptions of the Law's having been subverted through sin, and understood these as a condemnation of Judaism *tout court*. Thus, they too could subscribe to the view of the universe as fallen under the power of sin, and Christ as God's agent sent to effect humanity's rescue. But their view, different from the historical Paul's, complicated his ideas in interesting ways.

Axiomatic in Greek learned culture was the theological principle that the High God (a.k.a. "the One" or "The Father of All") could not be involved in change. The One was "perfect, free from passion, free from change"[9]—and, accordingly, free from any direct involvement in the physical universe. Taking this, Paul's condemnation of the god of this world, and Genesis, dualist Christians concluded that the god of the Septuagint who formed this cosmos was not, *could* not be God the father of Christ. Christ's father was the God above God, hidden before all the ages, pure spirit, pure love. The busy, jealous, opinionated God of Genesis—the evidently *embodied* god of the Jews—was a lower, inferior creator. God the Father had sent his son into this lower cosmos in the *likeness* of flesh, in the *form* of a man (Philippians 2:7–8) in order to bring saving, transforming knowledge of a God whose revelation could never be inferred from creation.

6.3.1 *Gnosis*

This revelation of hidden knowledge (*gnosis*) saved by awakening the knower to who he really was, and what his situation really was.[10] Who could receive this knowledge? Only he whom the High God elected, or called, or predestined: those whom Paul designated "the perfect" (*teleioi*, 1 Corinthians 2:6). Just as all are not chosen, so all are not redeemable. The issue is not choice, but nature: Only the spiritual man can understand the things of God. He alone can know and understand that his true self, a divine spark or higher spirit, was trapped in the cosmos the lower god, stuck in flesh essentially alien to it. But those in Christ, as Paul had promised, could be free of the power of the flesh. This theology implied an ethic of asceticism (food disciplines, sexual abstinence) in the effort to transcend the body as much as possible while still in it. We might see sexual abstinence as a kind of realized eschatology: absent sexual activity, within the body of Christ, there might really be "neither male nor female" (Galatians 3:28). Salvation, ultimately, was not from mere physical death—of course flesh dies—but from ignorance, torpor, spiritual death, existence *kata sarka*, "according to the flesh." Once the soul broke free of its immediately hostile material environment, the fleshly body, the "self" of the true gnostic could ascend past the astral spheres, their powers broken by Christ, and be united with him in a higher, spiritual heaven.

6.3.2 *Anti-dualism, Anti-docetism*

The later writings in the New Testament canon attest, in their hostility to it, the early advent of this way of understanding the Christian message. Pseudonymous epistles written in the name, hence on the authority, of first-generation apostles, roundly condemn a universal ethic of celibacy (1 Timothy 4:1–5; cf. 6:20, against "*gnosis* falsely so-called'), and warn that Paul's writings contain "things in them hard to understand" and easily susceptible of heretical interpretation (2 Peter 3:15–16). Those Christians who deny that Christ came in the flesh are not "of God" (1 John 4:2), indeed, are Antichrist (2 John 7). Those who say that the resurrection is already passed (i.e., has already been accomplished spiritually) "swerve from the truth" (2 Timothy 2:18).

The anti-dualist, anti-docetic branch of Christianity eventually won this struggle of interpretation, retroactively establishing itself as "orthodox" (hence the anti-dualist writings in the canon). But the classic heresiologists and apologists—Justin Martyr, Tertullian, Irenaeus, Hippolytus—also stood within the broad stream of Greek high culture, and thus also shared much of the philosophical and ascetic sensibility of their Christian opponents. They too read Paul's gospel as fundamentally anti-Jewish; they too took "flesh" and "spirit" to indicate moral orientation as well as ontology; they too held that same definition of the High God as changeless, asomatic, perfect. But in insisting that the Septuagint was also—indeed actually—*Christian* scripture,[11] these theologians bound created, fleshly reality more directly to their construction of God, of Christ, and of salvation. And while their assessment of the current human condition was no more rosy than that of the dualists, the resolution they imagined emphasized aspects of Scripture and of Paul which the dualists had perforce abandoned.

6.3.3 *Salvation of the Cosmos*

If the High God were ultimately the source of Creation, then Creation, albeit fallen, cannot be essentially alien to God. Unlike the dualist, then, whose soteriology envisaged an individual, spiritual passage through an evil cosmos intractably untransformed by Christ, the catholic imagined redemption as transformation of the cosmos itself. The suffering, ignorance, and evil that marked the human condition, proleptically overcome for those within the (true) church by the giving of the spirit, would be publicly, historically, communally overcome at Christ's Second Coming, when Creation itself would be healed of Adam's lingering damage and the flesh itself redeemed. Christ himself, therefore, had really had a body, and had shown in his own resurrection what the human flesh would become.[12] So too at his Parousia, the saints would rise in their own bodies, to reign with him for a thousand years in the glorious New Jerusalem of the redeemed and transformed earth.[13]

Where the dualists had taken Paul's contrast of Old Aeon/New Aeon morally and metaphysically, then, catholics retrieved as well his emphasis on time and history. Against the dualist rejection (Marcion) or counter-reading (Valentinus) of the Septuagint, catholics urged a temporal understanding of Old Aeon/New Aeon as Christian supersessionism: the "old age" of the Jews, Israel according to the flesh, had ceded to the "new age" of the Church, Israel according to the Spirit. And in their reading of the classical prophets contained in the book they now claimed as their own, these Christians constructed their own traditions of Christ's apocalyptic kingdom upon the ancient Jewish visions of a just society: this Kingdom would have agriculture, social arrangements, marriage and even births, as well as huge convocations in Jerusalem. God had authored flesh; Christ had assumed it for man's salvation. Salvation would not be realized, then, until flesh itself were redeemed.

6.4 Origen

Much of the Christian writing of the late first and second centuries is the intellectual equivalent of street-fighting: these authors struggle to make their case against the well-established communities they see as rivals—Jews, for the Bible; traditional pagans, for paideia—while continually honing their polemic against myriad other Christian groups as well. Coming to Origen (185–254), we enter a different world. With his massive (and well-placed) intellectual self-confidence, his creative mastery of traditional philosophy, and his command of the full range of biblical texts, Origen marked a new maturity in developing catholic tradition. The full measure of these excellences comes together in his ambitious *Peri Archōn* ("On First Principles"), the church's first systematic theology.[14] In four books—God (I), World (II), Moral Freedom (III), and Biblical Revelation (IV)—he proposes a coherent, indeed compelling, exposition of Christian redemption; and embedded within is a powerful diagnosis and description of the human condition. To grasp this, let us begin where he begins: with God.

6.4.1 God as Trinity

God, defined as Trinity, presided over an eternally existing universe of rational beings. These rational beings, though co-eternal, were *contingent* upon God, and distinguished one from the other by "the sole principle of differentiation," body. God, however, is uniquely *asomaton*, non-embodied.[15] (People who understand from Scripture that God has a body only expose their own unfortunate low level of understanding, since they read *kata sarka*—"according to the flesh" or "in a fleshly way"—and thus fail to grasp the true, higher meaning of the text *kata pneuma*, "according to the spirit."[16]) A crucial defining characteristic of these rational beings is their free will. Since they were contingent, they had a sort of built-in distractableness,[17] but this was offset by their moral independence, the freedom of the will that defines the rational being. In the time before time one of these beings, completely of its own free choice, loved God so intensely that it in effect fused with the Godhead: this was Christ.[18] All the rest, insufficiently attentive, lapsed, each to his own particular 'distance' from God.

6.4.2 Double Creation: Eternal and Spiritual, Temporal and Fleshly

To accommodate these distinctive and individual levels of merit in his creatures, and also to place them in a propaedeutic situation whereby they could come to choose, freely, to return to him, God graciously and out of nothing called into being the world of matter.[19] Rational souls thus find themselves in fleshly bodies proper to their situation, in respect of choices made before life in the body. Sun, stars, angels, devils, principalities, powers, humans—all are embodied enfleshed instances on a continuum of moral failure, the sin of turning from God. To think "human condition" then, for Origen, is to think too small. The entire visible cosmos is a fraternity in a "condition," one through which God graciously intends to redeem every one.

We must pause here to consider how this theology brilliantly satisfies some of the hoariest conundrums of both philosophical and Christian theology. Origen's doctrine of a "double creation"—one spiritual and eternal; one temporal and fleshly—at once spoke to classical formulations of God's essential changelessness (he was always eternally Father and Creator), asserted his absolute lordship over the physical cosmos (since he created it out of nothing), and relocated the problem of the one and the many to the ethical sphere. Further, his constant insistence on God's absolute fairness, and the will's absolute freedom, enabled Origen to appropriate the best of Platonic and Stoic thought in service of a Christian theodicy: will was free; each soul was to exercise its mind in pursuit of ultimate moral excellence, the love of God; and historical, situational evil—babies born blind, congenital diseases, the suffering of the innocent—shrinks in the perspective of eternity to a temporary learning situation for the soul.[20]

6.4.3 *Flesh*

Additionally—in light of Origen's intense commitment to a biblical Christianity, unsurprisingly—the status of "matter" or "flesh" is elevated. The dualist Christian and Origen might seem to make similar claims: life in the flesh is a burden, the measure of sin, a punishment; this world is not the native home of the soul; the fleshly body is not an essential part of the self. But where the dualist would denigrate flesh as a cause of the soul's sin, and this lower cosmos as the work of an inferior, hostile god, Origen praises flesh as the medium of redemption, and a dazzling index of the ingenuity of a generous, loving Creator.[21]

6.4.4 *Universal Salvation*

For God wants redemption for all his creatures—eventually, Origen thought, even the Devil would be brought round—and he has all the time in the world. The huge scope required by the capaciousness of this view of redemption was motivated in part by Origen's insistence on understanding God in terms of his two great biblical attributes, justice (all creatures are created exactly the same, and all are morally free) and mercy (God loves all his creatures, and works for their redemption). Yet it has the curious effect of shrinking key elements in the biblical story. "Adam's sin" can only be a figure for the prehistorical lapse of the entire species; Christ's resurrection, an exemplum rather than an epoch-changing event in itself. While history abets salvation, it does not define it.

6.4.5 *Salvation as Education*

The entire thrust of Origen's argument is intellectual, toward the education of the rational soul; and it is in terms of enlightenment that he understands the stark, Pauline contrast of Death and Life. Paul had embedded his description of the apocalyptic defeat of Death in his vision of the transformation of the body, the change from fleshly body to spiritual body by which both living and dead would join with Christ in God's Kingdom (1 Corinthians 15). Origen's variation on the Pauline theme had also retained redeemed bodies, but these have nothing whatever to do with flesh, which belongs intrinsically to the secondary, temporary order. The soul's body distinguishes it from other souls, and from God who has no body, but this body is literally *meta*physical. The defeat of Death, in this context, means the defeat of faulty understanding, of ignorance; life *kata pneuma* means understanding, and so loving, God. Its focus is not (as with Paul) the transformation of the body, fleshly or otherwise, but the transformation of the *nous*, the mind of the soul.

Hence Origen's principled concern with textual interpretation, and the huge mass of commentaries that he produced.[22] To live *kata pneuma* was to know the correct way to read, and so understand, the Bible: according to its spiritual meaning, which reveals the timeless truths of God. For the *Peri Archōn* faces off not only with Christian dualists; it strikes time and again against a more intimate enemy, those within the Church who understand her teachings and her scriptures *kata sarka*. These are the ones who, misreading the Bible, think that God has a body (I.1,1), that the saints, physically resurrected, will worship him in Jerusalem (I.1,4), that in this city resplendent with precious stones they will eat, marry, and celebrate (II.11,2–3). Such thinking, sighs Origen, is virtually Jewish, the pathetic advertisement of an impoverished intellect and spirituality (loc. cit.). But God is no fundamentalist; and for those trapped in time he wrote a text whose seeming simplicity requires the mind to seek its allegorical meanings. "The letter kills, but the Spirit gives life" (2 Corinthians 3:6), that is, it transforms the reader, and in so doing removes the veil between him and the Law so that "we shall with unveiled face behold in the holy scriptures the glory of God" (I.1,2).

6.5 Augustine

No one, looking around in 390, would have guessed that Augustine would be the next great architect of an innovative theological system. By that point, he had personally covered all these prior positions: raised by a fundamentalist Catholic mother, then joining a dualist Pauline heretical sect, he had flirted briefly with philosophical skepticism before settling into an allegorizing, cosmopolitan Catholicism retailed by Ambrose and shot through with Origen. His earliest post-conversion writings are modeled on philosophical dialogues; his first biblical commentary refutes Manichaean dualism with the standard tools of allegorical interpretation.

But the intellectual restlessness that compelled Augustine through a decade of intense religious reorientation did not subside with baptism. Returning from international Milan to the narrower world of North Africa, driven in public by a Manichaean interlocutor up against the glibness of his own understanding of evil—especially of that evil so evidently manifest in the human condition—Augustine plunged into a protracted study of the letters of Paul.[23] His new views on the relationship of grace and will, sin and salvation, that emerged from this period would define the tenor of Western Christianity for the next fourteen centuries. We see his most comprehensive statement of these issues in his great masterwork, *The City of God.*

6.5.1 Fleshly Creation, Fleshly Fall, Fleshly Salvation

When God created man in the garden, said Augustine, he created him male and female, with bodies of flesh joined *ab initio* to spirit or soul. From this seemingly simple reading of Genesis Augustine drew, for his tradition, radical conclusions. God's sovereign choice to make humans thus—with gendered, fleshly bodies—not only clearly implied that the flesh was the natural and God-willed habitat of the soul *even before the Fall*; it meant as well that God had always intended humans to be sexually active, to "be fruitful and multiply" precisely by the sexual union of male and female. Why else would he have bothered with gender? Paradisiacal sex, however, would have been different than sex has been since. Now, sexual union and, thus, procreation rely on a loss of control in orgasm and, prior, the loss of rationality as the mind (for Augustine always the premier sexual organ) must needs be moved by lust.[24] Then, however,

> without the morbid condition of lust the sexual organs would have been brought into activity by the same bidding of the will as controlled the other organs. Then, without feeling the allurement of passion goading him on, the husband would have relaxed on his wife's bosom in tranquility of mind and with no impairment of his body's integrity. . . . And the male seed could have been dispatched into the womb with no loss of the wife's integrity, just as the menstrual flux can now be produced from the womb of a virgin without loss of maidenhead. (*City of God,* XIV.26)

What had happened? Even though man had complete freedom of will, and was able to choose freely not to sin, he disobeyed the divine command. God thus struck him in the offending agent, the will itself; and, since soul and body stand intimately connected on the same continuum, this injury to the mind or soul manifested itself instantaneously in the flesh: "There appeared in their body a certain indecent novelty which made nakedness shameful, and made them self-conscious and embarrassed" (XIV.17). Whereas prior to the Fall the capacity for physical pleasure would have been coordinate with the will, thereverafter, it escaped conscious control. This basic disjuncture of body and soul echoed a further disjuncture with which the species, in every generation, was cursed: for the soul, though created to embrace and love the body as marriage partners had been created for one another, would be wrenched, unwilling, from the body at death.

From Adam on, then, humanity has found itself in a penal condition of ignorance and mortality, the affliction of its broken will passed on, precisely and necessarily, through the morbid condition of lust. Worse: not only can the will no longer control the body; as Paul laments in Romans 7, it can no longer control even itself: "The evil I do not want to do I do" (7:19). Wounded, divided, ineffective, the will—which term functions, for Augustine, as a code for the soul's affect—is turned in upon itself. Although the soul naturally longs to love God,[25] it writhes impacted in itself. The Fall turned the soul's natural *amor dei* to *amor sui*, the irretrievable human narcissism that transmutes every effort to genuinely love another into an exercise in (at best, covert) exploitation. Adam's prerogative not to sin (*posse non peccare*) has been replaced by a harrowing, but nonetheless culpable, inability: humanity cannot *not* sin (*non posse non peccare*). Human nature, body and soul, is now "carnal," fleshly, oriented toward ignorance and death. The entire race is a *massa damnata*, literally a lump of perdition.[26]

God justly condemned the entire race. But he has mercifully chosen to elect some individuals for salvation. He does so entirely at his own initiative (*gratia*), and for his own profoundly hidden (*occultissima*) reasons. Put differently: God does not save the just or the righteous, for there are only sinners; it is his grace alone that makes sinners righteous. For Augustine, the parade example of this principle is Paul himself, a murderer and persecutor of the Church, whom God inexplicably called to the Gospel.

But even those who have received grace still struggle with sin; even those God has elected for salvation die. How then, and when, will God resolve the terrible tensions marking the human predicament; how, and when, will he save? If one knows how to read the Bible, answers Augustine, one can know the answer.

6.5.2 *Reading the Bible*

The Bible must be read both for its spiritual meanings (*secundum spiritum*) and for its historical meanings (*ad litteram*). Here Augustine again comes up with arguments of astonishing originality. Against the Manichees who, like their second-century dualist predecessors, renounced the Old Testament and Judaism as carnal, *and* against prior Catholic tradition, which kept the Old Testament if read *secundum spiritum* but denounced the Jews as carnal, Augustine insisted that the New Testament and the Old, like the soul and the body, were intimately, fundamentally, essentially connected. The Jews had been right to keep the Law *secundum carnem*, literally and not figuratively; the first generation of apostles and Paul himself had realized this, and they, as Jesus himself, had been Torah-observant Jews. Through their actual, physical observance of the Law, the entire people of Israel, like a great prophet, foretold Christ not only in word (i.e., through their Scriptures) but also in deed, through their actions—blood offerings, food laws, Sabbath, and above all and especially circumcision.

6.5.3 *Whence the Saved, Flesh and All?*

This last most especially bespoke God's redemption. By placing his "seal of righteousness," as the Apostle designated it (Romans 4:11), on that most recalcitrant fleshly member and organ of human generation, God had Israel embody the fundamental mystery of Christianity: the *re*generation of humanity through the revelation of God in the flesh, in the Incarnation and Resurrection of Christ.[27] Now, in the Church, those whom God has chosen experience the first resurrection of the saints, which is spiritual, the regeneration effected through baptism. The second resurrection, however, will be physical, when God raises all humanity, body and soul, for judgment, reigning finally with his saints in his eternal Kingdom (XXII.30).

Only this last act of history will serve to finally resolve the human condition. The resurrection, accordingly, *must* be with a body made of flesh: only reunited with the flesh can the soul truly be complete. What then of Paul's pronouncement, that "flesh and blood cannot inherit the Kingdom of God" (1 Corinthians 15:50)? Of course, Paul was right, says Augustine. But by "flesh" he meant moral orientation, not physical substance. The fleshly body of the saved[28] will be raised spiritual, meaning that with the wound in the will closed and the soul healed, the body of flesh will again, without effort, follow the dictates of the spirit in all things: man will no longer be capable of sinning (*non posse peccare*).

Where do these spirit-directed bodies of flesh go? Where is the habitation of the saints? Millenarian Christians, especially those within Augustine's own North African tradition, in insisting on the redemption of the fleshly body, had likewise insisted on a redeemed earth, especially a redeemed Jerusalem, as the saints' new home. Those who had abandoned visions of terrestrial beatitude were either dualists, who repudiated the material realm altogether as inimical to the True God; or Origen who, though himself no dualist, had held flesh to be a providential and temporary dwelling-place of the lapsed rational being: the return back to God, for both, meant a permanent farewell to the material world, human flesh included.

Not so Augustine. The human being is raised with his body of flesh; but it will dwell in the heavens, with God. Earth is not redeemed: only humans are.[29] To protests that such a view was simply scientific nonsense—how could the weighty elements of flesh ascend to a realm past the moon?—Augustine counterposed the reciprocal miracle of birth:

> The world is full of souls animating these earthly physical frames, combined and bound up with them in a mysterious fashion. Why, then, if it is the will of the same God who made this living creature, cannot an earthly body be raised up to a heavenly body, if the soul, which belongs to a more exalted order of being than any body, even a heavenly body, could be linked with an earthly body? [. . .] The present state of things . . . has been cheapened by familiarity, but . . . is in fact much more wonderful than that translation which our philosophers find incredible. Why, in fact, are we not more violently amazed that immaterial souls, superior to celestial bodies, are bound within earthly bodies, than that bodies, although earthly, should be exalted to abodes which are material, albeit heavenly? (XXII.4)

6.6 Summary

This completes our quick march through the very variable terrain of ancient Christianity. As we have seen, interpretations of the Christian message, and especially of the human condition, differ significantly. Some points are constant: humans currently are in a dire predicament, caused somehow by an ancient fall; the High God has effected redemption from this predicament by sending his Son to undo this fall; ultimately, at least some—for Origen, all—will be saved. But the predicament is described and imagined variously, as is the definition of 'human' itself.

6.6.1 *Fall and Redemption*

For Paul, all creation has fallen, and all creation will be redeemed when Christ returns to defeat every hostile power and even death itself (Romans 8; 1 Corinthians 15). For dualists, material creation lies outside the scope of Christ's redemption, since God concerns himself exclusively with those whom he has called, the spiritual men (*pneumatikoi*) who can receive the knowledge of salvation. Their Christ does not really have a fleshly body, nor in a sense does the spiritual man: the body is a temporary incident, the self is the soul. For Origen, too, this material realm is not the object of salvation, but all fallen rational intelligences are. Hence Origen, like Paul, holds that *all* creation, not just humans, will be saved. Since the soul is eternally alive, and the rational being is in reality its soul, the enemy that Christ defeats is not physical death but intellectual death, the death that comes of not knowing God. For Augustine, human beings are by definition flesh and soul together; Christ really assumes flesh, and in doing so really dies, is really raised, and really signals forth the redemption of the flesh. But his soteriology is narrowly androcentric: *only* humans (and, arguably, only *some* humans) are the object of God's love. The rest of creation is backdrop; what remains, at the end, is God and man.

6.6.2 *Practical Renunciation*

What surprises me, in the face of these significantly different ideological orientations toward embodiment, is how similarly all these communities *acted*. The great social innovation of ancient Christianity, often described but never adequately explained, is the practice of permanent sexual renunciation on a large scale. It is this commitment that binds all these groups together, making them behaviorally much more alike than different. Whence the appeal, and the institutionalization of sexual renunciation?[30] Paul in 1 Corinthians 7 endorsed it, but only as a temporary measure, mutually agreed upon by spouses, to concentrate on prayer in preparation for the impending End. Marcion insisted that all members of his church be celibate, and did not baptize those not prepared to take this step. Unlike the Shakers, Marcion's group flourished, being one of the first Christian communities specifically targeted for persecution by Constantine after his conversion (Eusebius, *Life of Constantine* 64).

Catholic piety was likewise peopled with heroic virgins and lifelong renunciants. So serenely self-controlled was Origen that envious coreligionists gave vent to nasty rumors of self-castration and libido-inhibiting drugs.[31] Augustine quite specifically correlated joining the Church to becoming and staying celibate.[32] Like many perfectionist ideals, universal celibacy was, evidently, more honored in the breach; yet remarkably enough, the ideal remained. The Roman church's endorsement of marriage—specifically against the Manichees; and drawn up by celibate men—was typically ambivalent. Marriage was praised as from God; but the model of Christian marriage was the Holy Family, Mary and Joseph in the archtypical *mariage blanc*.

Perhaps, if in Christ the flesh was to be already somehow put off, celibacy for all these different Christians was a way to transcend existence *kata sarka*. To renounce sexual activity—as renouncing normal family ties to enter into a new fictive family of choice, the Church—was to escape the human condition despite being still trapped in it in the period before the Parousia. Celibacy within normal time, then, is the social expression of the Now/Not Yet paradox of Christian eschatology—the paradox that is itself the occasion of Paul's letters, the source of his congregations' confusions about behavior, and the measure of the degree to which God's *fixing* the human condition stands at the center of Christian hope.

6.7 Postscript: Terms of Comparison from the Seminar

Thus far, I have compared different forms of Christianity to each other in terms native to all types. How can we consider this religion in light of categories generated by the group's discussion?

6.7.1 *Obligation*

Given the complicated attitudes to concepts like "law" arising from the anti-Judaic reading of Paul and the gospels that marked orthodox Christianity, the vocabulary of the movement features praise of "freedom"—from the Law, from the bonds of sin, and with the anticipated resurrection (however imagined), from the bonds of death and decay. A discourse of obligation remains embedded in ethical behavior rather than theological rhetoric as such. The Christian is, thus, obligated to fulfill the commandment to love God and neighbor, radically extended in the Gospel of Matthew to love of the enemy as well (5:44). Christian apologists in the second century (and too many New Testament scholars in the twentieth!) divided the Law into ethical and "ritual" commands, arguing that the ritual ones, as specifically Jewish, were irrelevant to the Christian, only the ethical ones were still binding. Eventually, Christian culture evolved its own ethos of ritual obligation—feast days, the liturgical year, sacramental obligation, Lent, and so on; monastic communities, as we would expect, articulated and regulated this ethos to a very high degree.

6.7.2 *Loyalty*

I had not thought about the ancient communities that I work on in this way, and it has occasioned some interesting regrouping. The self-identities of groups can be seen as a function of loyalty to a progressively particular set of texts. At first, the great divide was over the status of the

Septuagint: which Christian group held it as sacred as well as revelatory, which groups merely as revelatory. Later textual loyalties called the first Christian canon into being: thus, the dualist Marcion held the Pauline corpus (the seven authentic epistles, plus Ephesians and Colossians) as the true textual patrimony of the Christian, along with one gospel (perhaps some version of Luke's: we don't know). Other Christians countered with allegiance to a larger canon—Paul's letters plus other deutero-paulines (1 and 2 Timothy, Titus, 2 Thessalonians; Hebrews); four gospels, other letters, one apocalypse, and all of the Septuagint. But how was one to interpret these texts and organize one's communities? Enter the creeds.

Two interesting observations. First, the loyalty to a scriptural canon did not produce a similar loyalty to a canon of authoritative commentary and interpretation, as is the case with rabbinic Judaism or with Confucianism. The authority of commentary—and so loyalty to it—rested with the prestige of the commentator. Accordingly, loyalties varied locally as well as temporally: good commentary in the second century (e.g., Irenaeus) would be outgrown by the fourth (hence the passive 'rewriting' of the millenarian fifth book of Irenaeus' *Against All Heresies* by the simple expedient, by the anti-apocalyptic Western church, of dropping that section when copying the manuscripts). Augustine's prestige in the West guaranteed him nothing in the East. Christendom never had anything like the Mishnah and Gemara.

Second, creeds become a sort of loyalty oath. In this regard, they fail: Athanasius was maddened that the Nicene creed, necessarily vaguely worded to pass through committee, could be endorsed by Arians: say what they might, he *knew* that they were *thinking* about Christology differently. And even creeds of supposedly universal import and application met with variable local reception and interest (at Nicea, amid the hundreds of Eastern bishops, we find only two from the Latin West).

Loyalties could cash out along lines of correct ritual, and the North African church, for example, notoriously divided over a disagreement about the admissibility of second baptism. The Donatists indeed are the parade example of the Church's obsession with group loyalty and intellectual uniformity. North African Catholics and Donatists were divided by no doctrinal differences. They shared exactly the same sacraments, the same calendar, the same saints; indeed, to the detriment of local harmony, they claimed the same church buildings and worshipped at the graves of the same martyrs. What separated them was their thought on sacraments and, thus, their practice of (second) baptism for the lapsed. The Christian obsession with a universal loyalty to the minute particulars of interpretation, reflected linguistically in the career of the term *hairesis*, eventually challenged one of the most conservative forces in late Latin culture, namely Roman law: how one *thought* could become—if one thought wrongly, that is, disloyally to the Church—a state offense.

Finally, loyalty in Christianity (Catholic and Gnostic) was loyalty to the new, fictive family of the members of the community, not to one's biological family with whatever social obligations that might adhere. The Christian hero transcends family bonds, indeed renounces them, even as he (and, with much less opportunity, she) renounces power and social position as well: This is a major theme of conversion stories. The bishop is "father," the head monk is "abba," one's community members are one's true "mother and brothers and sisters," as Mark's Jesus himself had preached (3:33–35).

6.7.3 *Utopian Visions*

Society after Adam, most Catholic Christians would agree, had not been overly marked by justice, peace, and harmony. Exceptions were imagined or allowed. The early *ekklesia*, according to Paul, at least *should* act as one body, with one accord. Cyprian argued that the church, as the unique ark of salvation, should be an orderly obedient community subject to the authority of her bishop. Orders of virgins, desert fathers (and mothers), extravagantly ascetic holy men, the learned literate retirement of *otium liberale* that eventually evolved into the bookish perfectionism of the Western monastery—all these societies saw themselves as proleptic pieces of heaven, their individual members transformed by the shared ethic, community property (hence individual poverty) and sexual celibacy into a *communio sanctorum*. As such, while still in this life, the individual who joined in such a group endeavor might slip the coil of the human condition while still, nonetheless, in the body.

6.7.4 *Memory*

Permit me here to focus on Augustine, because he does so much with this term and this idea. The very fact that we have memory is for Augustine a symptom of the Fall, for it is the measure of the soul's distension in time. Through memory, the turbid *Qi* of recollected loves pools and so compromises the choices of the soul—"my love, my weight." Habit forms through the memory of loves, leading to compulsive and thus inappropriate choices—Augustine's premier argument for the unfreedom of the will and radical necessity of grace. The means out of this predicament is grace alone, which can be solicited by no discipline, no study, no effective effort on the part of the individual who, grace apart, cannot but be misguided. (The *Confessions* is in this sense his demonstration of the truth of this claim by using the data of his own life: he could not turn to God until God turned him toward Himself.)

6.7.5 Transformation

This is the term that encompasses the most dynamic and dramatic forms of Christian address to the Christian construction of the human predicament. The primal negative transformation of Adam's sin, passed from generation to generation as Original Sin, can be turned around solely by the healing transformation of the grace of God through Christ. What does this mean on the level of ritual, community loyalty, and obligation? For starters, one must belong to the correct community: *extra ecclesiam nulla salus*, where 'extra ecclesiam' meant, originally, outside of *Cyprian's* church. The sacraments through which grace is mediated can be given only through the correct human medium—a churchman, however morally flawed himself, ordained in the Spirit because ordained through the correct episcopal hierarchy. Constantine and Theodosius only complicated this issue, but it existed in the Church long before the state took an interest.

The moral and spiritual transformations available in the ecclesia are a mere shadow, of course, to the ultimate transformation of the flesh at the resurrection of the saints. Here orthodox Christianity got to have its millenarian cake and eat it too—while renouncing millenarianism. The original context for the proclamation of bodily resurrection is the kerygma of the early church, an apocalyptic Jewish movement. Centuries and ethnic groups later, the sort of orientation toward time embarassingly captured in the canon—Paul's letters, Mark, Revelation—had been condemned by the hierarchy as heretical and interpreted out of the texts. But the transformation of the flesh as the ultimate measure of redemption, the resolution to the human predicament, remained nonetheless. Without it, Christ's incarnation lacked focus, his resurrection would flirt with gnosticism. *Malgré lui*, the Church kept it and the Resurrected Christ, in turn, stood as the model of saved humanity.

Finally, Christian eschatology expects as well the transformation of the soul. Paul spoke not just of being "in Christ"; he also spoke of Christ being in Paul: "I have been crucified with Christ; *it is no longer I who live, but Christ in me*" (Galatians 2:20). Origen's rational beings, once redeemed, will be back contemplating the Godhead, stripped of all the incidental particulars—gender, race, class—of life in the material cosmos (neither Jew nor Greek, neither slave nor free, neither male nor female). Augustine's saved humans, by contrast, are emphatically individualized, raised with the same flesh they traveled through history with, still gendered, identifiable as individuals. Yet the essential orientation of their ego will have changed, which accounts for their no longer being able to sin: the love of self, that hallmark of fallen man, will have been replaced by love of God. God replaces ego. Perhaps, then, in the eschatological speculations of these three very different thinkers—the apocalyptic Jew, the speculative theologian, the Late Roman bishop—we find something close to a doctrine of no-self.

Notes

1. My list is idiosyncratic. I am negotiating between my obligation to present a comprehensive sweep of several centuries, my pedagogical instinct to make my points clearly by using high-contrast cases, and my desire to focus on those thinkers whom I find most interesting—hence Paul, Origen, and Augustine. Let this declaration stand as my apology for not including other pertinent theologians (Athanasius and the Cappadocian Fathers being the most conspicuous absentees).
2. See esp. E. P. Sanders, *Paul and Palestinian Judaism* (Philadelphia: Fortress Press, 1977), 442–511, on understanding Paul's soteriology as an instance of the "solution" (i.e., Christ) preceding the "problem" (what Christ must save humanity *from*).
3. Paul is notoriously unclear on this point. Where the imagery of Temple sacrifice prevails, he speaks without complication of Christ's "blood" (again, Romans 3:25, 5:9) and of his "death" (e.g., Romans 6:3, 1 Corinthians 15:3; 2 Corinthians 4:10, and frequently; cf. on his birth, Galatians 4:4, "God sent forth his Son, born of a woman, born under the Law;" fleshly descent, Romans 1:3). Elsewhere, however, Christ is a preexistent cosmic figure, whose descent in obedience requires that he assume a human form (*morphos;* Lat. *forma*) or human likeness (*en homoiomati anthropo;* Lat. *in similitudinem;* Philippians 2:7–8), appearing "in the likeness of sinful flesh" (Romans 8:3). Later Christologies, as we shall see, resolve this ambiguity by rejecting one or the other of its implications.
4. For various lists of who or what these are, Romans 8:38–39; 1 Corinthians 15:24–26.
5. Again, enslaved, but by divine design: "for the creation was subject to futility, not of its own will but *by the will of him who subjected it in hope.*" (Romans 8:20). Presumably this subjection is somehow tied in with the sin of Adam, but Paul does not spell out the connection. My point is that, while Paul scripts "good" and "evil" forces ranged against each other, he is (unlike some of his later commentators) no dualist: the single High God of the Bible stands supreme.
6. On receiving the Spirit through baptism, e.g., 1 Corinthians 1–3 (where Paul segues to Temple imagery, this time applied to the believer, who, as the temple in Jerusalem, is likewise God's temple because "God's spirit dwells in

you," 3:16, cf. 6:19); 12:4–29 ("Now you are the body of Christ and individually members of it," v.27).

7. 1 Corinthians 1–3, chiding the Corinthians for their divisiveness; 5:1–7, condemning *porneia* within the congregation; 5:11 warnings not to associate "with anyone who bears the name of brother if he is guilty of *porneia*, or greed, or worships idols"; 6:12 again against *porneia*, specifically sex with a prostitute; 10:14–22 more warnings against idolatry; 11:2–16, confused ravings against a perceived breach of etiquette at worship; Galatians 5:19–24, another sin-list (the "works of the flesh"): "those who belong to Christ Jesus have crucified the flesh with its passions and appetites." By Romans, the last letter we have from him, Paul speaks of this desired moral conduct, tellingly, not in terms of "freedom from sin" but as "slavery to righteousness," 6:20–22.

8. On wrath, condemnation, and the destruction of those who will merit it on the Day of the Lord, 1 Corinthians 1:18; 2 Corinthians 2:15, 4:3; Philippians 3:19; cf. Romans 1:18, and the general warning in 1 Corinthians 10:6–12.

9. Sallustius, *Peri Theōn kai Kosmou* ("On the Gods and the World"), 1.

10. All gnostics were dualists, but not all dualists were gnostics. Marcion, a radical Paulinist (*fl.* c. 140), repudiated allegorical interpretation and, thus, the Septuagint, advancing the idea that Christians should have their own, new canon: more on this below. Gnostics such as Valentinus urged an esoteric interpretation on the Septuagint, and composed many charismatic gospels and revelations, as well as commentaries. Given their mutual polarization of spirit/flesh, High (Spiritual) God/Lower(Jewish, Fleshly) God, the christologies of both were necessarily docetic: the divine Son could never be too intimately juxtaposed to something as degenerate as flesh.

11. E.g., most famously, Justin, *Dialogue with Trypho* 29, where Justin, arguing with a Jew, refers to "your Scriptures" and then corrects himself: "rather, not yours, but ours."

12. These theologians were reading documents that Paul had not, namely, gospels that insisted that Jesus had been raised not simply bodily, but with a fleshly body—hence his eating fish in Luke (24:37–43), and forcing Thomas to touch his wounds in John (20:27–29). Paul, as we have seen, held to the redemption of the body, but not of the flesh per se. For Augustine's ingenious resolution to this problem, see below.

13. E.g., Justin, *Trypho* 81, referring specifically to Isaiah 65 and Apoc 20:4–5; Irenaeus, *Adv. Haer.* 5.26.1 and 30,3; Tertullian, *Adv. Marc.* 3. For a brief review of these traditions, P. Fredriksen, "Apocalypse and Redemption. From John of Patmos to Augustine of Hippo," *Vigiliae Christianae* 45.2 (1991): 151–83.

14. This masterwork fell victim to the posthumous controversy that surrounded Origen's theological legacy in the centuries after his death. As a result, the text itself is tattered, the scientific edition in *Griechischen Christlichen*

Schriftsteller (22, ed. P. Koetschau; Leipzig: 1913) a pastiche of various Greek fragments, texts from Justinian and the second Council of Constantinople anathematizing Origen in 553, and an early fifth-century Latin targum by Rufinus composed with an eye toward protecting Origen from the objections his work was already attracting. My observations about his arguments, accordingly, will sometimes be tentative. I draw on G. W. Butterworth's English translation of the Koetschau edition, *On First Principles* (New York: Harper and Row, 1966; orig. pub. 1936).

15. E.g., I.2,2; II.2,2.

16. Origen's opening salvo, I.1,1.

17. In the language of traditional theology (pagan and, eventually, Christian), only God is perfect, hence changeless; contingent beings, by definition, are susceptible of change.

18. "But whereas, by reason of the faculty of free will, variety and diversity had taken hold of individual souls . . . that soul . . . clinging to God from the beginning of the creation and ever after in a union inseperable and indissoluble . . . was made with him in a pre-eminent degree one spirit. . . . It is therefore right that this soul . . . because it received the Son of God wholly into itself, should itself be called . . . the Son of God," II.6,3; also II.8,2.

19. II.1,4–2,2.

20. I.8,1.

21. "[T]his matter, which is so great and wonderful as to be sufficient for all the bodies in the world, . . . God willed to exist, and to be at the call and service of the Creator in all things for the fashioning of whatever forms and species he wished, receiving into itself the qualities which he had willed to bestow upon it," II.1,4. Cf. his discussion in III.1,4, on sexual desire and the fundamental cause (*aitia*) of sin, which is choice.

22. With the exception of the systematic theology, and another important work of anti-pagan apologetic, the *c. Celsum*, virtually all of Origen's huge written legacy directly concerned biblical interpretation, whether to establish a scientific text of the Septuagint (the goal of his work of textual analysis, the *Hexapla*), or to comment on the texts themselves. He wrote on all the books in the OT and NT, sometimes on a vast scale: the commentary on John ran to at least 32 books, 8 of which are extant; on Matthew, 25 books, 8 of which survive; on Romans in 15 books; 13 books on Genesis, 46 on forty-one psalms; 30 on Isaiah, and so on—some 2000 treatises in all, according to Jerome. See the entry in J. Quasten, *Patrology* (Westminster: The Newman Press 1953) 2.37–100.

23. For a review of his work on Paul during this period, P. Fredriksen, "Beyond the Body/Soul Dichotomy: Augustine on Paul against the Manichees and the Pelagians," *Recherches augustiniennes* 23 (1988): 87–111, esp. 89–98.

24. "[Sexual] lust . . . disturbs the whole man. . . . So intense is the pleasure that when it reaches its climax there is an almost total extinction of mental

alertness; the intellectual sentries are, as it were, overwhelmed . . . and sometimes desire cools off in the body while it is at boiling heat in the mind" (XIV.16).

25. A point beautifully invoked in the opening lines of the *Confessions*: "You have made us for yourself, and our heart is restless until it rests in You" (I.1,1).

26. The image, again, from Paul, Romans 9:19–23, on God as the potter and humans as pots.

27. Augustine spells out the details of this argument in the *c. Faustum*. It serves as the foundation for his more summary presentation of the role of Israel in redemption in *civ. Dei* XV–XVIII. On the novelty of this reading of Judaism, and the ways it creatively articulates his own theological program, P. Fredriksen, "*Excaecati occulta iustitia Dei*: Augustine on Jews and Judaism," *Journal of Early Christian Studies* 3 (1995): 299–324; eadem, "*Secundum carnem*: God, history, and Israel in the theology of Augustine," *The Limits of Ancient Christianity. Essays on Late Antique Thought and Culture in honor of R. A. Markus*, ed. W. Klingshirn and Mark Vessey (Ann Arbor: University of Michigan Press, 1999), 26–41.

28. Those of the damned will also be raised fleshly, of course; but will proceed to eternal torment.

29. Hence his interpretation of Romans 8:8–24 taking the *creatura* who groan awaiting redemption as man himself, *Propositiones ex epistula ad Romanos* 53,4.

30. The most recent full study is Peter Brown, *The Body and Society. Men, Women, and Sexual Renunciationin Early Christianity* (New York: Columbia University Press 1990); also extremely valuable, Robin Lane Fox, *Pagans and Christians* (New York: Knopf, 1987), esp. his chapter "Living like Angels." In 1965, E. R. Dodds attempted to use psychoanalytic psychology to understand Christian asceticism, *Pagan and Christian in an Age of Anxiety* (New York: Norton, 1965). Ultimately, the effort fails—the theory necessarily sat loose of the unobliging evidence, and the chronological frame wobbled; but Dodds slim effort (138 pages) in no small part provoked the 1200+ pages of the two books cited above.

31. Eusebius, *Ecclesiastical History* 6.8, for the castration story; Epiphanius, *Panarion* 64.3.11–12, that Origen's remarkable chastity was due to drugs.

32. *Conf.* 6.12,21–15.25; 8:6,13 and passim.

7

The Human Condition in Islam

Sharīʿa and Obligation

S. Nomanul Haq

7.1 Preliminary Reflections

In the field of comparative studies of religions, one frequently comes across explicit scholarly claims that two given religious systems, upon a close comparative analysis, display a remarkable community of ideas and doctrines, and that they are after all not so far apart as they appeared at a first glance. Not so long ago, Ignaz Goldziher received tributes for what was considered to be a happy and rigorous conclusion that Islamic mysticism is nothing but a shadow of Buddhism.[1] More recently, Leo Schaya juxtaposed the two Semitic cousins, Islam and Judaism, and spoke of a very close doctrinal community between their mystical thinking, something that is hardly surprising, and something that has been explored in both general and specific terms by many other scholars before and since.[2] Then, among so many comparative studies, we received Sachiko Murata's painstaking *Tao of Islam*[3] with a glowing foreword written by Annemarie Schimmel—the same well-known author who had earlier, and in the same vein, co-edited a volume entitled, *We Believe in One God: The Experience of God in Christianity and Islam.*[4] In addition, scholars of religion are also familiar with the many writings of W. Cantwell Smith, which fall in the same genre, and such examples can easily be multiplied.

The corpus of contributions in this volume itself provides much happy material for the seeker of doctrinal similarities between Islam and other religious systems, similarities that sometimes appear to lie at such fundamental theoretical level that they tend to render the coinciding regions practically indistinguishable. Take, for example, David Eckel's account of the human condition in Buddhism in which he provides an exposition of the theory of "vision" *(darśana)* in Buddhist philosophy.[5] One would gather from this account that in the Buddhist philosophical system, vision and all its conceptual cognates—seeing, looking, witnessing, etc.—function both as cognitive and experiential categories; and that at the same time they are so central to Buddhist philosophers that their whole system "also goes by the name of vision." Wisdom, we learn, is a form of vision; indeed, "to know is to . . . see."[6] Recall here the Islamic declaration of faith, the very first pillar *(rukn)* of the Muslim creed, which is precisely a declaration of *Shahāda,* known as such in the Islamic tradition—*Kalimat Al-Shahāda*—that is, a declaration of *seeing,* or, alternatively and equivalently, of witnessing, testifying, or having the vision: "*Ashhadu* [I *see,* or, I witness, testify, etc., from the root *SH-H-D*] that there is no deity except Allah, and I *see* [or witness or testify, etc., the same word here] that Muḥammad is His creature and His Apostle." Recall also the Qur'ānic[7] Primordial Covenant: "And when your Lord extracted from the children of Adam . . . their entire progeny and made them *witness* upon themselves [alternatively and legitimately: made them *see* themselves, made them have a *vision* of themselves, etc.], saying, Am I not your Lord? And they replied, No doubt, You are, we bear *witness* [or, we *see,* we have the *vision,* etc.] . . ." (7:172–73).

But the similarity here is even more extensive and deeper, for it would appear that vision is the fundamental ontological category of Islamic religious metaphysics. We note that the Arabic language, of which the Qur'ān became both the historical and literary fountainhead, is inherently barred from rendering the concept of "existence" except by means of the noun *wujūd,* a noun derived morphologically from the verbal root *W-J-D,* which literally means "to find," and this is a cognate of the verb "to see." Thus, to be is to be found, and to be found is to be seen. Ultimately, then: *to be is to be seen.* Vision, therefore, is the primary category of being. And, let me point out, this is not a manufactured analysis unknown in the tradition, for in the Islamic religious literature God is frequently referred to as the *Shāhid* (The One Who sees, witnesses, looks, etc.—again from the root *SH-H-D),* and doctrinal sufi writings abound in discourses on vision, its levels and stations, its typology, its coverings and veils. In our own century the poet-philosopher Iqbal once poignantly implored in supplication:

O, The One Who sees (*Shāhid*),
Render me seen (*mashhūd*)!
By a single glance—
Bring me into being![8]

Note here that, as is the case with Buddhist philosophers, "vision" is functioning both at the cognitive and experiential level; but further: it is functioning at the primary ontological level—to cast a glance is to bestow being.

To illustrate another instance of what I would call "local overlap," let me very briefly take up the case of the human condition in Chinese religion presented in this volume by Livia Kohn. We learn from Kohn that the Chinese view concerning the root of all life is unity-oriented: "All is ultimately One, and the One is manifest in all."[9] And a little later: "Any object or being . . . partakes of the One yet can never be the One itself, which remains formless at the root of creation. Everything thus has always only partial access to the unity of the original, is never fully whole."[10] Again, these assertions can be applied, virtually without any formal adjustments, to Islam. Indeed, "All is He!" and "He is One!" are well-known exclamations of Muslim mystics, and the Qur'ān itself says, "Whithersoever ye turn there is the Face of God" (2:109).[11] Also, as I shall discuss below, a serious and central challenge faced by Muslim theologians and mystics is one of balancing Allah's transcendence against His immanence, for this logical tension arises out of the fundamental Muslim belief that all objects and beings "partake of the One yet can never be the One [Himself]."

Kohn also speaks of the Chinese world as rooted in the One, and the Chinese culture as a "one-centered" (as opposed to "zero-centered") culture. Now even though Islam is monotheistic as opposed to monistic, it is so radically grounded in the principle of *Tauḥīd* (holding God as One), a principle that lies so firmly at the very core of its faith, that Islamic culture may well qualify as a one-centered culture—this is the drift of the declarations, "All is He!" and "He is One!" Finally, there seem to be other regions too where the Chinese and Islamic worlds overlap. One such region lies in the notion of virtue that is, in both cases, largely defined in social terms; another exists in the admission in both systems of human will, namely "the power to think and act in disharmonious ways [for Islam, read: in contravention of *Sharī'a*] . . . [which] sets human beings apart from the rest of creation"; yet another overlap is to be found in the Islamic and Chinese ideas of memory that in both cases defines consciousness, the Islamic term being *dhikr*;[12] and so on.

7.2 Ambiguities in Comparison

But what is the meaning of these kinds of similarities? If we simply state them without further analysis, we have at best told only a part of the larger story; and at worst, what we have stated may not even form a "proper part" of the story; and if, as some scholars and numerous (well-meaning) popular writers do, we draw from these similarities hasty ecumenical conclusions, we have misled our audience: for surely, when considered in its totality, Islam is very different in its fundamental drift both from Buddhism and Chinese religion. The beginning section of Eckel's chapter is highly instructive here, carrying a message that can be summarized in a single sentence—whatever you are looking for with regard to the human condition, you will find it in Buddhism. Indeed, it is in principle possible to show, for example, that in the context of the question of the human condition, Islam shares some of the basic concerns even of the *Vedas;* or to provide evidence that the idea of Christian priestly authority, conceived functionally as a means to make sense of the human condition, is closely akin to the institution of Shīʿī *Imāmate;* or to demonstrate the irony that—and many a writer in the modern period has done just that—in terms of the historical conception of the human condition, Islam has much in common with socialism. In this vein, then, one can say equivalently: whatever you are looking for with regard to the human condition, you will find it in Islam.

Approaches of this kind, though they may bring some delight to us, suffer from a basic flaw in failing to recognize that similar or even identical doctrines or theories or ideas frequently function in altogether different ways in different systems; they have diverse careers in diverse religious environments, generating dissimilar social and moral structures, and giving rise to emotional and intellectual attitudes that are unique to their own respective milieu. Analyzing the notion of "one-centered" cultures, Livia Kohn speaks of some characteristics that such cultures would typically have, using the Chinese example as an illustration.[13] But insofar as Islam too meets the criterion of being one such culture, and I tend to think that in its own way it does, it shares none of these characteristics; nor does it share any of the stated features of "zero-centered" cultures. The fortunes of Islam's one-centeredness are simply different.

Speaking historically, ideas that appear similar to us grow in complex historical soils and turn into tenaciously espoused traditions, so much so that these traditions acquire a life of their own, fully differentiated and practically independent of the primary sources that are the carriers of the original idea. There is no predicting as to how the seed of a given religious doctrine will grow in a given soil, what kind of a social group it will generate, and what will be the nature of its cultural yields. There is no room for essentialism here. The fundamental idea of vision, for example, enjoyed a career in Islam that has little in common with Buddhism; and the vicissitudes of the Muslim one-centeredness generated a society far removed in its characteristics from the Chinese; and an Iranian Ayatollah (*āyat Allah*) today shows little resemblance to a Christian priest. The explanation of all this lies in the intricacies and complexities of the historical process.

Philosophically, this whole question of similarity or dissimilarity of two given bodies of doctrine is highly problematic. Let me once again invoke here the theory of "proper parts."[14] Isolated from the totality of which it forms an integral element, a given idea may appear similar to another idea plucked likewise from another totality. The round button on my shirt looks similar to the round wheel of my car. But then, the function of the button in the system we call "shirt" bears no similarity to the function of the wheel in the automobile system known as "car." Sheer roundness, then, does not, in this specific case, constitute the defining feature of a proper part. The button and the wheel are similar only in isolation, and this is what I call "local similarity (or dissimilarity)." Likewise, for example, just any piece of rubber does not form a proper part of my car; when I go to the auto parts store, I ask for a tire, or a washer, or a tube, not just any piece of rubber. In other words, a proper part is an integral whole in itself, it is a subsystem of a differentiated totality. In comparisons, therefore, we must first examine how two given elements from two given systems function within the system to which they each belong, and whether they each form a proper part of that system; only then will we be in a position to compare them meaningfully.

This does not mean, however, that the similarities between Islam and other religions I have noted above are all necessarily similarities-in-isolation; on the contrary, they appear so remarkable as to hold the promise of being very useful in a comparative study. But to make a categorical judgment one way or another will be seriously premature. My whole point simply is that the task of identifying "proper parts" of religious systems has yet to be done by comparativists, and that the relationship between the corpus of fundamental doctrines (e.g., normative texts) of a religious system and its developed tradition (beliefs, creed, rituals, etc.) still awaits a thorough historical investigation in a comparative perspective. And this is precisely what, as I understand it, the Comparative Religious Ideas Project promises to do.

7.3 The Human Condition in Islam

Robert Neville's learned search for comparative categories is effectively a search for what I have been calling proper parts, and his conception of vagueness and generality of these categories, among so many of their other features he conceives and articulates, promises in effect to ensure a degree of flexibility in our category choice so that in the process of comparative analysis they can, without breaking down, absorb the variegated historical development they have undergone in various cultures—in other words, the aim is to avoid essentialist explanations and historical emptiness. It is this understanding of mine that constitutes the methodological framework of my own approach.

7.3.1 *Obligation*

Neville's formulations, "Human condition is to live under obligation," and, "To be human is to lie under obligation"[15]—these have worked rather well in the case of Islam. To be sure, it has appeared that these formulations have, in terms of their vagueness and generality, sufficient explanatory power to give a degree of coherence to certain apparently disparate core doctrines of the Islamic faith as these doctrines appear in normative texts, the Qur'ān here being the supreme one. But more than that, these specific formulations seem to be such as to remain perfectly intelligible to the believer, hence they hold the promise for a cross-cultural comparison that is not only text-sensitive but one that is also tradition-sensitive. But let me now turn to a closer analysis.

7.3.2 *History and the Moral Order*

The Islamic notion of obligation is one that makes little sense if viewed in isolation from the Qur'ān's cosmic concept of history—history here meaning the arena of real life, that which has a temporal beginning and end, that in which natural phenomena unfold themselves with regularity, that in which human relations make their manifestations. The Qur'ān tells us that the purpose of the creation of humanity, indeed of the entire cosmos, is to bring about through God's guidance a moral order *here on earth,* that is, a moral order in history. Thus, the exit—exit or separation, not fall—of Adam from the Garden is ontologically equivalent to the creation of history.

The moral order of which the Qur'ān speaks exists in the non-human world solely through Allah's *amr*—the divine command that is the fundamental constitutive principle of each created entity, placing it under obligation to take its assigned place in the larger cosmic whole. This *amr* bestows upon the world of phenomena a "nature" (*ṭabīʿa,* functionally identical with but metaphysically distinct from Aristotle's φύσις) or, as most Muslim theologians would prefer to characterize it, a "custom" (*ʿāda,* a notion that explicitly denies the principle of natural causation precisely as Hume did) that is never violated.[16] In the human world, on the other hand, the moral order *ought to* come about, again *here on earth,* by the fulfillment of the human obligation: the obligation, namely, of observing Allah's Law (*Sharīʿa).* But a violation of *Sharīʿa* is possible, for human beings have free will, and it is this human freedom that provides the moral and logical scope for Allah's Justice—that is, the scope for ultimate reward or punishment at the end of history. And in this context emerges the Qurʾānic eschatology.

The Qurʾān bestows a historical reality both to nature and to humankind, and places them both under obligation that they are commanded to carry out in the *real world*—the former existing without the faculty of will and thus bearing no moral onus, and therefore meriting neither reward nor punishment; while the latter endowed with the ability to choose and therefore being morally liable. In other words, the *amr* of nature is the obligation to observe the created Law of Nature (*ṭabīʿa* or *ʿāda),* and the *amr* of humankind is the obligation to observe the Law of God (*Sharīʿa)—amr* being the *fundamental* constitutive principle of every created thing. Thus, it would be in keeping with the Islamic doctrine to say that to be human is to lie under obligation.

7.3.3 *Sharīʿa and Fiqh*

But what is the precise nature of *Sharīʿa* that humankind is under obligation to observe? And, more fundamentally, what is the ultimate source of *Sharīʿa?* Indeed, the search for, and the articulation, systematization, and codification of *Sharīʿa*—this whole process being designated as *fiqh* (literally, "understanding")—occupies the center stage in the development of the Islamic religious tradition. To be sure, the *summum bonum* of Islamic intellectual output lies precisely in the field of *fiqh,* a field most frequently referred to in Western literature as Islamic Law or Islamic Jurisprudence. This discipline saw such great giants, and became so all-embracing, that it became the articulation of the whole of Islam *as a function.*[17]

It should be noted that *Sharīʿa* and *fiqh* are conceptually distinct: the former is the moral imperative that remains after God's entry into history through Revelation; the latter is, as indicated before, the *process* of understanding this moral imperative.[18] But, as things developed historically, it so happened that *Sharīʿa* became practically identified with the *products* of *fiqh*. Thus after the formative period of the Islamic religious tradition (seventh to tenth century), *Sharīʿa* has been understood to be the codified corpus of juristic material written by (or issuing forth from) the masters of *fiqh,* this material including in its scope legal formulations, definitions, and corpora of legislation that, in principle, cover the entire range of human conduct—private, public, individual, social, domestic, personal; specifying rules ranging from those governing the use of a toothpick to those governing the performance of Hajj; from rules for clipping nails and cutting hair to contract law and state taxation codes. This grand body of Islamic law can legitimately be described as the outcome of the Muslim search for a functional understanding and codification of obligation.[19]

Note here that in the context of *Sharīʿa* we have to view obligation in functional terms, thereby giving this category a more defined, practical dimension. The aim of *fiqh,* human understanding, is none other than to concretize obligation—that is, to translate *amr* into *aḥkām* (legislative commands, rulings, statutes), and these *aḥkām* tentatively constitute the substance of *Sharīʿa*. I say "tentatively" because the dominating Islamic position on the issue is that *aḥkām,* even though they must be derived through correct procedure, are nevertheless products of a human effort which is subject to error; therefore, *fiqh*-laws remain epistemologically suspect and yet, until replaced by a better *fiqh,* they are legally binding on each and every Muslim.[20]

Aḥkām that *fiqh* yields are not, it should be noted, merely a corpus of proscriptions or penal codes; rather they constitute primarily a blueprint of Muslim life, and they embody a hierarchy and a taxonomy that is considered to comprehend every conceivable human conduct. Thus all human acts fall into one or the other of five classes: *farḍ* (obligatory), *ḥarām* (forbidden), *mubāḥ* (permitted), *mustaḥabb* (encouraged), and *makrūh* (discouraged). This is the whole of Islam in *functional* terms.

7.4 Allah, the Ultimate Source of *Sharīʿa*: Monotheism and the Creator-Created Duality

The principle of *Tauḥād,* as I have already indicated, constitutes the very pivot of Islam, a principle that makes this Abrahamic religion *radically* monotheist. Allah, in Himself, and nothing other than He, is the ultimate source of *Sharīʿa* that humanity is under obligation to follow. And Allah, and nothing other than He, is God, the Creator; all else is created by Him. There can be no compromise here. Indeed, the very first pillar of Islam, the *Shahāda,* is nothing but a resounding declaration of this very belief: "I testify [or see] that there is no deity except Allah and I testify [or see] that Muḥammad is his creature and messenger." Let us analyze this primary Muslim testimony.

The testimony begins with an uncompromising negation of all deities except Allah—the particle of negation here being *lā,* described by philologists as the universal or emphatic negation, as compared to other particles of negation that do exist in the Arabic language. In the second half, the *Shahāda* declares the entry of God into history through His revelations brought by His messengers—Muḥammad is one such messenger who conveys God's message, His *Sharīʿa,* to humanity. But then, a fundamental point to note is that the messenger is here explicitly declared only to be a *creature* of God, without any divine attributes or divine authority. Manifesting the radical monotheistic thrust of Islam, this first Muslim step of faith is one that embodies a strict commitment to the principle of Creator-created duality—that is, the principle of divine-human disjunction.

The Prophet, even though he received God's *Sharīʿa* by means of direct divine revelation, remained human in every way, that is, his existence is historical not transcendental. God's messengers are no gods; like every other human being they lie under the same obligation to follow *Sharīʿa.* On the other hand, God's entry into history consists solely in Revelation; God's substance or His essence (*Dhāt*) does not make a manifestation in this natural world—that is, God remains transcendental. A profoundly revealing characteristic of the Muslim formula of faith is that it at once links and separates the transcendental and the historical. The first half of the formula testifies to something transcendental ("There is no deity except . . ."), the second half to something historical (Muḥammad is His creature . . ."); the first has to do with the singular uniqueness of the Creator, the second concerns a created being who is a member of the bountiful plurality of creatures. But then, the two halves of the formula are conjoined by the linking "and," and further, the first half is semantically and inextricably linked to the second by the possessive "His." Indeed, for Muslims the *Shahāda* does not admit of any divisions, it is one integral whole; any separation of the two of its (grammatically) complete sentences has to be for the purposes of analysis only.

7.4.1 *The Disjunction between God and Other-than-God: Shirk*

But this analysis throws into bold relief many fundamental features of a wide range of Islamic doctrines, explaining also the drift of the historical development of the Islamic tradition. It explains, for example, why *shirk* (associating other-than-God with God/admitting any deity except Allah) is *the* cardinal sin in Islam—the Qur'ān is full of wrathful condemnation of *shirk;* indeed, in terms of its frequency, intensity, and rhetorical force, there exists hardly any theme in the Qur'ān that matches *shirk*. In one of the relatively well-known Qur'ānic chapters that evidently addresses Christian Trinitarians, a chapter significantly called "Purity [of Faith]," the matter is dealt with in no uncertain terms:

> Say: He is God,
> The One and Only;
> God, the Eternal, Absolute;
> He begetteth not,
> Nor is He begotten;
> And there is none
> Like unto Him.
> (112:1–4, A)

7.4.2 *Qur'ān: Created or Eternal?*

And as for the Islamic *tradition,* one finds in it what may be described as an obsession with *shirk,* an attitude manifesting itself throughout Islamic religious literature, constituting the central and burning preoccupation of all Muslim theologians. Indeed, it may strike one as curious that the two schools of Muslim theologians are divided primarily on the issue of the createdness of the Qur'ān, the famous and historically scandalous issue of *Khalq al-Qur'ān:* is the Qur'ān a creature of God? Or is it coeternal with God? The earlier of the two schools, the Muʿtazilite, made it its fundamental theological project to demonstrate that the Qur'ān—even the Qur'ān, the Word of God (*Kalām Allah*)—is only a creature of God, and does not share His essential attributes of being eternal and absolute. But in the context, this makes sense, for the Muʿtazilites were concerned that otherwise the Book will become another deity, besides God, and this will amount to *shirk*. Of course the ultimate source of *Sharīʿa* was the One Eternal God; admitting a plurality of deities would mean a plurality of the sources of *Sharīʿa,* besides creating the metaphysical problem of having to admit a plurality of eternals. No wonder that these Muʿtazilites branded themselves *Ahl al-Tauḥīd* (The Espousers of the Oneness of God).[21]

Given the text of the Qur'ān, a thoroughgoing monotheism gives rise to its own inner tensions and rational challenges; then, this whole issue has contingent historical dimensions too. It seems highly probable that the early Muslim theological focus on the issue of the Word of God has much to do with Islam's encounter with Christianity. Recall that in the

Gospel According to John, God is identified with the Word (λογος), the Word Which "became flesh and resided among us" (1:14)—that is, manifested Itself in history. The Qur'ān too refers to Jesus as the Word:

> Behold! the angels said:
> "O Mary! God giveth thee
> Glad tidings of a Word
> From Him: his name
> Will be Christ Jesus . . ."
>
> (3:45, A)

But, then, it quickly dismisses any claims of divine status for Jesus:

> Christ Jesus the son of Mary
> Was only
> An apostle of God
> And His Word,
> Which He bestowed on Mary,
> And a Spirit proceeding
> From Him: so believe
> In God and His apostles,
> Say not "Trinity": desist:
> It will be better for you:
> For God is One God. . . .
>
> (4: 171, A)

To be sure, if the Word of God is admitted to be a divine *substance*, then it is coeternal with God; and therefore if Jesus is the Word of God—as the Qur'ān itself says—then Jesus too is coeternal with God, participating in Godhead. But this was *shirk*, pure and simple, introducing a multiplicity of the sources of *Sharī'a*, and obliterating the divine-human disjunction.[22] Given all this, it is hardly surprising that there grew in the Islamic tradition an enormous and impressively sophisticated body of theological, metaphysical, philological, and polemical literature on Word (*Kalima*, from the root *K-L-M)*; in fact, the whole discipline of Islamic theology was called *'Ilm al-Kalām* (Science of Speech) or simply *Kalām* (Speech, from the same root), and theologians were designated by an active participle derived morphologically again from the same root, *mutakallimūn* (sing. *mutakallim)*, doer of *Kalām*.[23]

7.4.2.1 *The Mu'tazilite Position*

The Mu'tazilite position on this issue is that the Word of God, here specifically meaning the Qur'ān, is an accident (*'araḍ*, in Aristotle's sense);

like every word, it is made up of "letters serially arranged and sounds separately articulated," which God creates in one or other corporeal framework. And once God has created a word in a certain body, it is this body that would be the agency of speaking as a result. But, then, the speaker is not "he in whom the word resides, but he who produces the word."[24] The Qur'ān does the "speaking" by means of the ink that embodies its words, and the surface on which it is written; or by means of the phonetic articulation of sounds; and these are all accidents. By virtue of this reasoning, the divinity of the Qur'ān is dismissed, just as that of Jesus is dismissed. For the Mu'tazilites the expression "Word of God" signified that God created in contingent beings words and phrases so that He could communicate in the historical world His *Sharīʿa* which humanity is under obligation to follow.

7.4.2.2 *The Ashʿarite Position*

The opposing school of Muslim theologians, the Ashʿarite, rejects the theory of the createdness of the Qur'ān. But while the Ashʿarites do affirm that the Word of God is coeternal with God, they nevertheless manufacture a device to save themselves from having to admit that the physical body of the Qur'ān, written or vocally enunciated, is eternal—for again, this would be *shirk*. Thus they distinguish between the Word subsisting in the divine Essence, which is without speech, and its expression by means of letters or sounds in a corporeal body. It is the former that is eternal by virtue of being a divine attribute—a *disposition* of God, though not a separate divine *substance*. The latter is created and contingent.[25]

But then the question is: If the Qur'ān, as we have it, is not eternal but contingent, then why it is to be followed for all times to come? And if the Qur'ān is to be followed, then why are God's other revelations, the Torah and the Evangel, for example, not being followed? The standard answer is that the Qur'ān supersedes all the earlier revelations, and comprehends all earlier revelations, just as a tree supersedes the seed from which it grows, and comprehends within itself the principle of the seed. Besides, the earlier scriptures were extant only in a corrupt form, for God never promised to preserve them as he had done in the case of the Qur'ān, his final message. Note Islam's evolutionary view of God's revelation, but evolutionary in the teleological sense not the Darwinian one.

As for the question of non-eternity of the corporeal body of the Qur'ān, the standard resolution in the mature Islamic tradition is that the Book is the appearance in history of the (final) Message of God, and though its written letters and enunciated sounds are not eternal substances, they are nevertheless an immutable and unique carrier of something eternal; for

God's Message is indeed eternal, being an attribute of God. This carrier—the Qur'ān in its corporeal form—will lead to an understanding of the *Sharīʿa,* if only human beings would seek it sincerely according to their *fiṭra* (primordial nature), if only they would seek it sincerely and truthfully, if only they would reflect and ponder. Here enters the Qur'ānic doctrine of human effort—human beings *ought to* follow God's *amr*; and this is the whole meaning of the moral burden of humanity:

> [I swear] by man's personality and that whereby it has been formed, God has engraved into it its evil and its good. He who makes [an effort to render] his personality pure, shall be successful, while who corrupts it shall be in loss. (91:7–10, Re)

Success of the human effort is guaranteed because good has been engraved into the human soul. And furthermore, there exists a Primordial Covenant between God and human beings:

> And when your Lord extracted from the children of Adam—from their spinal cord—their entire progeny and made them witness upon themselves [or made them see themselves], saying, Am I not your Lord? and they replied, No doubt You are, we bear witness [or we see]. [The Lord did this] lest you say on the Day of Judgment, We were quite unaware of this, or lest you should say, All that happened was that our forefathers had committed *shirk.* . . . (7:172–73, Re)

In this covenant lies the Islamic theory of human conscience.

7.5 Maintaining the God-Human Disjunction

The Islamic doctrine of God-human disjunction has not always been easy to maintain. The Qur'ān no doubt speaks strongly and abundantly about God's transcendence, but it also says, and says it more than once, that after fashioning human beings God breathed "My own spirit" into them (15:29; 38:72; 32:9); and also that God is nearer to humans than their "jugular vein" (50:16); and that, as we have already seen, whithersoever we turn "there is the Face of God." This gives rise to a tension that has exercised many a religious thinker and all Muslim mystics. God is, then, at once transcendental and immanent. To be sure, there can be no obliteration of the divine-human divide, for this would be the obliteration of *Sharīʿa:* for if the Commander and the commanded are fused (the technical term here being *ḥulūl,* the dissolution of one into the other), then neither the commanded remains nor the Commander, nor indeed the Command. And yet, God is within every human being, for we all carry God's very spirit.

Those sufi-mystics who have felt God's presence in the depth of their being have even slipped into pantheism and monism. In referring to Chinese religion I had pointed out the standard sufi axiom that one can partake of the One, that is, one can—and should strive to—develop in oneself God's attributes, but one can never become the One or fuse into the One. In fact, the fundamental challenge of all sufi theory is precisely that of balancing God's immanence against His transcendence; and sufis have dealt with this tension most creatively. But not all of them could contain themselves at the delicate threshold; many of them lapsed, and some of them suffered a tragic end. Bāyazīd of Bisṭām had cried, "Glory be to me!" He has been called a sufferer of theopathy (*shaṭḥ*). The fate of the grand sufi al-Ḥallāj is known to us: in his rapture, he had ecstatically declared, "I am the Truth," and he was mercilessly executed in 922. Among other things, al-Ḥallāj was accused of *shirk*. The Andalusian mystic Ibn al-ʿArabā was charged with the transgression of *waḥdat al-wujūd* (ontological monism), and he has been bitterly condemned ever since.[26] These sufis had relaxed the tension.

The Qurʾān-based tradition of the Prophet's Ascension (*Miʿrāj)* is particularly relevant here. Tradition has it that he ascended through the seven heavenly spheres into the company of God, and he was only two "bow-lengths" away from God, or even nearer; but he did not look at God, he only saw His signs—and he returned back to the earth:

> While he was in
> The highest part
> of the horizon:
> Then he approached
> And came closer,
> And he was at a distance
> of two bow-lengths
> Or [even] nearer
> . . .
> His sight swerved not
> Nor did it go wrong!
> For truly did he see,
> Of the Signs of his Lord,
> The Greatest!
> (53:7–18, Ae)

This return of the Prophet is considered in the Islamic tradition to signify a fundamental prophetic message that has both moral and ontological dimensions: the Lord-servant duality must be maintained; and the obliteration of this duality is a metaphysical impossibility; and this is the whole logic of the human condition. Even Ḥallāj had been at pains not to blur the Creator-created nexus, something his political enemies refused to recognize.

7.6 The Linkage of the Transcendental with the Historical

But the transcendental God of Islam does operate on a historical plane. Thus the exit of Adam to the earth was not essentially a punishment for some kind of an Original Sin: God had planned to send him down even before creating him—"I am going to create a *khalīfa* (vicegerent) *on earth*" (Qur'ān, 2:30). The human exit from the Garden, then, was an ontological phenomenon, akin to natural birth—a baby coming out of a mother's womb, a bird breaking out of an egg, or a bud sprouting forth from a branch. Indeed, like nature, Adam had to evolve, morally, spiritually, intellectually—just as a baby grows into adulthood, and a seed grows into a lofty tree.

This explains why the human condition in Islam does not consist in a process of recovery from a fall, and thereby regaining some original glory; it consists rather in perpetually fulfilling a set of obligations, "to enjoin good and dismiss evil," and while fulfilling its obligations humanity reaches ever new glories. To be sure, both good and evil were provided in the world, and humanity had been placed in a state of moral tension; but this was a creative tension, for in order to avoid the ever present evil, humanity had to keep harking back to, and supplicating for the succor of, God—and this struggle kept intact a transcendental moral anchorage in human life. In fact, it is this very struggle wherein lay the unfolding of humankind's moral, spiritual, and intellectual potential. Note here that, like good, evil too is deemed to be serving a divine purpose; and it is for this reason that the image of Satan (Iblīs) in Islam is one that arouses sympathy, not condemnation, particularly among sufi circles.[27]

The linkage of the transcendental to the historical also explains two more fundamental attitudes of Islam. First, the Islamic attitude to nature. Nature is real; it is God's creation like everything other-than-God; nature is good since it follows God's *amr* without the possibility ever of violating it. Natural phenomena are God's *āyāt* (sing. *āya,* signs), and this is the same word that designates Qur'ānic verses, so there is a kind of significant equivalence between nature and the Word of God. The Qur'ān, of course, is full of references to natural phenomena—rains, clouds, stars, pearls, thunder, afternoon, dawn, dusk, the sun and the moon, trees, gardens and orchards, and so on. Indeed, man is a natural creation: in what is believed to be the very first revelation to the Prophet, the Qur'ān says:

> Recite!
> In the name of thy Lord
> Who created;
> Created the human being, out of
> A clot of congealed blood
> (96:1–2)

The other fundamental Islamic attitude explained by the transcendental-historical linkage is that which exits toward history and historical forces. Islam admitted no secular-religious dichotomy, no sacred-profane opposition, no mind-body problem. If history is the arena of divine activity, then historical forces must be exploited to achieve a moral end—hence a justification for *jihād*. It is most important to keep in mind that the whole notion of prophethood in Islam manifests a transcendental-historical linkage: prophethood has two elements—revelation (the transcendental element), and success in establishing a socioeconomic community *here on earth* (the historical element). A prophet, then, is practically *duty bound* to succeed in history. A hermit, pious as this individual may be, cannot be a prophet in the Islamic sense. As Rahman put it:

> A God to whom it is, in the final analysis, indifferent whether He is effective in history or not is certainly not the God of Muḥammad and the Qur'ān.[28]

And further:

> The Islamic purpose must be achieved, as an absolute imperative, and for this not only preaching but the harnessing of social and political forces is necessary. This is precisely why the Medinese career of the Prophet [during which the Islamic state was born], far from being a compromise of Islam with politics, is an inevitable fulfillment of Muḥammad's Prophethood.[29]

These attitudes are not only peculiarly Islamic, they have also, as a matter of historical fact, clashed with those of other faiths.

It seems to me, then, that obligation is a very promising comparative category in the Islamic case. It appears to be a "proper part," and by being able to trace through this category the core doctrines and their historical career in Islam, I hope I have been able to provide some groundwork for a thorough comparative analysis.

Notes

I would like to thank Celeste Sullivan, a doctoral student in anthropology at Brown University, for her help on this chapter.

1. See, for example, T. Duka, "The Influence of Buddhism upon Islam," *Journal of the Royal Asiatic Society of Great Britain and Ireland* (January 1904): 125–41.
2. L. Schaya, "Contemplation and Action in Judaism and Islam," *Contemplation and Action in World Religions*, ed. Y. Ibish and I. Marculescu (Seattle: University of Washington Press, 1977). A representative example of earlier studies of this kind is Abraham Katsh's *Judaism and the Qur'ān* (New York: Barnes and Company, 1954). For relatively recent works see, for example, K. Cragg, *The Privilege of Man: A Theme in Judaism, Islam and Christianity* (London: University of London Press, 1968); F. E. Peters, *Judaism, Christianity and Islam: The Classical Texts and their Interpretation.* (Princeton: Princeton University Press, 1990).
3. S. Murata, *The Tao of Islam* (Albany: State University of New York Press, 1992).
4. Co-edited with F. Abdoldjavad (New York: The Seabury Press, 1979).
5. See Eckel's discussion in chapter 3, esp. 3.3.
6. Ibid.
7. In citing the Qur'ān in this chapter, I have used several sources of translation indicated by standardized abbreviations after the specification of chapter and verse. Thus, A = A. Y. Ali. *The Holy Qur'ān* (Brentwood, Md.: Amana Corporation, 1983); Ae = Ali emended by me; R = F. Rahman. *Major Themes of the Qur'ān* (Minneapolis: Bibliotheca Islamica, 1980); Re = Rahman emended by me. When no source is specified, the translations are mine. All dates are specified in the Common Era (CE).
8. *Kulliyāt-i Iqbal (Farsi)* (Lahore: Ghulam Ali Publishers, 1973).
9. See Kohn, 2.2.
10. Ibid.
11. For a scholarly survey of the Islamic mystical tradition see A. Schimmel, *Mystical Dimensions of Islam* (Chapel Hill: University of North Carolina Press, 1975).
12. See "Dhikr," *s.v. Encyclopaedia of Islam, New Edition*, ed. H. A. R. Gibb, et al. (Leiden: E. J. Brill, 1954–).
13. Kohn, 2.2.
14. I am grateful to Professor A. I. Sabra for inspiring guidance here.

15. Robert C. Neville, *Normative Cultures* (Albany: State University of New York Press, 1995), 143.

16. For a fuller discussion of the Islamic theological problem of causality, see my "Ṭabī'a," *s.v. Encyclopaedia of Islam.*

17. A highly learned elucidation of the notion of *Sharī'a* is F. Rahman's chapter under this title in his *Islam* (Chicago: University of Chicago Press, 1979).

18. I must acknowledge that here I draw heavily upon Kevin Reinhart's excellent article, "Islamic Law as Islamic Ethics," *Journal of Religious Ethics* 11.2 (1983): 186–203. The usual disclaimers of course apply.

19. Sunni Muslims, the vast majority in the Islamic world, belong to one or the other of the four schools of law named after their masters: Abū Ḥanīfa, d. 767 (Ḥanafī school); Mālik ibn Anas, d. 795 (Mālikī school); al-Shāfi'ī, d. 820 (Shāfi'ī school); and Ibn Ḥanbal, d. 855 (Ḥanbalī school).

20. Cf. Reinhart, op. cit.

21. In recent years there has been a revival of scholarly interest in Islamic theology. For specialized studies the reader should consult the works of, for example, R. Frank and J. van Ess. For an introductory survey the standard work still is W. M. Watt's *Islamic Philosophy and Theology* (Edinburgh: Edinburgh University Press, 1962).

22. See A. H. Mathias Zahniser. "The Word of God and the Apostleship of 'Īsā [Jesus]: A Narrative Analysis of Āl Imrān (3): 33–62," *Journal of Semitic Studies* 37.1 (Spring 1991): 77–107.

23. Scholarly introductions to these aspects of the Islamic intellectual tradition are to be found in "Kalām" and "'Ilm al-Kalām," *s.v. Encyclopaedia of Islam.*

24. qu. D. Gimaret in his "Mu'tazila," *s.v. Encyclopaedia of Islam,* 788.

25. Cf. Gimaret, op. cit.

26. Cf. Schimmel, op. cit. For superb studies on al-Hallāj, see the writings of L. Massignon, which are still unsurpassed. For an introductory account of the life and doctrines of al-Ḥallāj see my introduction in *Dīvān-i Ḥallāj* (M. Iqbal tr. Karchi: Maktaba-i Daniyal, 1997).

27. On Iblis, see P. Awn *Satan's Tragedy and Redemption: Ibīls in Sufi Psychology* (New York: Columbia University Press, 1987). An incisive analysis of course exists in L. Massignon, *La Passion de Husayn Ibn Mansūr al-Hallāj,* 4 vols. (Paris: Gallimard, 1975).

28. Rahman, op. cit., 21.

29. Ibid., 22.

8

Comparative Hypotheses

Cosmological Categories for the Human Condition

Robert Cummings Neville
with Wesley J. Wildman

8.1 Introduction

Our concluding hypotheses are prefaced by some preliminary remarks that are both explanatory and evaluative in character. We begin by summarizing and evaluating the main lines of argument that we have been prosecuting and end by explaining the organization of our concluding chapters. In between we take stock of our project's progress and explain the limitations on our results.

8.1.1 Three Lines of Argument

This chapter and the next aim to conclude three lines of argument that have run throughout this book. First, and most fundamentally, our project has been conducted in the name of a particular theory of comparison. This understanding of comparison grounded the seminar discussions during the year devoted to the human condition; it is described in the preface, introduction, and first chapter, and is examined from many different angles in *Ultimate Realities*, chapter 8. Its implication in the actual discussion is analyzed in Wildman's Appendix A and it has influenced the purpose and presentation of the specialists' work presented in chapters 2–7. The theory of comparison defines the essential connection between those specialists' chapters and these conclusions. Chapters 8 and 9 aim to consolidate our argument on behalf of this theory of comparison by explicitly enacting the dialectic of vagueness and specificity that relates our hypothetical comparative categories and the religious phenomena analyzed in this book. The structure of these chapters, described later, reflects this goal.

Second, we have proposed a categorical scheme for facilitating comparison between the six religious traditions we have examined. Other schemes might have worked as well, as we have said in the preface, especially in view of the dynamic way that schemes are understood within the operative theory of comparison. Nevertheless, these concluding chapters aim to confirm the usefulness of the scheme we have adopted in two ways. On the one hand, the scheme registers many of the comparisons that are well established in the extant literature on comparative religion; if those comparisons seem obvious to our readers, then so much the better for our case. On the other hand, the scheme's categories permit new comparative hypotheses, interesting paths of comparison that have not already been well traveled.

Third, we are trying to make comparisons between the ways the human condition is viewed in a number of texts and subtraditions of the six religious traditions we have chosen. At this level our argument is twofold: that the comparisons we are making are important ones and that the comparative judgments they express are true. It is especially at this level that our comparative hypotheses are sometimes quite tentative. But since our goal in this book is not to present definitive comparisons but rather a snapshot of an ongoing, self-correcting process of comparison, we boldly take the risk of describing in this volume where we have come after one year. Our subsequent work has already taken us much further, resulting in corrections to what we present here. But that is a topic for future volumes.

8.1.2 Evaluating the First Year of the Project

Chapters 8 and 9 present an opportunity for us to evaluate in public how far we have come in establishing our three lines of argument. And what is the executive summary of the progress report? In brief, we are confident that the theory of comparison has been strongly confirmed by our work. We are relatively less confident about the value of our scheme of categories but still pleased with how it has handled and been enriched by the data and tests to which we have exposed it. And we are simultaneously delighted and anxious about the specific comparisons we have advanced.

It is at this point especially that our work is most clearly in its early stages. The reasons for this ambivalence with regard to the specific comparative hypotheses we make here need to be described in some detail and much of this introductory section will be given over to that purpose. Those partly evaluative and partly explanatory remarks also will serve to orient readers who plan to read this book backwards, though we strongly advise against that approach to trying to understand what we are up to in this project.

We have said that the examinations made in chapters 2–7 are highly selective. And we are aware that every one of the comparative hypotheses we suggest here can be shown to allow exceptions. Sometimes it has seemed that any comparative judgment can be put to death by a thousand qualifications. Nevertheless, however tentative and needy of further nuance, the hypotheses we can propose about the six religions' ideas about the human condition are broad in their sweep and suggestive in their indications for further study. They have the authority of having arisen from the project and are hence ready for correction. They are a particular constructive phase in the dialectic of comparison. To be more precise, they reflect much development of the comparative categories on the one hand, and much analysis of different ways of specifying the categories on the other, acknowledging that future study might correct both the categories and how we specify them.

In constructing our hypotheses we have often moved far from the terms of earlier discussion. In fact, none of the previous chapters has much sustained discussion of how to shape the categories or how the specifications differ from one another and these concluding chapters have more sweeping generalizations than the seminar had hoped. We recognize that this expresses the seminar's experience of a painfully steep learning curve as we tried to master the skills necessary to work the dialectic of vagueness and specificity. Specialists had to learn to make comparisons and to be explicit about the categories presupposed in those comparisons. Generalists had to learn to slow down and pay attention to details. Graduate students got to watch and contribute to this process of mutual retraining, learning how to do it themselves. We moved a long way in these regards in the first year and have come still further since that time. But we clearly recognize that the distance between our comparative hypotheses and the terms of earlier chapters expresses the level of our corporate skill at an early stage.

8.1.3 *Selectivity of the Study*

Our hypotheses are vulnerable to correction and improvement in several ways. The most obvious kind of vulnerability is that our own project might falsify them. Are the comparisons proposed made impossible by material contained in chapters 2–7? Or is there other evidence that would sustain them? In principle, everything said in chapters 2–7 should be interpretable as either specifications or vaguer categorizations of the comparative judgments proposed here. The most important kind of vulnerability is that the judgments we propose need to be sustained (or reformed) by the careful treatment of many texts, motifs, and traditions other than those studied in this book. So it is important here to rehearse the selectivity of our study and the diversity of our approaches.

Each of the religions has been approached on the one hand in terms of some of its ancient core texts and motifs about the human condition, and on the other hand in terms of certain later key texts interpreting those more ancient elements. Our judgments about both elements are provisional on being sustained when the core texts and motifs and the selected key texts are further interpreted from other angles. Every one of the specialists, with the possible exception of Haq in chapter 7, approaches his or her subject with the deliberate intent to confound expected comparisons as reflecting the bias of Western conceptions of religions. This is precisely what makes these comparisons good test cases for the comparative method, even if they give rise to unusual representations of the religious traditions.

So, Kohn more than the others provides general representations of Chinese religions, and from a predominantly Daoist point of view, with muted presentations of Confucianism or Chinese Buddhism. The texts she examines in detail are not the familiar ancient Daoist classics but medieval Daoist practical treatises. Moreover, more than the other authors she presents her general representations as core motifs rather than core texts.

Eckel begins with the Buddha's Four Noble Truths but moves quickly to a scholastic sixth-century text by Bhāvaviveka from Nāgārjuna's Madhyamaka school, emphasizing a kind of epistemological middle way between plain reference and subjectively determined fancy, all controlled by soteriological motives. This selective emphasis thus subordinates, perhaps even denies, such cosmological themes as karma, Buddha-worlds, world-ages, and the Pure Land that many assume are typical Buddhist affirmations. In the particular Buddhist line that Eckel pursues (and others as well), such "affirmation" is problematized. The comparative judgments made in the present chapter about Buddhism deal with that line's representation of it, not the more customary and expected cosmological views, except as noted.

Clooney is the least ready of our specialists to make general representations of Hinduism. Although he cites core pan-Hindu texts such as the Vedas, Upaniṣads, and the *Bhagavad Gītā*, he does so rather strictly from the standpoint of the special development of Advaita Vedānta in the *Vivekacūḍāmaṇi.* It was difficult to decide whether to call the present comparative hypotheses about his contribution "Hinduism," "Advaita Vedānta," or the "Position of the *Vivekacūḍāmaṇi*"; much of what he writes cannot be generalized to Advaita, let alone Hinduism. This is not being picky: what Western scholar would let Origin, Augustine, Aquinas, or Luther speak without qualification for Christianity? Chapter 4 illustrates quite sharply our thesis that the identity of religious intellectual traditions does not reside in a general essence but in core texts and motifs *variously* interpreted and deployed by layers of subsequent, often divergent, developments. Regarding titles nevertheless, in parity with the other traditions we keep the general designation, "Hinduism," with reminders to look closely at our text to see how far the comparative judgments extend in that tradition. Comparative judgments are always vulnerable with respect to how far they extend; most of the comparative judgments here concerning Hinduism are vague with respect to Advaita Vedānta and the particular brand of the *Vivekacūḍāmaṇi,* using the latter to illustrate points with wider application.

Saldarini sets his generalizations about Judaism in the context of an historical discussion of the emergence of Judaism as we know it from its early Second Temple form. He says little about the main core text, the *Torah,* especially the story of Adam and Eve in Genesis, but lays out his historical account of Judaism by an examination of a sequence of interpretations of that core. He make no claim to a complete history. Alone among the authors, however, he provides a review of the contemporary state of that historical trajectory in light of the Holocaust.

Fredriksen begins with the note that Christianity is another form of Second Temple Judaism, focuses on what Paul's Jesus is supposed to fix in redeeming the human condition, and then filters her interpretation of the historical development of Christian thought on the human condition through the problem of the "flesh" versus soul or spirit in the controversies over docetism and the writings of Origen and Augustine. Because so much recent Christian thought since Bultmann and Tillich has been anti-dualistic, this identification of Christian ideas about the human condition with the body-soul dualism might seem to many in our time to miss the point of Christianity, to be focusing on what has become a side issue. But that is just Fredriksen's purpose, to make Christianity strange to our modern Western eyes. And, after all, Bultmann and Tillich did not live in late antiquity: Paul, Origen, and Augustine did, and they were heavily focused on the problems of the flesh-spirit identity. Our comparative judgments here accept that late antique focus and have not been applied to modern anti-dualistic (or modern dualistic) positions. We (Neville and

Wildman) offer an interpretation of the divergence of the two forms of Second Temple Judaism, Christianity and rabbinic Judaism, that is not found in chapters 5 or 6.

Haq's approach is not as historical as some of the others but is the most explicitly comparative of all; moreover, it is the most explicitly cosmological in the sense that it focuses on the human condition as created by Allah and as the context in which human beings relate to God.

The result of this diversity and selectivity of approaches is that the scope of the comparative hypotheses summarized in the present chapter is not as broad as might be expected, and this in several ways. First, there are no simple comparisons of some traditions—of Hinduism and Judaism, for instance. Second, sometimes comparisons made here are grounded in chapters 2–7 on only one side, as when 8.3.6 vaguely sketches comparisons between Islam and Christianity on the role of the Word in the relation between God and the world, building on claims about Islam made by Haq that do not have parallels with anything in the Fredriksen chapter, and the references to the common philosophic traditions of Aristotelianism and Neo-Platonism are supplied by us (Neville and Wildman). Third, in order to rearticulate the separate points in chapters 2–7 so that they can be brought into comparison, we (Neville and Wildman) sometimes have had to adjust their presentations to make them more vague or specific, or to supplement them with material not found in the previous chapters. In general, we have brought the diverse traditions' points together to compare them at a slightly more vague level than presented in chapters 2–7, and then moved down to their specifics in order to distinguish them.

Vagueness and specificity are relative notions. The comparisons are always more than a mere lineup of specifications: they involve saying how the specifications are similar and different. But then each specification we articulate is itself vague and might be specified further. Our judgment is always vulnerable to the criticism that it deals with matters only at a vague level and that more precise judgment would require finer discrimination. Our specialist chapters differ among themselves with regard to the level of specificity, with Clooney attempting to say little about Hinduism or Advaita Vedānta in general and to speak only of the very specific *Vivekacūḍāmaṇi*, whereas Kohn and Haq operate with vaguer and more sweeping characterizations of their traditions, only illustrated by specific texts.

Of course, any comparative judgment is vulnerable to the criticism that it does not take into account this or that aberration from the identified specification—for instance a Chinese thinker who believes the universe is too chaotic (*hun-tun*) to be One, or a Buddhist who believes in a substantial self. For all of our efforts to say only what we mean and write in a posture defensive against objections, we hope these hypotheses about comparative judgments will be construed with sympathetic imagination, filling in with confirming detail as well as questioning the limits of the judgment with disconfirming detail.

In sum, this chapter makes comparative judgments arising in four ways: (1) a repetition of points made in chapters 2–7 or the seminar discussion pretty much in their own words; (2) a restatement of one or several sides in the comparison so as to express the points as specifications of a vaguer comparative category; (3) the translation of one or several sides in the comparison into a vaguer or more specific level so as to make comparison possible; and (4) the development of comparative judgments previously not discussed on the basis of what seems wanted by the cumulative array of judgments here.

8.1.4 The Structure of Chapters 8 and 9

The hypotheses in this chapter and the next will take the form of reviewing what has been learned about specifying the categories concerning the human condition listed in the introduction. Furthermore, our findings will be presented so far as possible and relevant in terms made vulnerable to correction according to four of the five sites of phenomenological analysis laid out in detail in *Ultimate Realities,* chapter 8. These are: (1) the intrinsic, or the ideas expressed and analyzed in their own terms; (2) the perspectival, or the ways the ideas determine a larger perspective on life, in relevant religious respects; (3) the theoretical, or the ways in which the ideas lead to larger theoretical considerations; and (4) the practical, or the implications of the ideas for practice. The singularity of the ideas, the special qualities that resist analysis of any sort by definition have no comparative capabilities and will not be discussed. Ideas in their singularity are grasped through becoming competent in their use and made accessible by metaphor, indirection, and naming (for those who know the names). Were we assured of infinite reader patience, however, we could talk about the singular and incomparable elements of the religious ideas, just to indicate what cannot be brought under more encompassing categories of comparison. We do not mean to say that everything in a religion's ideas can be expressed adequately in comparative hypotheses.

Reviewing the ideas from all the sites of phenomenological analysis tests our judgments by exposing them to at least four different angles of representation and understanding. Whereas the review through the four sites sometimes seems mechanical, it is a discipline that enhances vulnerability. It is also the discipline that most often has caused us to develop comparative judgments that had not occurred to us in the seminar or in the writing of chapters 2–7. Often in this chapter we abbreviate discussions of phenomenological sites where they are repetitive, obvious, or uninteresting, and the discussions in chapter 9 will abbreviate the rehearsal of the sites even more.

The structure of this summary of comparative hypotheses is to discuss each of four main cosmological categories. Under each category, first Chinese religion will be discussed, beginning with its intrinsic representations, then perspectival ideas, then theoretical implications, and finally practical implications. Next Buddhism will be discussed according to each site of phenomenological analysis, compared in each case with Chinese Buddhism. Next Hinduism in its Advaita Vedānta form will be discussed in like fashion, with comparisons to Chinese religion and Buddhism. And so on for Judaism, Christianity, and Islam with the multiplicity of comparisons getting more complex as the discussion proceeds. Not every religion compares with every other in all respects, but we aim to articulate the important and interesting comparisons insofar as we have noticed them. In the long run, the vague cosmological categories get specified in different comparable ways by most of the traditions in most respects.

Our comparative method calls for moving beyond the various specifications of a vague category to the rearticulation of the category as concretely filled in. That would require a kind of comprehensive summary of how the various specifications add up. So, it would be convenient to have in each of the following discussions a seventh section summing up unity, ontology, value, and causation respectively. But our comparisons are too fragmentary and selective to add up to fulsome characterizations of those categories. Therefore, we are left with the comparisons that are made in the discussions of each tradition.

The cosmological categories found to be most relevant for understanding the religious dimensions of the human condition are those articulating the unity, ontological status, and value of the cosmos, and causation, that is, how things of religious import work in the cosmos. All of these involve conceptions of the cosmos as expressed in important symbols in the traditions and our concern here is with how these cosmological conceptions bear upon the human condition. For reasons of ease of exposition, given the interconnectedness of the ideas, the discussions of the first several categories are longer than the others and anticipate many points that could have been made later. For this reason, too, chapter 9 will be briefer than 8.

8.2 Unity

Unity is an extremely vague notion, parsed in many different ways within each religious tradition studied here as well as in different characteristic ways among the traditions. Relative to the human condition, at the vague level unity means whatever coherence there is for the inclusive encompassing context or environment for human life. The religions differ quite significantly regarding what is to be included within that encompassing environment as well as regarding the kinds of coherence the elements might have. Stated in this vague way prior to specification, unity might seem to be merely cosmological and not interestingly religious. The specifications will help elucidate the religious aspects of unity, so that at the end the vague category made specific in these several ways will be much more informative.

8.2.1 Chinese Ideas of Unity

Kohn (2.2) is extraordinarily clear that Chinese religion is firmly and usually explicitly based on the conception that the cosmos is one and unified. Miller, in commentary on an early draft of the present chapter, observes that the Chinese focus on unity developed in response to issues of diversity, and that it is "more accurate to speak of a syncretistic drive towards achieving unity that eventually resulted in an elite unified cosmology that was capable of holding together Daoist, Confucian, and Buddhist ideas in a pan-Chinese worldview. This worldview is essentially Daoist, in that it is built up in commentaries on the *Daode jing* and the *Zhuangzi,* but in that process, Daoism is transformed, Confucianism becomes metaphysical, and Buddhism is sinified." We (Neville and Wildman) agree with this account of the evolution on Chinese notions of unity, but agree also with Kohn's claim to their centrality from the earliest times. Kohn cites Colavito's metaphoric distinction between religions of the One and those of the Zero. Chinese religions are based on the mythic suppositions of the One, an aboriginal mass of Qi that achieves differentiation in movements of yin and yang like vibratory patterns that remain functional processes and harmonies within the unity of the gigantic jelly bean of cosmic reality. This is a core conceptual motif that underlies all historical developments of Chinese religion, variously punctuated by the interactions of Daoism, Confucianism, and Buddhism.

The human sphere within the cosmos can be delimited by processes of human scale, but these processes are continuous with those of other scales, and there is nothing in the human condition that is not a condensation or rarefaction of processes otherwise making up the cosmic whole. The religious aspect of the unified cosmos is that people are in essential continuity with everything else, and hence never seriously alienated. The emphasis on cosmic unity is an intrinsic representation of the cosmos for Chinese religions.

The perspectival understanding deriving from the Chinese conception of unity intrinsically grasped is that the various features of the world are processes expressing and seeking harmony. The human condition thus is to be understood as resting in the harmonies of physical, biological, social, and personal process. And where the human condition has a predicament, it is that something has gotten out of harmony and needs to be reharmonized. Resolution of the predicament is the restoration of harmony and return of human life to full participation in the unity of the cosmos, the one. This reharmonization so as to return to unity has different specifications in Daoism, Confucianism, and Chinese Buddhism (2.1, 2.3.2).

The theoretical understanding of cosmic unity in Chinese religions is the conception of things in the world as falling into harmonically interlocked classes, or sets of balanced changes.[1] For instance, consider the classifications of things according to movements of yin and yang, the four seasons, the five elements and directions, and so forth. Human troubles, accordingly, are understood as things being out of balance, with the Qi moving too fast or slow, the diet being too hot or wet, projects undertaken in the wrong season, and so forth (2.2).

The practical understanding for Chinese religions follows from its conception of life as a project of harmonization so as to maintain continuity with the oneness of the cosmos. As Chinese medicine seeks to restore lost balance, and military strategy seeks to do things in the right season and know when to stop, so Chinese religion employs ritual to bring discords into harmony and advocates practices aimed at bringing people into harmony with heaven and earth, the society, the family, and details of personal life, for instance, as expressed in *The Venerable Lord's Wondrous Scripture of Exterior Daily Practice* (chapter 2.3.1). The interior life—see the *Scripture of Interior Daily Practice* (2.3.1)—is likewise to be managed so as to transform the person into a being with perfect union with the One.[2]

8.2.2 *Buddhist Ideas of Unity*

The situation is quite different for Buddhism, especially Indian Buddhism of the sorts analyzed by Eckel. With regard not only to unity but to all the other cosmological categories, the Buddhists might first tell the story (see 3.1) of the Buddha's question about the poisoned arrow asked in response to a series of high-powered metaphysical questions. Buddhists do, of course, have assumptions about the cosmos, assumptions diversely characteristic of their times and cultures. But these cosmological assumptions are not uniformly important for the religious dimension of the human condition. Eckel and Thatamanil in commentary on an early draft of the present chapter write:

> We feel that the "most important" thing Buddhists say about the human condition is that humans suffer and seek to bring suffering to an end. This does not mean that Buddhists have no developed views of the cosmos, either in the moral sense (in the six realms of rebirth) or in the physical sense (as a configuration of continents around a central mountain or whatever). And it does not mean that these views of the cosmos are lacking in "religious" significance, as in the concern to move on to a better rebirth or in Tantric meditation about seeking the still point of the mandala.

Nevertheless, the Madhyamaka line lets the cosmic conceptions of unity be a function of the individual's interest in release from suffering, rather than interpreting the individual's interest as arising from some kind of primordial cosmic unity. Or to put the point more finely in comparison with Chinese religion, whereas Chinese religion emphasizes the objective character of the cosmos and the religious importance of conforming to or harmonizing with that, the Buddhists in the Madhyamaka Mahāyāna line explored in chapter 3, take the religious import of the cosmos to be strictly dependent on the religious needs of individuals, as expressed, say, in the Four Noble Truths. Not that Buddhists need to deny objectivity to the cosmos when properly described—the no-self doctrine discussed in chapter 3 is affirmed as describing the way things are—but that the cosmos is not important for religious purposes except insofar as it is a function of those purposes.

So, for instance, regarding the unity of the cosmos, Buddhism in the Madhyamaka line analyzed by Eckel and Thatamanil is indifferent to questions such as totality and integration that exercise the Chinese, except perhaps to apply a negative dialectic if those questions seem to be given too substantialist a reference; other forms of Buddhism take the opposite rhetorical tack, as shown, for instance, in Garma C. C. Chang's *The Buddhist Teaching of Totality: The Philosophy of Hwa Yen Buddhism.* Buddhism in the line we have analyzed rather transforms the question of unity into what is relevant to the human condition as described in the Four Noble Truths. Universal statements are allowed, such as that everything is constantly changing, nothing has a self-nature, all experience is suffering, and so forth. Yet these are not so much objective descriptions asserted of reality as ways recommended for regarding reality in order for the poisoned arrow to be removed swiftly.

Thatamanil, commenting on an early draft of the present chapter, points out the some qualifications that need to be made comparing Madhyamaka and Yogācāra Buddhism:

> While it may be true that Yogācāra Buddhists may deny the objectivity of the world (in the sense of extra-mental reality), for Mādhyamikas the problem is substantiality or reification. In other words, while it is possible to read Yogācāra as a kind of "subjective idealism" or at least "idealism," it would not be possible to read Madhyamaka so. Though it is true to say that the imposition of intrinsic nature (*svabhāva*) is an activity of mental construction, this does not mean that Madhyamaka philosophers deny extra-mental phenomena. In this respect, Yogacara is both too reificatory in postulating the reality of mind-only (*samaropa*) and too negative (*apavada*) in denying the conventional reality of phenomena.
>
> Regarding unity, it may be that the Madhyamaka emphasis on *pratātyasamutpāda* has implications for "unity." To deny that the world is composed of entities with intrinsic nature or own-being is to allow for an experience of the world that is far more unified and characterized by non-duality than to imagine a universe of self-subsistent entities. However, to speak of the universe or reality as unified in such a way that the whole is reified makes language regarding unity problematic.

For some kinds of Buddhism such as Huayen the conception of the world's unity is regarded so much as a function of the religious imagination that many Buddha-worlds can be imagined, alternative realities each whole in itself, or perhaps nested so that an entire Buddha-world is contained in a piece of dust under a bed in another Buddha-world. Whereas the Chinese can imagine heavens and hells as various parts of the One world, particularly located relative to the Middle Kingdom, because there is only one world into which they all must fit, Buddhists, even Chinese Buddhists, can imagine alternative realities whose truth lies in their liberating function for the imagination rather than a plain assertion of correspondence to some part of reality. In answer to the question, how is the cosmos unified, Madhyamaka and many other Buddhists would answer something like this: the world's unity lies in being susceptible to the ideas of unity with which it is grasped for soteriological purposes, and the susceptibility is not to be tested except through the success or failure of the project of religious liberation. Whereas the Madhyamaka schools tend to emphasize the non-objective character of imagination, the Yogācāra schools tend to emphasize the positive qualities of the imagined worlds.[3]

Indian Madhyamaka Buddhism, minimizing religiously important conceptions of objective cosmic unity—in Nāgārjuna's case refuting them—does not take up a perspective on life based on cosmic unity. Rather, what unity there is to the cosmos is what results from the subjective perspective of the individual. This is not to say that the cosmos objectively is not unified, if that can be known; the objective cosmos per se is not religiously interesting.

By contrast with the Chinese objective classification of things so as to express the harmonious unity of the cosmos, Indian Buddhists such as Bhāvaviveka make few objective claims that are not undone by the negative dialectic discussed in 3.3. As a result, Buddhism, far more than ancient Chinese religion and indeed most other religions committed to a structured view of the religious importance of how the world is unified, tolerates many variant cosmologies. Buddhism has far greater tolerance for the cosmology of modern science, for instance, than those traditional religions committed to a specific view of the world's structure, precisely because Buddhism finds little of religious importance in such objective views, save when they are asserted as too objective.

The practical consequence of Mahāyāna Buddhism's non-commitment to an objective view of the world's unity is nicely expressed in the doctrine of two truths discussed in 3.1 and in Bhāvaviveka's discussion of vision (3.3; see also 3.4 on negation in comparative categories). Conventional truth expresses whatever unity and structure are taken to be objective in the world. This includes such things as laws of karmic accountability, the sense that nothing hangs together in times of social confusion, and it might even include the worldview of modern science. The ultimate truth is that these conventional truths are not really objective, but merely pragmatically feasible (or unfeasible) ways of projecting organizing ideas onto reality. And the doctrine of the two truths is that the conventional truths are as true in their way as the ultimate truth, and that one has to live in that conventional world of saṃsāra. Even one's religious life has to be lived in that world. A Madhyamaka adept realizes that the conventional world is the only home one has: nirvana is saṃsāra; a Pure Land adept takes another view.

8.2.3 Hindu Ideas of Unity

The question of cosmic unity in Hinduism is framed differently from that in either Chinese religion or Buddhism. The Hindu question concerns the unity of the personal self with the underlying divine self or Brahman, and the question of a multiplicity to be unified is either that of the falsely assumed distinction between the personal self and the divine, or that of the world's diversity construed as *māyā* (4.2.1). But as Clooney stresses in 4.6, a statement like that must be construed as extremely vague, with the understanding that the way it is specified by a text such as the *Vivekacūḍāmaṇi* in the Advaita Vedānta tradition is quite different from ways it is specified in other schools or in the *Bhagavad Gītā* or even in other Advaita texts, for instance, those of Śaṇkara. The exposition of the *Vivekacūḍāmaṇi* in chapter 4 makes explicit reference to the *Atharva Veda* and the *Taittirāya* and *Chāndogya Upaniṣads*, which are core texts for much of the Hindu tradition, and to ancient motifs such as the three gunas, tamas, rajas, and sattva; those core texts and motifs are developed very differently by other branches of the Hindu tradition. The comparative generalizations made here need to be understood in nuanced ways according to their reference to the vague core texts and motifs or to the specifications in the *Vivekacūḍāmaṇi* (4.6).

The unity of the personal self with Brahman is specified by the *Vivekacūḍāmaṇi* through a series of arguments showing that what might be construed as a separate personal self is not the real self. Thus, the eating body, the vital self, the mind, the intellect and bliss-enjoying self are not the true self, and the true self that is left is no other than Brahman (4.3). This is affirmed positively in accord with Advaita's non-mythic and rationally accessible specification of the classic *tat tvam asi* (4.4): any sense of distinction or separation of something real from Brahman is wrong. Hence the emphasis on negation in the doctrine: non-duality.

In contrast to the intrinsic notion of unity in Chinese religion, according to which human beings are proper parts organically related to the rest and internally resonant with cosmic oneness in its aboriginal incipient origins, the Advaita notion negates any possible diversity within Brahman or between Brahman and the personal self. In contrast to the Buddhist conception of unity as a function of the experiencing subject, the Advaita conception takes the ontological reality of Brahman as the only reality in the experiencing subject, a reality that can be discriminated only when the experiencing mechanisms of the personal self are transcended by discernment and transformation. Whereas the Buddhist approach studied here brackets questions of objective cosmic or ontological unity in order to focus on the experiencing subject, the Advaita approach teaches means to bracket all the elements in the experiencing self that are functions of change, *māyā*, in order to focus on the exclusive cosmic or ontological unity, Brahman. (It should be noted that the Advaita *Vivekacūḍāmaṇi*, ninth century, is later than the work of the sixth-century Buddhist Bhāvaviveka and the other writers on whom Eckel bases his argument; the Advaita position here arises in the context of responding to Buddhism.)

The conception of self-Brahman unity in Advaita Vedānta casts the diversity of things in the world in the perspective of being *māyā* (4.2.1–2). *Māyā* is problematic because non-discriminating people can be fooled by it. But the successful realization of the Advaita Vedānta path can lead to proper discrimination, or rather consists in the successive achievements of capacities properly to discriminate, so that one is not fooled (4.4). The world is viewed from the Advaita's theory of unity, not as a field of processes in potential harmony or disharmony, as in the Chinese case, but as a field of potential illusions that would have the effect of reinforcing the false sense that things other than Brahman have reality.

The *Vivekacūḍāmaṇi*'s Advaita Vedānta conception of the spread of the world as *māyā* does not entail the belief that it lacks structure or that one cannot relate pragmatically to human needs. Indeed, the laws of karma govern saṃsāra in the ancient imagination, and the laws of science can be accepted in the modern. The irreality of *māyā* consists in its appearance as duality whereas the real truth of things is their non-duality (4.2.2). Whereas in Chinese religion the field of harmonious processes is a matter of opportunities for religiously important action, the field of *māyā* has only preliminary religious bearing in Advaita, though in important ways: scriptures, teachers' meditation, and the entire religious quest coming to the knowledge of non-duality are part of *māyā*, as Thatamanil points out in seminar commentary. *Māyā* is not unreal in the sense that the son of a barren woman is unreal, to use Thatamanil's citation, and therefore we (Neville and Wildman) call it *irreal*. In contrast to the Buddhists whose world is unified according to the experience of persons, the advocates of Advaita take the real unity, that is, non-duality, of the world to be the truth behind any discriminations that themselves are dualistic *māyā*.

The practical consequence of the Advaita Vedānta view of self-Brahman unity might seem paradoxical. For, although the truth is the non-duality of self and Brahman, most people actually live in *māyā* without realizing it. So the practical point is to transform the self through the processes described, say, in the *Vivekacūḍāmaṇi* to have the powers of discrimination (4.4). This is a matter of serious work, involving study and the rigorous life of discipleship, and in the tradition of the *Vivekacūḍāmaṇi* the project is limited to smart, interested, male Brahmins who have the texts and a teacher at hand. In this regard Advaita is far closer to the Chinese project of maintaining and repairing one's harmonious relations than it is to the Buddhist change of attitude or realization of the Middle Path. On the one hand it is an illusion to believe that there is a religious problem in the human condition (4.1), but it takes a lot of work, a lifetime (or many lifetimes) project, to dispel that illusion. One of the most important points Clooney makes is the distinction between the abstract truth of non-duality and its concrete realization in experience (4.6).

Although there are many qualifications to the comparative generalizations among Hinduism, Chinese religion, and Buddhism, as expressed in the seminar commentaries of Eckel, Thatamanil, and Miller on early drafts of this chapter, they show that on balance the center of gravity is with the comparative hypotheses we have presented.

8.2.4 *Jewish Ideas of Unity*

In contrast to Chinese religion, Buddhism, and Hinduism, the three monotheistic religions of West Asia agree vaguely in asserting a dualism between God and the world, however variously they specify that dualism internally and in comparison with one another. Saldarini (5.1.1) makes for Judaism a claim that applies to Christianity and Islam as well: "*Human life and the human condition in all its complexity may be defined as life under, and in relation to, and responsive to God or as a deviation from that divinely ordered relationship.*" Dualistic as this vague claim might be, the three West Asian religions envision a totality inclusive of God and the world, with an asymmetrical relation between them.

Staying for a moment with the vague claim that God creates the world, the character of unity in that God-world totality varies most according to the sense in which human responsibility for being responsive to God or deviant is interpreted. Although East Asian and South Asian religions recognize disharmony and ignorance as existentially crucial religious problems, they downplay the ontological significance of that, and human responsibility for it, compared with the West Asian religions. That they downplay it does not mean they reject it. As Thatamanil points out in commentary, "The question of the locus of ignorance, a question that post-Śaṇkara Advaitins worry about constantly, is baldly ontological. Is Brahman the locus of ignorance or is it the individual soul? If the individual soul is itself the product of ignorance how can it also be the locus of ignorance?" In the West, the emphasis on morality and conformity to the divine will has been coupled with a problematic of human freedom such that it is inevitable that the question will be asked whether people can be in ontological opposition to God. That is, does the God-world dualistic totality tolerate a serious rupture in the totality? The three traditions share some core texts, for instance, the creation and fall stories in Genesis. How they differently develop those texts is interesting indeed.

Judaism affirms that God is the just and provident creator of the cosmos (5.1.2). Although there have been mystical movements within Judaism for which it might be inappropriate to use personalistic imagery for

God, the main part of the tradition has treated God as personal and intentional, so that it is always appropriate to ask why God does or allows things that are evil or seem to be so. With the exception of a few thinkers such as Richard Rubenstein (5.4.1) who believe that the horrendousness of evil in the world, especially in the Nazi holocaust, requires rejection of the existence of God altogether, Jewish thinkers from Ben Sira to Eli Wiesel (in a problematized way) affirm that God exercises just and provident control over the whole cosmos (5.1.2). The world as a whole is in God's hand. And therefore evil constitutes a problem for human understanding, as it would not be were God's justice and provident control to be partial. The cosmos is unified through being created and providentially ruled by one God. The unity of the whole is thus the dualism of a just, provident, personal creator and the creation that includes free and sometimes evil persons as well as much suffering.

From the perspective of Judaism's dualistic unity of just, provident, creator God and world, the human condition is the field in which one lives before God affirming and worshipping the divine person. Saldarini traces some extraordinary developments of this core motif that was interpreted principally in terms of how Israel, not the whole human race, relates to God. In Ben Sira's thinking this field is generally a well-managed order within which the Torah (5.2.2) provides the means by which the people of Israel rightly live before God and by which God generally keeps order. The stability of the Jewish state in Ben Sira's time included the flourishing cult of temple sacrifices and the leisure to practice pieties, which became a threefold interpretation of the way to God for Jews in the field of human endeavor. Even after the destruction of the Second Temple, rabbis remained concerned to interpret human events in terms of how they relate to the temple sacrifice. But slowly the study of Torah assumed preeminence as the key to what is important in life. The Torah is the revelation of the just and provident creator; life's crucial points are not focal points for harmony, as in Chinese religion, or for liberation from craving as in Buddhism, or for discerning illusions as in Advaita, but rather are focal points for obedience and thanksgiving as defined by Torah.

The theoretical ideas of how to live before God in the dualistic unity of Judaism are bound up with the problematic of the freedom to live obediently or disobediently before God. If God is the just and provident creator, then is God responsible for creating the evil tendencies in human life? If so, as Judaism has generally affirmed, how then are individuals or the collective responsible for their good and evil deeds, as Judaism has also generally affirmed? Saldarini point out that the questions of the goodness and unity of God as providential creator versus the capacity of human beings to rebel against divine order are rarely neatly reconciled. They might be downplayed in Ben Sira, or inverted in post-holocaust writers to ask God how He could allow evil (5.2.2.1). But they usually cannot be answered by giving up on either side.

Except in certain mystical strains, Judaism is frankly dualistic in practice both abstractly and concretely. Abstractly, God is just but creates a world in which there is sometimes evil, and both sides have their integrity (5.3.3.2). Concretely, God relates to this duality by practicing both justice and mercy: with either one of those alone, the person of God could not relate to the world created. From the human side, people are enjoined to relate to God by repentance, acknowledging their own responsibility, and by thankful obedience to Torah that includes both acknowledgment of God's justice and mercy and resolution to follow Torah more closely (5.3.4).

Judaism's dualistic unity makes for quite different comparisons with Chinese religion, Buddhism, and Advaita Vedānta. On the side of its claim for God's practice of justice and mercy toward the world, there is very little analogue in those three religions, none of which has such strong images of personal intention in a God. The motif of a creator God is strong in many forms of Hinduism, even if quickly transcended in Advaita; but even in theistic Hindu piety such as expressed in the *Bhagavad Gītā* or in Śaivism, there is not a degree of emphasis on the unity of the person of God to occasion the reconciliation of justice and mercy to be such agony as in Judaism.

8.2.5 Christian Ideas of Unity

Christianity, of course, arises from most of the same core texts and motifs as Judaism, beginning self-consciously as a movement within the people of Israel, one of many movements in Second Temple Judaism. But it differed very sharply from the other developments of Judaism at the time and since over the issue of Jesus as the Messiah, a point assumed in Fredriksen's chapter and given more direct analysis here.

This difference is clearly reflected in the Christian conception of the unity of the God-world totality. Jesus was taken by his disciples to be extraordinarily connected to God, and yet as depicted in the New Testament gospels he died young, with disappointing students, a fickle following, caught up in the political turmoil of Jerusalem and Rome that had little to do with his business, and was crucified in humiliation: according to such historical measures, Jesus was a failure. Moreover, although the disciples experienced Jesus as raised from the dead, he did not return to ordinary life like Lazarus and thus perhaps to raise an army to defeat

Rome and restore Zion: on the contrary he left the historical world to ascend to heaven. With Jesus ascended, according to Acts of the Apostles, the Holy Spirit is promised to come as advocate and guide for the people, but not to bring them historical victory. Rather, as argued in the "Farewell Discourses" in the Gospel of John, the function of the Holy Spirit is to comfort and shape their fragmentary and often persecuted lives and to bring them at last to God. So in stark contrast to most other forms of Judaism, which envision a Messiah who will bring peace and righteousness to Earth, restoring Israel for a long time, Christianity from its core New Testament texts onward views life as always finite and filled with frustration and suffering. Religious fulfillment is in relating to God within this life, and perhaps over or after this life, so as to take satisfaction in God's own glory, not history's.

Christianity has had many ways of specifying this view of history and fulfillment. One sort, keeping very close to the Jewish images of God in history, is apocalyptic, envisioning an end of time with a last judgment, or an end of historical time where the forces of evil lose power and a heavenly city comes to Earth, or a millenarian approach that can combine those two apocalyptic images; see Fredriksen's account in 6.3.3, 6.4.4, 6.5.6, 6.7.5. Another sort, "realized eschatology," interprets fulfillment as relating to the divine eternity now, not necessarily in an afterlife, supposing that history itself is but a partial dimension of the real reality that includes the possibility of people participating in the divine eternity; see the "Farewell Discourses" mentioned above or Colossians 2:8–3:4.

Christianity also has had many ways of specifying the conception of the creator God. It has always maintained the imagery of the personal God from the Hebrew bible. Yet, influenced more than Judaism by Hellenistic and then by the entire European tradition of speculative and metaphysical philosophy, decisively so in Origen (6.4), Christianity has given many different philosophic interpretations of the basis for that personalist or anthropomorphic imagery; Augustine, for instance, said that God creates time, and hence is not in time except by an action of divine intervention; Neo-Platonic Christianity identifies God with the One that is beyond all determination; Thomas Aquinas said God is a pure Act of To Be (*esse*), surely not a personal individual in any ordinary sense; Paul Tillich in the twentieth century said God is the Ground of Being, not a being at all.

With regard to the question of unity relative to the human condition in Christianity, therefore, it is important to distinguish the metaphysical from the existential respects in which unity is interpreted. Metaphysically, Christianity has been expressed in dualistic positions akin to Judaism, with integrity to the different realities of both God and world, and with the equivocations of asymmetrical and symmetrical relations between them (see 8.3.4, 8.4.4, and 8.5.4 on symmetry and asymmetry). But Christianity has also been expressed in such ways that the world is part of the active or creative divine nature, with no integrity of its own apart from God, as in Neo-Platonic theologies; and also in such ways that God has no nature as God apart from the creating of the world, as in some creation *ex nihilo* theologies. These last two approaches, not much discussed in chapter 6 or the seminar, are closer to monisms than to dualisms and they affirm that the human condition cannot ever be in total separation from God no matter how bad it gets.[4] At its worst, the human condition is bad for these nearly monistic views because human attention is just "turned in the wrong direction," to use Plato's, Plotinus' and Augustine's metaphor; in this respect, this kind of Christianity is closer to Advaita Vedānta than to dualistic monotheisms in its account of the separation of people from God as resulting from a mistaken perspective or way of looking.[5]

Existentially, Christianity finds unity only within God and in a divine life or heavenly world that transcends history in the ordinary sense. The Christian perspective on history in the ordinary sense is that it is a field of crucifixion; resurrection is transcendence, real full-bodied transcendence (6.1, 6.6) of the ordinary historical plane. Christianity thus involves an existential dualism in which ordinary history is taken to be at odds with the full reality in which human beings are existentially unified with God. That existential dualism is softened where the plane of ordinary history is taken to be a mere misinterpretation of the larger reality, a dream from which people should awaken (as in Jesus' "wake up" parables in Matthew). But often heaven is interpreted as a different place to which people go later, or the course of history is regarded as subject to ontological, not merely historical, transformation at the Second Coming of Jesus. For Christianity, there is no existential unity within history in the ordinary sense, as there is or ought to be for Judaism in the line traced by Saldarini.

The Christian perspective on the world derivative from its peculiar sense of existential dualism is expressed in its phrase, "in the world but not of it." Life is to be lived enthusiastically within the world, under the guidance and comfort of the Holy Spirit, encountering obstacles but continually attempting to be just and holy with a whole heart (6.6.2), expecting ultimate defeat and death in the ordinary historical sense. Gnosticism did not sustain itself as a Christian strain because it abandoned the importance of living fully in the world (6.3.1–3). On the other side, Fredriksen (6.4) cites Origen's attack on the Christian materialists who interpret scriptures "according to the flesh" and expect a material resurrection at

Jerusalem with a bodily God. At the same time, true human identity is a function of existential purified unity with God and is not a matter "of the world."

Christian experience has much the same practical perspective on the world regarding unity that Judaism does: on the one hand love God, for in that is true human identity, and on the other work to be just and holy, if not through Torah then through something very like that. But Christianity does not expect vindication in the flesh in history, in the restoration of justice and universal piety; it expects rather the transformation of the flesh to be vindicated in unity with God. At least this is the impact of the crucifixion-resurrection motif in most of the Christian tradition. (Contemporary liberation theology sometimes returns to a view of God's unification of history consonant with Judaism though lacking Wiesel's tragic disappointment.) The concern with history in the ordinary sense sets both Judaism and Christianity off over against Buddhism and Advaita Vedānta; Judaism insists that God be fulfilled in history, Christianity that history be transformed to be fulfilled in God.

Christians approach the existential dualism of God and history, and the unity of human life in relation to God alone, by means of a theoretical conception of Jesus as the Christ. Jesus was the paradigm of how to live in the world but not be of it. The synoptic gospels (Matthew, Mark, and Luke) stress his devotion and ministry; John concentrates on how he marks the pathway to God from within this life. Subsequent debates over what it means to be transformed bodily so as to be in union with God, such as those discussed in chapter 6, were fought over the interpretation of such core texts about Jesus. The Trinitarian controversies carried this out to elaborate philosophic detail. In respect of defining the proper course of human life according to the paradigm of a founder, Christianity has much in common with the theory of avatārs in Hinduism and with following the way of the Buddha. But more than those traditions, on balance, Christianity in its anti-docetic modes has stressed the importance of fully investing oneself in the world.

Christians early conceived the practical consequences of existential dualism and the unity of true human identity with God in terms of grace and sin. Grace is the divine action that keeps the existential option of human unity with God open, and sin is the human action and subsequent limiting condition that prevents or inhibits that unity. St. Paul intensified the Jewish notion of evil inclinations to be a depotentiating transformation of human powers so as to make people unable to return to unity with God, a unity he interpreted in terms of the Torah's covenant (6.2). He interpreted Jesus Christ as the man sent from God, the divine Son, who is the sufficiently powerful means of grace to retransform human nature. As Fredriksen relates (6.2), according to Paul the first man Adam corrupted human nature and Jesus, the second Adam, restored it. The practice of life "within the world but not of it," therefore, is the practice of human beings availing themselves of the various means of grace, which for Christians mainly has meant becoming disciples of Jesus in one historically conditioned sense or another. As Fredriksen says, Christianity has provided many ways of conceiving the problem of getting body and soul together to enter into the divine or heavenly life.

8.2.6 *Islamic Ideas of Unity*

Islam, like the other monotheistic religions, affirms a strong God-world dualism (7.4–7.5). At the same time, far more than Christianity, even more than Judaism, Islam emphasizes the unity or oneness of God the creator. Haq goes so far as to suggest a deep similarity of the Islamic stress on unity with the Chinese "one-centered" religion (7.1).

Three main points specify the Islamic approach to cosmic unity. First, there is the absolute unity of God, witnessed to in the primordial "vision" (7.1) and elaborated especially in opposition to any kind of polytheism and Christian trinitarianism (7.4.2). The Islamic preoccupation with *shirk,* idolatry, is less an attempt to establish a gulf between God and the world than an attempt to deny any multiplicity in deity (7.4.1).

Second, because the absolutely unified God absolutely creates the whole world, the world itself has a high degree of unity. The world's unity consists in the *amr,* "the divine command which is the fundamental constitutive principle of each created entity, placing it under obligation to take its assigned place in the larger cosmic whole" (7.3.2). It is in respect of each thing having a specific harmonic place within the larger whole that Islam is similar to the Chinese case. Natural things, for Islam, cannot do anything but express their roles as defined by *amr;* but human beings have the freedom to do otherwise, and hence the *amr* for humans is a matter of obligation that might be failed. Precisely because the *amr* of human beings, elaborated in *Sharīʿa* and proclaimed in *aḥkām,* is to live under obligation (of which much more in chapter 9), the world has a unity derivative from the absolute unity of Allah (7.3.1, 7.4, 7.6).

Third, the unity of Allah with the world, encompassing their dualism, is accomplished by the former being the total source of the latter. This will be elaborated further in discussing the cosmological category of ontological status (8.3.6). Here we note the tension Haq describes (7.5) that results in mystical tendencies to lose oneself in God or to find God in oneself, both of which are *shirk* but are almost unavoidable when entering into the Creator-created relation.

Islam stands in steady contrast with Buddhism, at least the Madhyamaka strain described in chapter 3, with its plainly objective reference to God and the world and their unity. Islam stands with Judaism, Christianity, and Chinese religion over against the *māyā* theme in Advaita Vedānta in emphasizing the unified real plurality of the natural and social world.

The emphasis on unity in Islam, both divine unity and the unity of the world, gives it the perspective on life of free people in society taking life as a field of obligations. Haq (7.3.2) describes the development of the Islamic notion of law as divine command, articulating the normative elements Allah establishes in nature and society. Moreover, the field of obligations is a unified one.

Judaism and Christianity share the perspective that life is a field of obligations, but specify that somewhat differently. Judaism, at least after Ben Sira (5.2.3), stubbornly acknowledges a kind of recalcitrance of evil, and a problematic tragedy in that field of obligations. The messianic theme in Judaism is that God and good people should be able to triumph in history, and that God is provident for that; nevertheless, the unity of the divine intent across history, the fulfillment of the promises, is not evident. Like Islam, Judaism sees the forces of evil to be part of creation, and thus subserving the divine purpose (7.6). But that purpose seems obscure, or at least not obviously fulfilled in what happens. Islam, by contrast, had its formative period when its political aspirations were on the ascendancy, in contrast to late Second Temple Rabbinic Judaism that was formed when Israel's low status was deteriorating to the complete destruction of temple worship and the abandonment of any pretence of a Jewish puppet state. Islam has a more nearly triumphalist obsession with the divine unity of the field of obligation, to be expressed in political exercise of Islamic praxis (7.6).

The Islamic perspective on the unity of the field of obligations contrasts also with the Christian perspective that the obligations are to be engaged with the expectation that life is filled with crosses. Unity in Christian perspective comes only through people's unifications with God that embrace dis-unified historical life in the transcendence of history. Islam, of course, is filled with visions of Paradise, but not a Paradise in radical discontinuity with historical life; in this respect Islam agrees with the Chinese position that there is only one world even though it contains more than is apparent to ordinary consciousness. Christianity views the kingdom of heaven or life before God as a transformation and transvaluation of ordinary historical existence.

Islam agrees with all the other religions studied that life is a field of responsibility points, specified in Islam as obligations in the sense expressed in *Sharīʿa* (7.3.3). Buddhism specifies the field of responsibility points as occasions for liberation from ego-induced cravings, and Advaita Vedānta as occasions for learning and practicing discriminations making apparent non-dualism. The personal and social dimensions of this field will be discussed later (9.3.6).

The chief theoretical implication of the Islamic approach to unity, especially the unity of the world, is the conviction that the world is rational and that therefore science is not only possible but a part of *fiqh*, the process of understanding the divine word (7.3.3). The theoretical emphasis on the divine word, shared with Judaism and Christianity, even though interpreted differently, promotes science and rational inquiry as an important virtue. Thus, whereas Buddhism of the sort studied here and Vedāntic Hinduism are tolerant of science as non-interfering with religion, Islam promotes rational inquiry as a positive pious virtue.[6]

The practical consequence of the Islamic approach to unity is enthusiasm for the engagement of the life of obligations, with a sense that all is working out God's unified plan. Chinese religion, Judaism, and Christianity are all committed to the goodness of life, but with reservations. The Chinese understand that the search for harmonies might be frustrated because the proximate disharmonious processes participate in vast harmonies beyond our reach. The Jewish sense of suffering and tragedy means enthusiasm is qualified by trips to the Wailing Wall. The Christian sense of the inevitable fragmentariness of life in its human dimensions means that practical commitments to life's responsibilities are always to be accompanied and supplemented by intentional involvement with the transcendent God.

8.3 Ontological Status

The vague category of ontological status relative to the human condition has to do with the contingency of human existence and the interpretation of this with regard to the cosmos as such. Ontological status is related to the unity of the cosmos in many ways, but is not reducible to it. How or why does the world exist (whatever its unity or lack thereof)? What is its power of existence? The traditions specify this in ways that at first look very different but that have more continuity than expected when reflected upon as specifications of the ontological question. "Ontology," of course is a Western philosophical category, and the "ontological question" is a phrase from Heidegger given theological currency within Christianity by Tillich. We mean ontology in a much vaguer sense than this, of which the Western tradition is only one line of specification, a vague sense having to do with how or why things exist, contingency, power, and the like. The

Chinese case is probably the harshest test as to whether this category picks up on an important respect in which religions interpret the world relative to the human condition.

8.3.1 Chinese Ontological Ideas

The ontological status of the cosmos in Chinese religions, given the mythic pattern of the One, is that the plural world ontologically arises from within, as it were, rather than from some source transcending the aboriginal unity. Kohn (2.2) cites *Daode jing* 42: "The Dao produces the One; the One produces the two; the two produce the three. . . ." In this case the Dao is the aboriginal or incipient unity and is present in all portions of the plural world as the incipient unifying ground of the existence and connections of manifest diversity. A similar point can be made for later representations in Wangbi or Zhou Dunyi[7] of non-being giving rise to being or the Great Ultimate and then to the manifold things: the one unified manifest world of changes does not depend ontologically on another one of any sort, but on a principle of ontological origination within the unity of the one world itself, not one of its parts but a self-starting incipience of its own diversified unity.[8] We in this chapter stress the difference of the ontological point from the unity problem more than Kohn does.

The Chinese ontological conception of incipience conduces to a perspective of deep appreciation of spontaneity in things and in human affairs. The Chinese of course also have a deep appreciation for the causal patterns and processes of nature, of which human social and personal life take part. But the relation between the flow of temporal causation and ontological spontaneity in the core motifs of Chinese thought is quite different from what it might be in Enlightenment European thought (2.4.3). In the modern European scientific worldview the processes of nature are often construed as controlled by a mechanistic determinism, relative to which spontaneity would be a breaking of law-governed process, as in Hume's approach to miracles; or the deterministic process of nature might be construed as compromised by islands of indeterminacy with regard to the future, in relation to which spontaneity is the individual decisions that determine what is otherwise an indeterminate option, as in Whitehead's process philosophy. The Chinese ontological conception is different: in its perspective, every happening within nature is both continuous with other processes and also ontologically spontaneous, arising from the Dao, the incipient one.[9]

For Chinese religion the theoretical implication of the ontology of incipient one-worldness is that the human condition is part of the unity of the cosmos in two senses. One sense has to do with harmonizing with the processes that make up the whole. The other has to do with finding oneself situated in those processes as a spontaneous product and agent of the ontological arising of the world, a depth dimension of human existence. For Chinese religion, spontaneity is not in competition with the ongoing processes of nature. On the contrary, one finds one's spontaneous depths by harmonizing more closely with the pervasive unifying forces of the cosmos. Spontaneity is not willfulness, but a merging of the will with the principles of harmonization ingredient in nature's or society's processes. Or better, spontaneity requires a deconstruction of selfish motives that put one at odds with the harmonies of the One and an opening of the will (to use a Western philosophic term temporarily) so as to be conformed to the principles of harmonization in the cosmos, a message of *The Great Learning* and *The Doctrine of the Mean* as much as of the *Daode jing* and the *Zhuangzi* (2.3.3–4).

Among the practical consequences of the Chinese ontological idea are the practices for cultivating openness and a feeling for one's grounding in the ontological spontaneity of existence. The Daoists do this with the inner alchemy discussed in 2.3, the Confucians with their cultivation of the sense of Heaven and its mandate (and the Neo-Confucians with the cultivation of Principle), and the Chinese Buddhists with their cultivation of a mind empty and open to the spontaneous suchness of things.

8.3.2 Buddhist Ontological Ideas

Whereas Buddhism in most of its forms, especially that studied here, does not have a religiously important sense of a unified objective world whose ontological status might be in question, it does have an extraordinarily important sense of the ontological contingency of everything that happens, as 3.1 points out. This is not contingency in the sense of lack of determination by the past. Nor is it contingency on an external ground as might be the case for some theisms, nor internal ground as might be the case for Chinese religion in the sense mentioned previously. Rather each thing in the world for Buddhism is contingent in the sense of not having its own being, having no "self," as Eckel says in 3.2. Everything, including persons, are mere congeries of constantly changing elements, only conventionally identified together and named. Given the constant flow of elements, there are no stable things in the world to which words refer; or, to put the matter the other way, the reality of stable things is contingent on the reference of words, not on the nature of the things. Any given "thing" to which a word might refer is reducible to the causal components that are passing one another in the object of reference. So things in the world are ontologically contingent in two senses for Buddhism, especially of the

Madhyamaka sort. On the one hand any given object in our experience is contingent on our conventional reference for its identity over against other things in the flow; on the other hand, any object is contingent in the sense of being wholly reducible to the array of conditioning causes.

With such a different ontology from the Chinese, it is perhaps surprising that Buddhism's ontological perspective on the world is similar in precisely this point: the radical contingency of things on their conditions and on conventional designation fills the world with openings for freedom. Or, as the point is expressed in 3.2, coming to realization of the non-self-identity of things means that you need not be bound by any of the attachments to false conceptions of self or of other things. From the perspective of Mahāyāna Buddhism's ontological contingency, life is a field of opportunities for spontaneity. In this regard, Buddhism's discovery of freedom as spontaneity in the midst of dependent co-origination is remarkably like Chinese religion's sense of spontaneity in the midst of temporal process.

The Buddhist ontology of radical contingency takes the world into perspective by seeing things in what Eckel characterizes as the Middle Way (3.3). That is, things are recognized or approached with an attitude ready to negate the descriptions with which they are designated or apprehended. The fact that putative reference is to change makes this understandable: to say an object has such and such a character when in fact it is on the way to becoming something else is to be ready always to take back what has been said. But change itself is not the only reason for finding the middle way between negations. The very lack of self-identity in things, and in the knowers referring to them, requires expression through the elliptical forms of assertion and negation.

There are thus two levels of comparative contrast between Chinese religion and Buddhism in their theories of the world extrinsic to their ontologies. Both agree in stressing change and denying anything like an Aristotelian enduring self-identified substance. The Chinese, however, describe things positively precisely as changes, as transformations, as shifting proportions of yin and yang; change, not substantial things, is the object of reference. The Buddhists, by contrast, assume that the objects of reference ought to be static things like words and therefore have to draw back from positive description to the elliptical forms of reference through assertion and negation. Perhaps the Sanskrit origin of Buddhist thinking has deep affinities with the other Indo-European languages that lead many West Asian thinkers to believe in substances-with-properties like subjects-with-predicates. Eckel and Thatamanil, in commenting on an early draft of this chapter, remind us to not make the comparison too strict: "Conventionally Buddhists are perfectly happy to use words. They criticize their literal significance when words are viewed from the ultimate perspective. Conventionally there is no need to be elliptical. Ultimately there is no need to refer." This qualification, however, makes the point of the comparative contrast with the Chinese happy readiness to refer to concrete things at all levels. This is one level of comparison.

The other level of comparison between Chinese religion and Buddhism is with regard to reference. Being of a piece with the entirety of the harmonious universe for Chinese religion, a person's referential abilities and the structure of human knowing need to be natural and continuous with the causal processes of what it knows. Knowing, in Chinese religion, is a cultivated way of being in harmony, connected on the one hand with the rest of the cosmos and resonating spontaneously with its depths; knowing is on the one hand practiced and on the other intuitive, in accord with the Chinese conceptions of harmony (2.3.3). By contrast, the Mahāyāna Buddhist notions of reference are problematically related to natural processes. Because things in nature cannot be taken with simple positive form (of change), reference is made a function of the subject's conventional delimitation of the world on the one hand and of the subject's being fooled into delusion by taking those conventions to be more than they are on the other. For Buddhism, as explicated in chapter 3, even the conception of "the world" is a result of a special Buddhist reading of reference as much as of a reading of nature. Whereas the Buddhist approach to reference is to refer in such ways as to become free from suffering, the Chinese approach is to refer so as to get it right about nature and thus be able to reconnect harmoniously.

Chinese Buddhism is continuous with Indian Buddhism in the respect just cited, namely, the practical cultivation of the apprehension of the spontaneous suchness of things, their no-selfness or emptiness. The radical ontological contingency featured in Indian Madhyamaka and Yogācāra means that people need to realize the freedom inherent in things in order to free themselves and exercise their freedom. The practices of Buddhist cultivation are aimed at this realization.

There is a striking comparative difference between Chinese and Buddhist religion at the practical level stemming from their ontologies, however. The Chinese practical bent is toward greater connectedness and harmony, both regarding the processes of the world and the return to the One in depth. The Buddhist bent in part is toward disconnection, toward escaping the binding connections resulting from hypostatizing conventional unities and self-identities, so as to be free. In other part, of course, the Buddhist bent is toward connection. As Thatamanil writes in commentary, "The limitless compassion of the bodhisattvas is grounded in the realization of dependent co-origination. To realize emptiness is also to realize mutual co-dependence. Consequently, there is both a moving away from connections based on reification and a moving toward all creatures and their suffering." The Neo-Confucians were extremely critical of the Buddhist meditative attempt to reach completely empty nonbeing; from the Neo-Confucian point of view, that would be to fall out of the One into a pure fiction, and would be entirely contrary to the religious intent to maximize harmony. (What would it be like for a Song sage wannabe to team-teach a course on quiet-sitting in the Hanlin Academy with a working bodhisattva?)

8.3.3 *Hindu Ontological Ideas*

One of Advaita Vedānta's primary concerns is ontological, namely, to discriminate what is really real in the context where life is tormented with illusions (4.1). Although it has been common in the West to associate Vedānta with the Perennial Philosophy,[10] akin to Neo-Platonism with its levels of reality reaching to higher and higher unity, the point of Advaita is that there simply is not any other reality, lesser or not. True, there are levels of discrimination; but anything dual is *māyā*. The ontological distinction is between Brahman, full reality, and *māyā,* which is not reality. Chinese religion, by contrast, does not distinguish significantly between true reality and a vast realm of *māyā,* though it does acknowledge that people can be fooled by their own selfishness and by being unpracticed in discerning the Dao. Buddhism would seem to share with Advaita Vedānta the view that the realm of saṃsāra has an illusory, deceptive, and binding character. But what is religiously real for Buddhism is the subjective experiencing non-self and the reality of the rest is a matter of religious indifference, whereas what is real for Advaita is Brahman relative to which the subjective experiencing self is unreal insofar as it takes itself to be different. For the Mādhyamikas, as Eckel points out in commentary, all reality is conventional, "including the subjective experience of Emptiness." But not all conventional realities are as religiously important as that experience.

That only Brahman is real for Advaita Vedānta means that all appearances to the contrary are *māyā*. Thus the field of experience from the ontological perspective of Brahman is ready for discrimination (4.3). The unrealized person takes the world into perspective and is fooled into believing that it is real. The realized person simply enjoys the world for what it is, happy as described in the citation of the last two verses of the *Vivekacūḍāmaṇi* in 4.4.

The theoretical ontological ideas in Advaita Vedānta are those distinguishing *māyā* from reality, as expressed in 4.2.1. What is religiously interesting about the world, from this standpoint, are what we might call the puzzle-points, the places where in particular some element of *māyā* is taken to be real itself and also capable of being unveiled, like apparent snakes shown to be ropes (4.3). Clooney analyzes one such puzzle-point from the *Vivekacūḍāmaṇi* in his discussion of the five layers of non-self that ordinarily are taken to be the real self (4.3). This differs from the extrinsic ontology of Chinese religions, which identifies action-points as where harmonies can be affected for the better, perhaps with some spontaneous depth. The Advaita theory is similar in many respects to the Buddhist emphasis on learning not to misconstrue experience because of existentially binding ignorance. With much mutual resonance, Buddhism focuses on removing the causes of the binding ignorance, namely cravings that suppose permanence and self-identity, while Advaita focuses on identifying the mistakes and developing the capacity of discernment necessary to distinguish the true Brahman in all things from the false or dual. Thatamanil writes in commentary on an early draft here:

> After all, both Mādhyamikas and Advaitins focus on removing a habitual cognitive mistake. For the former, that mistake is the imputation of intrinsic existence or own-being on both self and things. For the latter, the mistake is the superimposition (*adhyasa*) of the non-self on the Self. These mistakes are the basic cause for the perpetuation of the defilements (*klesa*) or faults that mark the human predicament. In Madhyamaka, these defilements are *raga, dvesa,* and *moha*. This list with variations also occurs in Advaita texts. Both traditions believe that fundamental ignorance is responsible for these problems but disagree on the nature of that ignorance.

The outcome sought by Buddhism is to be free because no longer bound in ignorance. The outcome for Advaita is to be free because identical with Brahman, fully realizing the truth, previous error itself being part of *māyā*.

A practical consequence of Advaita Vedānta ontology is the path of discipleship that binds a proper male Brahmin to a guru, perhaps in a community of disciples, reading texts and working on the transformations necessary to gain ever better discrimination of the distinctions between *māyā* and the real. Chapter 4.4 analyzes this as *bhavana*. Advaita Vedānta practice shares its transformative theme with Chinese religion and Buddhism, though with less of an emphasis on transforming the world than much Chinese religions exhibits and more of a sense of becoming attuned to the true reality than Buddhism, which makes no objective claims about true reality.

8.3.4 *Jewish Ontological Ideas*

The ontological status of the world for Judaism is obviously reflected in its claim that the world is wholly created by God and would not exist without God. This point it shares with Christianity and Islam as well as many forms of Hinduism. Judaism is distinct in its note that there is a special ontological status for the people of Israel, set within the larger ontological status of the created order. Israel is ontologically special because it is defined in relation to Torah, which is God's revelation and in some forms of Judaism is treated as preexisting the world as the means of the world's creation (5.1.2). This is an ontological difference for Israel, not just a superiority of civilization as in some Chinese religion, or a readiness of a certain class of people to receive revelation, for instance, smart male interested Brahmins with a teacher and a text at hand.

The perspective on the world from the Jewish ontology of creation and Israel's special status is that the world is a problem. The problem is that, whereas from the human standpoint we are free and responsible, from the divine standpoint all we are, good and bad, is the gift of God (5.3.3.2). Another way to express this is the following. From the standpoint of the ontology of creation, there is an asymmetrical relation between God and the world such that God is responsible for everything. From the standpoint of the ontological condition of Israel, and even the rest of the nations, there is a symmetrical relation of reciprocity between divine command and human obedience or disobedience, between divine justice and mercy and human repentance and recommitment, and so forth. Because Israel is commanded to be responsible, it treats God symmetrically as an Other to whom it is responsible, and this is problematic because the ontology of creation is asymmetrical. When these different standpoints come into conflict or press questions for interpreting God's person, generally the asymmetrical relation of creation trumps, but without ever denying the interactive symmetry of command (in Torah) and response (5.3.4.4).

One of Judaism's theoretical ontological ideas has already been mentioned, namely, the need to understand the world as a field in which to be responsible, including taking responsibility for one's own faulty actions, at the same time acknowledging that God is sovereign over all. This is focused by construing life through Torah such that occasions for obedience are at once choice-points for responsible freedom and acknowledgment points of God's creative sovereignty. Judaism thus shares with Chinese religion a proclivity to view the world as punctuated with decision points for the exercise of responsibility. But there is little in Chinese religion corresponding to the Jewish view that our responsibility is judged by a God construed in highly personalistic ways; even the Daoist gods who measure and reward human action are represented more as bureaucratic functionaries than as the highly individualistic God who has a personal history with Israel. The Jewish emphasis on conforming to Torah, especially loving God with all one's heart, mind, soul, and strength, for the sake of pleasing God, has little resonance in Buddhism or the *Vivekacūḍāmaṇi's* Advaita Vedānta that do not give much place for gods whom it is important to please. In some other forms of Hindu religion, there is a kind of reverse emphasis on human beings taking pleasure in God that has its analogue in Jewish scholars taking pleasure in studying God in the Torah.

One practical inference from Judaism's ontology of creation is a strong focus on the worship of God. That worship reflects the dualism of the ontology. On the one hand is the straightforward address to God in devotion and prayer. On the other hand is the worship that consists in the practice of Torah, and the working through of the problematic parts of life resulting from the symmetrical interactive relation with God, problems concerning who is responsible for the evil in the world, and also for doing good.

8.3.5 Christian Ontological Ideas

Christianity shares Judaism's ancient motif of creation of the entire world by a monotheistic God. Perhaps more than Judaism it has interpreted this according to a great variety of philosophical constructions, Origen's being analyzed in 6.4. The creation theme is common in many forms of Hinduism, and the contingency of the apparent world on an originating source has analogues in Chinese religion. The special ontological element in most strains of Christianity has to do with the role of Jesus whom the "Prologue" to the Gospel of John identifies as the incarnation of the Logos by means of which the entire creation takes place. There have, of course, been many specifications of what this might mean, often involving complex doctrines of God as Trinity. The special ontological point, however, is that because the world is constituted by the divine Logos it cannot have a separate existence over and against God, Deist fashion. In fact, the way to a unity between human beings and God is laid through the Logos. In practical terms, following Jesus as the incarnation of the Logos is supposed to lead people into proper harmony with God. This special ontological twist in Christianity surprisingly bears close relation to the Chinese ontological conception of the world arising from its own internal incipient ground; but whereas Chinese religion emphasizes the world with its ground, Christianity emphasizes in reverse God as creator whose creative act the world is, formed by the Logos and guided temporally by the Holy Spirit.

The perspective on the world from most forms of Christian ontology is that everything in the world is potentially interpretable as the Logos or God, and thus as a connecting point in the potential existential unity between God and people, especially insofar as each thing has a way to be pure. Neo-Platonic Christianity provides a specific philosophical theory of how God is to be found in the world. Yet in nearly all strains of Christianity, ancient, medieval, and modern, there is an ontological play on the double meaning of Jesus Christ: on the one hand, the historical Jesus from whom the Christian Church dates its life and, on the other hand, the cosmic Logos or principle Jesus was supposed to incarnate and that subsequently is grasped according to the symbols of Jesus Christ. Put in other symbols, the Christian perspective on the world is that it is the divine plenum, a notion central to the scientific mind of Isaac Newton and, as we have seen in 8.2.6, with the Islamic notion of the rationality of the world.

The Christian ontological perspective on the world as the divine plenum or as shaped by divinity creating has remarkable parallels in some forms of Hinduism, for instance in the *Bhagavad Gītā,* chapters 8–10. This point is not weakened by the fact that Christianity recognizes only one incarnation whereas Hinduism recognizes many. There is also some parallel with the Chinese perspective on the world as a field of harmony-points at which spontaneous freedom might be exercised; the parallel is that the spontaneous freedom arises from the incipient ground just as the Christian believes that a responsible action is expressive of the divinity within. Whereas Christianity's ontology often leads it to equate acts of human freedom with divine action (modern process theology is a counterexample), and hence the pursuit of responsibility is a way of intensifying the unity with God, Christianity does share with Buddhism the point that the free exercise of responsibility is the goal of practice.

Christianity shares with Judaism the conception of the world as a field of responsibility both for loving God and pursuing justice. More than Judaism, however, it sees the occasions for responsibility in that field as connecting points with God, shaped by the Logos in their very structure and capable of bearing responsibility in a Christ-like manner. Hence the Christian understanding of the prevalence of grace: though it is human responsibility, it is God acting in the responsible person (6.5.3). Hence also the extreme form of sin, according to Christianity in contrast to Judaism: to turn from God, as Augustine put it, whose Logos shapes the very being of people is serious indeed, an ontological denial more serious and debilitating than a mere acceding to evil inclinations.

Though sharing with Chinese religion the sense that the world is a field for responsible action, Christianity stresses the possibility of alienation from the world and its ground far more than is common in Chinese religion. Metaphors of destructive, even self-destructive, disharmony describe evil in the Chinese context; Christian metaphors have to do with ontological contradiction of self and of the unity between self and God.

The practical consequence of the Christian ontology is the pursuit of holiness by means of availing oneself of divine grace in the world. For the most part, this means life within the Church that presents grace in the form of symbolic encounters with Jesus, the saints, holy times and places, sacraments, and so forth. But it also means finding grace, and responding so as to become more holy, in nature and also events of social life. This is remarkably similar to the Neo-Confucian project of becoming a sage by availing oneself of Principle, which can be found in all things. The actual practices of holiness in Christianity might have many similarities with those in Buddhism, including meditation, monastic life, even asceticism; some Buddhist sects urge celibacy like the Christian sects discussed in 6.6.2. The Christian ontological emphasis on God graciously present in the world, helping human beings, is different from the non-ontological but pious Buddhist emphasis on the grace of the Lord Buddha in that the latter is usually represented as merely an expedient means of thinking.

8.3.6 Islamic Ontological Ideas

The principal Islamic ontological idea, in fact what might be regarded as the principal idea in all of Islam—so important is the ontological question—is that the entire world is wholly dependent on God its creator. The internal dialectic of Islam involves defining the boundaries of the world by test cases of idolatry, *shirk*. The dispute between the Mu'tazilites and the Ash'arites recounted in 7.4.2.1–2 concerning whether the Qu'rān is created or an eternal part of God is perhaps the central test case. A fundamental underlying intent is to deny multiplicity within God, and that means denying parts of God that are determinate so as to be different from one another. Hence, even the Ash'arites affirmed that the Qu'rānic Word expressed in spoken and written words is contingent and created whereas the eternal Word in Allah is a disposition that is not internally manifold (7.4.2.2).

Islam and Judaism vaguely agree that the entire world is contingent upon God as creator, and share core texts to that effect. But because of its fierce insistence on the unity of Allah, Islam specifies that the Creator be non-manifold or simple, at least so far as that can be conceived (7.4). Judaism, by contrast, construes the Creator very much in personal terms with purposes and regrets, and especially a tension between justice and mercy; for Jews to say that the Lord is One is to affirm integrity and organization to the divine Person, not to claim internal non-manifoldness. Judaism has been less influenced than either Islam or Christianity by the Hellenistic philosophic tradition that offers abstract conceptual options for interpreting the nature of the creator and the creator-creature relation.

Islam and Christianity share profound commitments to the ontological claim that the world is created by God, and also are jointly shaped by the dual streams of Semitic thought in the Hebrew Bible and by Hellenistic and late antique Greek philosophy.[11] Unlike Islam's very great rhetorical stress on divine unity, Christianity's rhetoric has been Trinitarian, affirming a manifold of divine Persons within the Godhead. Indeed, within one line of Christian thought that emphasizes the "immanent Trinity," the three Persons are taken to be internal to God eternally and apart from the world and God's creative activity; this line dominated the great Christian councils of the fourth century and appeared as the orthodox Christian position to the early Islamic thinkers. Another line of Trinitarian thinking, however, called "economic Trinitarianism," ascribes the three-Person distinction to the relation between the Creator and the created world; Catherine Mowry LaCugna has recently argued that this was the better position all through the Patristic period.[12]

The range of philosophical conceptions articulating economic Trinitarianism overlaps in many interesting ways with the range of Islamic conceptions for the Creator-creature relation, with disputes about the status of the Word as Second Person of the Trinity mapping the Mu'tazilite-Ash'arite debate. Aristotle's insistence on self-sufficient simplicity, Neo-Platonism's metaphors of creation as overflowing plenitude, and *creatio ex nihilo* models of creation competed in both Islam and Christianity to afford adequate conceptualities for affirming the complete contingency of the whole world on the Creator-God while maintaining also that God is genuinely revealed in a divine Word expressed in the world. Islam, of course, never identified that Word in the world with a person in whom its worldly expression is incarnate, as Christianity affirmed about Jesus. But concerning the Creator-world relation, the perhaps surprising parallels between the Islamic and Christian dialectic are exhibited in the theology of Thomas Aquinas. Influenced by direct interaction with the Islamic philosophers as well as by the Neo-Platonic and Aristotelian elements of his Christian tradition, Thomas began his *Summa* with a discussion of the existence and simple unity of God, subordinating the Trinitarian distinctions to second place, and making them philosophical negligible.[13] Thomas conceived God's dispositions to be non-manifold within the divine simplicity, manifold only as expressed in creation; God can know separate creatures by knowing their simple origin within the creative disposition, not by distinguishing them in separate acts of knowledge. Thus in many respects Thomas' position has more in common with the Ash'arite Islam than with the immanent Trinitarianism of the fourth-century Christian councils. Although our seminar discussion did not explore the philosophical aspects of the Creator-world relation in any detail for either Islam or Christianity, it did indicate that this is a fruitful avenue for comparative research.

Islam shares with Advaita Vedānta the ontological idea that the manifold world is totally contingent on God as Creator. It would be another interesting research project to explore the uses in Advaita Vedānta of conceptions of Iśvara as creator and of the distinction between Saguṇa Brahman (with qualities) and Nirguṇa Brahman (without qualities), as Hindu attempts to affirm the total dependence of the world while at the same time affirming that the Creator can be known somehow in the world, a project like Islam's. The sharp difference between Islam and Advaita Vedānta concerning the relation between the Creator and the world has to do with the world. Islam affirms a strongly realistic and objective view of the world of nature and society, with little patience for construals of the world of ordinary experience as *māyā*. Advaita Vedānta's central claim about the importance of discriminating non-dual Brahman within the field of *māyā* puts the central religious focus on precisely that point where Islam has difficulty keeping the human from sliding into God or humans claiming divine presence, both forms of *shirk;* see 7.5 on the sufi mystics. That is, the common vague Creator-world affirmation is specified dualistically in Islam and monistically (or non-dualistically) in Advaita Vedānta.

The ontology of Chinese religion is epistemologically realistic, like Islam's, but not concerned to define a transcendence for the creative ground by a sharp distinction whose boundaries are marked by potential *shirk*. On the contrary, Chinese religion internalizes the ground to the Oneness of the cosmos by making it a deeper level of incipient determinate multiplicity. In fact, in certain core Chinese expressions there is not a single distinction between ground and manifold world but a series of nested incipient orders; Zhou Dunyi thus wrote of non-being (*wuji*), being (*taiji*), yang, yin, elements, and the ten thousand things, each item generating its successor, and only the last being the multiple organic world of processes.[14]

Because the strain of Madhyamaka Buddhism we studied ascribes ontological matters to subjective functions of human experience, it does not provide interesting comparisons with Islam at the ontological level, save in that very point: realistic ontology is not ultimately important for this Buddhist approach to the human condition.

The perspective on life deriving from the Islamic ontology of the total dependency of the world on Allah as Creator has what might be called three dimensions. First and most obvious is the complete and total submission of each person, and of social groupings such as family and state, to Allah, acknowledging and witnessing to, seeing, the dependence (7.1). The second dimension is the commitment to follow *Sharī'a* in all one's ways, personally and politically; as Haq puts it (7.3), to be human is to live under obligation and therefore take life to be a field of obligations. This dimension is part of the means to submission to Allah in the first dimension. The third is associated with Sufism and is the finding and worshipping of Allah in the world, with all the risks of *shirk* this entails (7.5–6).

All of the religions we studied take up a perspective on life as a field of occasions of responsibility, and this vague perspectival agreement derives from their ideas of unity, value, and causation as much as from their ontological ideas. Different aspects of the diverse specifications of responsibility are discussed in this chapter at appropriate points. The point to emphasize here, concerning the perspective coming from Islam's ontological ideas, is that the ground and goal of responsibility is the ontological relation between human beings (and the world more generally) and Allah the Creator. This consideration is not of much importance in Chinese religion and Buddhism, at least of the sort we studied. Various forms of Hinduism, including Advaita Vedānta, acknowledge that the ground of obligation and the contingent content of each person's obligations come from the contingency of human life generally on Īśvara as Creator; there is a religious element in the obligatoriness of one's obligation, as Arjuna discovered in the *Bhagavad Gītā*. But the pursuit of obligation is not the heart and soul of religiosity derivative from the human ontological status, as it is in Islam.

Judaism, Christianity, and Islam share certain themes derivative from the shared conception of God and the created world. They agree that one should love the Creator with heart, mind, soul, and strength, including submission to the divine will, the first dimension. They agree that social life should be structured by the Word of God, variously specifying that Word as Torah, Christ-the-Logos, and the Qur'ān-*Sharī'a*, the second dimension. And they agree in their mystical strains that God is to be found in the world and human soul, variously specified, the third dimension. But Islam more than the others stresses that the emphasis on obligation is definitive of the ontological status of human beings (7.3). The others would not deny the point, but they would soften its force. Judaism softens the point by attributing to God some of the responsibility for evil, whereas Islam tends to put a positive spin on evil as serving God's purpose, part of the maturation process for human beings (7.6). Christianity softens the point by saying that even faithful fulfillment of obligations may be fragmented and frustrated, and should be understood in terms of the supplementary relation to God, whereas Islam has no doubt that God's purposes are being served in history. Historical moral life in the Jewish perspective is puzzling, in the Christian perspective unrewarded, but in the Islamic perspective triumphant.

The theoretical implication of the Islamic ontology regarding the human condition is that it ought to be possible rationally (through *fiqh*) to conform to a consistent divine plan (7.3.3). Without dismissing the ambiguities involved in casuistry, and the fallible nature of specific juridical judgments, Islam attempts to conceive the world as a consistent expression of a moral Will. As noted before, this is a strong motive for scientific inquiry. Judaism shares Islam's faith that God is provident, but wrestles with the fact that apparent counterinstances to a fundamental moral ontological structure are so strong, according its interpretation, that it is hard simply to explain them as hidden purposes: human freedom is an ontological stumbling block to an ontologically moral and divinely ruled universe. Christianity says that the ordinary historical plane of the cosmos is not moral, however obliged people are to try to make it so, and that the providence of God involves transcendence of that historical plane.

The practical implications of Islam's ontology, of course, are an intense practice of worship—prayer five times a day for everybody, not just monks and nuns—and moral conformation of life to the law. Parallels to this exist in Judaism and Christianity, but often with the recognition that such intensity is a matter more for heroes than for everyone.

8.4 Value

The category of the value of the cosmos, and of human beings as part of the cosmos, is specified by different approaches to value in the religious traditions. But for the human condition, the vague meaning of value is how and whether human life is good, given the value constitution of the cosmos.

8.4.1 *Chinese Ideas of Value*

The Chinese conception of value at the cosmological level is expressed in the metaphors of harmony and unity (2.1). A thing is good by virtue of what it harmonizes and how it harmonizes with the whole. Things are better the more they are in harmony with the cosmic processes articulating the one (2.2). Miller, in commentary on an early draft of this chapter, puts the point with a stress on nature:

> The most important thing to say, I think, is that because the constitution of all human processes is the same as everything else in nature, there is not a great distinction between humanity and nature. Consequently the highest aesthetic value is placed on things that reflect most closely natural patterns, and promote the harmony of man and beast. As a consequence of this life of all sorts is intrinsically valuable and good, because it is natural. Nature is not amoral, wild, dangerous and beautiful, but exquisite when fully harmonized with human beings.

The perspective on the human condition of the Chinese conception of cosmic value as harmony is that life is basically good because it cannot help but be an element in the larger harmony. Even when things go wrong and people suffer, that suffering is possible only because of cosmic processes that tolerate it, processes that might be local setbacks in harmony, or because human consciousness allows for local obstructions of the otherwise good movements of nature and society (2.3.3).

The theoretical consequence for the human condition of the Chinese ideas of value as harmony is the articulation of a practical worldview highlighting occasions for harmony and disharmony as of prime pragmatic significance (2.3.2). Enjoyable things are enjoyed because they create, exercise, or celebrate human connectedness, harmony, and inner balance, particularly reflecting patterns of nature in human life; for instance, music and ritual, art and poetry, family life and cuisine are articulated as expressions of harmony. Contrarily, the pains of life are articulated in the Chinese worldview as elements of disharmony, disconnection, and inner imbalance. Given the Chinese ontological idea of internal incipient oneness, harmony is interpreted both horizontally, as it were, wherein one thing harmonizes with the processes connecting it across the cosmos, and vertically wherein the harmony enjoyed includes an openness and spontaneous sincerity regarding ontological roots (2.3.3).

The Chinese practical consequences for the human condition of the idea of value as harmony have to do with the religious practices of attaining or restoring both external and internal harmony, as discussed in 2.3. The practical intent is to make possible enjoyable harmony both with the rest of the cosmos and also with the spontaneous grounds of one's being.

8.4.2 *Buddhist Ideas of Value*

The Buddhist approach to value is somewhat different from the Chinese. Rather than treating it as a characteristic of things in the world, or the world as a whole that the Chinese perceive as pervasively good, Buddhists of nearly all sorts focus on the subjective mechanisms of valuing. The first approach to value in the Buddhist analysis examines the values imposed by our attachments and cravings. Mainly these are things falsely believed to be valuable but in fact are disvalues, negative and harmful valuings. There are at least three kinds of attachment-driven values/disvalues, corresponding to the three levels of suffering analyzed in 3.2. These include the plain pleasures and pains that please or hurt, the values and disvalues shaped by the fact of impermanence, and those arising from the deep illusion of self-identity.

A second approach to value in our Buddhist analysis is to revalue things instrumentally as means or blocks to liberation. What might be good for the liberation of some people might be harmful to others: the value of a thing is instrumental and contextual. This instrumental approach explains some of the more striking valuations associated with Buddhism, for instance, the ego-breaking menial and boring work in Chan monasteries, or the "excesses" of sexual tantrism.

A third approach to value in Buddhism is to say that, after all the above subjective analyses and practices are acknowledged, there still are more or less objective goods and evils in the world and these should be attended to in devising a life. For instance, the Eightfold Noble Path stresses the importance of a moral life and clean living as a condition for more intense spiritual development. In evaluating social conditions, justice is better than injustice, personal freedom than political imprisonment, health than illness. Buddhists should be committed to values such as these even though they know that, in the path toward true liberation, oppression, imprisonment, and sickness can be just as salutary instrumentally (as in the second approach to value) as their opposites. A truly liberated person, for Buddhism, will be more discerning about what is publicly and objectively valuable than one confused by binding cravings; but Buddhism, unlike Chinese thought, does not focus on an analysis of what makes such values objective as having any religious relevance; a Buddhist might engage in metaethics, but not as a religious consideration.

Things come into the Buddhist perspective on value according to the unliberated structures of their attachments. Buddhists on the path see things as having instrumental value or disvalue for their liberation and for that of other sentient beings. Buddhists freed enough to recognize the importance of responsibility in public life look to the real values of things in an objective sense, even if those values play no special role in spiritual bondage or liberation.

The fact that the first two approaches take value to be a matter of human projection or instrumentality already expresses a theoretical vision of how the world takes on value because of human subjectivity. This is a way of saying that for Buddhism, in contrast to most of the other religions, the intrinsic character of value *relative to religion* is a function of subjectivity, not of some objective character.

The very heart of the Buddhist approaches to value appears in the phenomenological vantage point emphasizing practice. Buddhist practice, as enjoined in the Four Noble Truths, especially the Fourth, aims to deconstruct the values that are functions of attachments. It does so by pursuing or avoiding things whose instrumental value for liberation is positive or negative respectively. And it concludes with a commonsense or public appreciation of things as good or bad for life when life is approached from an enlightened perspective. Whereas the Chinese practices are aimed to change one's actual connections with the rest of the world and its underlying oneness, the Buddhist practices are aimed to change one's attitude or relation to the world, after which things will fall into place (3.3).

8.4.3 Hindu Ideas of Value

Advaita Vedānta in the *Vivekacūḍāmaṇi*, like Buddhism, and unlike Chinese religion, does not thematize objective inquiry into why things are valuable or disvaluable in the ways they are. It recognizes the various affective elements in experience, of course, and relates these to the religious problem and its solution. Chapter 4.1 quotes the disciple's apprehension of the tormenting fire of saṃsāra, and longing for the nectar-like speech of the guru. But all of these values are functions of *māyā,* of dualisms set at odds with the Advaitic truth. This is not to say that within *māyā* there are no serious value distinctions. It is only to say that when properly discriminated as Brahman, those valuable things are no longer dualistically set apart from the disvaluable ones. The adept is at peace with Brahman as such, regardless of its manifestations in *māyā* (4.6). Brahman is not value-neutral or empty, however. It is bliss, as well as being and consciousness (satcitananda). Whereas a person's bliss-experiencing self is not the true self because of its transience (4.3), the true self, Brahman, is pure bliss, which many forms of Christian and sufi mysticism, for instance, would identify in their different specific ways with the fullness of goodness in God.

Ordinary people, according to Advaita Vedānta (4.2.1), live within the value-discriminating world of *māyā*, pursuing good projects perhaps but even at their best fundamentally unhappy because alienated from their true self. For the prepared male brahmin, the project of realizing the true self of Brahman results from the perspective in which the illusoriness of the world is sensed, at least in its pain and alienation, and the promise of a greater reality, visible in the guru, has come into view. This perspective on the world, viewing ordinary valuations as problematic functions of ignorance, is similar to Buddhism's first approach to value in noting pleasure and pain. But whereas Buddhism accounts for the error as mistaking impermanence and the empty no-selfness of things, Advaita Vedānta accounts for the error as not discriminating the non-dual reality from the apparent dualisms in *māyā*. The world for Advaita Vedānta invites the project of getting it right; for Buddhism, the world invites the project of stopping the desire to get it in its own being. As mentioned earlier, Advaita Vedānta looks upon the value structure of the world of *māyā* as an indication of opportunities for improved discrimination, but not as chances to harmonize things better rather than worse, the Chinese case.

Advaita Vedānta would say that value has no intrinsic character save for the bliss of Brahman, if that counts. Rather, the values of things in the world are functions of dualistic mis-discriminations that constitute the world of *māyā*. For those who have not realized the non-dual character of reality, those values are apparently real and guide such things as householding and even the taking up of the religious life. But if one is an adept with a "theory of life" based on the truth, there is no religiously interesting theory of why things have different worths and why that is important. Rather, the adept lives discriminatingly, "hearing, knowing, doing, but not speculating" (4.6).

The practical consequence of the Advaita Vedānta approach to value is to direct an appropriate person (a smart, interested male brahmin with texts and a guru at hand) to give up the major pragmatic considerations of life, determined as they are by *māyā*, and attend to Vedāntic study. The course is to transform one's self so as not to be hurt, or helped, by the values of *māyā* but to see through them to Brahman. Then one can live within what others see as *māyā* without being fooled.

8.4.4 *Jewish Ideas of Value*

Judaism agrees with Chinese religion in taking the world and its contents to be good. This is so because it is the product of a good Creator (5.1.2). The value of the world is resident in the world, not merely imputed to it because God creates it. As Genesis 1 says, God looks at the things created and sees that they are good. The world's goodness reflects its Creator's goodness. So the world can be read as an expression of divine goodness, beauty, and glory. Judaism is not particularly associated with a philosophic theory of the nature of goodness, for instance, value as harmony, as in the Chinese case. In most instances, the goodness of the world is measured by its appropriateness and support for human life. But the world's goodness is not limited to the domesticated realm of human habitation. The heavens themselves declare the glory of God. Judaism values things in the world in real and objective ways, not especially concerned about either projections or illusions.

The Jewish approach to the world's value provides a powerful perspective on the world that, on the one hand, should be enjoyed as God's handiwork and gift for human life and, on the other, should be dealt with according to the strictures of Torah. Life lived by Jews in accordance with Torah is itself a praise of God for the world's goodness. At the same time, the rabbinic focus on the study of Torah recognizes how complex the values of the world are and how complex people's responses need to be. Chapter 5 traces the increasing complexity perceived by the tradition. So, whereas Judaism shares the general appreciation of the world expressed in Chinese religion, it adds the revelatory dimension of Torah as a guide to navigating through the world. The rabbinic tradition of detailed analysis of experienced values and permissible responses is somewhat like Buddhists' detailed analyses of experience to identify egoistic projections and Advaitins' detailed discriminations of illusions. The Jewish problematic is not a matter of fundamental ignorance, however, not ego-based projections or illusions, but rather is a concern about selfishness, aggressiveness, partiality, and lack of wisdom, as well as for misreadings of the revelation.

The theoretical consequence of the Jewish idea of value, namely, that the world is good, is that life should be approached with the expectation of satisfaction and happiness. This means that life should be embraced vigorously and with enthusiasm, and also with hard work to make good things happen. There is no tentativeness in Judaism about life being illusory or objectively value-neutral, with only experiential projections making it seem valuable. On the contrary, life is to be invested with all one's energies. And when life holds more troubles or suffering than usual, then questions should be raised as to what is going wrong, questions that might examine conscience or conduct, or even that put God's intent on trial (5.3.3.2).

The practical consequence of the Jewish approach to value, of course, is for the Jew to embrace life through faithful obedience to the Torah. The prescriptions for this life include not only positive ways of appreciating the good things of life, of working to deliver and secure them and to use them for praising the Creator, but also remedies for restoring the moral covenant and ritual purity when they are spoiled. Although all the religious traditions have careful prescriptions for practice that come from their approach to the world's values, Judaism perhaps more than the others save Islam makes this the prime form for its general religious practices as such. For Judaism, because the world including ourselves (even with some evil inclinations) is good, and because that goodness displays the goodness of God, we should live in the covenant defined by Torah to enjoy, praise, and fulfill our roles. Chinese religion stresses more the importance of the human contribution to creating that value, not merely playing covenantal roles but playing constituting roles. Far more than either Buddhism or Advaita Vedānta, Jewish thinkers stress the religious importance of enjoying, fostering, repairing, and securing the good things in life, objectively or realistically construed, and hedging against the evil (5.3.3.1). Although Jewish thinkers point out many conditions when things are wrongly valued, and bear the internal debate about just how good the world is, as discussed in chapter 5, they would think that distrust of all experiential valuing as ego-driven projection or serious illusion are attitudes of impiety. Undue suspicion of the world's felt goods denies the goodness of the Creator manifest in them, and the goodness of the Creator's intent for human life.

8.4.5 Christian Ideas of Value

Christianity for the most part agrees with Chinese religion and Judaism about the goodness of the world (6.1), and its history has been powerfully shaped by the Platonic theme that to be at all is to be good. Its special stress is on the point that the goodness of the world is not merely a reflection of the Creator's character, a main point in Judaism, but is the real presence of the Creator; this "incarnational" theme was sounded early, in the Gospel of John, and gradually became a pervasive Christian motif.

The world from the perspective of the Christian idea of value is of course not only the manifestation but the living presence of God, the Spirit of God resident in nature, society, and persons. For this reason, the early modern scientific project of treating the world as value-free had a devastating effect on Christian sensibilities. Deism was a first step of retreat, abandoning the principle that the Logos is resident in the world as its shaping creator. Beyond that, value was seen as merely aesthetic and non-cognitive, hence subjective, or constituted by the human moral will (Kant); at all events non-revelatory. Much of modern Christianity has flourished either in forms that emphasize its moral dimension, perhaps coupled with aesthetic mysticism, or in forms that stress the Christological and Pneumatological symbolism of liturgies and other practices that do not treat the cognitive dimensions of science as religiously interesting.

The Christian theoretical interpretation of value agrees with the Jewish regarding the importance of life as a field of occasions for investing oneself wholeheartedly, with the added stress that this is one important way to participate in God's presence.

The practical consequences of the Christian idea of value include those mentioned for Judaism, with the contrasts to the other religions. The Christian contrast with Judaism in the practical sphere is that it does not suppose that the values of the world can be embraced with full satisfaction or that the human project will be properly rewarded in history. Rather, the value of things in the world is both simply what they are worth and also the fact that these valuable things are connecting paths to the true human fulfillment in unity with God.

8.4.6 *Islamic Ideas of Value*

Islam agrees vaguely with Chinese religion, Judaism, and Christianity that the cosmos is fundamentally good and that human life is good, though of course each religion specifies that differently. Islam agrees with Chinese religion in a point stressed far less by the others that there is a unity to the good of the cosmos, that human beings participate in a singular cosmic good, mirroring the whole somewhat in their own lives. Chinese religion provides a naturalistic account of this cosmic goodness whereas Islam attributes both the goodness and unity of the world to its Creator.

Islam, Judaism, and Christianity agree in specifically attributing the goodness of the world to its Creator. As already noted, Islam has far more confidence than Judaism that the world's apparent evil and suffering are integrated into a larger divine goodness in the world. Judaism in the forms studied here, save a few thinkers in the twentieth century, continues to affirm faith in God despite the incomprehensibility of evil, including in that faith a confidence that God will somehow keep the divine promises. Islam is less ready to admit the incomprehensibility of evil and suffering, in light of God's thorough presence throughout creation. For Islam, everything in creation, even the devil, participates in God (7.6).

Islam shares with Christianity not only the belief that the world is good because God creates it but also much of the European philosophic tradition deriving from Plato that to be is to be good. In the Neo-Platonic scheme, even though the material elements of the world are far down the scale of existence from the One and Soul, they still are overflowings of goodness: evil has no positive reality. Christianity in most of its philosophic dispositions insists that the natural goodness of the world, its beauty and nobility, is finite and fragmented, and that human life on that plane alone has no guarantee of fulfillment, however beautiful, gracious, and satisfying its parts might be; but taken in proper transcendent relation to the Creator's loveliness, human life participates in a divine glory that perfects historical life. Islam stresses more the goodness of the world on its own account because of the presence of God in it. Islam and Christianity share a range of mystical interpretations of God in the world and the world in God like that recounted in 7.5, with Christianity being less uneasy about idolatry. For at least some forms of Christianity, especially the Orthodox and Roman Catholic forms, the world can be conceived as a sacrament of God without idolatry (a point with which the Reformed Protestant Christian tradition is in some tension).

The Islamic idea of value shapes the world in perspective much the way the topic is approached in Judaism; that is, the world is to be savored for its beauty and the presence of God, and people should work to the utmost to follow *Sharīʿa* and fulfill their part in the plan. More aesthetic than early Christian asceticism or Calvinism, more rigorous and action-oriented than many forms of Roman Catholicism, Islam combines gracious thanksgiving and delight in its perspective on the world with an extremely rigorous view that people are defined by their obligations.

The theoretical implications of this include an emphasis on the world to be known as beautiful and expressive of divinity, though not in idolatrous forms. Thus like Christianity, Islam emphasizes science but is uneasy with the modern Western conception of science as value-free.

The practical implications have already been mentioned and compared with others, namely, an aesthetic approach to life coupled with moral rigorism.

8.5 Causation

The category of causation is difficult to state vaguely except in Aristotle's way of saying that a cause is something that answers to the question "Why?" The supposition is that "Why?" is asked about changes, about the occurrence of one pattern rather than another, about composition, about existential placement, about purpose, about value, about existence, indeed, about anything that can be conceived to be other than it is. Even in this vague statement it is necessary to recall that the "thing" to be explained is itself problematic, as the Buddhist emphasis on the nothingness of things asserts. There are wide differences among the ways the religious traditions conceive causation in relation to the human condition. Causation, as answer to the question Why? includes correlative causation when that is taken to be explanatory, as well as linear or ontological causation.

8.5.1 *Chinese Ideas of Causation*

The Chinese conception of causation is extremely important for its understanding of the human condition because the human sphere needs to be harmonized causally with the rest of the cosmos, and with its spontaneous ground. There are two lines of metaphors for causation as reflected in Chinese religion. One is the account of temporal change in which processes come together and diverge in a multitude of ways, not so much in linear fashion but in synchronic balances (2.2). This account analyzes causation as a function of the interchanges of elementary yin and yang movements, organized as the five elements, which in turn combine and recombine to form the ten thousand things. The wave-like shape of yang extension and yin return allow variations of amplitude and frequency, thus giving rise to different, changing, and interacting vibratory patterns (2.2). Some of these temporal changes are regular, even cyclical, such as the movement of the stars and the rotation of the seasons, and the Chinese carry this forward in the sequence with which the elements can transform into one another. Correlative causation, as analyzed by Graham and Hall and Ames,[15] is of this temporal sort, with the temporality being patterns of simultaneous processes. Others of the temporal changes are irregular and accidental such as unexpected earthquakes or the sudden appearance of the barbarians over the hill. Of special importance for the religious dimension of the human condition are the irregularities that result from human selfishness and disharmony. Miller, in a paper presented to the seminar, wrote:

> It was the cosmologists of . . . the Han who first succeeded in regularizing the patterns of correspondence between heaven, earth and humanity in terms of the five phases, an eternal hierarchical cycle of arising and decaying. What made this possible was the compilation of histories (the greatest literary and intellectual figure of the Han, Sima Qian, was a historian) from the analysis of which patterns of interaction between heaven, earth and humanity could be deduced. . . . More interesting to the Han cosmologists than the observation of causality between two temporally successive events in one particular situation, was the observation of correspondence between two different situations that are temporally simultaneous.
>
> Correspondence rather than causation is the underlying principle of investigation, and a continuous intra-related universe rather than a temporal contiguity of discrete objects its metaphysical presupposition.

(Miller uses "causation" in a narrower sense than Why? in order to contrast it with correspondence.)

The other line of causation in Chinese religion is the ontological one according to which the whole temporal flow as just analyzed itself results from being or *Taiji,* which in turns results from non-being. Put the other way, the aboriginal unity of nothingness gives rise to the undifferentiated unified plenitude of being that then has articulation in the differentiations of yin and yang. This "line" of causation is usually expressed sequentially, but real temporal sequences does not occur except as the transformations of yin and yang and what they comprise. So this second line of causation is expressed as spontaneity that can be appreciated anywhere along the temporal line of causation (2.3.3). It is thematized in the various uses of the term *sheng*, meaning "giving rise or birth to."

The temporal and spontaneous lines of causation are both crucial to the conception of the human condition in Chinese religions. The first articulates the breakdown of harmony with other things in the cosmos as well as provides the causal mechanisms to repair that, as in the *Exterior Daily Practice* (2.3). The second articulates the relation of human beings to the unity of the cosmos, indeed the aboriginal unity upon which the dance of movements depends as spontaneously produced; Daoist alchemy, certain projects of Confucian sagehood, and certain Buddhist meditations aim to reconnect the individual with the One, as in the *Interior Daily Practice* (2.3.1, 2.3.4). The temporal and spontaneous lines of causation cannot really be separated because any thing or movement is to be grasped as involved in both at once. This unity of the two lines of causation is itself a vague idea, because the different Chinese schools specify it differently.

From the perspective of the Chinese conceptions of causation as temporal and spontaneous, the human condition is to be viewed primarily as a project. The project is to stay in harmony along both causal lines and, if that harmony is broken, to repair it. That human life is a project does not necessarily mean a creative or aggressive project, although some elements of Chinese religion take that position. Confucians (2.3.2), for instance, believe that human beings need to create a civilization based on conventions that define family life, political responsibility, friendship and the like, and that complete or bring to fruition the excellent potentials supplied by heaven and earth; similarly, individuals need to be deliberate and aggressive in creating their own character. Others, however, emphasize the negative elements in the human project, the elimination of selfish preoccupations and attachments, for instance, that inhibit both harmonizing with the other ten thousand things and returning to the unifying Dao in all. The point of calling life a project is that, if everything is constantly changing, one must engage in constant rebalancing even to stay steady. This is one of the crucial points at which the spontaneous line of causation coincides with the temporal: to be human requires a constant activity of maintaining poise among the changes of the cosmos.

The implications of the Chinese conception of temporal and spontaneous causation for the theoretical conception of the human condition have to do with viewing life under the aspect of identifying changes, both regular and irregular. As Kohn points out (in the Japanese case, 2.4.2), the dates of seasonal transformation are more important than actual temperature for determining when to turn on the furnace. In deciding what to do, the location of things in ongoing identifiable processes is of paramount importance. Perhaps more than any metaphysical dispute about the priority of process over substance in the Aristotelian sense, the Chinese view of life as having to deal with things that are implicated harmoniously or disharmoniously in processes expresses its basic sense of causation.

The practical consequences of the Chinese ideas of causation have to do with practices that sustain or deepen one's harmony with nature and society, and the original one, or that repair disharmony in those respects. Music, dance, and ritual are exercises in harmonization, in bringing concordance and mutual resonance. Gymnastic, diet, and Chinese medical arts are ways of restoring balance. The Confucian and Daoist techniques mentioned earlier are based on effecting changes understood according to the Chinese conceptions of causation, including correlative causation. Miller writes, in commentary, that "what is religiously interesting in China is the relationship between earthquakes, revolutions, plagues of beetles, and an itchy scalp."

8.5.2 Buddhist Ideas of Causation

The focus on causation is central to Buddhism in ways quite different from its role in Chinese religion. Elaborated in the earliest Buddhist schools to articulate the impermanence of things, it was given detailed metaphysical expression in the Madhyamaka of Nāgārjuna as the doctrine of *pratityasamutpāda* or dependent coorigination and developed even further in the Yogācāra schools to express the constant change and instability of even ideas in the mind. Some of the early schools allowed for continuity amidst change, and even for the self-identical reality of some of the dharmic elements. But gradually, by the time of the Buddhist flowering in the early centuries of the common era analyzed by Eckel in chapter 3, the doctrine of causation amounted to something like this. On the one hand, everything is changing and any identity is impermanent. On the other hand, change itself is literally inconceivable if things are conceived to have any self-identity or own-being whatsoever: this was one of the main points of Nāgārjuna's metaphysics. Therefore, change has to be conceived in such a way that everything that can be the object of inquiry, or referred to in words, can itself be reduced to the multitude of causes on which it depends; and each of the causes can in turn be so decomposed, *ad infinitum*. Thus everything including the whole is empty of self-identity. The Yogācārins abandoned even the apparently objective reference to changing things in Madhyamaka (Nāgārjuna's argument was not really committed to objective reference, except hypothetically: if you believe that substantial things change, think again) and asserted the doctrine of dependent coorigination for even mental experience that alone is accessible for analysis. As noted in chapter 3 and above here, the Buddhist notion of causation is central to its fundamental interpretation of the Four Noble Truths.

The first and most obvious comparative point to make about the Buddhist doctrine of causation is that, despite its centrality and thorough development, it was never transformed into an ontological metaphor. The theistic religions use causal metaphors to say that God creates the world; Hinduism in one form or another says much the same, allowing for interesting variants such as that the world is the body or dance of the deity or Brahman; even Chinese religion says that the temporal passage of causation analyzable as yin and yang movements is itself "mothered" by a deeper Dao or aboriginal One. Not only does the Buddhist approach to causation not extend in that metaphorical direction, it asserts what is in many respects the very opposite: *pratātyasamutpāda* is such that there is no real ontological creation or dependence. Causation for Madhyamaka Buddhists is appealed to not to explain why things are as they are, not as a principle of sufficient reason, but to deconstruct the solidity of apparently stable and self-identical realities.

A second point of comparison with Chinese religion is that Buddhist thinkers frame their causal interpretations so as to loosen up the connections between things and create a space for freedom, as mentioned above. The Chinese look to causation in order to identify ways of enhancing harmonious connections. Whereas both Chinese religion and Buddhism affirm thoroughgoing interconnectedness, the former takes this observation as part of an apprehension of an organic wholeness to reality and the latter resolutely fail to make that inference. Even for Huayen Buddhism, according to which the Jewel Net of Indra contains gems in its knots each of which reflects every other gem with infinite symmetrical mutual mirroring,[16] there is no sense in which one gem is in palpable touch with the rest: between the gems is empty space and cords of karma. For most forms of Mahāyāna Buddhism, though not Theravada, and in contrast to many non-Advaita forms of Hinduism, karma too is empty.

Human life from the perspective of Buddhist dependent coorigination is exactly the opposite of the Chinese: not a project. To believe in the continuous self-identity of a person required to organize life as a project is precisely the problem for Buddhism, and embodies all the errors involved in the attachments that lead to suffering. Rather, for Buddhism one should learn to abandon taking life into the perspective of one or a number of human projects and attain to the objectivity of seeing life as it is—a vast swarm of changes determined by dependent coorigination. To be sure, Buddhists should pursue good goals, such as getting an education, building a house, or becoming a better Buddhist. Indeed, the entire symbol system of the bodhisattva, the person who takes the vow to become a Buddha but to postpone the fulfillment of that until all sentient beings are helped to enlightenment, is powerfully goal-oriented. Despite the vow, however, the bodhisattva's path cannot be followed many steps before it is required to abandon any sense in which one's self is committed to the vow; rather, one forgets self and transforms the vow to the great compassion for others. As Sung-bae Park argued, the key to the bodhisattva's vow is the "patriarchal faith" that one is a Buddha already, and therefore fully (or emptily) self-less.[17]

The Buddhist theoretical implications of causation similarly construe happenings in the world as intricately related in causal conditions. The force of the Buddhist observation of this is not to call for greater harmony but to back up and look at the attitudes of people toward the changing things. More to the point, the Buddhist emphasis is on the affirmation-negation approach, the middle way, to describe and assess the causal connections. From a religious standpoint, the Buddhist concern is not to make or break causal connections but to see them as empty, and therefore as providing openings for spiritual freedom.

The practical consequences of the Buddhist ideas of causation have to do with practices that break the attachments to self-identity's projects and that cultivate an attitude of enlightened freedom that can take things to be such as they are, and respond then appropriately. Unlike the consequences the Chinese draw from their conception of causation, which are to *do* something, Buddhist consequences have to do with taking up a new relationship to the causal process, including that within oneself, so as to be free.

8.5.3 Hindu Ideas of Causation

Causation in Advaita Vedānta has nothing like the religious centrality that the topic has for Chinese religion and Buddhism because it is put down to *māyā's* dualism. Within *māyā*, of course, it recognizes causation of many sorts. Advaita Vedānta (4.2.1) accepts the three gunas theory of natural change and causation, an ancient motif given clear expression in *sāṃkhya*; this is specifically different from but generally parallel to the Chinese conception of change and causation in nature as the dance of yin and yang vibratory patterns in the Qi. Like in Buddhism, thinkers in Advaita Vedānta believe in the causal powers of karma, and articulate religious success as liberation from those powers, though in a different sense of liberation from the Buddhist. Like in Chinese religion, thinkers in Advaita Vedānta entertain the problematic of the ontological creation of the world and consider what Brahman must be as Īśvara to create a material world. Unlike both Chinese religion and Buddhism, which take causal change to be pervasive and stable identities to be only temporary or conventional projections, the assumption in Advaita Vedānta is that causal change is a mask for ultimately stable unity and substantiality.

The driving force of Advaita, perhaps in distinction from Viśiṣṭādvaita Vedānta, however, is to learn to discriminate the true non-dual reality of Brahman in all the dualities of causation—natural, karmic, and ontological. Even the pedagogical causation involved in the project of transformation (*bhavana*) is preliminary to the discrimination of the non-dual truth that is accomplished by the transformation (4.4). None of this is to say that Advaita fails to be effective in causal ways: it is a school for personal realization. But its interpretation of that causation rejects the duality in what causation seems to be: it is in reality only Brahman, one and unchanging.

Advaita Vedānta agrees with Chinese religion over against most Buddhism (bearing in mind the ambiguity of the bodhisattva's project) that personal life is a serious project, at least for ready male brahmins. The project is that of realizing one's true identity with Brahman, and there are social and personal as well as intellectual elements to the project. The project of realization of true identity results from the perspective on life created by the Advaita Vedānta approach to causation. But of course the successful prosecution of that project eliminates the dualism even in "perspective." Like the patriarchal faith of the bodhisattva that he is already Buddha, the Advaitin conviction is that one is always and already only Brahman and therefore the externality or dualism in having a "project" is something that will be understood differently, as non-dual, in the end.

Within the realm of *māyā*, Advaita Vedānta accepts causal accounts of nature and society appropriate for understanding natural change and for maintaining the social institutions supportive of households in the life of the castes. Moreover it attends to a careful institutionalized pedagogy for those included in the Advaita Vedānta path. The *Vivekacūḍāmaṇi* is a wonderful pedagogic instrument, as described in chapter 4. The causal elements of personal transformation so as to make possible the realization of identity with Brahman are special to the Advaita

Vedānta path. But they remain characteristic of the duality of *māyā*. Brahman as the one reality is not transformed.

The practice of Advaita Vedāntins is as engaged as the Daoists' attempt to reach personal unity with the Dao or the Confucians' project of becoming a sage. It is less like the Buddhist view of enlightenment as changing one's attitude toward things so as not to be bound or hurt by them, or the middle way's combination of affirmation and negation: for Advaita Vedānta there is a clear, convincing, and univocal truth and, though it cannot be said except in dualistic self-betraying terms, there is a way to it. Even though Advaita lacks the impulse in Chinese religion to change the world to make it more harmonious, it shares with Chinese religion and Buddhism a sense that a fully realized adept is at home in the world and fully free.

8.5.4 Jewish Ideas of Causation

Judaism has not been wedded to any religiously important philosophical account of natural causation, such as the yin-yang theory of the Chinese or dependent coorigination in Mahāyāna Buddhism. So it has been free to think in terms of causation in Hellenistic philosophy, the alchemical theories of medieval Europe, and the categories of modern science.

The interesting question about causation for Judaism is how God interacts with the human sphere. We have already traced some of the questions concerning God's role in creating the conditions of suffering and the evil inclinations within human beings. There is also the issue of miracles, interventions by God to change what would have happened otherwise. Even modern Jewish thinkers, however, who believe in the determinism or quasi-determinism of modern science still ask how God could allow something as terrible as the Holocaust. How could God allow a world in which the deterministic laws of blood and psyche could produce the Nazis? How could God allow a world in which the people of Israel are targeted for genocide? Whereas secular thinkers, or thinkers from at least the non-monotheistic religions, could respond to those questions by saying that the Holocaust was a tragic accident, a disastrous chance encounter of various social and psychological forms of causation, Jewish thinkers are haunted by the idea that either God is involved or there is no God (5.4.1). God's involvement is to be understood according to both the asymmetrical creation relation and the symmetrical covenant relation discussed above under ontology.

Life for Judaism surely is a project of living in accordance with Torah to praise God and enjoy creation. The causal perspective for Judaism, assuming some sense of natural causation and how to get things done, has two dimensions. One is to live life before God in a fitting way. Saldarini describes the evolution of this way from the three joined points of temple sacrifice, study of Torah, and pious works, to the more exclusive focus on study of the Torah. The shape of this behavioral causation is to live according to law. The other dimension, cutting through the first but not limited to it, is the more direct encounter with God in which things that happen in the world are taken to be divine acts with intent and significance to which human beings respond. The shape of this second dimension of causation is like that of personal interactions. In respect of the first dimension, Judaism is similar to many religions that stress life lived according to law or dharma. But in respect of the second dimension, Judaism differs from the non-monotheistic traditions, and agrees with the other monotheistic ones, that a crucial part of piety is a personal relationship with God. There are, of course, many ways of specifying "personal relationship with God," and perhaps Judaism rarely approaches the anthropomorphic extremes of some kinds of Protestant Christianity. Nevertheless, the persistence within Judaism of the Why question addressed to divine intent marks the importance for Jewish piety of personal relationships between God and the people.

The theoretical idea of causation in Judaism, of religious significance, is the conception of human life as an engagement with God. This involves both the covenant role-playing of life according to Torah, in which God is engaged in praise, obedience, and repentance, and also the more direct saga of the people's and individuals' interpretation of life's meaning and the significance of its projects and frustrations in terms of their interaction with God. In respect of the former, the rabbinic tradition has stressed the conception of life as a plan of conformity to Torah, or inquiry into how to conform in problematic situations. In respect of the latter, far more than the non-monotheistic religions Judaism requires narrative to make sense of life: the relationship with God is a matter of story. Especially in the modern period, whether Israel or an individual lives rightly according to Torah is a point of interest within the larger story, not the other way around in which the stories would be instances of obedience or disobedience to Torah.

Whereas freedom is an important value in Judaism, both in political and in personal senses, it is not as important as competence and faithfulness at the pious life of Torah. Like Chinese religion, Buddhism, and Advaita Hinduism, Judaism employs ritual, prayer, and shared community practices to cultivate and reinforce competence and faithfulness. Judaism shares with Advaita Vedānta a dimension far less stressed in Chinese religion and Buddhism, namely the spiritual importance of the study of the sacred texts. Chapter 5 traces the development of this stress.

8.5.5 *Christian Ideas of Causation*

Like Judaism, and unlike Chinese religion and Buddhism, Christianity and Islam do not have any special theory of natural causation. The theories espoused by Christian and Islamic thinkers have been functions of the philosophic and naturalistic, if not scientific, theories of their various contexts.[18] Like Judaism, both Christianity and Islam take special religious interest in how God interacts with the world and with human beings; that is the first sense of causation that bears especially upon the human condition.

The Christian vague affirmation that God relates to the world as its creator has been specified in a wide range of ways. From earliest times to the present day the biblical metaphors of God as a personal individual with whom people interact have been powerful in Christian thinking. To the extent this is so, Christianity has shared with Judaism the perplexing conundrum of both asymmetrical (God creates the totally contingent world) and symmetrical (God and people interact) causal relations. But as Fredriksen points out, from the earliest times Christianity has also incorporated the Hellenistic conviction that the High God, as they put it, is eternal and beyond change; moreover, if individuation comes from being bodied in some sense, however spiritual (Origen), the High God is not an individual (a point made in other ways by Christians as distant as Aquinas and Tillich). This Hellenistic conception makes for a very strong stress on causal asymmetry between God and the world. God's eternal reality has to be something like a singular act that together creates the world, fills it with grace, responds to the Fall, and elects the to-be-saved (some or all of humanity). Chapter 6 traces variations on what this act has to do in the thought of Paul, Origen, and Augustine.

Because of the Christian diminution of the symmetrical interactive causal relations between God and the world, it was pushed to treat biblical stories of patriarchs and others wrestling with God in metaphorical, even allegorical ways. Christianity then stressed a different collection of metaphors for the human (and world's) causal relation to God, namely, those of the human ascent to God and of human turning to God. In these metaphors the change is on the human side, and God acts only in the singular multiplex creative act, subsequently drawing people and the world to union or enjoyment or cognizance of the divine by non-active attractiveness, the beatific vision. Chapter 6 traces several ways of specifying this point. Insofar as Christian spiritual life requires an interactive tussle, it relates to Jesus as the interactive partner.

Obviously there is a second sense of causation that is religiously important for Christianity, and that is the matter of human freedom. Most of the issues concerning freedom will be discussed in detail in chapter 9. The following can be said here where the focus is on the cosmological aspects of the human condition. In vague agreement with all the other religions, each specifying the point in its own way, Christianity acknowledges that life is a field for responsible behavior in which people ought to do the better, can and sometimes do the worse, and in which the bounds of freedom are variable conditions (not being in jail, having the relevant knowledge, training, etc.).

In vague agreement with Buddhism and Advaita Vedānta, but not with Chinese religion, Judaism, or Islam, Christianity holds that in ordinary life there is a special religious inhibition to freedom, a special bondage to sin and to the "powers" of the world (6.2). The ordinary state is thus a "fall" from what ought to be the normal conditions of finite freedom, and in the fallen state people are powerless to deal with that special inhibition of freedom, however skillful they might be at exercising responsibility in a more general sense; chapter 6 traces several ways of specifying the conception of the fall. Restoration of the full sense of religious freedom then requires a gracious transformation in which people are turned back to God or brought to God in some kind of union; and because the matter is one of freedom of knowledge, will and action, the "whole person," body and soul, needs restoration; Fredriksen explores pivotal conceptions concerning "bodily resurrection."

The perspective on life coming from the Christian ideas about causation in divine action and human freedom is thus less of an interactive model between God and human beings, as in Judaism in the texts and motifs we studied, than a model with a two-way orientation: human transcending of the ordinary world through turning toward or union with God in some sense, and human commitment to exercise freedom responsibly in the world without guarantee of worldly success. Even where asceticism and sexual abstinence are intended to model transcendence in immanent worldly life, the distinction is maintained between transcendent transformation of the human, body and soul, and historical practice. Sometimes, as in Origen (6.4), the transcendent transformation is not of the fleshly body but of the eternal spiritual body defined by intellection.

Christianity shares with Chinese religion, especially medieval Daoism, its emphasis on bodily transformation. But whereas Chinese religion supposes a unified cosmos within which the transformation of the Daoist adept is continuous with the processes of the universe, the Christian conception of transformation is transcendent as well as immanent. For Christianity, only because one can turn (or return) toward God and thus not be in bondage to the powers of the world and its fragmentary, frustrating character, is it possible to turn back to the world with loving commitment and proper spiritual, holy, freedom. Further study of the Chinese and Christian conceptions of transformation is very important. Just as Fredriksen says (6.6) that despite all the diversity, even contradictions, within Catholicism, and among Catholicism and gnostic and docetic brands of Christianity, their practices regarding bodily discipline were remarkably similar, so the differences between Chinese and Christian transformations might not be so great in practice as in theory.

The theoretical and practical implications of the Christian ideas of causation have already been spelled out.

8.5.6 Islamic Ideas of Causation

As noted several times, Islam shares with Judaism and Christianity the vague conception that God creates the world and the world is wholly dependent on God, an asymmetrical causal relation. Islam would regard a strong symmetrical interactive relation between Allah and people as *shirk* and, like Christianity, give metaphorical interpretations to popular expressions of divine-human interaction. With Christianity, Islam affirms that Allah as High God is beyond change on account of unity.

Like Christianity, Islamic thinkers believe that if one properly turns toward God in submission, one is free to act in the world in accord with *Sharīʿa*, properly playing out one's destiny in the divine Word (7.3.3). But most Islamic thinkers do not agree with Christianity's extreme interpretation of the fall (6.1; 7.7), and therefore do not suppose that a special religious bondage needs to be removed before proper human freedom is possible. Rather, for Islam the fall is a good part of creation: "The human exit from the Garden, then, was an ontological phenomenon, akin to natural birth. . . . Indeed, like nature, Adam had to evolve, morally, spiritually, intellectually—just as baby grows into adulthood, and a seed grows into a lofty tree" (7.6). More of this in chapter 9.

Although vaguely agreeing with the other monotheistic religions that the causal patterns of the world are the result of the divine creative will, Islam stresses the triumph of the divine will in worldly affairs, especially history. Because of this, religious life is required to be political (7.6). Jewish thought, by contrast, after Ben Sira acknowledges the power of evil and suffering to thwart at least temporarily the divine intent for just rewards; Christian thought, by contrast, sees history as not the full expression of divine goodness, which also requires human transcendence into unity with God. Far more than the other monotheistic religions, Islam stresses the creation as a unified totality expressing the goodness of Allah, a totality within which natural and historical causal processes play religiously significant roles.

The perspectival and theoretical consequence of this Islamic stress on the unified totality of the world with its causal processes is that all dimensions of life are seen as religious, as avenues for playing out one's submission to Allah and following of *Sharī'a*. In a variety of senses, all of the religions we studied claim that everything in the human condition has a religious dimension. But none other has maintained as consistently as Islam that everything in life, down to manicures and politics, is governed by religious obligation (7.3.3). This is because of the stress on unity in its conception of cosmological causation. Recent scholars have criticized the Western notion of *religion* as parochial, reflecting a European privatization of religion and division of life into related but distinguishable and partly separable dimensions; such a conception of religion cannot treat Islam fairly, it is argued, because Islam involves no distinction of religious from secular life.[19] But this is not entirely a matter of biased Western epistemology; it is also a function of the different ways thinkers in religious traditions conceive the causal connectedness of the world. Religion might still be one dimension of life among many but relates to those others in different ways for each tradition according to the conception of causation in that tradition. For Islam but not most other religious traditions, the causal totality of the world as God's expression is such that there is no obligation that is not religious. More on obligation in chapter 9.

The practical implications of the Islamic approach to causality have already been noted, namely, the imperatives to witness to and worship Allah (7.1) and to live life as the opportunity to follow the demands of *Sharī'a*. The singularity of the Islamic conception of causation is its extraordinary unity, not only the coherence of the world and its history but the coherence of that with God's creative action. Indeed, most of what is to be said about Islam's specifications of the cosmological categories for the human condition derives from its specification of the first, unity. Because of this, the important comparisons we made with other religions have already been expressed.

Many fascinating comparative projects yet remain regarding causation in the human condition. For instance, in respect of the totalizing presence of the Creator in the world, according to Islam, it would be interesting to relate this to the model of the world as God's body, say as expressed in Rāmānuja's non-advaita Vedānta, an equally totalizing conception. Whereas Islam strongly emphasizes human freedom of choice, thus accentuating obligation to divine will, the God's body model emphasizes the presence of God in individuals enabling blissful knowledge and holy action, dancing God's dance. What difference does that make? That question is beyond the scope of this study. Our comparative work continues in the next chapter in which the personal and social categories of the human condition are given vague and specific elaborations. Many of those topics, especially concerning freedom and obligation, already have been broached.

Notes

1. See John S. Major, *Heaven and Earth in Early Han Thought: Chapters Three, Four, and Five of the Huainanzi* (Albany: State University of New York Press, 1993); David L. Hall and Roger P. Ames, *Thinking through Confucius* (Albany: State University of New York Press, 1987); and Anne D. Birdwhistell, *Transition to Neo-Confucianism: Shao Yung on Knowledge and Symbols of Reality* (Stanford: Stanford University Press, 1989).
2. See also Edward J. Machle, *Nature and Heaven in the Xunzi: a Study of the 'Tian Lun'* (Albany: State University of New York Press, 1993).
3. Garma C. C. Chang, *The Buddhist Teaching of Totality: The Philosophy of Hwa Yen Buddhism* (University Park: The Pennsylvania State University Press, 1971); and Francis H. Cook, *Hua-yen Buddhism: The Jewel Net of Indra* (University Park: Pennsylvania State University Press, 1977).
4. See Robert C. Neville, *Eternity and Time's Flow* (Albany: State University of New York Press, 1993).
5. See Thatamanil, *Non-duality and Ecstasy: Śankara and Tillich on Theological Anthropology.* Ph.D. dissertation, Boston University, 2000.
6. Syed Nomanul Haq, *Names, Natures and Things: The Albhemist Jabir ibn Hayyan and his Kitab al-Ahjar (Book of Stones)* (Dordrecht: Kluwer Academic Publishers, 1994).
7. Wing-tsit Chan, *A Source Book in Chinese Philosophy* (Princeton: Princeton University Press,1963), 321, 463.
8. See also Zhuxi's "Treatise on *Jen*" in Chan, ibid., 593–596.
9. The line of interpretation of Chinese cosmology taken by Kohn in this book, and followed in most respects by Neville and Wildman, stands in at least rhetorical contrast to that initiated by A. C. Graham (e.g., *Disputers of the Tao: Philosophical Arguments in Ancient China* [LaSalle, Ill.: Open Court.1989]); and developed in beautiful detail by Roger T. Ames and David L. Hall in *Thinking through Confucius* (Albany: State University of New York Press, 1987); idem., *Anticipating China: Thinking through the Narratives of Chinese and Western Culture* (Albany: State University of New York Press, 1995); and idem., *Thinking from the Han* (Albany: State University of New York Press, 1998). According to Hall and Ames, notions such as transcendence, linear causation, being, and truth have only a western provenance and do not apply except mischievously to Chinese culture. One of their most mature and carefully argued defenses of this is in chapter 9 of *Thinking from the Han.* The rhetorical contrast between the two lines of interpretation is more apparent than real, we (Neville and Wildman) believe. Our own comparative

project does indeed employ comparative categories whose origins lay outside the Chinese tradition, and comparativists ask questions of texts and traditions that might not arise natively. Thus we need to be especially careful not to import foreign elements falsely into intrinsic representations of the Chinese cases; ironically, within our project we (Neville especially) are accused of forcing a Chinese, mainly Confucian, frame on the approach to comparison. On their side, Hall and Ames are vigorously committed to a polemic against such notions as transcendence, linear causation, being, and truth, which leads them to bias their representation of the Chinese case with what Whitehead would call "negative prehensions" and to represent Western conceptions in ways far too narrow for identification with much of the outgrowth of that tradition in the present situation (i.e., Neville and Wildman's own various views). There are perhaps two matters of substantive disagreement. One is our belief that Hall and Ames emphasize correlative causation in Chinese thought to the exclusion of the linear causal theme of roots and branches, the ethical concern to locate false starts and broken connections in development, the fairly constant desire to be centered because from that flows beneficial consequences for affairs. Hall and Ames recognize the many Chinese references to these phenomena, but do not accord them the dignity of a style of causation different from the correlative and more like that developed in Western thought (though not according to patterns of law, admittedly). The other substantive disagreement concerns their nominalism, their assertion that only particulars exist in particular connections, with a consequent denial that something else lies behind or within the particulars at hand. Against this we would argue that for the ancient Chinese the particulars of a given situation exhibit underlying patterns such as those described in the *Yijing* or the interactions of yin and yang; later thinkers such as Wangbi and Zhou Dunyi developed hierarchies (or "lowerarchies") of underlying presupposed levels of reality articulating the paths of incipience, e.g., from the ten thousand things to the five elements to yin/yang to the Great Ultimate to Nonbeing (*wuji*). If one is to raise the question of nominalism versus realism, or particulars-only, in the Chinese case, a very western kind of question, then we think the Chinese are realists of some sorts. See Ames and Hall, op. cit., esp. chapter 9.

10. See, for example, Huston Smith, *Forgotten Truth: The Primordial Tradition* (New York: Harper & Row, 1976); and Frithjof Schuon, *The Transcendent Unity of Religions* (Wheaton, Ill.: The Theosophical Publishing House, 1984), esp. the introduction by Huston Smith.

11. Haq, op. cit.

12. Catherine Mowry LaCugna, *God for Us: The Trinity and Christian Life* (San Francisco: Harper Collins, 1991).

13. Ibid., chap. 5.

14. Chan, op. cit., 463.

15. See Graham, op. cit.; and Hall and Ames, op. cit.

16. See Francis Cook, *Hua-yen Buddhism: The Jewel Net of Indra* (University Park: Pennsylvania State University Press, 1977).
17. Sung-bae Park, *Buddhist Faith and Sudden Enlightenment* (Albany: State University of New York Press, 1983).
18. See, e.g., Richard Sorabji, *Time, Creation, and the Continuum: Theories in Antiquity and the Early Middle Ages* (Ithaca, N.Y.: Cornell University Press, 1983); and Haq, op. cit.
19. For instance, Talal Asad, *Genealogies of Religion: Discipline and Reasons of Power in Christianity and Islam* (Baltimore: Johns Hopkins University Press, 1993).

9

Comparative Hypotheses

Personal and Social Categories for the Human Condition

Robert Cummings Neville

9.1 Introduction

The human condition is shaped not only by its setting in the cosmos but also by conditions defining the human, both individual persons and persons in social interconnection. Our seminar discussion ranged widely over the possible respects in which religions could be compared on the topic of the human condition at the personal and social levels. At one point we had twenty-nine comparative categories. One draft of this book had two cosmological categories and twenty-three personal and social ones, dealing with such things as memory and authority. But as the discussion progressed, we realized that our comparative hypotheses grouped around four main approaches to the human condition: *personal identity*, *obligation*, the senses in which the human condition is a *predicament* to which religion is a response, and the ways by which human *affiliations* cut across these issues.

The procedure in this chapter is like that in chapter 8, to discuss each of these comparative categories in turn. Within the discussion of each category, I shall sketch how Chinese religion specifies it, add to that Buddhism with a comparison to the Chinese, similarly adding Hinduism, Judaism, Christianity, and Islam. The sources for these hypotheses include chapters 2–7, the seminar discussion, and the reflections of the author of this chapter that have arisen from the process of putting it all together. As with chapter 8, to frame the hypotheses here it has been necessary sometimes merely to repeat comparisons made in previous chapters or the discussion, to rephrase points from there to put them into the language of the comparative category, to make points either more vague or more specific so as to bring them into comparison in relevant respects, or to develop hypotheses that had not come to our previous attention in order to address structural issues raised by laying out specifications of our four main categories.

The four categories discussed in chapter 8 obviously overlap and intersect with one another in interesting ways and that is true of those discussed here as well. In fact, the previous discussions of ontological status and value anticipate the discussion of obligation here. The category here of affiliation cuts across personal identity (socially and individually defined), obligation (conjoint and individual), and predicament (communal and personally existential). Yet the issue of the relational definition of the human condition has an integrity of its own, and so we have treated it separately.

What follows are hypotheses for comparative projects, proposed comparative judgments that bear further exploration and qualification. Perhaps these comparative judgments are simply wrong, not merely subject to qualification and further specification, but wrong. Most likely, further exploration would bring in surprising detail. Surely, further specifications will change their affective tones. I have tried to formulate the comparative hypotheses to make them friendly to further study, not so general as to be either clichéd or obviously foolish, nor so specific as to be uninteresting to those who deal with different texts and approaches.

9.2 Personal Identity

The vague category of personal identity has to do with how thinkers in religious traditions understand such matters as the differentiation among individuals, continuity of individual life through time, mental and physical existence, moral worth, subjectivity and objectivity, and individuation in relationships to others, to groups, and to aspects of the natural environment, all as generic aspects of the human condition. Thus the category is vague enough to tolerate Buddhist "no-self" answers to these issues as well as heavy-duty Western substantialist, "ātman is Brahman," and karmic transmigration answers. Our interest here is not so much in the anthropological differences registered in different religious cultures as in how they use these issues to articulate the religious dimension of the human condition.

9.2.1 *Chinese Ideas of Personal Identity*

The most important stress we found in discussing the Chinese approach to personal identity is that "groups predominate in all respects over individuals in Chinese society. That means that anyone is first a member of a family, clan, village, or state before he or she is an individual with needs and wishes. Justice, as a result, is a group affair; often entire families are executed for the treason of one, and typically groups of five families stand responsible for the neighborhood order" (2.4.2). The sense of personal identity in Chinese religions thus is closely related to its sense of affiliation, discussed in 9.5.1.

Human individuals themselves are complex harmonies of multitudes of processes in the Chinese cosmos; some of those processes run through individuals to the larger environment, and some have to do with organs and ways of behavior internal to the individual, with many mirrorings of patterns large and small. The shape of personal identity has to do with growing through the stages of life and their appropriate roles in family, neighborhood, and sometimes public life, individuating the person in those roles relative to the institutions and people involved, for instance, through the changing roles in family membership. Much in these various roles is ritualized, and ritual helps shape the integration of the roles into a complex dance in which many individuals participate in changing ways.

Moral aspects of identity are also predominantly social, measuring how individuals fulfill their obligations in their social roles. So, loyalty and filial piety are more important than the more personal virtues of honesty and perseverance (2.4.2), though the personal virtues are present too. It is in this context of social orientation to morality that the countercultural models of the Daoist recluse or the Neo-Confucian committed to the interior life of sagely perfection are to be understood. Miller, in commentary on an early draft of this chapter, suggests that "perhaps one could contrast learning (*xue*) as the achievement of personal identity on the Confucian hand, and forgetting (*wang*) as the unachievement of personal identity on the Daoist hand, the former being the full development of the root, the latter full regression to the root." To this Birdwhistell has commented that concepts such as *xue* and *wang* are gendered concepts, though the literal markers are not there. So Miller's astute Confucian/Daoist distinction is with reference to men only, or at least primarily.

With regard to mind and body, the Chinese assumptions about the universe as containing various modulations of Qi dictates a monistic conception, with mental activities being speedier modulations than physical ones. Physical processes (*xing*) and spiritual ones (*shen*) are both manifestations of the pure Qi of creation (2.4.3). When special desires and the evaluative consciousness develop ego-centeredness, mind and body are driven apart in personal behavior, part of the human predicament. The Chinese distinguish conscious knowledge from intuitive wisdom. Whereas some other religions put knowledge and wisdom at the service of the self, the Chinese think rather that the self is a bad idea, and emphasize instead the person as concretely embodied in relations and affiliations.

The perspective on life derivative from this complex sense of personal identity is heavily oriented to participating in webs of relations with other people, formal and informal institutions, and nature in various scales; see the discussion of affiliation in 9.5.1. This requires a theory or vision of reality that expresses the harmonic patterns of family, society, and nature in which one participates and an articulate sense of how that participation takes place. It also involves an understanding of participation as the root of one's connection with the unity and ontological grounding of the cosmos. The practical implications, in contrast to the senses of self characteristic of so many other cultures, involve not the development of a substantial self but the development of poise in being oriented to and participatory in all the various webs of relation within which one should be in harmony.

9.2.2 *Buddhist Ideas of Personal Identity*

The first approach to the Buddhist notion of personal identity needs to begin with Eckel's discussion of the no-self doctrine. In contrast to all traditions that view persons, selves, or souls as continuous substances that undergo or entertain changes, Buddhism, in the widely shared core text of the *Questions of King Milinda* and elsewhere, has held that the identity of a person is but a conventional designation, like "chariot" designating chariot parts. Every part of the self is only a conventional collection of parts, and so on down. Continuity of the person through time is similarly a matter of conventional designation.

The conventional designations of continuous personal identity would be fine for conventional purposes, in contrast to ultimate truth, if it were not that people suffer such pain from it. Believing that the continuous personal self is ultimately real, people languish in the ignorance that gives rise to suffering (3.2). Rising to the wisdom of ultimate truth, one sees things as they are without conceptual distinctions or conventional aggregations.

The real truth, however, for the Buddhism of the sort treated by Eckel, is neither the extreme of conventional truth nor that of ultimate truth but the middle way (3.3), a path threading through both conventional and ultimate truth to freedom.

So the more profound Buddhist approach to the question of personal identity lies in the metaphor of the journey, underpinned by the complex philosophical analysis traced in chapter 3. A person is a traveler on a journey. Most people wander about lost, but bodhisattvas have found the Middle Way to genuine freedom. Eckel and Thatamanil point out that much of the Middle Way is negative; this accords with the cosmological discussions noted in chapter 8. The no-self doctrine is part of this negative approach, and much of the journey of personal identity is getting rid of ignorance and the baggage it drags along. At the same time, personal identity can be viewed as the attainment of goals, of nirvana, or reaching the Pure Land.

The contrast of the sort of Buddhism we studied with Chinese religion regarding personal identity is not as great as might be expected. To be sure, whereas most (though not all) Chinese religious thinkers assume a positive and objective approach to reality, and take it fundamentally to be good, Buddhist thinkers often hedge affirmations with negations, treat conventional designations as functions of subjectivity, and emphasize the theme of suffering. Where Chinese religion treats personal identity as very much a matter of relations to others, society, nature, and to elements of one's own person, Buddhism has a much more individualistic focus, though with an ideal emphasis on compassion. But there is an unexpected similarity in that both traditions affirm that personal identity is a matter of harmonizing parts and relations. Chinese religion puts a very positive spin on harmony, whereas Madhyamaka Buddhism seems to say that life is nothing but harmony (dependent coorigination). The practical significance of life as a project of harmonizing brings both traditions into connection. It is not difficult to see why, in this respect, Buddhism could easily enter into Chinese religion. Of course, insofar as Buddhism emphasizes the negative aspect of the no-self doctrine, it cannot conceive of life as a project. But insofar as it emphasizes the pursuit of the Middle Way, it is a project of liberation. Thatamanil, in commentary on an early draft, objects to this distinction because "the contrast between no-self and the Middle Way is unwarranted. The truth of the no-self is the Middle Way." Perhaps in Hegelian fashion *the truth* of the no-self doctrine is identical with the Middle Way; nevertheless, it can be used negatively, as it was by Nāgārjuna, to block belief in causal progress and striving and yet alternatively to recommend the spiritual journey of the Middle Way. Eckel adds in the same commentary the point that "freedom from the cycle of death and rebirth might seem to be a pretty poor project to a tradition that seeks eternal life (Christianity), but this does not make it any less important in the context of the Indian view of saṃsāra."

9.2.3 *Hindu Ideas of Personal Identity*

The principal Advaita idea of personal identity is "the ultimate unity of interior reality (the ātman, self) and the ultimate cosmic reality" (4.1), and this point is common to many forms of Hinduism, itself a theme in some early Upaniṣads. Why is the identity of the self with Brahman not obvious? Because the self ignorantly identifies itself with the non-self (4.3). Thus there are two steps to the realization of the identity of the self with Brahman, discrimination or learning to distinguish the self from the nonself, and the practical transformation of life to realize the true self (4.4).

At one level it is true that only Brahman, one and undifferentiated, is real, and that finite human selves are nothing more than that, different only as a function of *māyā* (4.2.1). But at the more important level for defining personal identity, the self is sufficiently complex as to be able to have the project, first, of learning to discriminate the self from the non-self and, second, of achieving practical integration (*samādhi*). The self is no undifferentiated unity but is brought to full realization by means of hearing, reading, reflection, meditation, and integration (4.4). But personal identity in this second sense is inclusive of *māyā*. Many of the issues we have taken to comprise the topic of personal identity—continuity, subjectivity and objectivity, moral identity—are what the *Vivekacūḍāmaṇi* would call the non-self: the body and its material connections, the vital self, the mind, the intellect, even the realization of bliss (4.3). All of these are non-self because they change and are multiple.

So, whereas Advaita Vedānta recognizes the sorts of discriminated elements of personal identity recognized elsewhere, it disqualifies them for the true self. In the long run, personal identity is *not* an interesting or real topic for Advaita. The interesting topic is Brahman.

The sharp contrast between Chinese religion and Advaita Vedānta concerning whether ultimate reality is constantly changing or changeless manifests itself in their approaches to personal identity. For the Chinese, personal identity, defined through affiliations, is the very locus of the individual's approach to the ultimate: to live better is to improve poise in balancing relationships and harmonies. For Advaita, that sense of personal identity is harmful and one should instead withdraw identification with involvements and focus on integration and identity with Brahman.

Where Madhyamaka Buddhism denies any underlying substantial and unchanging element in personal identity, Advaita Vedānta uses that as the very criterion of reality.

Perhaps the most interesting comparative contrast has to do with what the realized adept looks like. For Chinese religion, it would be the person most deeply engaged and exquisitely sensitive to the changing harmonies of the cosmos, and transcendently connected to the foundations of the cosmos. For Buddhism, the adept would be free and able to engage in the things of the world without attachments. For Hinduism in its Advaita form, especially as analyzed in the *Vivekacūḍāmaṇi* (4.4), "the sage lives alone, enjoying the sense-objects while yet being the very embodiment of desirelessness; he is always satisfied with his own self, and himself is established as the self of all."

9.2.4 *Jewish Ideas of Personal Identity*

Unlike Chinese religion, Mahāyāna Buddhism, and Advaita Vedānta Hinduism, Judaism does not have an important cosmological or metaphysical story to tell about personal identity. Rather, what is important about personal identity for Judaism is (1) one's relationship with God; (2) moral life and the moral dimensions of identity; and (3) membership (for Jews) in the Jewish community and what this entails as a people living under Torah as that has developed from late Second Temple times. The last point will be discussed under affiliations in 9.5.4.

"Wrestling with God in an Imperfect World," the subtitle of chapter 5, a reference to the story of Jacob wrestling with God or an angel (Genesis 32:24–32), neatly marks out the Jewish sense that human personal identity is founded in the relationship with God. As noted in chapter 8, this is a difficult relationship because it is both asymmetrical and symmetrical. The asymmetrical element is that God creates the entire world, including the people in it in their entirety; that world also includes pain and evil. The symmetrical side is the human-like interaction between God and human beings. When the former side is stressed, the human sphere is subordinated to the divine as in Islam or in, say, Neo-Platonic strains of Christianity. When the latter side is stressed, God is represented very anthropomorphically, and human beings can complain to God about the pain and evil in the world, its apparent injustice. Judaism, especially in the rabbinic line discussed in chapter 5, maintains both stresses, never letting one totally suppress the other.

Now personal identity for human beings, in this double relationship with God, is that character that ideally is formed by acknowledgment and worship of God as creator of the world and of Israel at the same time that one insists on independent judgment about good and evil and the right to apply this judgment to God: why is there this evil when there should not be? And why is it in ourselves? Chapter 5 traces the increasing seriousness of this wrestling match from Ben Sira to Elie Wiesel.

The result of this character formation in the course of a developing relation with God, both asymmetrical and symmetrical, is extraordinary interior depth in the personhood of both God and human beings, a depth that can contain contradictions and still affirm fundamental goodness on both sides. This is not to suggest that there is no depth to personal identity in the other religions studied; Christianity and Islam rather follow Judaism in this point though stressing the asymmetrical side of the relation. And Chinese religion finds the Dao in the heart of the person (specified variously by Confucianism, Daoism, Chinese Buddhism, and Neo-Confucianism. Buddhism finds the contradiction between craving and freedom in the (no)self. Advaita Hinduism finds the contradiction of *māyā* causing the mis-experience of non-dual reality. But in Jewish conceptions of personal identity there lurks the suspicion that the interior contradiction is between two wills: for humans the will to goodness and obedience versus the will for aggression and evil; for God the will to create and hence control completely versus the will for engaging people in responsible interactions, almost as equals.

The other element noted above in the Jewish approach to personal identity is that (Jewish) human beings live under the obligations of Torah, that is, in community with God and one another defined by the covenant. Torah is the revelation of God, and so people are the ones, Jewish people the special ones, in and to whom God reveals the divine command. All of the religions studied here note that human beings are special. Chinese religion, at least in its Confucian form, says that human beings form a trinity with heaven and earth, completing what nature cannot do by itself. Yet human beings for the Chinese are of the same stuff and processes as the rest of the universe, and may not be as speedy and smart as gods and other higher beings. Buddhists are concerned with all sentient beings, not just human beings; but humans have sign-using capacities and hence can be preached to about the Four Noble Truths. Advaita Vedāntins say that what is special about human beings is that they are Brahman (not that this distinguishes them from anything else), not just creatures of or like Brahman but identical with it. But Judaism, emphasizing God's self-revelation and initiative in establishing the covenant, affirms that God makes human beings, especially those of Israel, special as those who have been brought into a special relation with God, receivers of revelation. Christianity and Islam follow Judaism here in their own ways.

9.2.5 *Christian Ideas of Personal Identity*

The first Christian approach to personal identity, especially in Paul, is very like the Jewish focus on the relation with God and the contradiction of good and evil within the soul, with at least these two differences.

First, in the relationship between God and human beings, the asymmetrical side is stressed over the symmetrical side, and the interactive wrestling element is directed at human interactions with Jesus and the Holy Spirit, both of whom are represented as being (at one time or another) in the worldly wrestling arena. By the time of the third and fourth centuries concerns to give a metaphysical conception of the Trinity, relative to which both Jesus and the Holy Spirit are located in the immanent trinity rather than on earth, symbols or icons of the persons of the Trinity functioned as partners in interactions. In both Origen (6.4) and Augustine (6.5), God's gracious saving actions are associated with the aboriginal creative act (hence the concerns about predestination) rather than timely interactions.

Second, concerning the internal contradiction of good and evil, whereas Judaism attributes the source of both in human beings to God, Christianity in Paul attributes the source of human evil to human beings alone in Adam's fall (6.2). This protects the asymmetry of the relation between the creator and creation. It also allows for a somewhat different disposition of the contradiction. On the one hand, if God is not the source of human evil, then God might not have personality in that deep sense that involves intentional contradiction; Christian thinkers have been far readier than Jewish ones to subordinate personal characterizations of God to "higher than personal" ones, for example, Light, Love, Creator of persons, Act of Esse, Ground of Being. On the other hand, in Paul human beings are existentialized as internally contradictory in spades! There is another sense, for most Christianity (though not perhaps for Paul), in which God is indeed the source of evil, namely in creating a world of nature and history that is not fulfilled by divine justice but that is fragmentary and finite.

A second element in the Christian treatment of personal identity is the problematic of soul and flesh, thematized in chapter 6. To understand this requires reference to the Christian approach to the human predicament (9.4.5). On the one hand, salvation is cosmic (6.3.3, 6.4.4, 6.5.6), and on the other hand historical life is a bunch of crosses—witness Jesus the paradigm. The simplest way to reconcile these points is to get the soul out of the body and save it while leaving the body to history and unredeemed suffering and death; this was the way developed by gnosticism and docetism but rejected by Catholic Christianity (6.3). The Catholic, henceforth orthodox, position has been that salvation is of the whole person, flesh and all, imagined somehow after history, or above it, or a combination of the two; Origen (6.4.2) and Augustine (6.5.1–3) have brilliant specifications of this point. Christianity often has stressed an eternal dimension to God, an eternal creation (for instance, in both Origen and Augustine), providing a trans-or-non-temporal locus for "resurrection of the body." Where the separation of salvation from ordinary nature and history is very sharp, theological supernaturalism is the result (6.5.6). Some thinkers, however (e.g., Origen), just expand the scale of nature and creation so that "our world" is a small part of a larger whole.

The Christian temptation to separate soul and body (gnosticism was declared unorthodox but did not go away) has no parallel in Chinese conceptions that see such distinctions only as matters of degree of vibratory activity of the Qi, save perhaps in Daoist meditative and alchemical attempts to develop the soul part of the body from the coarser rest of the body. Nor is there any parallel of the problematic of salvation in-and-out of nature and history in Chinese religion; the medieval Daoist conceptions of a multitiered cosmos have interesting similarities to Origen's levels of spheres of reality, both affirming one world overall.

Christianity would seem to have little resonance with the Buddhist conception of the no-self, emphasizing as it does the salvation of embodied selves. Yet there are interesting parallels. Paul (Romans 6–7) says that the evil in him is not really him but sin, and the good in him is not him but God, and he himself has no integral reality; but for Paul, that is a problem, not merely a fact as it would be for Buddhism from which to make practical inferences. Buddhism condemns strict asceticism as contradictory to the Middle Way, and so has much of Christianity; but both traditions in fact have emphasized extreme discipline and sometimes celibacy and mortification (6.6.2).

Catholic Christianity, especially in Augustine's form, would have nothing to do with a Hindu distinction between *māyā* and the true reality of the self's identity with Brahman. But gnostic strains of Christianity indeed have some parallel if *māyā* might be construed as a "lower and grosser" form of reality, something not strictly possible on an Advaita basis.

9.2.6 *Islamic Ideas of Personal Identity*

Islam is closer to Christianity than to Judaism in stressing the asymmetry of the relation between the creator and the world including human beings. But it is closer to Judaism than to Christianity in that it attributes the source of evil to God. These two points are reconciled in its view that evil itself is part of the purpose of God and will result in good (7.6). So whereas both Judaism and Christianity vaguely agree that human beings are at the mercy of evil, and hence personal identity cannot be defined exclusively in terms of moral identity, Islam can indeed make moral identity the key.

So Haq says that, for Islam, to be human is to lie under obligation (7.3.1). This is a function simply of being created in a world shaped by divine law, *amr*, "the divine command which is the fundamental constitutive principle of each created entity, placing it under obligation to take its assigned place in the larger cosmic whole" (7.3.2). That obligation is trivial for creatures that cannot do otherwise. But for human beings who can in fact do otherwise, it is what defines their personal identity: their cumulative career as moral agents living before God.

Judaism and Christianity share with Islam the conception of personal identity as including one's moral identity before God. They differ from it, however, in stressing the almost necessary sense of contradiction in personal identity between the good and evil will, and the peculiar sense of depth this gives. A moral agent, for Islam, can contain contradictory impulses, and indeed does almost as a means of growth (7.6); but it need not be a defining contradiction unless the person makes it so, only an instrumental one for God's purposes. For in any case, for Islam, God's purposes are served.

Although both Buddhism and Advaita Hinduism acknowledge moral identity and the importance of moral striving for religious discipline and for living out the fulfilled life, for neither is it at the center of defining personal identity as it is for Islam. Chinese religion does take moral identity as central, but interprets it in somewhat different ways from Islam, emphasizing the work of harmonizing properly (*yi*, righteousness). Islam construes duty to involve harmony, or playing out one's "assigned place in the larger cosmic whole." But the religiously important part of duty for Islam is that it is part of obedience or submission to God.

9.3 Obligation

Obligation is a vaguer category than might be connoted by the term. We use it to refer to any sense of ideal or norm for human behavior, any sense in which it would be better to do or be one thing rather than another. Thus it is far more general than categorical imperatives or obedience to law with which the term has sometimes been associated in Western philosophy. Obligation also extends beyond matters of moral behavior. In our vague use of the category it is an obligation to be in harmony rather than disharmony, according to Chinese religion, to be enlightened instead of ignorant or deluded. Obligation thus means those things the religions believe to define the ideal or normative form of the human condition, and the religions differ in this.

9.3.1 *Chinese Ideas of Obligation*

As mentioned, for Chinese religion the obligation is to be in harmony and to promote the harmony of processes in which one participates. This of course has many dimensions. Kohn in 2.1 and *passim* distinguishes the this-worldly from the transcendent; see the discussion in 2.2 on harmony and 9.5.1 on affiliations for expressions of the diversity of relevant harmonies in which there is ideal participation. At the same time that harmony is normative, Kohn points out that an evaluative and judgmental spirit is a vice (2.4.3). Rather, the sense of obligation should be intuitive for thinkers such as Mencius and Zhuangzi, a matter of deep wisdom, instead of calculative or sophisticated learning; a thinker such as Xunzi would hedge the intuitive element with solid training.

The perspective on life deriving from the idea that harmoniousness is good and obligatory is complex. First, life itself is perceived as good; indeed the whole cosmos is good because it is fundamentally one and harmonious (2.1–2). Appreciation is thus a large part of the Chinese perspective. Second, because there are many points at which people can affect the harmonious processes in which they participate, people need to cultivate both discernment of what is harmonious or not and competencies to do the right thing. Both texts in 2.3.1 deal with cultivation in these senses. Third, because most people are not adepts whose adjustments to subtle shifts in harmony are accurate and instinctive, ideal relationships are codified in principles and rituals. Miller, in commentary, stresses the fact that rituals (*li*) "are not rules or laws in the Western sense, but rather styles of performative enactment by which obligation may be expressed. What Confucius worried about was not what norms were true but how actually to interpret them in his life." Thus one's perspective on life is focused and stereotyped to lift up issues such as "the five relationships"; there are, of course, many other human relationships, but these five are given paradigmatic status in terms of which the others are perceived (2.3.2). Fourth, because harmony is so important and disharmony so hurtful of the whole, a blanket of rigid rules overlays the East Asian perspective on life, amusingly illustrated in the refusal to turn on the furnace until the official start of winter, regardless of the cold (2.4.2).

A major theoretical implication of Chinese religion's sense of obligation as harmony is the analysis of the way things work and are to be classified in synchronic and interactive causal systems (2.4.1). See the discussion in 8.5.1 on the Chinese approach to causation. The practical side of this is the discernment and nurture of what makes for harmony, often a matter of counterbalancing.

9.3.2 *Buddhist Ideas of Obligation*

The principle Buddhist ideal is liberation or enlightenment. As Eckel points out (3.1 and *passim*), this can be approached either as a flight from ignorance and suffering or as a pursuit of a goal. The ordinary actual state of affairs, to be bound in ignorance, is painful and provides a motive for the work of liberation. At the same time the Buddhist tradition is replete with attractive images of liberation and enlightenment.

In contrast with Chinese religion's major focus on the ideal of harmonization, understood as running from the personal to the cosmic scales of things, Madhyamaka Buddhism focuses on liberation from the bondage and suffering of ignorance. To this end it emphasizes harmonization as an expedient means to the attainment of that goal. And it can understand the enlightened life as one that takes up the perspective of harmonizing with other people, social institutions, and nature. But harmony, or the individuation of harmonious relations, is not the goal for most Buddhism, rather only a by-product of reaching the goal.

9.3.3 *Hindu Ideas of Obligation*

There are many layers and kinds of obligation in Hinduism; the discussion in the *Bhagavad Gītā* is one of the most famous treatments of duty in all world literature. Our own interest in the *Vivekacūḍāmaṇi* was much more limited and focused on the sense of obligation involved in the distinction between living trapped in *māyā* and living in a way that realizes the identity of the self with Brahman. Clooney presents this in a dual way, as a matter of discernment or enlightenment (4.3) and as a matter of transformation or actualization (4.4). The ideal for this stream of Advaita Vedānta is to be enlightened so as not to be fooled by *māyā* and practiced at living with the realization of one's identity or non-duality with Brahman. See 4.2.1 and 4.2.2 for discussions of *māyā* and the true human condition. The Advaitic ideal is to live in the truth of non-duality. This is one specification of a somewhat vaguer Hindu conception of the ideal as living in proper realization of what is truly real as opposed to living in ignorance of what is real.

Compared to the obligation to participate harmoniously at the center of Chinese religion, Advaita has a deep distinction between the apparently and truly real that has little serious counterpart in ancient China.

The Chinese of course recognize mistakes and understand self-deception;[1] they also understand that there are deeper and deeper levels of reality to be discerned by the wise. But the deeper levels of reality are interesting because they exhibit levels of harmony in which people can participate but would ordinarily miss: "the Dao that can be named is not the true Dao."[2] As has been said, participation in the harmonies of all the things with which people are affiliated (9.4.1) can be corrected and intensified, made more individuating for persons; but it is not a matter of rising from ignorant commitment to what merely appears to be real to a realization of a deeper identity. The medieval Daoist project of transcendence or return to oneness with the origination of the universe bears practical resemblance to the Advaita *bhavana* as a form of discipline (2.3.3). But the Daoist project is to make oneself into a spiritual being who borders on the emergence of form at the foundation of the world's creation; it is not to realize what one already really is. The Advaita obligation is to be true, not to make oneself into something new.

For the sake of clarity it is important here to recall that our broad use of obligation extends beyond the way that word would be used in most Advaitic thought. Thatamanil points out in commentary on an early draft the following context for the use of the words:

> The Advaita tradition, particularly Śaṇkara, rejects the notion that liberation can be the object of an obligation. Obligations require action (*karma*). However, liberation cannot be produced by any action. Furthermore, only persons who think of themselves as agents are obliged to act, and it is precisely the notion of agency that Advaita seeks to dispel. Ātman is changeless and therefore not an agent. Not only do obligations not apply to ātman but since the ātman is eternally liberated, no action or obligation is necessary. . . . Scriptural texts which appear to impose injunctions such as "The self is to be heard, should be reflected on, should be meditated upon. . . ." (Brhad II.iv.5) are presented by the opponent as an indication that liberation requires the performance of action. Śaṇkara responds, "We say that they are meant for weaning one back from objects toward which one inclines naturally. . . . These [texts] turn him back from the objects, naturally attracting his body and senses, etc., towards them, and then they lead him along the current of the indwelling Self." In technical terms, these texts are not injunctions but are merely eulogistic (*arthavāda*) and serve only to motivate persons away from their natural appetites (BSBh I.i.4).

On the one hand, the vow of a bodhisattva is: "May I attain enlightenment for the sake of all sentient beings." On the other, Mahāyāna Buddhism takes the fundamental obligation to be to attain liberation, even if for others before oneself. In many respects, this is not so different from the Advaita Vedānta ideal, particularly as expressed in the closing lines of the *Vivekacūḍāmaṇi* (quoted in 4.4). But for Advaita liberation comes from attaining a true discernment and actualization of one's fundamental reality, and for most forms of Madhyamaka Buddhism there is nothing like fundamental reality, though sometimes "even Mādhyamikas use such language as a metaphor for Emptiness," as Eckel points out in commentary on an early draft of this. Thus for Advaita, discernment and actualization are ontological attainments, realizations of an ontological state; one attains them by surmounting ordinary ignorance and the corrupting practical effects of *māyā*. There is no obligation to ontological attainment in Madhyamaka Buddhism, only the personal goal of liberation and the spillover duty to exercise compassion.

9.3.4 *Jewish Ideas of Obligation*

Obligation in Judaism is established by divine command, a command for justice for everyone and the command establishing Israel in the Sinai covenant. As Saldarini describes it (5.3.2.1), the rabbinic tradition found three things in the covenant: the Torah and its study, ritual, and acts of piety. Although the ritual involved has not been the actual temple sacrifice ritual since the destruction of the temple in 70 CE, those three remain central to Jewish conceptions of obligation. To be sure, the Jewish tradition has developed a conception of universal morality that has been extraordinarily influential on other religious and secular cultures. But, strictly speaking, that universal morality is binding on Jews because of their involvement in the covenant.

Obligation as variously specified in Chinese religion, Buddhism, and Advaita Vedānta has the vaguely common factor of being an ideal that should be attained. It is simply better to be more attuned and harmonious, to be liberated from cravings that cause suffering, to be enlightened with discernment and transformed to actualize Brahman. With Judaism, by contrast, being obligated by one's relation with God and by being in the covenant is simply what one is. Fulfilling the obligations does not enhance the human or attain special virtues so much as it is a properly thankful response to God's creation and self-revelation. It is a way of taking possession of the human gift of a special relation with God. And human beings cannot deny their obligations even though they can fail them: their obligations define them as human beings. It is always possible for people to acquiesce in their disharmonies, sufferings, and ignorance.

Thus the Jewish perspectives on life, deriving from these ideas of obligation, take life as the field in which human beings work out their personal relationship with God, and that is done by addressing the obligations.

9.3.5 *Christian Ideas of Obligation*

Christian ideas of obligation are very like the Jewish ones save that the notion of covenant is somewhat different. The universal covenant (symbolized by that with Noah) and the Mosaic covenant of the Torah are not in disrepair just because of giving in to evil impulses or failing ritual purity regulations, according to Christianity, but because human nature has seriously fallen and internalized the breaking of the covenant. Therefore the obligation defined by the divine law, while obligatory, itself can get in the way and cause sin (6.2).

The overarching obligation, then, is to restore the possibility of fulfilling obligations, and this cannot be done by fallen humanity alone. For this reason, according to St. Paul, God sent Christ to set aside the fallen nature in the ways Fredriksen cites in 6.2. The Christian, then, who follows Christ or is "in Christ" addresses two senses of obligation. One is to pursue the ordinary life of morality as far as possible, including the imperatives to bring others into relation with Christ. But this moral life can never be satisfied or fulfilled in itself, however much we give ourselves to it. For this reason the second sense of obligation is to "participate" in Christ so as to share his transcendence (resurrection) of the world to connect with God. That participation in Christ is the only way, for Pauline and Augustinian Christianity, in which human beings can fulfill their created status, otherwise ruined by an internalized fall.

Christianity thus shares with Mahāyāna Buddhism and Advaita Vedānta, but not so much with the other religions studied, a two-level approach to obligation: one level is the morality of ordinary life, and the other is the removal of existentially defining constraints to the plain pursuit of the morality of ordinary life. For Buddhism, ignorance has to be removed, with the liberation from craving, before ordinary morality can be taken at face value, and one's religious identity is a function of removing that ignorance. Similarly for Advaita Vedānta, human beings are ordinarily blinded and distorted by *māyā* and cannot find their true self that allows for ordinary morality at face value without learning Advaitic discrimination and personal actualization. Buddhism, Advaita, and Christianity give different specifying accounts of the second-level problem of obligation. For Chinese religion, Judaism, and Islam, there is continuity between ordinary morality and ultimate obligation.

9.3.6 *Islamic Ideas of Obligation*

As discussed in 9.2.6, the Islamic idea of obligation is that it is a created part of the world, the divine *amr* according to which each thing is an expression of the Creator's will. Obligation becomes especially operative in the case of free beings such as humans who can do otherwise. Obligation is expressed in the Qur'ān and *Sharīʿa* where it is understood to be a pattern of life.

The central singularity of the Islamic idea of obligation is the observation of the distinction between Allah and everything else, failure to do which is idolatry or *shirk* (7.4.1). This expresses the even more central point of Islam, namely, the witness to God as the one and absolute creator.

Comparisons of the Islamic idea of obligation with others have already been made under the heading of personal identity (9.2.6).

9.4 The Human Predicament

All the religions we studied suppose that the human condition includes a predicament. Something is wrong in the human condition at a basic level that partly defines the religious dimension, and religion addresses that predicament. The predicament of the human condition is manifested variously in disorientation and disharmony, in physical and emotional suffering and in destructive and immoral behavior. Religions differ in what they take the roots of the predicament to be and in what they say to do about that.

9.4.1 *Chinese Ideas of the Human Predicament*

The human predicament in Chinese religion, of course, is disharmony, some failure to pattern part of human life after the great patterns of the cosmos, and it is manifested in broken political and social relations, broken human relations, psychological and physical sickness, and failures of transcendence or identification with the One (2.2). Because of the Chinese conception of the cosmos as unified and composed of interrelated harmonious processes, it is difficult to understand how disharmony is possible. The answer is that the whole tolerates some harmonies whose integrity is disruptive of other harmonies. In the human case, this consists usually in some otherwise harmonious tendency being taken too far (2.2), for instance, due caution turning to fear, reasonable preparation turning to greed. Kohn points out that human beings differ from most other natural things by virtue of consciousness and memory within which extreme reactions become "part of the individual's repertory of reactions. Thus the human predicament arises with emotions and desires, which in turn influence conscious thinking and give rise to evaluations of things as profitable or harmful, good or bad. Self-perpetuating, these emotions, desires, and conscious evaluations are much harder to get rid of than to get into" (2.2).

Chinese religion's responses to the human predicament are various and need to be studied as different specifications of restoring harmony. Chapter 2.2 cites Confucian propriety, Daoist lessening of sensory inputs and the practice of nonaction, Legalist laws, cosmologists' "seasonal commandments," and popular control mechanisms for tying into "inherent cosmic rhythms." The medieval Daoists, influenced by Buddhism and influencing Neo-Confucianism, emphasized the cultivation of a character that returns to the root Oneness of creation, to the pivot-point where form emerges from the formless.

9.4.2 *Buddhist Ideas of the Human Predicament*

The human predicament for Buddhism is explicitly expressed in the Buddha's first sermon that includes not only an analysis of the predicament but also prescriptions for what to do about it. The discussion of suffering provided by Eckel (3.2) begins to show how complicated and deep the notion of suffering is supposed to be. They distinguish plain suffering, the suffering due to change, and the suffering "that consists of conditioned states."

Chinese religion, even that not inclusive of or influenced by Buddhism, recognizes physical and psychological suffering, as well as the misfortunes of communities. This is similar to the plain suffering (*dukkha-dukkha*) of Buddhism. Miller, in commentary on this point, urges us not to make too much of it:

> Suffering is not really a problem that Chinese religion goes out of its way to address. Perhaps it is in Confucian political theory, or Daoist medical theory, but I think it is fair to say that it does not conjure up in the Chinese imagination the sort of generalized misery that afflicts the western consciousness. Confucius said that to be a gentleman meant not being hurt when others didn't recognize you. Zhuangzi mocked those who were concerned with their name or reputation. But that's about as far as it gets.

The Chinese (except Chinese Buddhists) would not take change itself to be a cause of suffering, however, because things are always changing anyway, a fact that offers opportunities for improvement and gain as well as for loss. Nor would the conditionedness or ignorance of the emptiness of things be viewed as a profound suffering or source of suffering. Underlying the Buddhist approach to suffering is a hunger for stability and substantial own-being, a hunger not so important in ancient Chinese religion, which expects change and problems of harmonization instead. The Chinese, to be sure, would associate *disorder* with suffering, though not all change is disorder. Elaborating on this point in an early draft, Eckel writes:

> "Hunger" is an interesting metaphor. You are absolutely right when you say that the only solution the Indian tradition will accept is one that is permanent and free from the change and suffering of *saṃsāra*. This is why Buddhists will accept nothing less than the permanent cessation of a process that is characterized completely by change. It also is the reason why Mahāyāna Buddhists smuggled in the word "eternal" (*nitya*) when they spoke about the Buddha, even though it is a fundamental axiom in the tradition that nothing is eternal (*sarvam anityam*). One might be tempted to conclude from this that the Buddha is nothing. Ultimately this is not far from the truth. To carry the point further, however, you have to acknowledge a higher level of cessation: not merely a cessation of *saṃsāra* but a cessation of the distinction between *saṃsāra* and nirvāṇa.

The difference in perspective between Indian Buddhism and Chinese religion has much to do with tone, insofar as it is a function of differing views of the human predicament. Even when things are bad, Chinese religion has a deep confidence in the larger and higher harmonies of the cosmos; although one's proximate life might be in disarray, with psychological and physical suffering, that life is still assumed to be in continuity with the larger harmonies. Indian Buddhism has a dour side: life is like living with a poisoned arrow in one's flesh, the removal of which displaces the delightful discourse of thinkers on the imponderables of the universe.

9.4.3 *Hindu Ideas of the Human Predicament*

The human predicament according to the *Vivekacūḍāmaṇi* is *māyā*, and the analysis of *māyā* in that text is not that it is mere epistemological ignorance but what Clooney calls an ontological condition (4.4.4). Specifically, the three guṇas, *tamas, rajas,* and *sattva,* in their very material workings conceal, project, and cognitively guide the self so as to live in confusion; society thus is confused. *Māyā* is the creator of the material world: "Difference—as objective, as projected by the mind—is due to *māyā* (*Vivekacūḍāmaṇi* 444); it is the power of the Lord experienced as the material world on the one hand, and embodiedness on the other (444). The world as we know it is knowable only in and through *māyā*" (4.2.1). But one does not have to experience the world as objective and full of difference, taking that to be real. "*Māyā* is ignorance with body and with power; it is comprehensive, functioning on multiple levels, as a powerful, world-disfiguring force that requires a comparable response. But the solution is possible, precisely because ignorance is not essential to human nature; it is a mistake which can be remedied, dispelled" (4.2.1).

Much of the comparison with Chinese religion concerning obligation applies here as well, obligation being relative to the predicament. In contrast to Advaita Vedānta's deep metaphysical distinction between *māyā* on the one hand and on the other living with discernment and an actualization of one's identity with Brahman, the Chinese construe the human predicament as consisting simply of disharmonies that block the natural processes of life and inhibit the kind of transcendence that constitutes a higher level of harmony. For the Chinese, the processes of nature are fundamentally good, and human disharmony is possible only because we unwittingly can turn small harmonies against larger ones, dropping heavy objects on our feet or pushing caution to cowardice. For the *Vivekacūḍāmaṇi*'s Advaita, those natural processes are already unreal and deceptive. To experience the world as manifold is natural and wrong, leading to deep anguish.

Buddhism and Advaita do not share a common analysis of the human condition. For the former, the problem is thinking something is real in the permanent sense when it is not; for the latter the problem is thinking something changing is real when only the permanent is. For the former, the predicament is that things are in fact empty, if only we understood in discerning ways; for the latter, the predicament is that things are in fact full, pure Brahman, if only we could see beyond the deluding appearance of *māyā*. Buddhism and Advaita do share much the same practical response to the human predicament, namely, to learn to discern what is real (or is not) and to transform oneself so as to live in light of that discernment. Discernment and transformation are subjects for deeper comparative analysis.

9.4.4 *Jewish Ideas of the Human Predicament*

Despite the goodness of God and the divine creation, human beings are in a predicament because that creation includes evil impulses. Thus the predicament is created by God. "The Rabbis held God, not Adam, responsible for the general state of human life with its ambiguities and evil and thus the complexity of life was to be explained through complexity in God" (5.3.3.2.2). Nevertheless, human beings are obliged to be good, and therefore must work strenuously against their evil inclinations (5.3.4.2). Moreover, God on the one hand will be just and reward good and the struggle against evil, and on the other hand will be merciful to those who do evil and repent.

The modern period has not been gentle with the Jewish conviction that the human predicament is not so bad that strenuous effort and a merciful God will bring the rewards one would expect of a good and provident God. Chapter 5.1.1 points out that the leader of modern orthodox Judaism, Rabbi Joseph Soloveitchik, reaffirmed the centrality and sufficiency of life under Torah, with the modern concerns about repentance and anxiety serving to reconstitute the self and repair the human-divine relationship. But post-Holocaust modern writers question how God can be conceived at all as good and provident in light of the Nazi atrocities. And the particular atrocities against Jews are not the only sign that God seems neither just nor merciful. So part of the modern human predicament, for Jewish as well as Christian and secular writers, is that the personal Creator and Wrestler God seems to have abandoned the human scene. In face of this, a radically discontinuous interpretation of the human predicament is attractive to many Jewish thinkers, namely, that there is no personal God and the belief in divine providence, justice, and mercy is simply mistaken.

Not Chinese religion, nor Buddhism, nor Advaita Hinduism construe the human predicament as a complication of the relation between a personal creator God and people. There are various creation themes in those religions (perhaps least in sophisticated Mahāyāna Buddhism) and there are all sorts of complications between people and what is really real. But none interpret the human predicament as the failure, or at least inevitable breaking, of a covenant. Like all the other religions studied here, Judaism affirms the importance of effort in standing against and correcting evil impulses, selfish behavior, corrupting cravings, and ignorant perversions of reality. But unlike them, it finds a deeper part of the human predicament to rest in the divine responsibility for evil.

9.4.5 *Christian Ideas of the Human Predicament*

The human predicament for Christianity is complex, surrounded as people are by the demons and powers of this world and rendered impotent by their own fallen nature (6.2). But the human predicament is not merely this tough situation. Early Christianity quickly gave up this interpretation of the predicament when Jesus did not return quickly to fix things up in ordinary history. Rather, as said earlier, by the time of the late gospels such as Luke's, Jesus' resurrection was not to ordinary life to do battle against evil but readying to a further ascension into heaven, joining with God, showing human beings the way there, and sending back the Holy Spirit to guide people in their life on earth.

So the human predicament is that finite life itself is fragmentary and that moral rewards and punishments do not add up in ordinary history even for the saved. In this sense, evil is indeed part of creation whose source is God. Salvation requires doing the best people can in ordinary life but also connecting to God, a connection made possible by Christ. As mentioned earlier, this contrasts with both Judaism, which hopes for redemption within history despite the deep worries about why that seems not to be happening, and Islam, which is confident of redemption within history and in connection with heaven, a part of the larger created order, without much worry about the recalcitrance of evil. Christianity is one with Buddhism and Advaita Vedānta, in a vague respect, in taking ordinary life never to be perfectly fulfilling on its own. Rather, the proper attitude toward ordinary life must be taken up from a perspective outside that ordinary context, a transvaluation of values, as it were. Of course Christianity, Buddhism, and Hinduism specify this point very differently.

9.4.6 *Islamic Ideas of the Human Predicament*

As chapter 7 makes clear, the human predicament for Islam comes from the fact that there is a divine law and human beings are free to disobey it. Moreover, the world has temptations to do that, although there is no necessity of disobedience. Moreover, through Muḥammad Allah has revealed the divine law in the Qur'ān so that there need not be much confusion about it, particularly in light of the development of the legal tradition.

The central problem in the human predicament, so important that Haq calls it an obsession (7.4.2), is idolatry, *shirk*. Idolatry is not just a simple mistake about God, nor merely an expression of human selfishness, narcissism, or grandiosity, though it might be those things. Rather, precisely because of the immediate asymmetrical relation between the Creator and the creation discussed in chapter 8, there is no buffer between God and the world. So God is immediately present to human beings, nearer than their jugular vein. Or from the standpoint of the mystics, mystical ecstasy can take them up into God or fill them with the divine presence, depending on how you look at it. Haq (7.5) discusses the very great difficulty the Sufis face of avoiding *shirk* while enjoying God. This is the most difficult part of the human predicament.

Much of Christianity, by contrast, celebrates successful idolatry as incarnational religion or *theosis*, the divinization of human beings. For such Christianity, the revelation in Christ does not have to be classified as either eternal and wholly divine, or temporal and wholly created, although those were terms in famous controversies. Rather, Jesus and the Holy Spirit are both interpreted as extensions of God into the world, manifested in creaturely ways and "partaking of both natures" as the Trinitarian discussions put it. Thus the vaguely shared conviction that God wholly creates the world that is wholly dependent on the divine creative act is specified in two very different ways: in Islam there is a sharp break between God and His creatures, whereas in Christianity the creative act provides continuity, though the direction of action is still asymmetrical.

The chief difference between Islam and Judaism regarding the human predicament, as has been mentioned often, concerns the significance of evil. Whereas both agree that human wickedness is part of the divine creation, Judaism, especially in its later developments (5.4), cannot affirm easily that it can be justified by being put to good use. Chinese religion, Buddhism, and Advaita Vedānta do not have much that is like the Islamic problematic of *shirk* or the Islamic conception of the necessary victory of God.

9.5 Affiliations

Under the category of affiliations fall those aspects of the human condition that are to be conceived primarily as relations. For instance, societies in their religious dimensions are affiliations defining the human condition, as are interactions of individuals and groups with elements in the natural environment. Although all the religions we studied acknowledge individuals and religiously important aspects of individuality, sometimes the more important "unit" for the human condition is a group, community, or relation.

9.5.1 Chinese Ideas Concerning Affiliations

As has been stressed in chapter 2 and throughout chapters 8 and 9, Chinese religion regards the human condition as *primarily* affiliative, and the affiliation is with the entire cosmos, not merely human society or the environment. Moreover, humanly important affiliations are to many things of different scales, often arranged hierarchically. For instance, the *Exterior Daily Practice* (2.3.1) advocates properly harmonious affiliation first with the most encompassing sphere, heaven and earth, then with the more proximate sun and moon, then with the society's law, then the model of kingship, and then parents, closest to home. With respect to each scale of thing there is an appropriate kind of harmony involved in proper affiliation: with those mentioned they are respect, honor, fear, following, and obedience. These are all instances of deference in a vague sense, but deference of an appropriate sort—you could not "obey" heaven and earth as you can parents. That text goes on to list many other things or people, affiliation with which defines the human condition, harmonious affiliation defining virtue and disharmonious affiliation constituting some aspect of the human predicament: superiors, inferiors, good things, bad things, perfect people, debauched people, high knowledge, deep knowledge, luxury, human perfection, others' flaws, others' virtues, skillful means, one's neighborhood, the wise, the good, outlandish spectacles, poverty, wealth, action, repose, one's own ego, jealousy, hate, stinginess, greed, cunning, the oppressed, hoarders, promises, truth, the poor, the orphaned, the homeless and indigent, those in danger and trouble, hidden merit, compassion, killing, loyalty, scheming hearts, and the transcendent. Some of these things are external and others, such as one's own ego, are internal; but all are things with which one must take up some kind of orientation or relation.

Because all things in Chinese religion, including individual people, are harmonies of processes and participate in many ongoing harmonic patterns, ultimately in the unity of the cosmic processes, how one relates to one's ego, knowledge, or tendency to scheme are all to be understood as taking up or amending affiliations. The theoretical implications of the Chinese approach to affiliations thus have to do with conceiving everything as composed of and participating in harmonies. The practical implication for the religious dimension of life is twofold. On the one hand, one needs to get each of the affiliations right, and many if not all can be problematic. On the other hand, one needs to integrate or keep in harmonious balance all of one's different affiliations. The latter is where one's inner or personal harmony mirrors the deep or transcendent unity of the cosmos; Daoism, Confucianism, and Chinese Buddhism specify this in diverse ways.

9.5.2 *Buddhist Ideas Concerning Affiliations*

Among the religiously significant ideas about affiliations in most forms of Buddhism are those having to do with the Saṅgha, and we did not treat that topic in any detail. The monastic idea, however, stands in sharp contrast with Chinese religion except Chinese Buddhism. Withdrawal from the world to a monastery or closed community was taken to be an affront by Confucians who criticized Buddhists for neglecting their families and civic duties. Daoists might be more tolerant of recluses, and the medieval Daoism represented in the texts in chapter 2 included the foundation of temples and monasteries for the purpose of perfecting the meditative life, including its transcendent dimension. But even in medieval Daoism there is the injunction to affiliate properly with the heavens, the sun and moon, the law, the king, one's parents, and all the characters one meets in life, as illustrated in the texts discussed in 2.3.1.

A truly free bodhisattva will be in harmonious relation with human and natural surroundings. But improving one's affiliations is not the very stuff of the Buddhist life in most of its branches, as it is for Chinese religion. In Buddhism, it is possible to see affiliations as cravings, the source of suffering, and these must be given up before freedom is attained and non-bondage affiliations are possible.

9.5.3 *Hindu Ideas Concerning Affiliations*

If it is true as suggested in 9.4.1 that Chinese religion conceives the human condition primarily as affiliative, the opposite holds for Advaita Vedānta of the sort expressed in the *Vivekacūḍāmaṇi*. Precisely because difference itself is *māyā*, affiliation too is *māyā*. So on the level of true non-dual reality, there is only Brahman from which no one is different and hence no real affiliations.

Within the realm of *māyā*, however, are the affiliations of daily life, with a brahmin family structure for the community of the *Vivekacūḍāmaṇi*, a political and social structure, and various relations with the natural environment. Moreover, the adept can live within all these affiliations without misconstruing them as dualistic: "sometimes a fool, sometimes a sage, sometimes possessed of regal splendor, sometimes behaving like a motionless python, sometimes wearing a benign expression, sometimes honored, sometimes insulted, sometimes unknown—thus live the wise ones, every happy in the highest bliss" (*Vivekacūḍāmaṇi* 542; cited in 4.4).

Clooney has emphasized the exclusionary aspects of the *Vivekacūḍāmaṇi* and its community. This particular religious community was limited to male brahmins who were literate and could study and who wanted to pursue the path it describes. As an exclusive community devoted to study for the purpose of discernment and transformation, this Advaita community bears some similarity to Buddhist and Daoist monasteries, whose differences deserve closer study.

9.5.4 *Jewish Ideas Concerning Affiliations*

As already mentioned, affiliation is a primary and central component of personal identity for most forms of Judaism, a point it vaguely shares with the Chinese sensibility though specifying it in terms of the covenant. For a Jew, to be a person is to be in covenant with God. The affiliations involved in the covenant include those with God of the sorts addressed above, with other Jews within the People of Israel, with non-Jews, with the human habitat, and especially with the land of Israel as the place for Jews as stipulated in the covenant.

The Jewish sense of obligation as covenant is also intensely affiliative. Unlike, say, a Kantian interpretation of commands and categorical imperatives, which can be formulated as universalizable maxims, the Torah enjoins worship of God, participating with others in ritual, interacting with others in moral and pious ways, and, as later developed (5.3.1), common study. These are positive communal commitments.

The special importance of the People of Israel is so great for most periods of Judaism that it is almost as if Israel rather than individual persons is the human subject interacting with God. Daoist and Buddhist monastic groups, Confucian and Vedāntic schools, are special communities within which people practice religion. But with Judaism it is nearly the other way around: Israel relates to God by means of the individuals playing particular roles. This point needs heavy qualification, of course, because it is individual Jews who worry about the People of Israel. Nevertheless, in Chinese religion, Mahāyāna Buddhism, and Hinduism, especially Advaita Vedānta, the communities are situations and instruments for personal religion. In Judaism, religion is the acts of individuals defined in relation to one another by the covenant, including relations with non-Jews.

9.5.5 *Christian Ideas Concerning Affiliations*

The early Christians transformed the idea of the Mosaic covenant community, Israel, to the idea of the Church, the New Israel. There were thus two major divergences in late Second Temple Judaism with regard to the heritage of Moses. Judaism in its Rabbinic form defined the covenant community primarily (though not exclusively) in ethnic and kinship terms relative to Torah whereas Christianity defined it in voluntary terms as the Church relative to Jesus. Christianity transformed kinship terms to universal ones so that all people are brothers and sisters and God is Father of all.

This difference between Christianity and Judaism manifests itself in difference between the ways they relate their primary covenant communities to the surrounding society. For Judaism, the relation ideally ought to be something like one family living amidst other families, all under God but with special issues for the family of Israel. For Christianity all people are one family finally and those people who are not part of the Church are unsaved brothers and sisters; hence the strong impulse to proselytize. This is not to say that Christianity necessarily has to deny that salvation is possible outside the Church; one's brothers and sisters might find other ways to God and there is no principle in Christianity that can limit the grace of God. Jesus thought that Judaism "worked" even if Paul was doubtful (6.2). Even Paul appealed to Stoic natural law ethics and to the unknown God of the Greeks. But Christianity has most often been exclusivistic because of its view that all human beings are to be understood as one family under God.

Christianity shares with Chinese religion, Judaism, and Islam the strong conviction that the created world is fundamentally good, albeit containing suffering and evil. The good "image of God" remains even in fallen human nature. Therefore there is an obligation to affiliate with nature in appreciative ways. Modernity has somewhat undercut this by representing nature as value-free; this has allowed for Christian individualism and an instrumental attitude toward nature rather than an appreciation for it as part of God's good creation.

9.5.6 Islamic Ideas Concerning Affiliations

Islam shares with Christianity over against Judaism the conviction that all people are one family and that the same law applies to all, or should apply if they were to know it. Like Christianity, from this follows a strong commitment to proselytizing. From the Islamic confidence in the clarity of God's purpose and inevitability of divine expression in history follows a strong political expression (7.6). Indeed, Islam tolerates no distinction between a political order and Islam as a religion. Christianity often has taken the same line, though it recognizes the fragmentary and unfulfilling quality of history as in Augustine's contrast between the city of man and the city of God. For Christianity, the image of the crucified Christ as the paradigm for the human condition should give pause regarding the coincidence of religion and politics; Islam gives Jesus an important place but denies that he died by crucifixion [Qur'ān 4:157–58] because that would not befit one of God's prophets.

The Islamic ideal for the human community is for it to be bound together by the dictates of *Sharī'a*. The ideal social affiliation thus takes the form of rules or principles that interlock roles. That the form of social affiliation be the following of a pattern of rules or principles is vaguely common to Confucianism, many traditional Hindu societies, and Judaism insofar as this applies to Israel under Torah. This contrasts with the primarily mission-oriented affiliation model of the Mahāyāna Buddhist bodhisattva ideal and of Christianity. Monastic communities in any religion conceive their affiliation to be governed by rules, but in some cases, for instance Christianity and Zen Buddhism, as a rule-defined community that is instrumental for a larger mission or purpose.

The Islamic sense of affiliation with nature is double-sided. On one side it seeks to distinguish nature from God so as to avoid *shirk*. On the other it sees nature as expressing Allah, the divine *amr*, and hence can come close to nature mysticism, especially in sufi life. This double-sided sense of affiliation with nature distinguishes the Islamic sensibility, at least in some parts, from the Jewish and Christian that in other respects it joins in celebrating the goodness of creation.

9.6 Postscript

It should be said once again that the comparisons expressed in chapter 8 and here are suggestions that have arisen out of our study for further examination. They have taken the form of showing how different religions share a common idea vaguely but specify it differently. Sometimes the comparisons have started from the differences and sought a common respect for comparison, and sometimes they have arisen from vague similarities and moved to the differences. The enormity of the task of following out the comparisons, checking on the specifications, and specifications of specifications, refining the statement of common respects in which comparisons can be made, and cross-referencing the categories, is truly daunting.

But we hope to have shown (1) that comparisons are made by articulating both vague respects for comparison, which the compared things hold vaguely in common, and the various specifications by virtue of which differences are registered. Comparisons consist in saying what the similarities and differences are. We hope also to have shown (2) that our collaborative discussion has made real progress in identifying how religions, at least in the branches we studied, do have vague comparative elements in common and specify them differently in something like the ways we suggest. All of this is subject to further investigation. Indeed, the boldness of our comparative hypotheses has been intended to spur further, more systematic, study. Expressing our hypotheses in terms of the interconnected categories of unity, ontological status, value, causation, personal identity, obligation, predicament, and affiliations, we hope to have made them vulnerable to correction. They can be approached from different angles of comparison, in terms of different branches of the traditions we studied, and in terms of different texts. These very categories can be approached critically from the standpoint of other categories, as indeed they will be in our next volume on ultimate realities.

Notes

1. See Roger T. Ames and Wimal Dissanayake, eds., *Self and Deception: A Cross-cultural Philosophical Enquiry* (Albany: State University of New York Press, 1996).
2. This is the opening line of the *Daodejing*, as translated by Chan in *A Source Book in Chinese Philosophy* (Princeton: Princeton University Press, 1963).

Appendix A

On the Process of the Project During the First Year

Wesley J. Wildman

The Comparative Religious Ideas Project, or CRIP as we affectionately call it, might well have been called the Comparative Religious Ideas *Process*. The project was designed on the assumption that it is not possible to implement and evaluate a cooperative, self-correcting methodology for the comparison of religious ideas without also creating a community of scholars to serve as medium and laboratory. The members of this community would have to teach each other, write with each other in mind, criticize each other, and be drawn out of their usual modes of scholarly work to embrace unfamiliar approaches. All that involves intellectual excitement and discomfort, lots of time, many shared meals, endless discussions, writing and rewriting papers, and moments of laughter, frustration, disagreement, exhaustion, satisfaction, and breakthrough insight.

The three volumes of the Comparative Religious Ideas Project represent its formal output. They were written mostly in sequence and, despite later editing rearrangements, it is easy to see that the three volumes are quite different from one another in ways that suggest a process of development. There is a fascinating story to be told about this process, one that illumines the crucial corporate aspect of the method that was used in the project. This appendix is the first of three, one at the end of each volume, that jointly attempt to expose this process of development to scrutiny by scholars in religious studies interested in comparison. The three appendices are designed to be read together but also to make sense as standalone accounts. All three appendices have been written *after* the entire process is complete. They are, therefore, *retrospective analyses* of the process rather than simple descriptions of it. They draw on and occasionally quote from a large stack of meeting reports that were distributed to project members throughout the years of meetings as a kind of feedback mechanism aimed at helping the group to reflect on its discussions and to develop a sense of its overall direction. The retrospective analysis in these appendices is in large part also my own reading of the group process, informed by more or less extensive discussions with project members and thorough involvement. Indeed, more than one project member would argue that my meeting reports were also to a large extent my own reading of what happened during our meetings rather than objective reporting! The perspectival quality of such reporting and analysis is inevitable and, accordingly, the style of objectivity sought is not that of the biologist sketching plants or the architect drafting a plan but rather that of the ideally imaginative and observant writer seeking to illumine the pluripotent reality of a complex group process in a way that evinces agreement from those involved, albeit grudging or limited agreement. It follows that this set of appendices is as much a part of the group process as the events and developments discussed.

The project group several times debated whether to make the group process that lay behind the books more evident to the reader, perhaps by including the meeting notes in the volumes or by publishing them on the Web. We were concerned, frankly, that this would not be at all effective; many of the interesting moments are alluded to in the notes but it is a case of the reader having had to be there to make the connections. Frustrated with the problem of conveying in writing something so viscerally important to the method, and having made a couple of attempts, we resigned ourselves to relying on the various descriptions of the method itself that are scattered through the three volumes. After all, those descriptions stress the importance of a community of inquiry and, as Frank pointed out at the end of the first year, "Past projects of this sort have not succeeded when they have tried to initiate readers into the process of the project." We remained uneasy with this solution, however, and our advisors at the project's concluding conference confirmed our concerns. All of them insisted that it is vital to portray the group process for the readership of these volumes. They argued that descriptions of its importance in philosophical chapters on method would never succeed in conveying what this aspect of the project's method was all about. Our suspicions thus decisively confirmed, we were convinced that something had to be said. We remained no closer to having a good way to say it, however, and we are still somewhat at a loss for words.

This series of appendices adopts a somewhat experimental approach to the problem of conveying the social background for CRIP. Two challenges need to be met. First, while the main body of each volume can remain an approximately faithful snapshot of where we were at the end of each year, the description of the social background needs to be different; it cannot be hobbled by the very real limitations in perception that we suffered along the way. The retrospective approach is intended to meet this challenge. Our perspective at the end of the project also needs enrichment, of course, but it is significantly more adequate because of the process that produced it than our self-understanding at any point prior to the culmination of our work together. Second, the social background needs to be conveyed in a way that permits personality and humor to shine through. To that end, the appendices often use a narrative style and the picturesque language needed for conveying the color of the group process. This is meant to invite the reader imaginatively to enter into the group's work and struggles together.

With these introductory remarks in place, therefore, I turn to describing and analyzing the group process that enabled the Comparative Religious Ideas Project.

The Setting

Picture an ordinary seminar room on Commonwealth Avenue, Boston University. This is where CRIP meets on most occasions. In the middle stands a large rectangular table surrounded by sixteen purple chairs. On meeting days, there stands in one corner a small trolley with breakfast supplies secured by Susan Only, the CRIP coordinator, traffic cop, arranger of details, and money person. There are urns of coffee, glass bottles of orange juice, plastic bottles of water, and plenty of *Dunkin' Donuts'* creations, sometimes with colored icing (my personal favorites). Bob Neville, the principal investigator, always pokes his head in early but, if the room is empty, he dashes back across the corridor to his office where he quickly dictates a letter or two, eager to make the most of spare minutes. A few minutes before nine o'clock, people start arriving. Frank Clooney (Hinduism specialist) and Tony Saldarini (Judaism) show up early, traveling the short distance from Boston College together. Friendly greetings are exchanged with whomever happens to be in the room. The local Boston University folk drift in, usually beginning with co-principal investigator John Berthrong with the hat and outfit of the day and his latest load of stories. David Eckel (Buddhism) and Livia Kohn (Chinese religion) typically arrive right on time and Paula Fredriksen (Christianity) a little after that. The greetings multiply like latticework and people cluster around the food and drink. Peter Berger, the other co-principal investigator, is often late but warms the room with his big smile when he arrives. No shortage of jokes and stories there, either. Nomanul Haq (Islam) has the real commute and, being more at the mercy of the transportation gods than the rest of us, has a less predictable arrival. But the hardest arrivals to predict are the six graduate students, most of whose lives are not yet steadied by age or an unyielding need for sleep to the point that they have consistent morning habits (or morning appearances, for that matter). Yours truly arrives early, of course, because I have to get the note-taking computer set up and do initial editing of the document that is to record my observations of the day's work. But I have time to grab too many donuts and a bottle of orange juice as I say or wave hello to arrivals.

Ah, food and greetings. If it weren't for food, we never could have worked together. According to our experience, it is the number one precondition for successful corporate comparative work. We often speculated on the most fitting big-deal topics for imagined fourth and subsequent volumes (heaven forfend!) and repeatedly came back to food. Not only is food one of the central themes in all religions, sharing food together was our most spiritual practice. It brought and kept us together in a way that intellectual adventuring alone could not. In this sense, Susan Only's ministrations of food and drink served as midwife to the strange birth of our group's identity, or perhaps as the priestess of the caloric sacrifices that wrung a kind of togetherness from the gods of religious studies who so often seem to prefer dispersal and mutual incomprehensibility.

We are arrived, we have food and drink, and we are prepared for our corporate task with the social fuel of greetings and smiles. Of course, someone might be missing, for some reason, and as time went on we felt such absences more acutely. Even the quieter graduate students are missed when they aren't there, perhaps especially because of their stellar attendance records. But in various configurations—everyone on most occasions during that first year—we are arrived.

We work for an hour and a half and then break for more food, drink, and mingling. Someone seeks out Susan for some administrative question. Someone else finds me to point out that I had mischaracterized a remark in my report for the last meeting, enabling me to make a correction. A graduate student raises a question with a researcher. Academic business is transacted. Then work resumes. After another ninety minutes, it is off to lunch, which was consistently good food, inexplicable considering its institutional origins. We chat as we line up for the salads and sandwiches. Kosher meals off to one side, cookies at the end of the table, drinks in the ice-filled bowl—but you had to get there early to snag an orange soda. At one point a complaint about the scarcity of orange soda somehow reached all the way to Susan's ears and, sure enough, more orange soda appeared next time. The Boston University people might try to squeeze in a few minutes of phone-message checking before returning for the afternoon session. Frank eats fast to leave time for his midday constitutional walk along the Charles River. If you want to walk with him, you have to walk fast and he will even stipulate that as a condition of sharing his company. That's a serious walker. When I went with him I had to slow my usual pace a bit, but I never let on.

When lunch is over, the student carrion from around the building, though knowing little of CRIP, can sense food. Gathering for the leftovers, they tentatively approach the lunchroom, sometimes with encouragement from their professors or each other. After lunch the morning pattern repeats, with two ninety-minute sessions separated by a thirty-minute break. The afternoon break has a different quality. The remaining lunchtime cookies, if any, are rescued from the lunchroom lest they be consumed by hungry students and thus are preserved for afternoon tea but sometimes there is not much to eat. Usually the colorful orange juice is gone by now and only bottles of water remain for drinking, unless it is an afternoon cup of coffee. People are tired after three sessions of intense thinking and arguing. Sometimes they are confused or frustrated, sometimes they want to clarify some point with a colleague. The energy level is lower. People are starting to think about going home. But we all dig in for the last ninety minutes and, to our own surprise, sometimes the final session of the day is marvelous. A few people have to leave early, perhaps, but most remain to think all the way through the three hundred and sixtieth minute of session time. Come the end of the day, the circle of work complete, dispersal is rapid. Farewells are abbreviated compared to morning greetings and people move on to their next obligation quickly.

Twenty-five times we did this, eight times in the year devoted to the study of the human condition, 1995–1996. A few times we had guests, including during the final meeting of the first year, when advisors Rabbi Jordan Pearlson from Toronto and Prof. Max Stackhouse from Princeton Seminary joined us. It felt strange to have visitors with us, people who had not been formed by the food and the drink and the rhythm of the days the way the rest of us had been. But they were welcome and made us think about what we were doing from new perspectives. The fact that there could be an "otherness" about visitors was telling, at least to me: despite our differences, we were becoming a group with an identity focused by doing meaningful work together.

The Diversity

People with wicked imaginations, presumably mostly Bob Neville, designed the working group. Pandering to the aforementioned desire of the religious-studies gods for chaos and mutual incomprehension, perhaps, the project designers juxtaposed people with utterly different working styles. While the working group design has been described abstractly in the general preface and elsewhere, there are vital details to convey.

There are six tradition specialists, each devoted to historical details and linguistic nuances and thus allergic both to historical anachronism in all its subtle and not-so-subtle forms and to generalizations that obscure diversity or paper over awkward facts. Having worked for years on historical Jesus research, Paula has seen plenty of projecting backwards onto historical figures the interests of contemporary interpreters and her allergic reaction to historical anachronism is correspondingly acute. Frank and David have been interested in comparative theology for many years yet both have a fine-tuned sensitivity to the way that generalizations about religious ideas mask all-important differences. Frank is quick to point out that our own interests are surreptitiously present in the making of comparisons, which really are a type of generalization, and that self-awareness is necessary for right understanding. David's immersion in Madhyamaka Buddhist philosophy has sensitized him to the dangers of generalization as a kind of naming, which is always also a making of reality that distorts perception. Noman, Livia, and Tony have similar sensitivities to anachronism and generalization but they are less extreme. Tony is happy to make generalizations about Judaism if they are warranted but is sharply aware of how comparison can make Judaism look similar to something else while the internal diversity of Judaism is never registered in the comparison. Livia is as sensitive to details as anyone but has no time for tiptoeing around generalizations; she wades right in and says with rare courage what Chinese religion is about; this boldness proved extremely helpful for the group. Noman is determined to convey the nuances of key Arabic terms and distinctions, reading to us in Arabic, and helping us with transliteration; yet his work in a tradition that has a relatively clear sense of identity gives him a heightened readiness to make generalizations and to entertain comparisons.

None of these six tradition representatives is personally affiliated with the religion he or she studies except for Noman. That is another design feature but it is hard to determine its value for the group or its results because there is no alternative arrangement to which we can compare our process in that respect. It is possible to note that Noman was the most concerned of all the specialists to convey to the group the hypothetical adherent's view of his or her religion ("Islam is what Muslims say it is," he would say); this is apparent in his chapters for the three volumes. This concern was only a little more evident in Noman than in the other specialists, however, and I could not discern any impact on the group process or results because of it.

Four other scholars who, by design at least, represent the interests of comparison complement the six tradition specialists and their commitment to fidelity of description. Bob is the archetypal metaphysician, dreaming up seven theories before breakfast, all in the abstract language of his burgeoning philosophical system. Shockingly for a metaphysician, however, he wants to test and improve his theory of comparison. Peter is the archetypal sociologist and brings to the table a practiced eye for plausible generalizations, along with the intellectual gift of being able to frame elegant questions that consistently drive to the heart of a confusing discussion. John is a hybrid: trained in Chinese religion, especially Confucianism, he complements Livia's expertise in Daoism, yet he also works actively and eclectically in the comparison of religious ideas. As for me, my training in contemporary theology, philosophy, and science made me, besides the taker of notes, the representative of an unadvertised seventh tradition: the scientific naturalism of the modern West.

The six graduate students, one for each specialist, were invited both to watch what happens when six-and-a-half scholars nervous about generalizations work alongside three-and-a-half scholars for whom generalizations are the stuff of intellectual life (I count John standing half on each side of this fence) and to involve themselves in the process. Amazingly enough, there was turnover in only one of the six student positions during the whole course of the project (their names are listed in the general preface). At the beginning most of the students were quiet most of the time. Eventually, however, some of them started to talk or were forced to talk by virtue of being assigned presentation tasks by their specialist advisors. At times, the confusing currents of debate seemed to frustrate one or more of them and, certain that he or she could not do worse, a brave student soul would wade into dangerous waters in an attempt to rescue the struggling experts. It rarely helped much because their point was usually already taken for granted by those stuck in the swirling confusion but real insights were offered, confidence built, and rites of initiation passed in such moments. On occasion, a student would confront his or her mentor, which was especially gratifying and exciting.

For example, the most active student participant, John J. Thatamanil, now teaching his own students, attempted at one point during the first meeting to keep alive the possibility of a reality that helps to cause religious ideas to come out a certain way. This was in reaction to what John sensed was David's Madhyamaka-like readiness to see all categories as constructions. Here is how the notes record the exchange:

> David expressed the importance of vagueness in comparative categories when he suggested that the quest for comparative categories had to be understood as a search of "placeholders" in systematic representations of religious traditions. In reply, Thatamanil emphasized the perspective that truth-seeking is native to the human condition, and so these placeholders should correspond to joints in reality itself, and that the reality of these joints was the ground of the possibility of cross-cultural comparison of religious ideas.

What the notes do not record is the energy of the exchange, including several sharp rejoinders. It illustrates how CRIP served as a place of exploration and wing-stretching for the graduate students.

The First Blank Look

In a group this diverse, there is mutual incomprehension at times. Indeed, the design calls for blank looks but also for their gradual overcoming as scholars learn the ways of thinking of their differently brained and trained colleagues. The first blank look was not long in coming. In fact, on the very first meeting day, a large-scale blank look occurred around the required reading for that day: Bob's theory of comparison in *Normative Cultures*. Most people really didn't understand what they read. They knew that Bob is smart and that it probably all makes some sort of sense but for many the reading experience was akin to staring at the Rosetta Stone: the book is written in some strange sort of code and interpreting it rightly seemed pretty much out of the question. Of course, on the first day, saying that directly also seemed pretty much out of the question, so we struggled along politely. The usual symptoms of such a situation were present: the group rarely took up a technical point of theory but concentrated instead on talking about relevant issues that were well understood before the encounter with Bob's theory of comparison. The result was not unlike an interview, with Bob taking up one objection or concern after another and trying to expound the corner of his theory that deals with it.

This might be entertaining to some—I smile to remember it now—but sitting there watching all this politeness I was half convinced that the whole project was impossible, that the group was too diverse to achieve anything, that the method was impossible to test, and that we would never become sufficiently comfortable with each other to speak up when we didn't get it. And I doubt that I was the only one with such thoughts. Peter can be enormously encouraging at moments like these because he is probably the most self-assured of our group and almost certainly the most likely to say, "Bob, I think I discerned the general drift of your book but, to be frank about it, I really did not understand much about this theory of comparison. I could not penetrate your specialized language enough to decide whether my sense of the general drift was correct or not." Peter was restrained on this occasion, unfortunately, though I believe I have represented his actual view correctly. He would be this helpfully blunt at other times.

Afterwards I went home and worked *hard* on those meeting notes, trying to convey what Bob means by his theory of comparison in a less specialized language, more accessible to a broader range of scholars. I was slightly desperate, perhaps—anxious that CRIP should not be sunk before it had even left port. I feared that my explanations would be no clearer than Bob's but I kept refining the meeting notes. It was the beginning of my self-appointed role in the group as the one who keeps trying to help everyone understand each other. But it is a role that I probably need not have taken on; it is the controlling instinct of the young scholar—the young person—and, as every wise person knows, most good things in groups happen in spite of attempts to control the process. Good things would happen to our little group of scholarly adventurers but, on this first day, we had both blank looks and excessive politeness. It could only get better in those respects.

The Possibility of Comparison

The first meeting also had encouraging dimensions as classic issues familiar to every scholar in religious studies were debated. Reservations about comparison came out quickly as we struggled not particularly with Bob's theory of comparison (as I have said) but with the much more general question of the very possibility of comparison. Almost every facet of this problem must have been raised, from the power-analysis questions of "Who decides, who benefits, and who gets left out?" to the biographical-motivational line of "Why this project here and now in your life?" (a question Frank memorably directed to Bob, evoking an intriguing answer). In what follows I comment on three dimensions of the problem of comparison's possibility that were raised in that first meeting and returned to several times during the first year and beyond.

First, there is the problem of the big-deal categories that determine the topic for each of the project's three years: the human condition, ultimate realities, and religious truth. Each category fits some traditions more naturally than others and there is always the worry that some surreptitious agenda is being served by allowing such categories to determine the direction of work. For instance, Tony pointed out that beginning with the human condition is a bit forced for Judaism, though there is no problem with the category as such. Paula later asked the other specialists which category they would choose to begin with, confessing that she quite liked beginning with the human condition. The answers were as follows: Tony—God or creation; Noman—history; Frank—food or ritual; Livia—cosmology (David was not present at this moment). The answers show that the problem has two wings: the order in which categories should be taken up and the choice of which categories to use. We all knew that there is a degree of arbitrariness about these categories, partly due to the need to write grants before the project begins. And we also knew that all categories used in the description and comparison of religious phenomena have questionable parentage. Some emerge from early translations of sacred texts that stick, others from trailblazing works in the study of religion. Even more worryingly, some categories seem so obvious that we can't say for sure where they come from or what influences are set loose by their use. We discussed these issues back and forth and realized that one of the premises of the method of comparison we are using is correct: as David put the point, "We begin the process of comparison of religious ideas in the middle, for we already possess comparative categories (by default, in translations and traditions of discussion). The aim must be to correct, sharpen, and enlarge the collection of categories rather than to start over." It's like the strategic decision about whether to plant a lawn: you can never get pure soil and pure seed; except in extreme cases, it is almost always better to improve the lawn you have, gradually.

Second, the "human condition" is such a vague category that we were forced to wonder whether any meaningful comparisons can be made by means of it. We had lots of discussions about the vagueness of general categories and about how vague categories are given specific content by the comparisons made by means of them. That is all a part of the formal method we were supposed to be testing and refining, as described in a number of places and ways throughout the project volumes. In practice, however, we all struggled with how the specification of the human condition is supposed to be carried off without undue arbitrariness. The notes record that "Tony stressed the difficulty involved in trying move back and forth between comparative categories and detailed descriptions of specific situations, citing two common problems in support of his point, and illustrating each with reference to Eliade. First, the comparative categories are frequently overly conditioned by one particular religious tradition, usually that of the comparativist. Second, the categories themselves simply don't work that well at the level of detail." This is closely related to the problems of translatability and commensurability that are as familiar to anthropologists as to scholars in religious studies. An anthropologist makes comparisons under the vague category of "marriage" or "family" across cultures only by deciding what counts as marriage or family in each culture studied, and that is such a famously perilous decision that plenty of anthropologists have given up and opted for incommensurability of cultural forms instead. The specialists in our group were keenly aware of this problem and so skittish about deciding what counts as the human condition in all of the traditions we were considering.

Third, there was the question about the moral justification of embarking on a comparative enterprise. The notes record the following exchange, questioning Bob:

> Noman raised the question about whether it was permissible within the scope of the project to question the very desirability of comparison of religions. Frank pointed out that that in some groups there was even a religious objection to comparison, especially where it was perceived as a threat or as somehow demeaning or insulting. Bob replied that the strategy of the project is to proceed with this as an open question, one to be settled empirically. He conceded that the interest in comparing is the characteristic chiefly (though not only) of pluralistic Western culture. However, he is prepared to argue that, on balance, comparison is desirable. He listed three reasons: (1) we can't understand ourselves without understanding others; (2) healthy intercultural political interaction demands civilized conversation and mutual understanding; and (3) personal life requires orientation to the world, and the most worthwhile orientations are hard-won, requiring the labor of comparison. This moral argument for comparison outweighs the obligation to respect the religious allergy to comparison of individual traditions, thinks Bob, without thereby conferring carte blanche license to pry and poke where such curiosity is not welcome.

The group found itself looking over its shoulder repeatedly at these and other questions bearing on the advisability of spending time in comparing religious ideas across cultures. The moral justification of comparison, in particular, is a concern that simply never dissolved in our group consciousness.

The Struggle to Compare

In this first meeting, we settled on a routine that held steady for all three years. There were eight meetings each year, four in the Fall semester and four in the Spring. The first meeting of the year introduced and discussed the topic for the year—for the first year, the human condition. The six specialists introduced and led discussion of paper drafts at the remaining three Fall meetings, two each time, with the papers read by the group in advance. These exploratory papers were to expound what each tradition has to say about the human condition. The first three meetings in the Spring followed the same pattern except that the second set of papers were supposed to engage and synthesize what was presented in the first set, aiming to make comparisons where possible. The final meeting was a wrap-up discussion and contemplated how the year's volume would be structured.

From this arrangement it follows that the specialists, even those skeptical of the possibility or value of comparing, would not only represent their tradition for other scholars but also work toward making comparisons across traditions themselves. It wouldn't only be *other* people making the comparisons; the specialists themselves would do it, as called for in the method. But the making of comparisons involves the making of generalizations, hazards anachronism, and flies in the face of the current religious-studies convention of leaving comparison to genius experts with enough professional seniority that they can risk the associated notoriety. No religious studies scholar makes his or her professional reputation by comparing any more than a psychologist begins a career by leaping directly into an experimental study of human sexual behavior. First you work with texts and translate and interpret until everyone knows that you know what you are doing, at least in one tradition or subtradition. Then and only then, if at all, do you venture to make comparisons. By design, the specialists are mid-career, active publishers with at least two or three books and a host of articles in their respective fields already under their belts. They are in a position professionally to consider making comparisons of religious ideas in public or already have done so. But there is understandable reluctance for several reasons.

First, in most cases the specialists were not used to making the kinds of comparisons required. They were perfectly well aware that even their mono-traditional descriptions and translations inevitably use comparative categories. Moreover, all of them make comparisons between culturally and temporally proximate situations or texts, usually with some direct causal connection between them to give the comparison a solid historical basis. But comparison across such large cultural distances, often between traditions with no significant contact, is a task for which few are prepared by training or scholarly experience.

Second, the basis for this sort of long-distance comparison was obscure. Comparison of the "This religious idea in Hinduism is rather like that idea in Judaism" sort is a recipe for disaster; we do not need any more opinions about similarities. Yet neither was the project adopting any of the standard ways of furnishing a basis for comparison—say, a theory of archetypes or a theory of evolutionary development. Worst of all, we had only a fuzzy understanding of how we were supposed to make good use of the mass of details that were emerging in our discussions. It wasn't all so grim; we had made advances. For example, we had improved over the impression-of-similarity approach to comparison because we had detailed descriptions at our disposal that were capable of refuting initial impressions of similarity as more details were drawn into the interpretative picture. We had succeeded in making our comparisons vulnerable to correction by amassing details that comparisons, thought of as interpretative tools, needed to take properly into account. Thus, we were sometimes able to tell when a category was too vague, and thus arbitrary in its application, or when a category was not vague enough, and thus distorting in its application (usually because it was too much in thrall to one particular tradition). In this way we were able to reject many comparative categories as not useful. Indeed, it is striking how many categories for comparison were raised, explored, and then rejected as insufficiently illuminating; only a small portion of those listed in the meeting reports survived into the published volumes and the reports themselves do not mention every category raised and discussed. These advances are important and they were evident fairly quickly in the group's work together. But at this stage we were not able to explain to our own satisfaction why it made sense to reject a category as "insufficiently illuminating," "arbitrary," or "distorting." That is a philosophically subtle issue bearing on the justification of categories that was not addressed satisfactorily in Bob's prior work on theory of comparison and one with important implications. Basically, though it sounds harsh, I think we were all somewhat confused at this stage, even Bob. Bob was giving instructions using terms like "vulnerability" and "dialectic of vagueness and specificity" but they were not always translating into manageable tasks for those who had to follow them. The problem turned out to be twofold. On the one hand, as described in the Introduction to *Ultimate Realities*, we had not completed our own methodological procedure by translating comparisons made back into the terminology of the vague category, which is to say that we were not using the comparisons to infuse the concept of human condition with meaning. We needed to develop a theory of the human condition that expressed what we had learned from the multitude of detailed comparisons, we later decided, but all we had was a list of categories, subcategories, and comparisons. On the other hand, we had not isolated theoretically what was required to justify comparative categories as adequate. We were relying on adequacy to phenomenological description of the things compared but we did not yet realize that there were other important dimensions to the task of justifying comparative categories. We would figure out the answers to these questions later in the second year as we became more accomplished at working together.

Third, the subcategories guiding the discussion of the human condition—the cosmic, the social, and the personal (each with their subcategories)—did not emerge until well into the second year, as we were finishing the rewriting of the first volume. Distinctively Chinese in tone and origin (Livia proposed and first used them), they emerged as an appealing way to specify the vague category of "human condition" but they emerged so late in the process that the specialists had little time to work with them. Moreover, there were other proposals for subcategories to specify the human condition. David made a strong case for a narrative approach that stresses the way we come from somewhere and encounter various situations on the way to going somewhere else, which is an approach congenial to Buddhism with its stress on the problem of the human condition and the way of its resolution. This would have led to a set of comparative subcategories that would configure religious ideas across cultures rather differently than the set recommended by Livia. It took the group some time to decide what to do and it seems probable that both approaches would have worked well. But the timing made using the categories to guide the specialists' comparisons problematic. This was the downside of something rather positive: a genuinely empirical procedure leading to consensus around a set of subcategories that was deemed to make best sense of the amassed data about the human condition.

Fourth, the scope of the specialists' discussions was dramatically different, which made comparison quite difficult. Here is an excerpt from the notes on this problem, which was discussed on several occasions and is broached in the Introduction to *Ultimate Realities*. It shows both Peter's delightful bluntness and Frank's pleasantly ironic sense of humor.

Peter: I'd like to take a step back to assess the volume as a whole for a moment. I think it is fine for us as individual scholars to develop our reflections in relation to views that enjoy widely varying representation in our respective traditions—Livia can work from a cosmology that she thinks enjoys 90 percent representation in China, and Frank from a text that relishes its .01 percent representation in India. However, the book will look a bit odd if chapters next to each other are so different in the way they balance generalized judgments about traditions and specific interpretation of texts.

Frank: Perhaps we should have the eventual publisher make the chapters detachable. Then chapters disliked by individual readers could be disposed of efficiently. More seriously, one way to conceive the project is that we have a common problem and we are all looking for solutions to that problem. Alternatively, it may be that we are trying to solve different problems entirely.

Peter: If one person does something different, OK. But if everyone does entirely different things, then the project has failed.

The general point expressed in this extreme instance concerns whether the specialists should seek to characterize entire traditions or rather focus more narrowly on particular texts. In the first year, the diversity of genre and scope in the specialists' work made comparisons difficult to frame both for them and for the generalists trying to draw conclusions. This problem was to ease in the second and subsequent years as most of the specialists tried to juxtapose characterizations of traditions as a whole with analysis of the particular text or theme on which their research focused, the approach required by the method. Some of the specialists were deeply uncomfortable with characterizations of entire traditions as a counterpoint to their more detailed analyses while others, aware of the dangers, just dove in and did it anyway. The following excerpt from the notes on the year's final meeting illustrates this issue, with both visiting advisors chiming in.

Bob: Last time we agreed that each chapter of the book should combine generalized conceptions of a tradition with analysis of a specific viewpoint or text. Livia has found a way to do this that stresses the generalizations.

Frank: But the broad conceptions of a tradition do not need to be flat, comprehensive generalizations; to some extent they can be induced from the more specific analyses.

Bob: Indeed—and we don't have to agree exactly on the approaches we take, either.

Jordan: As we create ways of looking at these traditions by means of careful generalizations, we must always keep close at hand our knowledge of the realizations in actual places and times of each tradition.

John B: Livia's view is bold and will probably be attacked in a number of ways, but it is particularly useful in that it forces scholars to grapple with large-scale questions. For example, is there a pan-Chinese worldview in relation to which any Chinese cosmology can be articulated?

Max: How would you articulate the objection you anticipate to Livia's approach?

John B: The criticism would assert that Livia's view distorts too much of what actually happened by setting up a dominant paradigm within which certain majority views show up easily and others are effectively suppressed.

Bob: In this seminar to date, the theoretical device for taking account of these questions has been "vague categories." Livia has an hypothesis here that is worthy of testing; if the generalizations turn out to be too wooden or too narrow, then that is a criticism of the vagueness of the categories, to the effect that they are not vague enough in the right ways.

Finally, and closely related to this last point, there was the worry that making comparisons would lead to anachronism by abstracting ideas from their historical contexts. Paula held the lamp high in this resistance movement throughout the years of the project, resisting every attempt to characterize Christianity as a whole and confining her attention to the specific episode or thinker she was investigating. From the first meeting she signaled her concerns about anachronism, as the following passage illustrates.

> Paula described the criterion of "anachronism" that is used (too infrequently, according to her!) to judge the absence of depth in historical work. While the history of religions *as history* can always make use of this criterion, what might function similarly in the case of comparisons? In particular, philosophy seems singularly insensitive to the problem of anachronism; that's worrying because philosophers are frequently those who take up the generalist roles in comparisons.
>
> Bob entered a reply to this none-too veiled expression of concern about the entire project, partly granting the charge against philosophy but defending the sensitivity of *some* philosophical traditions to the historical conditioning of ideas and giving an example of how anachronism might be detected in the comparative task. This was a moment of genuine intellectual excitement: archetypal historian meets archetypal philosopher in a critical dialogue. It's just as good as historian meets phenomenologist, or tradition-specialist meets comparative-generalist.

The Drafts of Volume 1

The first volume reflects the intricate complexities of this struggle to compare during the first year. Apart from introductory material, the volume consists of individually fascinating specialist chapters that richly describe the human condition from various points of view while offering a few comparisons. Then there are two concluding chapters that (1) have to set up comparisons (to overcome the scope problem described above), (2) make comparisons (instead of summarizing them), (3) amass them into a formidable grid (in accordance with the group's much debated goal for the first volume), (4) without finally saying much synthetically about the human condition. These conclusions also had to juggle numerous subcategories and the phenomenological sites of importance, making them extraordinarily difficult to produce. In fact, a confession is on order: I simply could not do it. Although I composed most of the introductory material to the conclusions, as second author on those chapters I was overwhelmed by my task of enhancing Bob's drafts. I was unable to juggle all the variables and to manage the different scopes of the specialists' descriptions without becoming paralyzed by the need to enter thousands of caveats for which there was no space. Bob, even more aware of the needed caveats than I, somehow managed to press himself through the process in the name of fulfilling the group's stated goals for the first volume. I was personally amazed by Bob, just as I am by those who write dictionaries for a living and by any scholar who can by mental discipline unaided by threats against their personal safety or family members force himself or herself to go, machine-like, through the agony of drafting such chapters. I know he found it agonizing, though there were a few moments of excitement and satisfaction—and he had to do it twice more in later rewrites. It was not only an act of astonishing discipline, however, it was also one of enormous confidence, not to say hubris, to compare everything to everything else from multiple points of view in numerous respects. And each comparison made drove home Bob's worry about the project because he was not summarizing the specialist's comparisons but having to make the comparisons himself.

In any event, the introduction to *Ultimate Realities* describes the difficulties fairly well and I shall not go into it here any more than I have already. Instead, I shall give a retrospective analysis of the first volume's strengths and weaknesses and then I shall try to convey something of the group's own reactions to it.

With regard to analysis, the volume's weaknesses are obvious. First, the specialist chapters make some interesting comparisons but they are out of sync with respect to scope and sometimes topic. Second, the conclusions take the form of a grid that makes for lousy reading and the grid is overdeveloped relative to the degree of our control over the details of the data, indicating some possibly unnecessary yet nevertheless lurking arbitrariness in the subcategories used. Third, the linkage between specialist and concluding chapters is constructed mostly in the concluding chapters on the basis of the group's conversations and Bob's imagination whereas more of that linkage should be explicitly in the specialists' chapters themselves. Fourth, but more subtly, the categories used in the comparisons are justified only implicitly by virtue of their claim to make sense of the mass of data but this is insufficient warrant, as we see the matter after working on the second and third volumes. Fifth—and this is the result of deliberate decision as our apologies for being differently focused show—the volume almost completely neglects important, high-profile issues in the current study of religion, including especially power-analyses of texts and traditions, looking for missing voices and the experiences and ideas that are suppressed as a result.

These and other weaknesses are easy to point out and we were more painfully aware of them than anyone. But we battled on because of a number of less obvious strengths in the first volume, strengths that are rare in literature on the comparison of religious ideas and directly relevant to our goal of using and improving a particular method for comparison. First, the chapters by the specialists are fascinating and make serious contributions to the study of the human condition within each tradition and in religious studies generally. Second, the systematic character of the conclusions is quite unusual and valuable, even though it impairs readability. Particularly important is the procedure of using the five phenomenological sites of importance (actually, only four were used, as the fifth is intrinsically unsuitable for comparative work). That, together with the exhausting comparison of each pair of traditions within each subcategory, allows the human condition to be presented from a large number of angles. The comparisons ventured are but the tip of the iceberg, of course, but they are thought-provoking and they enrich our interpretation of the human condition while exposing it to constructive scrutiny from other experts. That systematic approach was to disappear in subsequent volumes but it is a virtue that should not be overlooked. Third, the subcategories under the general category of the human condition were arrived at in genuinely empirical fashion, late in the process of discussing masses of details, by means of trying out hypotheses and improving or rejecting them. This is unquestionably rare and genuinely refreshing in religious studies, which tends to be plagued by attempts at description that falsely pretend to be free of comparative categories or by the use of arbitrary categories that are never made vulnerable to correction. We mean forcefully to commend these categories to the community of religious studies specialists and, though their justification even in our own project was incomplete, we take them to be considerably less arbitrary than going alternatives and far better placed to profit from correction. All this is evidence of the positive value both of corporate work within groups of diverse scholars and of the method used in our group.

With regard now to the group's reactions to the first volume as it took shape, I have space for only a few remarks. Although the members of our group were always polite even when they were blunt, I think that the specialists and indeed others in our intrepid band were almost at a loss for words when they initially saw the first draft of the concluding chapters. I took this to be an indication of the limited possibility of politeness under the circumstances. It is quite amusing in retrospect. My sense was that the specialists believed there had to be a better way. Bob's viewpoint was that there certainly was a better way and it is what happened in subsequent volumes, especially the third in which the conclusions truly summarize the specialist's comparisons.

As a group we were sorely tempted to abandon the structure of the concluding chapters and to produce instead something more colorful, punchy, and less systematic. Some might think it professionally prudent to have done just that! Looking back on it now I smile to recall how gentle the specialists were when they probably wanted to scream in horror. I think it was David who made the breakthrough remark suggesting that we give up the goal of fully cooperative comparisons for the first volume and allow the generalists to say what they wanted in the conclusions, so long as it was accurate, while the specialists would be content to take responsibility for their own chapters only. This brought a welcome sense of freedom to everyone, none more than Bob who was now liberated from the curse of having faithfully to tie the conclusions to the scope and content of the specialist chapters. But it also indicated a partial failure of our method. While we could rectify the breakdown of joint ownership of conclusions to some extent by abandoning systematic grids and the use of phenomenological sites of importance in the second and third volumes, we never completely achieved the goal of cooperative work that took us as a group all the way from data to consensus conclusions. We had consensus as far along in the process as the construction of the comparisons used to draw conclusions (which is no mean feat in itself) but no further. Conclusions remained subject to criticisms from the group concerning accuracy and judiciousness but after the partial failure of the first year no mechanism was introduced to seek and achieve consensus around those conclusions.

As for the temptation to abandon the grid-like structure of the concluding chapters even in the first volume, we resisted it out of a real desire to proceed empirically. During the first year, the group had several times discussed its goal in terms of a network or a grid of categories, together with a commentary on how each tradition specifies each category and subcategory, thereby to infuse the higher-level categories with content from the lower-level details. That is precisely what we achieved in the two concluding chapters and so it is a fair record of our self-consciousness at the time. Moreover, though we all felt dissatisfied with the outcome in terms of its reference-work style, which is as fragmentary as it is overbearing even in the published version, it constitutes a powerful argument to the religious studies community that the category of the human condition and the subcategories by which it is elaborated should be used in future comparative work, thereby to test and refine those categories. There was much to be pleased about, accordingly. We had only begun to work collaboratively, however, and as that dimension of the project improved, despite the decision to abandon consensus conclusions, the strength of the comparative method we were using would become more evident.

The End of a Year

There were two endings to the first year: the eighth meeting and the end of the first round of revisions on the first volume, which was much later. It was in between these two endings that our working group had to go through the pain of confronting the dual problems of specialist chapters without much comparison and conclusions that said little synthetically and even less beautifully about the human condition. The two endings themselves were fairly positive events, however, with an air of celebration and, I think, a quiet determination to do better even when there continued to be misgivings about the project.

Many themes surfaced during the first year that I have not mentioned. Standard concerns in religious studies showed up repeatedly in discussions yet appear in the first volume only rarely or not at all. There were numerous stories and jokes, crucial debates about how to conceive of the project and how to organize the first volume, and many breathtaking distinctions of lasting value that are recorded only in the meeting reports and will probably never see the light of day, except perhaps in the work of a graduate student who keeps and rereads those reports or who made his or her own notes. Fortunately, comprehensiveness is not the goal of these appendices. Their point is rather to describe and analyze the way that our motley group of researchers made use of a collaborative method for comparative work. To be sure, the method was not always clearly understood and it changed as it was used—points broached here and to be considered more in another appendix—but it *was* used and it *did* produce results. Those results would improve as the specialists became bolder in the making of comparisons, the generalists more attuned to details, and everyone more vocal in their opinions. And through it all, improbable though it may seem given the levels of diversity and controversy, we became fond of each other and learned to appreciate the differences among us as enabling.

Appendix B

Suggestions for Further Reading

The Comparative Religious Ideas Project was designed to involve students both as participants in the seminar meetings and in background tasks. One of the more adventurous student projects has been the development of a set of twelve annotated bibliographies on a number of topics relevant to the project. These bibliographies are suggestions for further reading in each topic covered. I am grateful to the students involved in the annotation project: Marylu Bunting, John Darling, Greg Farr, Andrew Irvine, He Xiang, Mark Grear Mann, Matt McLaughlin, David McMahon, Glenn Messer, James Miller, and Kirk Wulf. I am also grateful for the suggestions of books to annotate that we received from Profs. Jensine Andresen, John Berthrong, Frank Clooney, Jonathan Klawans, and Frank Korom. The one bibliography in this volume contains suggestions for further reading on the topic of the volume, the human condition.

—Wesley J. Wildman

Annotated Bibliography: The Human Condition

Alter, Michael J. *What Is the Purpose of Creation? A Jewish Anthology.* Northvale, NJ: J. Aronson Inc., 1991.

This work brings together many primary sources from the Jewish tradition. All focus on the question of "What is the purpose of creation and life?" The collection begins with a critical examination of the *Tanakh* and includes excerpts from the works of major thinkers such as Philo, Moses Maimonides, Baruch Spinoza, Moses Mendelssohn, Albert Einstein, and Abraham Joshua Heschel.

Amy, William O. and James B. Recob. *Human Nature in the Christian Tradition*. Washington, DC: University Press of America, 1982.

This work is a collection of ten introductory lectures on the theme of human nature in the Christian tradition. These lectures were intended for undergraduates at Otterbein College. The authors explore human nature with references to Christian concepts including the image of God, salvation, sin, and the nature of human being as related to time and eternity.

Angell, J. William and E. Pendleton Banks, eds. *Images of Man: Studies in Religion and Anthropology*. Luce Program on Religion and the Social Crisis, vol. 1. Macon, GA: Mercer University Press, 1984.

This volume gathers essays fostering comparative inquiry between theologians and anthropologists. Eight contributions are included. The initial descriptive essays of the collection include the following topics: "Images of Man in the Hebrew-Jewish-Christian Tradition," "Order and Disorder in the House of Islam," and "Images of Man, Nature and the Supernatural in the Buddhist Scheme of Salvation." Several Christian theologians are represented, and their contributions range from an argument for theology as an indispensable key to anthropology (Edward Farley), to an examination of cultural forms of religion after secularization (Harvey Cox). James L. Peacock proposes a vision of the "good life" arising from reflection on anthropological method.

Aune, David Edward and John McCarthy, eds. *The Whole and Divided Self*. New York: Crossroad Publishing Co., 1997.

This work combines the resources of biblical and theological reflection to address what the contributors see as a split in the modern conception of self as either an ideal of wholeness or a position marker that is inescapably divided. In an introductory essay, Robert A. De Vito and William French trace the development of the modern concept of self through a consideration of Charles Taylor's *Sources of the Self*. Six topical essays follow dealing with the concept of self in the Hebrew scriptures as imbedded in the community, in Paul as a microcosm or the macrocosm, in the Psalms as used by Augustine, in the autobiographies of two monks in the Middle ages, and as needing a fundamental re-evaluation in theology as theologians become sensitized the ecological issues. The final two chapters contain Paul Ricoeur's heretofore unpublished eleventh Gifford Lecture, "The Self in the Mirror of the Scriptures" and a transcript of a 1994 interview with Ricoeur.

Belkin, Samuel. *In His Image: The Jewish Philosophy of Man as Expressed in Rabbinic Tradition*. Ram's Horn Books. London, New York: Abelard-Schuman, 1960.

Belkin explicates the religious underpinnings of Judaism's legal definitions of man and society. His central thesis is that Jewish philosophy is essentially theocratic. All doctrines and laws find their meaning with reference to God as creator. Belkin is concerned with how theocracy ought to play out in human affairs and explores his view as it is applied to equality, community, public consciousness, and law. He concludes, "It must be recognized that even our love for man ultimately is dependent upon our love of God."

Brandon, S. G. F. *Man and His Destiny in the Great Religions: An Historical and Comparative Study Containing the Wilde Lectures in Natural and Comparative Religion Delivered in the University of Oxford, 1954–1957*. Manchester: University Press, 1962.

Brandon's study proceeds by way of extensive chapters on paleolithic cave art, the ancient religions of the Near East, and South and East Asia. Brandon concludes that all the religions evince a characteristically human "detachment of attention from immediate experience" for the sake of grasping temporal existence. Such existence is pictured in religions in various ways: as bounded by the limits of physical life, or as the life of a soul that owns one or another sort of kinship with divinity. Similarly, gods may exhaust their relevance to humans within the activities of the physical world (i.e. they may be relevant only with regard to judgment in an afterlife), or the divine may be considered an impersonal principle to which humans should conform. For Brandon, all religions express a common endeavor to gain personal and communal security against changes brought by the passage of time.

Burrell, David B. *Freedom and Creation in Three Traditions*. Notre Dame, IN: University of Notre Dame Press, 1993.

This book, a sequel to the author's *Knowing the Unknowable God*, takes up the problem of human freedom as it relates to the doctrine of creation *ex nihilo* and, as this problem is addressed by three Medieval representatives of the so-called Abrahamic traditions: Ibn Sina, Maimonides, and Aquinas. Burrell's explicit comparative approach exhibits the strengths of thinking within a tradition and of eliciting mutual questioning. Burrell concludes that each tradition bears a doctrine of creation constituted around three elements: a source of all being and meaning (God), the word of revelation pointing to God as creator, and a community receiving the word. Moreover, recognition of this common core shows how each distinct tradition may correct the others with regard to excessive emphasis upon one focal element to interpret the other two.

Burtt, Edwin A. *Man Seeks the Divine: A Study in the History and Comparison of Religions.* 2nd ed. New York: Harper & Row, 1964.

In this work, Burtt argues that we should view religion from the perspective of how people have thought about the divine rather than from the perspective of the truth of divine matters that he sees as largely inscrutable. He claims that such a humanist perspective is a warranted and practical since "religion best reveals the deep seated forces which shape the course of human events." He urges a twofold methodology of "sympathetic appreciation" and "'inclusive impartiality" when approaching each religious tradition. He contends that if one does not appreciate how religions function to give meaning to individual believers, one cannot hope to understand religious belief. By the same token Burtt contends that if it is helpful to understand one religion, it is more helpful to understand many. In line with such claims, Burtt begins his exploration of the Daoist, Confucian, Buddhist, Christian, and Islamic traditions.

Carter, John Ross, ed. *Of Human Bondage and Divine Grace: A Global Testimony.* La Salle, IL: Open Court, 1992.

This book contains twenty contributions, arising from lectures given to undergraduate level students in 1981. The essays primarily address the central topics from within a tradition, and do not entail detailed lexical or theological comparison. The terms "bondage" and "grace" are shown to exhibit a considerable variety of positions of relative significance for religious practice, from focal to mistaken. Perspectives drawn from Śiva and Viṣṇu devotion, Theravāda and Mahāyāna Buddhist paths, Shintoism, Ancient Greek religion, Judaism, Eastern and Western Christianity, and Islam are discussed.

Cenkner, William, ed. *Evil and the Response of World Religion.* IRFWP Congress Series. St. Paul, MN: Paragon House, 1997.

The nineteen essays constituting this book are grouped into four categories: "Responses from the religions of the book," "Responses from Asian traditions," "Responses from African traditional religion," and "Contemporary responses." Jewish, Christian, Islamic, Buddhist, Hindu, Yoruba, and Unificationist perspectives are included, as well as essays with liberationist, ecological, process metaphysical and interreligious interests. Evil is a traditional and major concern in each of the religions, but no one definition of evil, of its source and its metaphysical status, or its remedy, can yet claim universal assent.

Chirban, John T. *Personhood: Orthodox Christianity and the Connection Between Body, Mind, and Soul.* Westport, CT: Bergin & Garvey, 1996.

This work presents a dialogue between Orthodox Christianity, psychology and medicine. Its contributors argue that while each discipline must focus on its own strength, all can and should work in complementarity to assist individuals in growth toward wholeness. They further argue that each discipline's commitment to the growth of human persons constitutes a foundation for cooperation. Topics covered include, "Spiritual Discernment and Differential Diagnosis," "Identity in Psychology and Religion," and "Addictive Adaptation," among others.

Coakley, Sarah, ed. *Religion and the Body*. Cambridge Studies in Religious Traditions, vol. 8. Cambridge: Cambridge University Press, 1997.

These careful essays arise from contemporary Western preoccupations, but seek also to review and correct those same preoccupations. Part I takes stock of contemporary Western perspectives on 'the body,' their sources and orientations. Part II reorients the contemporary scene by way of an examination of the Western religious inheritance concerning the body bequeathed by Judaism and Christianity—these essays are especially concerned to debunk glib characterizations of Christianity, or Western religion more generally, as 'negative' about the body. Part III looks at attitudes towards, and constructions of, bodies in Eastern religious traditions.

Cobb, John B. and Christopher Ives, eds. *The Emptying God: A Buddhist-Jewish-Christian Conversation*. Faith Meets Faith. Maryknoll, NY: Orbis Books, 1990. Essays by Masao Abe, with responses by seven Jewish and Christian writers.

Abe Masao has been a diligent leader in interreligious dialogue since the 1960s. This book contains Abe's major theological statement, "Kenotic God and Dynamic Sunyata," together with seven responses from Jewish and Christian theologians. Metaphysical questions feature prominently, but there is an experiential perspective fundamental to a number of the inquiries: for example, Cobb's "On the deepening of Buddhism," Catherine Keller's response "On feminist theology and dynamic self-emptying," and Schubert Ogden's "Faith in God and realization of Emptiness."

Collins, Steven. *Selfless Persons: Imagery and Thought in Therāvada Buddhism*. Cambridge: Cambridge University Press, 1982. Originally presented as the author's doctoral thesis under the title *Personal Continuity in Therāvada Buddhism*, Oxford University, 1979.

This book was written to aid comparative projects by disclosing the historical, philosophical, sociological and religious roles of the Therāvada "no-self" doctrine. Thus Collins is able to address the apparent disjunction between scholastic deconstruction of, and ritual care for, selves as a matter of "soteriological strategy." "No-self" is the highest truth of existence, but it means different things for people at different stages along the path of existence. Moreover, this differentiation is reflected in the textual tradition, giving rise to the doctrine of two truths. However, diverse concepts of self and "no-self" are also harmonized through imagery, including images of flowing rivers, growing vegetation, and decaying houses.

Cragg, Kenneth. *The Privilege of Man: A Theme in Judaism, Islam and Christianity*. Jordan Lectures in Comparative Religion, vol. 8. London: Athlone Press, 1968.

"The privilege of man" is humanity's divinely instituted role to have dominion in nature, or to be God's caliph in the world. The book exposits this theme of 'humanity under God' as it has been developed in each tradition, but it does so also with an eye to Cragg's concern that humanity is losing itself for the sake of technological possession. The first lecture presents this concern. The central lectures meditate on three aspects of the experience of Abraham corresponding to distinct emphases of each tradition. Two concluding lectures offer the theme of the "privilege of man" as hope in the contemporary situation. The book comprises Cragg's eight Jordan lectures, delivered in 1967.

De Silva, Lynn A. *The Problem of the Self in Buddhism and Christianity*. Colombo: Study Centre for Religion and Society, 1975.

De Silva argues that the Theravāda Buddhist doctrine of *anatta* ("no-self") and Christian teaching about *pneuma* (spirit) are mutually enriching religious resources. The first part of the book surveys Theravadin thinking about *anatta*, concluding that there are problems in this thinking that require a doctrine of God for their resolution. Bearing this problem in mind, De Silva casts fresh light on Biblical themes regarding the self. Spirit is not an immortal substance but is divinely given and maintained relationality. De Silva advances a synthetic notion of *anatta-pneuma*, as "non-egocentric relationality or egoless mutuality."

Duffy, Stephen. *The Dynamics of Grace: Perspectives in Theological Anthropology*. New Theology Studies, vol. 3. Collegeville, MN: Liturgical Press, 1993.

Duffy chooses the "theology of grace" as his topic because it "addresses axial questions: what it means to be a human person, how God is experienced by humans, and how God, humans, and their history are interrelated and made one in Christ." Chapter 1 considers the roots of thought about grace in the Hebrew Bible and New Testament. This investigation is then followed by a detailed review of some focal periods and figures in the Christian theological tradition (i.e. early Christian anthropologies, Augustine, Aquinas, Luther, the Council of Trent, Rahner, and Liberation theologies). Duffy considers that modern philosophies and theologies that emphasize a view of human beings as free agents confuse finitude with sin, and salvation with self-fulfillment. Grace, then, should not be considered as the rightful freedom of a self-constituting subject, but a transforming divine-human encounter.

Eliade, Mircea. *Cosmos and History: The Myth of the Eternal Return*. History and Historiography, vol. 11. New York: Garland Publishers, 1985 [1959]. Translation of *Le Mythe de L'éternel Retour*.

Eliade explicates the fundamental difference he sees between archaic man and modern man. He characterizes archaic man according to archaic ontology that is built on myths of participation and archetypes that make this participation possible. For archaic man, Eliade argues, reality comes through participation in the archetypes. Through the archetypes, the whole of the cosmos and human society is drawn into the realm of the sacred. For modern man, on the other hand, reality comes from participation in history. Faced with the "terror of history"; that is, with the need to justify or explain great tragedies in human existence; modern man finds it necessary to depend on an omnipotent god. Christianity, in Eliade's view, is thus the religion of modern man because it gives him a meaningful structure within which to make sense of history as a meaningful process from the fall to the incarnation to salvation to the final judgment.

Fingarette, Herbert. *Confucius: The Secular as Sacred*. New York: Harper & Row, 1972.

Fingarette, a noted philosopher, looks to identify the true teaching of Confucius through a focused analysis of the first fifteen books of the *Analects*. Emphasizing the ritual performance of moral codes, Fingarette starts with the thesis of human community as holy rite and ends with a Confucian metaphor; namely, the noble person is a holy vessel. This work is one of the first modern Western studies to suggest that the 'Confucian Way' can make great contributions to our contemporary understanding of the world and society.

Friedman, Maurice S. *To Deny Our Nothingness: Contemporary Images of Man*. 2nd ed. Chicago: University of Chicago Press, 1978 [1967].

In this study of thirty-two thinkers, Friedman pursues the hypothesis that the image of the human in each author studied is of significance because of its implications for moral philosophy. He argues that moral philosophy ought to be concerned with the values that are authenticated in human lives. Among those authors surveyed are Steinbeck, Bergson, Huxley, Weil, Jung, Dewey, Tillich, Berdyaev, Buber, and Wiesel.

Goodman, Lenn Evan. *Judaism, Human Rights, and Human Values.* New York: Oxford University Press, 1998.

Goodman argues for a Jewish philosophy of justice based on the metaphysics of 'deserts.' Each being's deserts are proportional and identical with its claims, in balance with the claims of other beings. He traces the development of the idea of rights in Jewish sources and applies his metaphysics of deserts to the issues of abortion, personal liberty, and nationhood.

Graff, Ann Elizabeth O'Hara. *In the Embrace of God: Feminist Approaches to Theological Anthropology.* Maryknoll, NY: Orbis Books, 1995.

This collection of essays deals with the topic of theological anthropology from a feminist, catholic perspective. The contributors are white, Hispanic, and Asian feminists who discuss such related sub-topics of anthropology as sexuality, learning, suffering, sin, ecology, eschatology, and the re-thinking the image of God. The overall methodology flows from the insight that humans live, move, and have their being in God. The contributors draw out the implications of the fact that despite this commonality of life in God, elements of social location affect the experience of each individual.

Greenspahn, Frederick E., ed. *The Human Condition in the Jewish and Christian Traditions.* Hoboken, NJ: Ktav Publishing House, 1986.

This volume is one in a series arising from symposia sponsored by the University of Denver's Center for Judaic Studies. The method is not explicitly comparative; rather, it is one of juxtaposing Jewish, Catholic and Protestant interpretations of three themes: human nature, sin and atonement, and eschatological hopes. In his introduction, Greenspahn provides a helpful historical view on distinct emphases that differentiate Judaism and Christianity.

Gregory, Peter N. *Inquiry into the Origin of Humanity: An Annotated Translation of Tsung-Mi's Yüan Jen Lun with a Modern Commentary.* Classics in East Asian Buddhism. Honolulu: University of Hawaii Press, 1995.

Tsung-mi was a Buddhist master in ninth-century China. His *Inquiry* is a systematic overview and classification of major teachings within early Chinese Buddhism, and as such, offers insight into contemporary Confucian, Daoist and Buddhist dialogue. In it, Tsung-mi develops an account of human nature as fallen from its true identity, locating the Buddha-nature at the root of all experience. Buddhism, then, is envisaged to provide the means to liberation. Also of central importance in this text is its discussion of the inculturation of Buddhism into China and its subsequent spread to Korea and Japan. Gregory provides a valuable introduction and running commentary as well as a glossary and a guide to supplemental readings.

Hamilton, Sue. *Identity and Experience: The Constitution of the Human Being According to Early Buddhism*. London: Luzac Oriental, 1996.

While much scholarship has addressed the Buddhist doctrinal formulation of *anatta* or "no-self," Hamilton argues that very little scholarship has addressed exactly what the human being is that can be said to have "no-self." The main body of her work is devoted to a detailed analysis of the five constituent parts (body, feelings, apperception, volition, and awareness) that the Buddha saw as constitutive of the human being. She describes each of these in detail with reference to the Pali cannon and with careful attention to their roots in Brahmaic religion. She concludes that the Buddha was not concerned with the ontological status of these parts or of the human person, but sought rather to explicate how their mutual functioning produced the illusion of a self through a process of dependent origination.

Hefner, Philip J. *The Human Factor: Evolution, Culture, and Religion.* Theology and the Sciences. Minneapolis: Fortress Press, 1993.

Hefner, a Lutheran theologian and avid participant in the dialogue between science and religion, urges a reevaluation of traditional Christian anthropology in light of science and in light of the destruction which humans have wrought on the ecosystem in their application of technology. He sees humans as created co-creators whose purpose is to create the most wholesome future possible for humans and the ecosystem they inhabit. Religion, in his view, is an evolutionary, adaptive mechanism of human culture that came about and ought to help humans to understand and act responsibly in the world. He seeks to challenge, on both theological and scientific grounds, any anthropology that would separate humans from nature.

Helminiak, Daniel A. *The Human Core of Spirituality: Mind as Psyche and Spirit.* Albany: State University of New York Press, 1996.

The author seeks a scientific approach to spirituality that is applicable outside the confines of religious traditions. He argues that spirituality is fundamentally a human quality that is a function of consciousness. As such, spirituality resides in the domain of psychology and has to do with the search for more authentic and self-aware living. Helminiak follows

Lonergan in viewing the human a composition of spirit, psyche, and organism, in the sense that these determinants are distinct but inseparable elements of the whole human person.

Hersch, Jeanne, ed. *Birthright of Man: A Selection of Texts.* Paris: UNESCO, 1969.

This work celebrates the twentieth anniversary of the Universal Declaration of Human Rights. It contains quotations from diverse time periods and cultures roughly paralleling in subject matter the major themes of the Declaration.

Hick, John. *An Interpretation of Religion: Human Responses to the Transcendent.* Basingstoke: Macmillan, 1988.

Arguing from a Kantian perspective, John Hick defends the position that all religions are human expressions of their experience of the same ultimate reality, which he terms the Real. The Real is analogous to Kant's noumena for Hick, whereas religious traditions are analogous to phenomena. Hick gives an apologetic for the reality of religious experience, arguing that religious believers can trust that their experience is of some existing thing; that is, the noumenal or the Real. Moreover, he defends the view that religious plurality can be affirmed on the grounds that all true religious traditions not only refer to an experience of the same Real, but also are salvifically efficacious for human participants in these traditions.

Holm, Jean and John Westerdale Bowker, eds. *Human Nature and Destiny.* Themes in Religious Studies Series. London: Pinter Publishers, 1994.

A collection of introductory essays that outline the anthropology of various religious traditions. This work seeks to illustrate the diversity of beliefs about the human condition and human ends both within and among the religious traditions that are described. The authors approach these topics not only by means of an historical description of the traditions' beliefs, but also with special reference to contemporary issues, such as gender, race and class.

Holm, Jean and John Westerdale Bowker, eds. *Women in Religion.* Themes in Religious Studies Series. London: Pinter Publishers, 1994.

This is an introductory text that deals with the role and status of women, historically and presently, in Buddhism, Christianity, Hinduism, Islam, Judaism, and Sikhism, as well as, in Chinese and Japanese traditions. The editors notice two striking facts that cut across these studies. First, equality between men and women was to a large extent greater in the earlier periods of each religion's development. This, in part, is attributed to the fact that the initiators of religions were far more radical with regard to gender than either their cultures or their followers. Second, in most of the traditions, there is great disparity between core teachings that by and large advocate gender equity and the practice of discrimination by these traditions' adherents. Some signs of hope are also noted. Rita Gross, writing the section on Buddhism, notes that as Buddhism becomes more established in the West, many women are being trained as leaders and taking leadership roles in practicing communities.

Jacobs, Louis. *Religion and the Individual: A Jewish Perspective*. Cambridge Studies in Religious Traditions, vol. 1. Cambridge: Cambridge University Press, 1992.

Jacobs seeks to rectify what he sees as an overemphasis on the role of the group in contemporary Judaism to the detriment of Judaism's traditional respect for the individual. Referencing the Mishnah, Talmud, and rabbinical literature, he traces this traditional respect for the individual from early Jewish sources to the present.

Kennedy, Leonard A. et al., eds. *Images of the Human: The Philosophy of the Human Person in a Religious Context*. Chicago: Loyola University Press, 1995.

An anthology of selections from Plato and Aristotle to a variety of twentieth century thinkers, men and women, advancing diverse views of what it is to be human. Thirteen college professors each take responsibility for a particular figure. Each selection is preceded by an overview of the person and his or her writings, as well as tips and/or questions to help readers engage the selection thoughtfully. A commentary and suggestions for further reading conclude each section.

King, Sallie B. *Buddha Nature*. SUNY Series in Buddhist Studies. Albany: State University of New York Press, 1991.

The author gives a detailed exposition of 'Buddha Nature' according to the mid-Sixth century Chinese *Fo Xing Lun* ("Buddha Nature Treatise") and interprets it in light of Western thinking about the being and existence of persons, and the development of Buddhist tradition in the West. The book begins with an introduction to the history and traditional importance of the motif of Buddha Nature and of the *Fo Xing Lun*. Succeeding chapters present the Chinese text's theory of Buddha Nature with respect to soteriology, selfhood, ontology, spiritual cultivation, and implications for Western religious thought. Central to King's interpretation is the non-substantial character of Buddha Nature; that is, it is saving action.

Kippenberg, Hans G.; Y. Kuiper; and Andy F. Sanders, eds. *Concepts of Person in Religion and Thought*. Religion and Reason, vol. 37. Berlin: Monton de Gruyter, 1990.

This volume explores the concept of personhood from diverse disciplinary perspectives including anthropology, philosophical hermeneutics, and sociology, and in view of Egyptian, Jewish, Christian, Hindu, Islamic, Ancient Indian, Hopi, and West African religious perspectives. While it is clear to the editors that the concept of personhood is a trans-cultural concept, they seek to show in this work that diverse meanings are attached to this concept in diverse contexts, and, therefore, a premature agreement on a universal understanding of personhood should be avoided.

Krejcí, Jaroslav and Anna Krejcová. *The Human Predicament: Its Changing Image: A Study in Comparative Religion and History*. New York: St. Martin's Press, 1993.

There are five basic paradigms, associated with five cultural centers, by which human beings have made sense of their life and death according to the author. These paradigms include Theocentrism (ancient Mesopotamia), Thanatocentrism (Pharaonic Egypt), Anthropocentrism (Classical Greece), Psychocentrism (India "throughout the ages"), and Cratocentrism (China). From these five paradigms, Krejcí offers explanations concerning the development and form of at least seven world religions, in terms of 'encounter,' 'flirtation,' 'mutation.' The last two chapters consider the future of religions and their import for global relations.

Krishna, Daya. *The Problematic and Conceptual Structure of Classical Indian Thought About Man, Society, and Polity*. Delhi: Oxford University Press, 1996.

Krishna directs his book against two misconceptions: that Indian thought has exhausted its creativity and usefulness in a repetitive commentarial tradition, and that non-Western modes of knowledge have been superseded by Western modes. The human person, "as a self-conscious being, finds himself embedded both in nature and society and yet considers himself apart from them in an essential sense. . . . A similar situation, though on a subtler level, exists in terms of his relationship to reality as a whole, in both its transcendent and immanent aspects." Krishna articulates the ways this problematic of an empirical and a true self was handled in the ancient texts—especially through the formulation of a scheme of life-stages and life-aims—and delineates the conceptual structures that gave sense and connection to the various solutions.

Lauer, Eugene J. and Joel Mlecko, eds. *A Christian Understanding of the Human Person: Basic Readings*. New York: Paulist Press, 1982.

This anthology contains excerpts from contemporary theologians pertaining to the concept of Christian personhood. The editors contend that Christian personhood is essentially relational and involves four basic relationships; namely, to God, to the material world, to other human persons, and to oneself. Four sections of this work are organized around these four relationships, and are linked with two additional sections discussing the role of religion in becoming human and Jesus as an ideally related person. Included are selections from Ninian Smart, Huston Smith, Harvey Cox, Carl Rahner, Wolfhart Pannenberg, Thoman Mann, and Elizabeth Kubler Ross, among others.

Lawson, E. Thomas and Robert N. McCauley. *Rethinking Religion: Connecting Cognition and Culture*. Cambridge: Cambridge University Press, 1990.

The authors of the work seek an explanatory and interpretive structure for religions. They focus on rituals of as a facet of religions that is self-limiting and therefore more readily analyzable theoretically. Building on the insights of linguistics and cognitive science, they propose a new-intellectualist view of religion, in which religion is a mental phenomenon analogous to language and the participant in ritual analogous to native speakers of a language whose intuitions about the rules of the ritual or language may not be precise, but are nevertheless trustworthy. They then seek universal principles of ritual structure.

Munro, Donald J. *Images of Human Nature: A Sung Portrait*. Princeton, NJ: Princeton University Press, 1988.

Munro argues that Zhu Xi's theory of human nature can be understood in relation to particular images such as the stream, the plant, and the mirror that occur repeatedly in Zhu's works. These images, Munro contends, help Zhu Xi to bridge two fundamental polarities of the human condition; namely, duty to family versus duty to state and self-discovery of moral truth versus obedience to objective rules. The images Zhu Xi employs serve both a structural and an emotive function, giving Zhu Xi's audience a sense of how human relationships work and why they should work that way. Munro concludes by exploring how Zhu Xi's ideas can be related to those of Western philosophy and how Zhu Xi's ideas continue to resonate in contemporary Chinese society and moral theory.

Neufeldt, Ronald W., ed. *Karma and Rebirth: Post Classical Developments*. Albany: State University of New York Press, 1986.

Contributions attend to the understanding of karma and rebirth in modern India, as well as in Sri Lanka, Southeast Asia, Tibet, China, Japan, and the West. Part I considers the influence of figures and movements of the Hindu Renaissance in India in the nineteenth and twentieth centuries. Part II looks at conceptions of karma in both Theravāda and

Mahāyāna Buddhist traditions. Part III looks at Western intellectual developments including theosophy and new religious movements.

Neville, Robert C. *Soldier, Sage, Saint*. New York: Fordham University Press, 1978.

This philosophical study develops a theory of spiritual freedom, freedom in respect to the divine, in terms of three models of human perfection. Each has its philosophical ground in one of the Platonic components of the soul: thus, will—soldier, intellect—sage, desire—saint. However, the models are also offered as a mode of comparative theology. They are found embodied in symbols of religious perfection and normative humanity in living religious traditions. The practice of the soldier, sage, or saint is said to make specific claims on the practitioner, leading the aspirant to engage in the ultimate contrast between the contextual world and the conditional possibility *that* there is a world at all. These practices, though distinct, all enhance responsible freedom in the world.

O'Flaherty, Wendy Doniger and J. Duncan Derrett, eds. *The Concept of Duty in South Asia*. New Delhi: Vikas Publishing House, 1978.

Arjuna's plea to Kṛṣṇa in the *Bhagavad Gītā* is to "show me where my duty lies." Part I of this collection of essays, "The Ancient Period: Duty and *Dharma*," examines duty through the conceptual lens of *dharma*, and traces the notion of duty from its oldest appearances in Vedic literature and early Buddhist interpretations to legal hermeneutics. Part II, "The Medieval and Modern Period: Muslim, British and Nationalist Concepts of Duty," evinces the rich and changing understanding of duty that so much cultural confluence has worked in India.

O'Flaherty, Wendy Doniger and Joint Committee on South Asia., eds. *Karma and Rebirth in Classical Indian Traditions*. Berkeley: University of California Press, 1980.

The essays in this volume consider the origins and establishment of theories of karma in India. No shortage of tension is evident in relating theories of karma to the varied religious stations a person may pass through in Hindu society, or during his or her own life (or lives). Questions are raised and addressed from a variety of methodological perspectives. Part I studies the emergence and development of the idea of karma in the literary roots of Hinduism, both Aryan (northern) and Tamil (southern). Part II looks at Buddhist and Jain approaches to karma. Part III reflects on philosophical traditions and their contributions to an understanding of karma.

O'Shaughnessy, Thomas J. *Creation and the Teaching of the Qur'ān*. Biblica et Orientalia, vol. 40. Rome: Biblical Institute Press, 1985.

This work's primary focus is the development of the concept of creation in the Qur'ān with special reference to the influence of other religious traditions. Through a careful study of the verbs and nouns used regarding creation, especially the creation of humans, O'Shaughnessy attempts to trace the development of the idea of the human person in Muḥammed's thinking. The author pays special attention to Syrian Christian, rabbinical and polytheist sources that may have influenced the development of Muḥammad's thought during the twenty-two years of the writing of the Qur'ān.

Organ, Troy Wilson. *The Hindu Quest for the Perfection of Man.* Athens: Ohio University, 1970.

Organ begins this long book by characterizing Hinduism as a quest, which subsequent chapters specify as a quest for reality, spirituality, integration, and liberation. The ideal of the perfected human is discussed in terms of relationship to the surrounding world, society, divinity, and as realization and practice. The author is much influenced by Hindu modernists such as Roy, Tagore and Vivekananda. He concludes with a commendation of Hinduism as a "catholic religion" for all humanity.

Panikkar, Raimundo and Scott Eastham. *The Cosmotheandric Experience: Emerging Religious Consciousness.* Maryknoll, NY: Orbis Books, 1993.

Panikkar, who holds doctorate degrees in philosophy, religion, and science, unites his knowledge of these three disciplines in his argument that the world is and must become more meaningfully inter-related because environmental destruction, overpopulation, and the unequal distribution of resources pose serious challenges to the survival of humans, as well as to many other species. He asserts that "divine, human, and earthly . . . are the three irreducible dimensions which constitute the real," and argues that his vision of the 'cosmostheandric spirituality,' which brings together cosmos, theos, and andros, offers a viable option that could inspire appropriate action.

Park, Andrew Sung. *The Wounded Heart of God: The Asian Concept of Han and the Christian Doctrine of Sin.* Nashville: Abingdon, 1993.

Park contends that the Christian notion of sin has failed to take fill account of the pain that accrues to the victims of sin. He uses the Korean notion of *han* to elaborate on this deep pain and bitterness caused by sin. Just as the Christian tradition sees sin as fundamental to the human condition, *han,* Park argues, is also fundamental. Therefore, *han* should also be treated in any conception of salvation. Park sees grounds for interfaith dialogue with Buddhism, Hinduism, and Judaism as traditions that have already developed implicit or explicit analyses of *han*. Finally, he argues that in order to have a holistic view of salvation one must include not only forgiveness of sins but also resolution of *han*. Park calls for religious people to unite against global capitalism, patriarchy, racism, and cultural discrimination that Park sees as the primary perpetrators of *han* today.

Park, Sung-bae. *Buddhist Faith and Sudden Enlightenment*. SUNY Series in Religious Studies. Albany: State University of New York Press, 1983.

Park explores the relationship between faith and sudden enlightenment in the Mahāyāna Buddhist tradition, particularly the Korean Rinzai school of Ch'an (Zen). He outlines the fundamental difference between "doctrinal faith" and "patriarchal faith." The former is founded on the faith that one may *become* the Buddha through a long process of learning and practice. The latter is founded on the faith that one is *already* the Buddha. While enlightenment is thus gradual in the former, it is immediate and sudden in the latter. For Park, patriarchal faith is the true faith of Mahāyāna Buddhism, particularly Zen. A life of patriarchal faith consists of continual meditative reaffirmations of one's essential Buddha nature. Throughout, Park draws parallels between these two Buddhist notions of faith and Christian notions of faith drawing particularly on Tillich and Kierkegaard, with an especially interesting section on 'backsliding'.

Ricœur, Paul. *Fallible Man*. Rev. ed. New York: Fordham University Press, 1986 [1965]. Translation of *L'homme Faillible*.

This work is the second volume in Ricoeur's series on the *Philosophy of the Will*, which includes *Freedom and Nature* and *The Symbolism of Evil*. In this volume, Ricoeur explores a phenomenology of human fallibility. He argues that fallibility is inherent to human nature by virtue of the fundamental "disproportion" of human existence. Because humans always have a pre-philosophical, pre-reflective experience of existence, their self-consciousness is always a second order reflection. It is this fragile "fault" resting in the tension between pre-reflective and reflective, pre-philosophical and philosophical that opens the space for fallibility and therefore, according to Ricoeur, lends to human nature the "capacity for evil."

Rouner, Leroy S., ed. *Is There a Human Nature?* Boston University Studies in Philosophy and Religion, vol. 18. Notre Dame, IN: University of Notre Dame Press, 1997.

This is a collection of essays focusing on the question of human nature. The contributors voice various positions. Bhikhu Parekh argues that human nature has a three-fold character—universal, cultural and self-reflexive. He notes that this tripartite conception takes into account Western (universal), Chinese (cultural), and Hindu (self-reflexive) conceptions of human nature. Daniel Dahlstrom argues that humanness rests on the recognition of one's humanity by others. He points to economic disparity, desire for superiority, and xenophobia as currents that militate against such recognition. Tu Wei-Ming calls for a reconsideration of Confucian filial piety within the context of the global environmental crisis. He argues that a conception of human nature as relational must go beyond human relations to include the earth. Other contributors include Lisa Cahill, Ray L. Hart, Robert Neville, Stanley Rosen, and Sissila Bok.

Sachs, John Randall. *The Christian Vision of Humanity: Basic Christian Anthropology*. Zacchaeus Studies. Collegeville, MN: Liturgical Press, 1991.

A brief, introductory work covering biblical visions and Catholic traditions regarding human nature. Topics include the divine image, freedom, individuality and community, gender, body and soul, sin, grace, death and resurrection, destiny, and Christian life. Suggested readings accompany each chapter.

Schimmel, Solomon. *The Seven Deadly Sins: Jewish, Christian, and Classical Reflections on Human Nature*. New York: Free Press, 1992.

Schimmel, a psychotherapist and professor of education and psychology, reflects on the contemporary human situation in dialogue with classic texts of the three traditions named in the subtitle. The writers of these works were "profound psychologists," whose insights into the persistence of sin can correct what the author sees as the psychological profession's amorality and scientistic arrogance. Seven chapters treat of pride, envy, anger, lust, gluttony, greed and sloth. Schimmel concludes with a consideration of sin and responsibility.

Segundo, Juan Luis and Centro Pedro Fabro de Montevideo. *Grace and the Human Condition*. Maryknoll, NY: Orbis Books, 1973. Trans. by John Drury from *Gracia y Condición Humana*.

Segundo argues in the work for a dynamic conception of Christian anthropology. He sees grace as the freeing agent in human life. It is an "irresistible force" that frees people so that they may participate in the "common task" of creating a "history of love in all its fullness." Grace is the force that liberates humanity to seek its true condition as free in whatever dynamic form this freedom takes.

Shari'ati, A. *Man and Islam: Lectures*. Danishgah-i Mashhad, vol. 103. Mashhad, Iran: University of Mashhad Press, 1982. Trans. by Ghulam F. Fayez from *Insan va Islam*.

Shari'ati, who was active in the Iranian renewal and liberation movement of the 1970s as well as exiled and murdered in 1977 as a result of that involvement, here argues that the answer to Iran's problems will not be found in Westernization (which he calls "westomania") or religious conservatism, but in a renewed understanding of the two-dimensional anthropology of Islam. The human in Islam is both "clay" and "spirit," this-worldly and other-worldly. Shari'ati sees Islam as superior in this formulation both to Christianity's emphasis on ascetic, other-worldliness and to Judaism's emphasis on historical, this worldliness. He concludes that any Islamic state must balance these two dimensions, not only respecting the religious tradition but also the free will and choice of the individual.

Shari'ati, A. *On the Sociology of Islam: Lectures*. Berkeley: Mizan Press, 1979. Trans. from the Persian by Hamid Algar.

Shari'ati argues from the concept of *tauḥīd* or the unity of God (entailing also the unity of the cosmos as God's creation) that 'the masses' are the most fundamental and conscious factor in determining history and society. He sees Islam as unique both in propounding this unity and in realizing the sociological importance of the masses to any movement for change.

Sharma, Arvind, ed. *Women in World Religions*. McGill Studies in the History of Religions. Albany: State University of New York Press, 1987.

This collection examines the role of women in world and aboriginal religions. The traditions that contributors cover include Hinduism, Buddhism, Confucianism, Daoism, Judaism, Christianity, Islam, and Australian aboriginal religion. The contributors employ phenomenological and historical approaches, using sacred texts as their primary sources. The work contains a helpful introduction by Katherine Young that examines broadly how and why these various traditions became patriarchal.

Soloveitchik, Joseph Dov. *Halakhic Man*. Philadelphia: Jewish Publication Society of America, 1983. Translation of *Ish ha-halakhah, galui ve-nistar*.

Soloveitchik describes the world view of Halakhic man (the person who is formed by the Torah) in counterdistinction to what he calls *homo religiosus* and cognitive man. Where 'homo religiosus' seeks to flee the material world for the eternal, Halakhic man seeks to bring the eternal into the material realm to make reality into the ideal. Where cognitive man dissects reality for its own sake, Soloveitchik contends, Halakhic man dissects reality with the *a priori* categories of Torah. Halakhic man's aim is to view the correspondence between the Torah's ideal and the real. Soloveitchik concludes that Halakhic man represents a singular creative potential since his ultimate aim is to mold the world that presents itself everyday into the world which he possesses in his ideal image from the Torah.

Soper, Kate. *Humanism and Anti-Humanism*. Problems of Modern European Thought. London: Hutchinson, 1986.

Soper offers an overview of recent humanist and anti-humanist anthropology. Soper pursues the question, "Does human really make history," while defending humanism (albeit a humanism qualified with limit views of agency and individuality). She provides a concise analysis of the roots of humanist positions in Hegel, Marx, Husserl and Heidegger, as well as the roots of anti-humanist positions in Levi-Strauss, Foucault, Althusser, Lacan and Derrida.

Thangaraj, M. Thomas. *The Crucified Guru: An Experiment in Cross-Cultural Christology*. Nashville: Abingdon Press, 1994.

Thangaraj, a Tamil from South India teaching in the United States, argues that his conception of Jesus as the crucified guru has the potential to bridge the gap between traditional Christology and the Śaiva tradition of Hinduism that is practiced in his home region. He critiques previous Hindu Christian avatar christology because they failed to speak to both Tamil Hindu's who see incarnation as inimical to avatars and to Tamil Christians who saw avatar christologies as minimizing Jesus' humanity. The guru, a human revealer of the divine, remains true on the other hand both to its Hindu origin and to the balance between human and divine in christological orthodoxy. Moreover, Thangaraj argues, the vision of Jesus as guru emphasizes the role of the community of followers or *sisya* that is enjoined not only to follow, but also to carry out the guru's message in the world. Overall, the book provides a detailed example of a comparative, cross-cultural, contextual christology.

Tu, Wei ming. *Confucian Thought: Selfhood as Creative Transformation*. Rev ed. SUNY Series in Philosophy. Albany: State University of New York Press, 1985.

Through the nine essays collected in this book, Tu Wei-ming attempts to answer the question posed to him by Robert Bellah: "What is the Confucian self?" Taking seriously the centrality of self-cultivation in the Confucian tradition, Tu Wei-ming explores the many subtle dimensions of Confucian thought by trying to understand Confucius in the light of the writings of Mencius and the thought of Mencius in relation to the teachings of Wang Yangming.

Ward, Keith. *Religion and Human Nature*. Oxford: Clarendon Press, 1998.

Ward seeks to explore, critique, and enhance a Christian view of human nature in genuine encounter with the view of human nature in other religious traditions. Ward categorizes concepts of human nature in two groups. There are those who argue that the self is an illusion, a manifestation of the one spiritual reality, and there are those who argue that the self is a unique, individual with a unique individual reality, whether material or spiritual or a combination of both. In dialogue with their major living teachers, Ward considers the International Society for Krishna Consciousness, Ramakrishna, Theravādin and Tibetan Buddhism, Judaism, and Islam. He then argues for a revised and enhanced Christian view of human nature that would occupy the middle ground between "no-self" (Vedic religions) and "embodied self" (Semitic religions) perspectives.

Warne, Graham J. *Hebrew Perspectives on the Human Person in the Hellenistic Era: Philo and Paul*. Mellen Biblical Press Series, vol. 35. Lewiston, NY: Mellen Biblical Press, 1995.

This work examines the Greek and Hebrew concepts of human personhood through an exploration of the concept of "soul" in Philo and Paul. Warne attempts to judge how much Plato's understanding of the soul influenced both Philo and Paul. He does not find a unified view of the soul either in Philo or in Paul, but concludes that traces of Greek as well as Hebrew ideas can be found in each of these writers. The work provides a detailed analysis of first century social, religious, and political settings, as well as an in-depth etymological studies of the word groups relating to the soul in Greek and Hebrew.

Weingart, Peter et al., ed. *Human by Nature: Between Biology and the Social Sciences*. Mahwah, NJ: Lawrence Erlbaum Associates, 1997.

This work is a reappraisal and experiment in the relationship between biology and the social sciences. It traces the historical development of these two disciplines, as well as the development of mutual distrust between them. In two sets of studies, one based on homology (the human is an animal) and one based on analogy (the human is like an animal), it reviews current conceptions of the human and explores the potential benefit of an "integrative pluralism" in which the methods of both social science and biology could be brought to bear in developing a more nuanced view of the nexus of biological and cultural factors that shape individual humans and human communities.

Wetherilt, Ann Kirkus. *That They May Be Many: Voices of Women, Echoes of God*. New York: Continuum, 1994.

Wetherilt argues for the transformation of authority structures, epistemology, and praxis so that diverse voices may be heard efficaciously in theological discourse. She argues that theological discourse ought rightly be called theo-ethical discourse since it should be an example of the enacting of an inclusive ethic. She proposes that women challenge traditional structures of authority by claiming their own voices and means of expression. She argues that epistemology must be transformed to accommodate embodied and other personal ways of knowing. Finally, she urges the transformation of individualist praxis into coalitions of praxis that would have the effect of combating the one-sidedness of the limited socially located knowing of solitary individuals.

Wilson, Edward Osborne. *On Human Nature*. Cambridge: Harvard University Press, 1978.

He argues that humans and their society, with its concomitant social institutions, should be viewed primarily as the products of biological evolution. He argues that such things as aggression, altruism, religion, and hope ultimately have their basis in the evolutionary drive to preserve the species. Moreover, he makes a plea for the union of biology and social science so that the biological basis of human nature, individual and cultural, might be better understood and thereby contribute to a more informed choice of the kinds of institutions and values that will truly be beneficial to humanity.

Contributors

PETER L. BERGER is University Professor of Sociology of Religion emeritus at Boston University and Director of the Institute for the Study of Economic Culture. He is the author of a several widely acclaimed books in the field of sociology of religion.

FRANCIS X. CLOONEY, S.J., Professor of Comparative Theology at Boston College, is past president of the Society for Hindu-Christian Studies. He specializes in certain Sanskrit and Tamil traditions of Hindu thought and their implications for Christian theology.

MALCOLM DAVID ECKEL is Professor of the History of Religion at Boston University and does research and teaching in Buddhism.

PAULA FREDRIKSEN is the William Goodwin Aurelio Professor of the Appreciation of Scripture and Professor of New Testament and Early Christianity at Boston University. She has a particular research interest in Augustine of Hippo, and has also published in the areas of Hellenistic Judaism, Christian origins, and Pauline studies.

S. NOMANUL HAQ is currently on the faculty of Rutgers University and a visiting scholar at the University of Pennsylvania. He has published extensively in the general area of Islamic intellectual history, including theology, philosophy, and science.

JOSEPH KANOFSKY recently received his Ph.D. from Boston University. His primary focus of his work is Judaic studies.

LIVIA KOHN is Professor of Religion and East-Asian Studies at Boston University. She is a specialist of medieval Daoism.

ROBERT CUMMINGS NEVILLE is Professor of Philosophy, Religion, and Theology, and Dean of the School Theology at Boston University. Neville is the past president of the American Academy of Religion, The International Society for Chinese Philosophy, and The Metaphysical Society of America.

HUGH NICHOLSON is a Ph.D. candidate in the Theology Department at Boston College and is currently writing his dissertation relating Indian philosophical thought to theological and philosophical questions and concerns of the Christian West.

ANTHONY J. SALDARINI is Professor in the Department of Theology at Boston College. He teaches courses in early Judaism and Christianity and publishes in the area of early Jewish–Christian relations.

TINA SHEPARDSON is a Ph.D. student at Duke University, specializing in Early Christian Studies, and is currently writing her dissertation on the thought of St. Augustine.

JOHN J. THATAMANIL is a member of the religious studies faculty at Millsaps College, and recently completed his dissertation comparing the thought of Paul Tillich and Śaṇkara.

WESLEY J. WILDMAN is Associate Professor of Theology and Ethics at Boston University. He teaches and does research in the areas of contemporary Christian theology, philosophy of religion, and religion and science.

Index of Names

Index of Subjects